DK DORLING KINDERSLEY
—HANDBOOKS—

TREES

DORLING KINDERSLEY
—HANDBOOKS—

TREES

ALLEN J. COOMBES

LEARNING ZONE
NORTHOP COLLEGE

Photography by
MATTHEW WARD

DK

A Dorling Kindersley Book

Dorling Kindersley

LONDON, NEW YORK, AUCKLAND,
DELHI, JOHANNESBURG, MUNICH,
PARIS and SYDNEY

DK www.dk.com

Editor Gillian Roberts
Art Editor Vicki James
Design Co-ordinator Spencer Holbrook
Editorial Consultant Roy Lancaster
Production Caroline Webber

Tree illustrations commissioned by
Mustafa Sami

Plant material photographed at
Sir Harold Hillier Gardens and Arboretum,
Ampfield, Hampshire

First published in Great Britain in 1992
Reprinted with corrections 2000
by Dorling Kindersley Limited,
9 Henrietta Street, London WC2E 8PS

10 9 8 7 6 5 4 3 2

A CIP catalogue record for this book is
available from the British Library

ISBN 0-7513-2746-8

Computer page make-up by
The Cooling Brown Partnership,
Great Britain

Text film output by
The Right Type, Great Britain

Reproduced by
Colourscan, Singapore

Printed and bound by
Kyodo Printing Co., Singapore

CONTENTS

LOOKING AT TREES

Whether standing in isolation on a windy hillside, crowded together in dense forest, or lining a city street, trees form an important element of nearly every landscape. The almost infinite variation of trees through the seasons – not only in shape, size, colour, and texture, but also in the finer details of leaves, flowers, fruit, and bark – makes the study of these familiar plants an ever-changing, yet enduring, source of delight.

THE FACT THAT trees survive almost everywhere means that you can appreciate and study them wherever you happen to be. In the countryside, they grow, hopefully but not always, as nature intends; in urban environments, planted along streets, and in parks and public gardens, they give comfort and solace among man-made structures. Of course, while there is nothing to compare with seeing trees growing wild in their natural habitat, towns and cities are still excellent places for observing and learning more about them.

THE TREE SELECTION

This book includes only those species of tree that grow wild in the temperate regions of the world. In the northern hemisphere, this covers most of Asia, North America, Europe south to the Mediterranean, the Himalayas, and most of China; in the southern hemisphere, it includes South America, the cooler regions of Australia, and New Zealand. From within this extensive area, I have made a selection of plants that illustrates the amazing diversity of trees that can be found throughout the world. At the same time, I have tried to include most of the species that you are likely to find planted in gardens and along streets, as well as a few that are unusual or more rare.

BEECH WOOD IN AUTUMN
An English beech wood is one of the glories of autumn. Its densely leafy canopy allows little light to penetrate, with the result that little else can grow beneath it.

ORIENTAL BEECH (*Fagus orientalis*)

CONSERVATION ISSUES

In recent years, the destruction of the tropical forests has excited a good deal of attention, and rightly so: these last great areas of natural diversity are home to numerous plants and animals, whose continuing existence may be of vital importance to mankind. Faced with so large a debate, it is easy to forget that most forests in temperate zones have already suffered the fate that is threatening those in tropical regions. In the developed world, extensive areas of natural woodland have been lost through man's demand for paper, building materials, and other wood-based products, as well as through the need for agricultural land, creating the relatively unnatural countryside we see today.

CHINESE CHESTNUT (C. mollissima)

In developing parts of the world, temperate woods are still under threat in places like the Himalayas and South America. Particularly in areas of heavy rainfall, the felling of trees – with scant regard to the far-reaching consequences of this action – causes problems such as flooding and mud landslides, when the vegetation that once stabilized entire hillsides is gone.

The majority of species are distributed over a wide enough area to be able to endure partial felling and survive without the danger of extinction. Some have a much more limited range, however. One

THREATENED SPECIES
Diseases can nearly destroy a species. Chestnut blight from east Asia has killed all but a few wild American chestnuts (Castanea dentata, p.149). The Chinese chestnut (C. mollissima, p.149) is being used to help breed resistant trees.

single example is the Spanish fir *(Abies pinsapo,* see p.56), which grows wild on very few mountainsides in a small area of southern Spain. Years ago, its timber was a valuable local resource. Now, any further cutting might extinguish these glorious forests for ever. We must make special efforts to protect this and other such endangered species.

SURVIVOR FROM CHINA
The bark of Magnolia officinalis *var.* biloba *was once harvested to produce medicines, causing the species to become extinct in the wild. Cultivation has ensured that it still grows in gardens.*

ADAPTATION FOR SURVIVAL
The larches (Larix, see pp.60–61) grow wild in the harshest conditions. They produce their foliage on numerous short side shoots – an adaptation that allows them to take advantage of favourable conditions as they come into leaf.

HABITAT AND ENVIRONMENT

By adapting to an extensive range of environmental conditions, trees are able to grow in many different habitats. Generally speaking, it is the conifers that inhabit the most hostile situations. Their slender shape minimizes damage by snow; evergreen leaves make the best use of a growing season that may be short, and mean that the plant can survive extended periods of drought when the ground is frozen; and wind pollination eliminates the need for insect visitors, which may be sparse or non-existent in unfavourable habitats.

Friendlier habitats produce a longer growing season, and encourage deciduous species. Here, there is time for the plant to produce new leaves, and shed old ones, every year in a continuous cycle of regeneration. In shady places, large leaves are needed to intercept as much sunlight as can filter through; in wet areas, tapered tips allow for the rapid shedding of water; in dry areas, grey or silvery leaves reduce water loss; and fragrant or showy flowers ensure a good chance of pollination by insects.

ILEX X
KOEHNEANA ▷

◁ TARAJO
HOLLY (*Ilex
latifolia*)

HYBRID PLANTS
A hybrid is produced when two different species cross together. The plant that results usually shows characteristics that are intermediate between the two parents. Some hybrids occur only through cultivation in gardens, because the parent plants do not grow together in the wild.

△ PARENT ONE
Tarajo holly (Ilex latifolia, see p.112) has rather large leaves, which are toothed at the margin but not spiny.

◁ COMMON HOLLY
(*Ilex aquifolium*)

THE HYBRID ▷
Ilex x koehneana (see p.112) has the large leaves of I. *latifolia. The spiny margin of the leaves is inherited from* I. *aquifolium.*

△ PARENT TWO
The familiar common holly (Ilex aquifolium, see p.109) has leaves that are typically edged with spiny teeth.

A FAMILY TREE

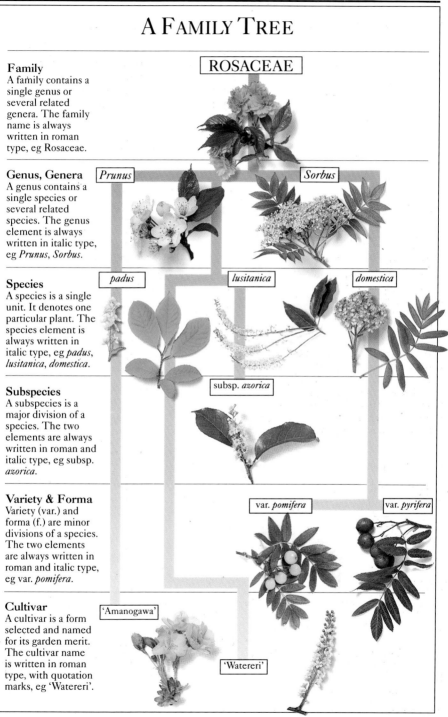

ROSACEAE

Family
A family contains a single genus or several related genera. The family name is always written in roman type, eg Rosaceae.

Genus, Genera
A genus contains a single species or several related species. The genus element is always written in italic type, eg *Prunus*, *Sorbus*.

Prunus

Sorbus

Species
A species is a single unit. It denotes one particular plant. The species element is always written in italic type, eg *padus*, *lusitanica*, *domestica*.

padus

lusitanica

domestica

Subspecies
A subspecies is a major division of a species. The two elements are always written in roman and italic type, eg subsp. *azorica*.

subsp. *azorica*

Variety & Forma
Variety (var.) and forma (f.) are minor divisions of a species. The two elements are always written in roman and italic type, eg var. *pomifera*.

var. *pomifera*

var. *pyrifera*

Cultivar
A cultivar is a form selected and named for its garden merit. The cultivar name is written in roman type, with quotation marks, eg 'Watereri'.

'Amanogawa'

'Watereri'

OBSERVING AND RECORDING TREES

Keeping written notes about the trees you see is not only an enjoyable activity at the time: it also makes interesting reading at a later date. Choose half a dozen favourite trees close to where you live or work. Visit each one several times during the four seasons and build up a fact file that records their special features at different times of the year.

MEASURING A TREE'S HEIGHT

Cut a straight piece of stick that is the same length as the distance between your eye and your fist. Hold it vertically at arm's length and walk towards or away from the tree to align the top of the stick with the top of the tree and the base of the stick with the base of the tree. Mark the point at which you are now standing and measure the distance on the ground to the base of the trunk. This distance equals the height of the tree.

long, 30m (100ft) tape for measuring height, and trunk circumference •

MAKING BARK IMPRESSIONS
Rubbing bark can be an effective way of capturing its diverse patterns and textures. Hold a piece of paper flat to the surface of the trunk, and rub lightly with a wax crayon. Label your rubbing with the date, the tree's name, and its location.

TAKING FIELD NOTES
Jot down the tree's height, the circumference of its trunk, and the colour and texture of the bark. Note details of its leaves, flowers, and fruit (depending on the time of year), its location, and the date. Expand your notes at home.

coloured pencils for making sketches •

small sketchbook for visual note-taking •

reference photographs •

wax crayon and paper for making bark impressions

cut specimen to take home for more detailed examination

magnifying glass •

• label with string tie for cut specimens

HOW THIS BOOK WORKS

THE BOOK IS ARRANGED according to the major groups of tree: Conifers and their Allies, and Broadleaves. The groups are divided, alphabetically, into families. A short introduction to each family tells you how many genera and species it contains, and describes the general characteristics and features of the plants that belong to it. The entries that follow are arranged, alphabetically, by genus and by species within each genus. They give detailed information, in words and pictures, about selected species that are found in that family.

Each entry begins with the common name, or the scientific name if there is no single, accepted common name for that plant. Many plants do not have a common name: indeed, they are well enough known under their scientific name not to need one. This example shows how a typical entry is organized.

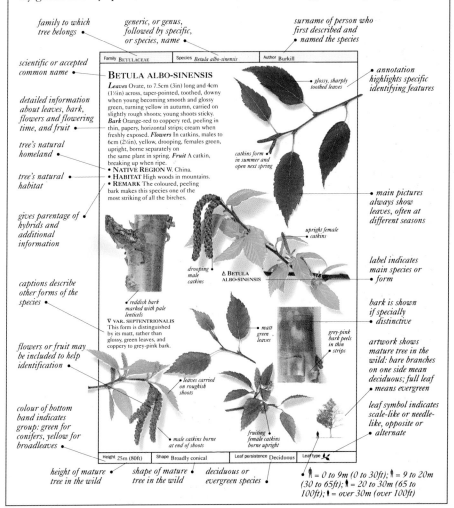

family to which tree belongs •

generic, or genus, followed by specific, or species, name •

surname of person who first described and • named the species

scientific or accepted common name •

detailed information about leaves, bark, flowers and flowering time, and fruit •

tree's natural homeland •

tree's natural habitat •

gives parentage of hybrids and additional information •

captions describe other forms of the species •

flowers or fruit may be included to help identification •

colour of bottom band indicates group: green for conifers, yellow for broadleaves •

• annotation highlights specific identifying features

• main pictures always show leaves, often at different seasons

label indicates main species or • form

bark is shown if specially • distinctive

artwork shows mature tree in the wild: bare branches on one side mean deciduous; full leaf • means evergreen

leaf symbol indicates scale-like or needle-like, opposite or • alternate

Family BETULACEAE   Species *Betula albo-sinensis*   Author Burkill

BETULA ALBO-SINENSIS
Leaves Ovate, to 7.5cm (3in) long and 4cm (1½in) across, taper-pointed, toothed, downy when young becoming smooth and glossy green, turning yellow in autumn, carried on slightly rough shoots; young shoots sticky. *Bark* Orange-red to coppery red, peeling in thin, papery, horizontal strips; cream when freshly exposed. *Flowers* In catkins, males to 6cm (2½in), yellow, drooping, females green, upright, borne separately on the same plant in spring. *Fruit* A catkin, breaking up when ripe.
• NATIVE REGION W. China.
• HABITAT High woods in mountains.
• REMARK The coloured, peeling bark makes this species one of the most striking of all the birches.

glossy, sharply toothed leaves

catkins form in summer and open next spring

upright female catkins

drooping male catkins

△ BETULA ALBO-SINENSIS

reddish bark marked with pale lenticels
▽ VAR. SEPTENTRIONALIS
This form is distinguished by its matt, rather than glossy, green leaves, and coppery to grey-pink bark.

matt green leaves

grey-pink bark peels in thin strips

leaves carried on roughish shoots

male catkins borne at end of shoots

fruiting female catkins borne upright

Height 25m (80ft)   Shape Broadly conical   Leaf persistence Deciduous   Leaf type ⚊

height of mature tree in the wild •

shape of mature tree in the wild •

deciduous or evergreen species •

⚊ = 0 to 9m (0 to 30ft); ⚊ = 9 to 20m (30 to 65ft); ⚊ = 20 to 30m (65 to 100ft); ⚊ = over 30m (over 100ft)

WHAT IS A TREE?

A TREE IS a living thing. It has a woody stem, the trunk, a root system, and branches clothed in season with leaves. It may have flowers and, later, fruit.

Size and habit distinguish a tree from a shrub. A tree usually attains 5m (17ft) or more and has a single stem that may divide; a shrub is usually smaller and has many stems growing from the base. Habit is related to habitat. A species that is a tallish tree in a fertile valley may be only a low shrub on an exposed hillside. Open sites allow the plant to develop a spreading crown; in dense forest, where the trees are crowded, it may form an altogether narrower shape.

chlorophyll may be obscured by other pigments

a flat leaf surface works most efficiently.

leaf veins conduct water and nutrients

all leaf types have the same function

variegated leaves have areas that lack chlorophyll

LEAVES
Chlorophyll is the pigment that makes leaves green. It enables the plant to convert water and carbon dioxide into sugars and oxygen, using the energy from sunlight (photosynthesis).

TRUNK AND BARK
The trunk conducts water and food to the leaves, and nutrients from the leaves to the roots. It supports the branches and their foliage. The layer of bark on the outside protects the delicate living tissues beneath.

bark is composed of dead cells

growth rings in the trunk show annual increase in size

ROOT SYSTEM
A mature tree has large, main roots that anchor it into the ground and support it. The surrounding network of very fine roots takes up water and minerals for transporting to its actively growing parts.

BUDS AND SHOOTS

Young leaf growths inside a layer of scales form buds on the shoots during winter. The scales protect the young leaves until they are ready to expand in spring. The shoots carry water and nutrients, and support the leaves.

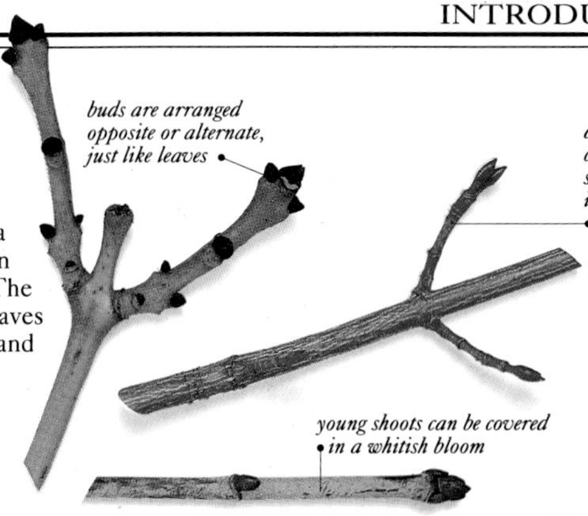

buds are arranged opposite or alternate, just like leaves •

distinctively coloured buds and shoots can help to identify deciduous • species in winter

young shoots can be covered • in a whitish bloom

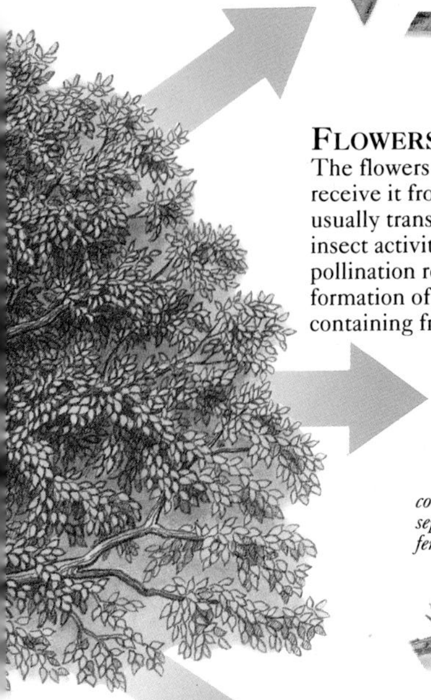

FLOWERS

The flowers produce pollen and receive it from other plants. It is usually transferred by wind or insect activity. Successful pollination results in the formation of seed-containing fruit.

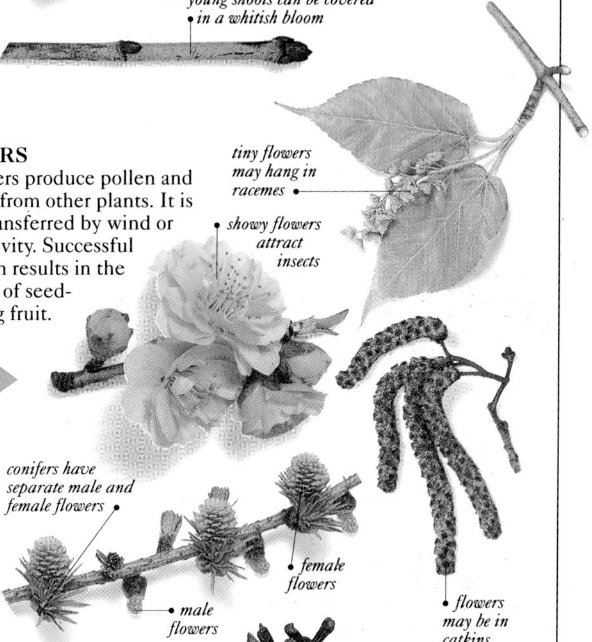

tiny flowers may hang in racemes •

• showy flowers attract insects

conifers have separate male and female flowers •

• female flowers

• male flowers

• flowers may be in catkins

FRUIT

The fruit protects the seeds as they ripen, and helps to disperse them when they are mature. Fleshy fruit is usually eaten by animals, which travel and spread the seeds; dry, winged fruit is carried away by wind.

fleshy fruits are often brightly coloured •

• cones carry their seeds exposed on their scales

dry, winged fruits •

some fruits have only one seed •

a nut has a hard outer shell

• seeds may be inside cone-like scales

THE PARTS OF A TREE

BECOMING FAMILIAR with the principal parts of a tree, and their variety, can help you to identify trees at any season of the year; and it is useful to recognize the special words that describe them.

These pages illustrate typical leaves, flowers, fruit, and bark. If you can relate the words to the pictures, you can see in your mind what the parts of the tree look like as you read the entries.

TEN BASIC LEAF SHAPES

Leaves occur in a great variety of shapes; each also has variations within its basic shape. Every leaf may not fit exactly into one of the shapes shown below: it may be between two different ones. These shapes apply not only to simple leaves, but also to the individual leaflets of compound leaves. A simple leaf is one that is not divided into separate parts. A compound leaf is divided into two or more parts: each separate division is known as a leaflet.

Needle-like leaves are parallel-sided and taper-pointed.

Linear leaves are parallel-sided and have a blunt tip.

Rounded leaves are more or less circular in outline.

Oblong leaves are parallel-sided or nearly so.

Elliptic leaves are broad, narrowing at each end.

      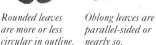

Heart-shaped leaves have a deep indent at the base.

Ovate leaves are widest below the middle.

Obovate leaves are widest above the middle.

Lanceolate leaves are slender and widest below the middle.

Oblanceolate leaves are slender and widest above the middle.

THE PARTS OF A FLOWER

Whereas leaves may vary greatly within any one genus, the flowers of related species and genera are usually similar, at least in structure. Those found on trees are often small, sometimes insignificant and without petals, or even inconspicuous; alternatively, they can be large and showy. Some tree flowers are fragrant; some smell unpleasant; some have no scent at all. How they are borne – singly or together in clusters – is also a notable identifying feature.

each anther is borne on a thin filament •

each style ends • in a stigma

petals are not distinct from • sepals

petals are • often showy

sepals look like petals •

• stigmas are arranged spirally

• anthers split to release pollen

ADVANCED FLOWER ▷
Most flowers are of this type. They have petals that are usually distinct from the sepals.

sepals do not look like • petals

PRIMITIVE FLOWER ▷
These flowers have no very clear distinction between the petals and sepals, which are known collectively as tepals.

TYPES OF FRUIT

Fruits develop from flowers, and so it follows that – as with flowers – the type of fruit a tree bears is characteristic of the genus or even the family to which it belongs. Most fruits originate from a single flower. Others, such as the fig *(Ficus carica, see p.219)*, are derived from several flowers, which fuse together to form multiple fruits.

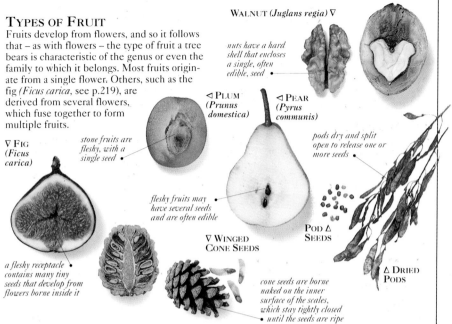

WALNUT *(Juglans regia)* ▽

nuts have a hard shell that encloses a single, often edible, seed •

◁ PLUM *(Prunus domestica)*

◁ PEAR *(Pyrus communis)*

pods dry and split open to release one or more seeds •

▽ FIG *(Ficus carica)*

stone fruits are fleshy, with a single seed •

fleshy fruits may have several seeds and are often edible

▽ WINGED CONE SEEDS

POD △ SEEDS

△ DRIED PODS

a fleshy receptacle • contains many tiny seeds that develop from flowers borne inside it

cone seeds are borne naked on the inner surface of the scales, which stay tightly closed • until the seeds are ripe

TYPES OF BARK

Trees develop their characteristic bark patterns and textures as a means of dealing with the increasing circumference of the trunk as they grow. Because the outer bark is composed of dead cells, it cannot grow and so, as the trunk expands, the bark cracks or peels in various ways. Bark is a useful feature in identification, since it can be used at any time of the year.

• smooth bark is dotted with lenticels

• bark of young tree was all white

• younger bark can be seen at base of ridges and fissures

Smooth bark is a feature of many young trees. It may crack or peel as they age.

Plates are irregular areas of bark, often flaking, with fissures or cracks in between.

Ridges and fissures may develop as thick bark cracks. They can be raised and prominent or deep.

• freshly exposed bark is distinctively coloured

• peeling bark by hand harms the tree

• flaking bark shows many ages and colours

Vertically peeling bark often hangs and falls from the tree in long strips and ribbons.

Horizontally peeling bark may unwind from the tree in paper-thin strips and wide sheets.

Irregularly flaking bark reveals different age layers, and gives the trunk a shaggy appearance.

CONIFER OR BROADLEAF?

IN ORDER TO DISCOVER all there is to know about a specific tree, scientists often use microscopic characters that are not visible to the naked eye. These provide vital, yet hidden, clues towards the positive identification of a species (although even scientists can, and do, make mistakes). But for most people,

careful, detailed observation of what is immediately visible must do. If you can recognize the distinctive features that categorize the two major groups, it is easy to distinguish conifers and their allies from broadleaves, and vice versa. The main characteristics are described and illustrated on these two pages.

CONIFERS AND THEIR ALLIES

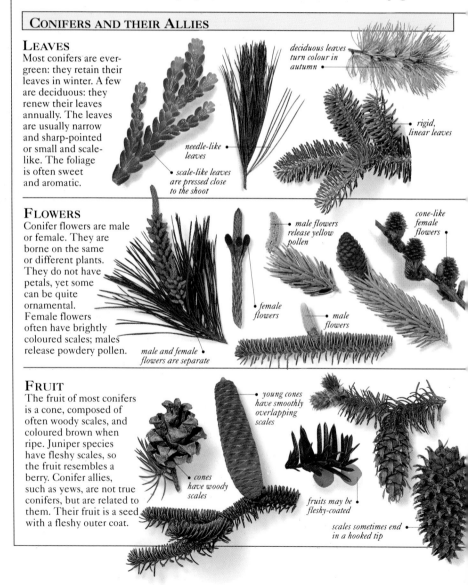

LEAVES
Most conifers are ever-green: they retain their leaves in winter. A few are deciduous: they renew their leaves annually. The leaves are usually narrow and sharp-pointed or small and scale-like. The foliage is often sweet and aromatic.

deciduous leaves turn colour in autumn •

• rigid, linear leaves

needle-like leaves

• scale-like leaves are pressed close to the shoot

FLOWERS
Conifer flowers are male or female. They are borne on the same or different plants. They do not have petals, yet some can be quite ornamental. Female flowers often have brightly coloured scales; males release powdery pollen.

• male flowers release yellow pollen

cone-like female flowers

• female flowers

• male flowers

male and female flowers are separate •

FRUIT
The fruit of most conifers is a cone, composed of often woody scales, and coloured brown when ripe. Juniper species have fleshy scales, so the fruit resembles a berry. Conifer allies, such as yews, are not true conifers, but are related to them. Their fruit is a seed with a fleshy outer coat.

• young cones have smoothly overlapping scales

• cones have woody scales

fruits may be fleshy-coated •

scales sometimes end in a hooked tip •

THE BOTANICAL DIFFERENCE

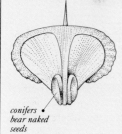

CONIFERS
Conifers and their allies are classed as gymnosperms: plants with naked seeds not enclosed in an ovary. They are considered to be more primitive than broadleaves.

conifers bear naked seeds

broadleaves have ovules inside an ovary

BROADLEAVES
Broadleaves are classed as angiosperms: plants with ovules enclosed for protection in an ovary. Following successful fertilization, the ovules develop into seeds.

BROADLEAVES

LEAVES
Broadleaves are evergreen or deciduous. The leaves are simple or compound, usually flattened, and have a distinct network of fine veins. They vary greatly in shape. The foliage may have an aromatic scent, but lacks the resinous quality of conifers.

deciduous leaves turn colour

compound leaves have leaflets

evergreen leaves stay green

veins are easy to see

leaf margin often has teeth or spines

FLOWERS
Broadleaf flowers are usually bisexual: male and female parts are in the same flower. Separate males and females are borne either on the same or different plants. Both types usually have petals, and are often fragrant. They can be small or large.

small flowers are often borne in clusters

sexes may be separate

broadleaf flowers usually have petals

bisexual flowers are usual

FRUIT
The fruit of broadleaves has much more diversity than that of most conifers, and comes in many forms. It may be a berry, acorn, capsule, nut, or pod; woody, fleshy-coated, or dry; spiny, rough, or smooth; inedible or edible; and any colour when ripe.

winged fruits

fleshy-coated fruit

woody fruits resemble cones

berry fruits can be brightly coloured

TREE IDENTIFICATION KEY

THE KEY on pages 18 to 33 uses leaf characteristics to help you to identify the trees that are described in this book. **Stage 1** (see right) establishes whether your tree is a conifer, broadleaf, or palm. **Stage 2** divides conifers and broadleaves into groups, according to leaf type. **Stage 3** divides each of these groups into more detailed groups that each contain two or more genera.

STAGE 1: WHICH GROUP?

The trees are divided into two major groups: Conifers, and Broadleaves (including Palms). Conifer features are described on page 16. Broadleaf features are described on page 17. Palm features are described on page 19.

CONIFER   BROADLEAF   PALM

STAGE 2: CONIFERS – DECIDUOUS OR EVERGREEN?

Only a few conifer species in this book are deciduous; most are evergreen. Deciduous species lose their leaves in autumn. In spring, their pale young leaves are clearly visible. Evergreens keep their leaves in winter, so they are easy to distinguish. In spring, look for pale young leaves together with dark old leaves. If your tree is deciduous, turn to pages 20–21. If it is evergreen, decide whether your leaf is not scale-like or scale-like, then turn to pages 20–21 or 22–23.

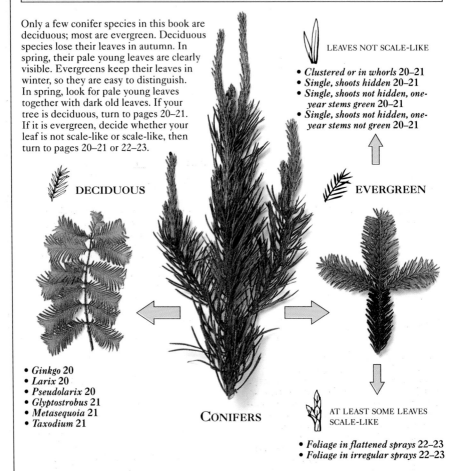

LEAVES NOT SCALE-LIKE

- *Clustered or in whorls* 20–21
- *Single, shoots hidden* 20–21
- *Single, shoots not hidden, one-year stems green* 20–21
- *Single, shoots not hidden, one-year stems not green* 20–21

EVERGREEN

DECIDUOUS

CONIFERS

- *Ginkgo* 20
- *Larix* 20
- *Pseudolarix* 20
- *Glyptostrobus* 21
- *Metasequoia* 21
- *Taxodium* 21

AT LEAST SOME LEAVES SCALE-LIKE

- *Foliage in flattened sprays* 22–23
- *Foliage in irregular sprays* 22–23

STAGE 2: BROADLEAVES – OPPOSITE OR ALTERNATE LEAVES?

All broadleaves have their leaves arranged in one of two ways: either opposite or alternate. Opposite leaves are borne in pairs or threes, one directly opposite the other, on either side of the stem. Alternate leaves are borne singly, staggered on alternate sides of the stem. Leaflets are opposite or alternate, too. If your leaf is opposite, turn to pages 22–25. If it is alternate, turn to pages 24–33.

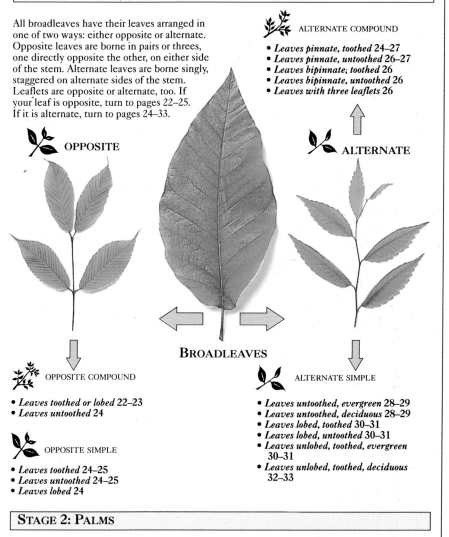

ALTERNATE COMPOUND

- *Leaves pinnate, toothed 24–27*
- *Leaves pinnate, untoothed 26–27*
- *Leaves bipinnate; toothed 26*
- *Leaves bipinnate, untoothed 26*
- *Leaves with three leaflets 26*

OPPOSITE

ALTERNATE

BROADLEAVES

OPPOSITE COMPOUND

- *Leaves toothed or lobed 22–23*
- *Leaves untoothed 24*

OPPOSITE SIMPLE

- *Leaves toothed 24–25*
- *Leaves untoothed 24–25*
- *Leaves lobed 24*

ALTERNATE SIMPLE

- *Leaves untoothed, evergreen 28–29*
- *Leaves untoothed, deciduous 28–29*
- *Leaves lobed, toothed 30–31*
- *Leaves lobed, untoothed 30–31*
- *Leaves unlobed, toothed, evergreen 30–31*
- *Leaves unlobed, toothed, deciduous 32–33*

STAGE 2: PALMS

Palms are often tree-like in habit, but are not true trees. They have a single, unbranched stem that does not increase in girth with age, and distinctively divided leaves. Most palms are native to warm regions, but some species grow in warm temperate regions, such as the Mediterranean and the southern United States. Chusan palm *(Trachycarpus fortunei)*, included in this book of largely temperate plants as an example of palms, is the hardiest species. If your leaf belongs to this palm, turn to page 31.

PALMS

STAGE 3: CONIFERS

This final stage in the identification key will guide you quickly to the correct section of the book. If you have turned straight to this part of the key, go back to pages 16 and 17, where the main characteristics that distinguish conifers and their allies, and broadleaves, from each other are illustrated and described. Having noted these features, move on to pages 18 and 19 and read through Stages 1 and 2 of the key. Now you are all set to start Stage 3.

Each individual leaf in the key represents a genus. You have already decided which type of conifer leaf you have – whether it is deciduous or evergreen, not scale-like or scale-like. You

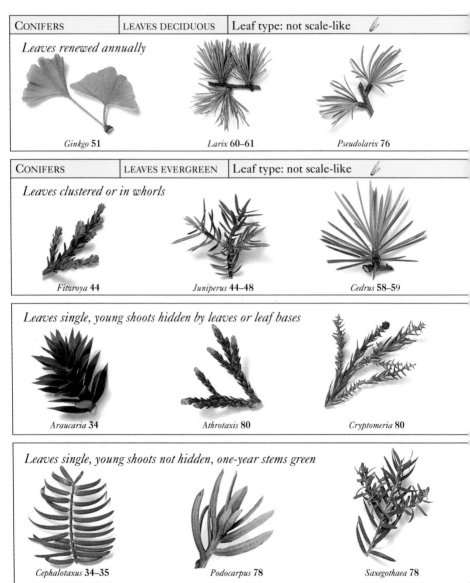

CONIFERS	LEAVES DECIDUOUS	Leaf type: not scale-like

Leaves renewed annually

Ginkgo **51** Larix **60–61** Pseudolarix **76**

CONIFERS	LEAVES EVERGREEN	Leaf type: not scale-like

Leaves clustered or in whorls

Fitzroya **44** Juniperus **44–48** Cedrus **58–59**

Leaves single, young shoots hidden by leaves or leaf bases

Araucaria **34** Athrotaxis **80** Cryptomeria **80**

Leaves single, young shoots not hidden, one-year stems green

Cephalotaxus **34–35** Podocarpus **78** Saxegothaea **78** will see that each large group has been further divided into several smaller groups. These give you an additional layer of information, which points you to finer detail; for example, whether the leaves are borne in clusters or whorls, or singly. Compare your leaf carefully with the leaves shown in the bands of each section, and decide to which group your leaf belongs. Compare your leaf to the leaves in the final group, and find the individual leaf that it most closely resembles. The genus to which it belongs is written below the photograph of the leaf. Turn to the page(s) indicated beside the genus name to find the relevant species entry or entries.

Glyptostrobus 81

Metasequoia 81

Taxodium 83

Pinus 66–75

Sciadopitys 82

Sequoia 82

Sequoiadendron 82

Taiwania 83

Taxus 79

Torreya 79

Cunninghamia 81

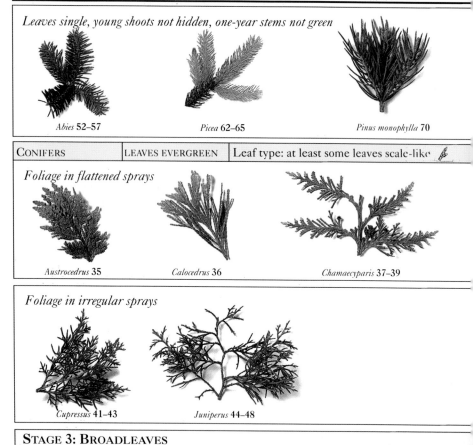

Leaves single, young shoots not hidden, one-year stems not green

Abies 52–57

Picea 62–65

Pinus monophylla 70

CONIFERS	LEAVES EVERGREEN	Leaf type: at least some leaves scale-like

Foliage in flattened sprays

Austrocedrus 35

Calocedrus 36

Chamaecyparis 37–39

Foliage in irregular sprays

Cupressus 41–43

Juniperus 44–48

STAGE 3: BROADLEAVES

This final stage in the identification key will guide you quickly to the correct section of the book. If you have turned straight to this part of the key, go back to pages 16 and 17, where the main characteristics that distinguish conifers and their allies, and broadleaves, from each other are illustrated and described. Having noted these features, move on to pages 18 and 19 and read through Stages 1 and 2 of the key. Now you are all set to start Stage 3.

Each individual leaf in the key represents a genus. You have already decided which type of broadleaf leaf you have – whether it is opposite or alternate, compound or simple. You will see

BROADLEAVES	LEAVES OPPOSITE	Leaf type: compound

Leaves toothed or lobed

Acer 84–104

Eucryphia 146–148

Aesculus 178–181

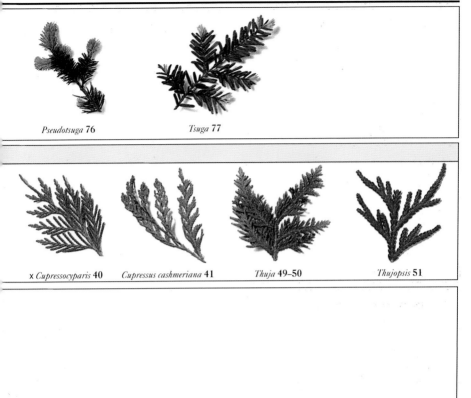

Pseudotsuga 76

Tsuga 77

x *Cupressocyparis* 40   *Cupressus cashmeriana* 41   *Thuja* 49–50   *Thujopsis* 51

that each large group has been further divided into several smaller groups. These give you an additional layer of information, which points you to finer detail; for example, whether the leaves are toothed, untoothed, or lobed, evergreen or deciduous. Compare your leaf carefully with the leaves shown in the bands of each section, and decide to which group your leaf belongs. Compare your leaf to those in the final group, and find the individual leaf that it most closely resembles. The genus to which it belongs is written below the leaf photograph. Turn to the page(s) indicated beside the genus name to find the relevant entry or entries.

Fraxinus 228–230

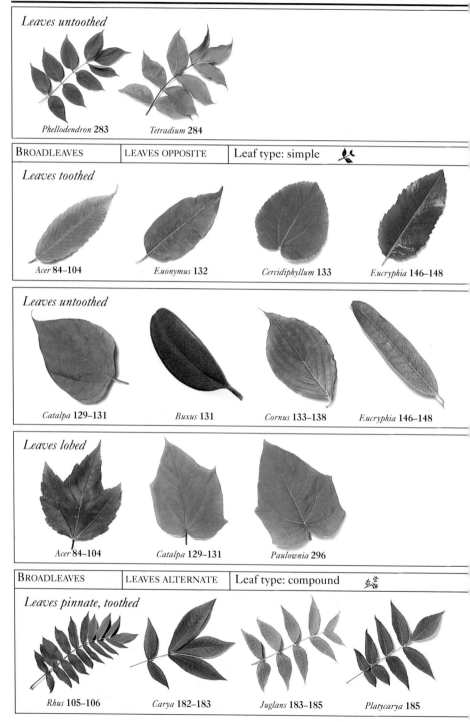

Leaves untoothed

Phellodendron **283**

Tetradium **284**

BROADLEAVES	LEAVES OPPOSITE	Leaf type: simple

Leaves toothed

Acer **84–104**

Euonymus **132**

Cercidiphyllum **133**

Eucryphia **146–148**

Leaves untoothed

Catalpa **129–131**

Buxus **131**

Cornus **133–138**

Eucryphia **146–148**

Leaves lobed

Acer **84–104**

Catalpa **129–131**

Paulownia **296**

BROADLEAVES	LEAVES ALTERNATE	Leaf type: compound

Leaves pinnate, toothed

Rhus **105–106**

Carya **182–183**

Juglans **183–185**

Platycarya **185**

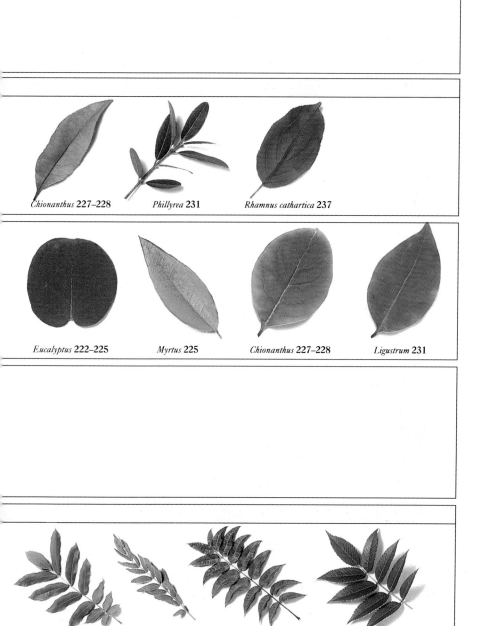

Chionanthus 227–228

Phillyrea 231

Rhamnus cathartica 237

Eucalyptus 222–225

Myrtus 225

Chionanthus 227–228

Ligustrum 231

Pterocarya 186–187

Gleditsia 195

Toona 217

Sorbus 274–282

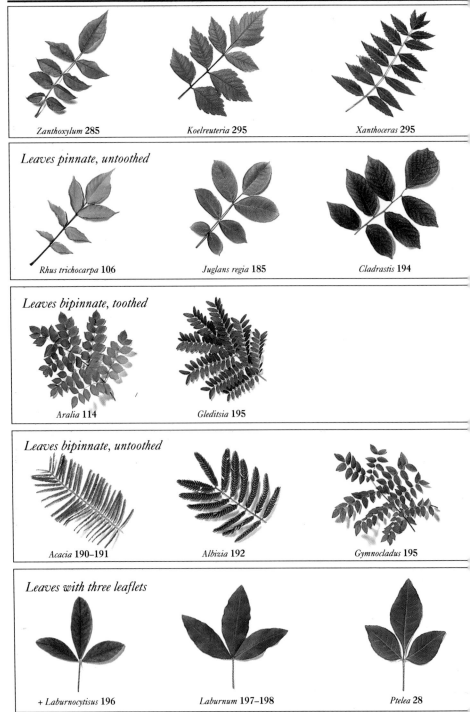

Zanthoxylum 285

Koelreuteria 295

Xanthoceras 295

Leaves pinnate, untoothed

Rhus trichocarpa 106

Juglans regia 185

Cladrastis 194

Leaves bipinnate, toothed

Aralia 114

Gleditsia 195

Leaves bipinnate, untoothed

Acacia 190–191

Albizia 192

Gymnocladus 195

Leaves with three leaflets

+ *Laburnocytisus* 196

Laburnum 197–198

Ptelea 28

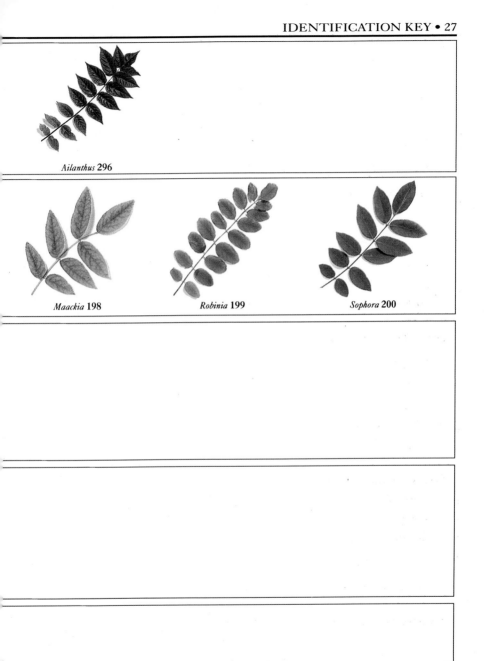

Ailanthus 296

Maackia 198

Robinia 199

Sophora 200

BROADLEAVES	LEAVES ALTERNATE	Leaf type: simple

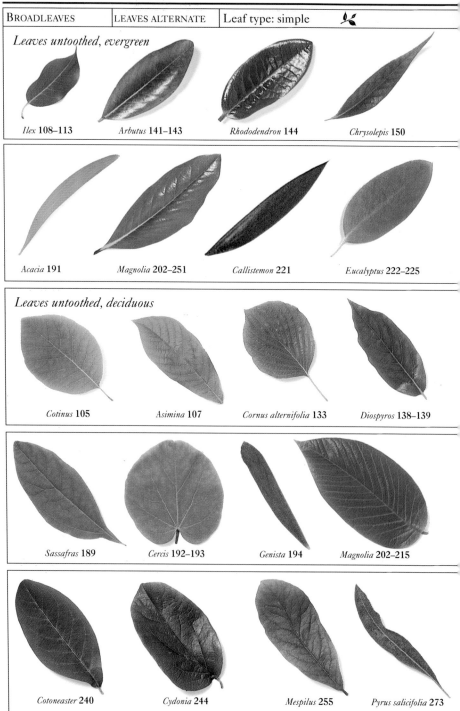

Leaves untoothed, evergreen

Ilex 108–113

Arbutus 141–143

Rhododendron 144

Chrysolepis 150

Acacia 191

Magnolia 202–251

Callistemon 221

Eucalyptus 222–225

Leaves untoothed, deciduous

Cotinus 105

Asimina 107

Cornus alternifolia 133

Diospyros 138–139

Sassafras 189

Cercis 192–193

Genista 194

Magnolia 202–215

Cotoneaster 240

Cydonia 244

Mespilus 255

Pyrus salicifolia 273

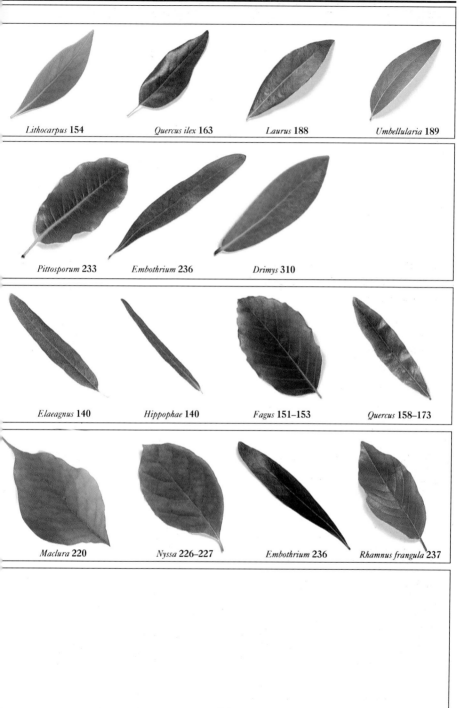

Lithocarpus 154

Quercus ilex 163

Laurus 188

Umbellularia 189

Pittosporum 233

Embothrium 236

Drimys 310

Elaeagnus 140

Hippophae 140

Fagus 151–153

Quercus 158–173

Maclura 220

Nyssa 226–227

Embothrium 236

Rhamnus frangula 237

Leaves lobed, toothed

Kalopanax 115

Quercus 158–173

Liquidambar 175–176

Broussonetia 218

x Crataemespilus 244

Malus 245–254

Sorbus 274–282

Populus alba 286

Leaves lobed, untoothed

Quercus 158–173

Sassafras 189

Liriodendron 201

Leaves unlobed, toothed, evergreen

Ilex 108–113

Pseudopanax 115

Maytenus 132

Azara 174

Photinia 256–257

Prunus 265

Ficus 219

Morus 220

Platanus 234–235

Crataegus 240–243

Tilia mongolica 304

Trachycarpus 232

Arbutus 141–143

Nothofagus 155–157

Quercus 158–173

Trochodendron 306

Leaves unlobed, toothed, deciduous

Alnus 116–117

Betula 118–125

Carpinus 126–127

Corylus 127

Fagus 151–153

Nothofagus 155–157

Quercus 158–173

Idesia 174

Morus 220

Davidia 226

Amelanchier 238–239

Crataegus 240–243

Pyrus 273

Sorbus 274–282

Populus 286–290

Salix 291–294

Tilia 302–305

Celtis 306–307

Ulmus 308–309

Zelkova 309–310

Ostrya 128

Oxydendrum 143

Eucommia 145

Castanea 149–150

Parrotia 177

Parrotiopsis 177

Hoheria 216

Broussonetia 218

Malus 245–254

Mespilus 255

Photinia 256–257

Prunus 258–272

Halesia 297

Pterostyrax 298

Styrax 298–299

Stewartia 300–301

CONIFERS
AND THEIR ALLIES

ARAUCARIACEAE

TWO GENERA AND ABOUT 30 species of large, evergreen trees belong to this family. In the main, they are native to the southern hemisphere, but extend into South-east Asia. Many are important timber trees. The monkey puzzle *(Araucaria araucana)* is the most well-known member of the family.

Family ARAUCARIACEAE	Species *Araucaria araucana*	Author (Molina) K. Koch

MONKEY PUZZLE

Leaves Ovate, to 5cm (2in) long and 2cm (¾in) wide, broad at the base, with a spiny tip, glossy dark green, overlapping, all around the shoot. *Bark* Grey, wrinkled. *Flowers* 10cm (4in) long, males brown, clustered, females green-brown, singly, on separate plants in summer. *Fruit* An ovoid, brown cone, to 15cm (6in) long.
• **NATIVE REGION** Argentina, Chile.
• **HABITAT** Mountains.

brown male flowers borne in clusters

rigid leaves end in sharp point

long, pointed cone scales

Height 50m (164ft)	Shape Unique	Leaf persistence Evergreen	Leaf type

CEPHALOTAXACEAE

ALTHOUGH FOSSIL EVIDENCE shows that this family was once widely distributed, it is now restricted in the wild to the Far East. The species in the only genus are small trees or large shrubs, with linear leaves and plum-like fruits. Male and female flowers are borne in clusters on separate plants.

Family CEPHALOTAXACEAE	Species *Cephalotaxus fortunei*	Author W.J. Hooker

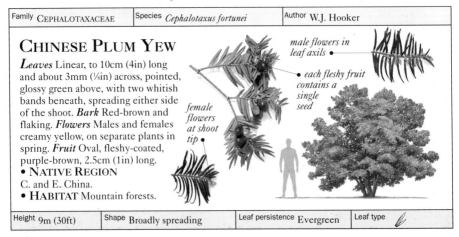

CHINESE PLUM YEW

Leaves Linear, to 10cm (4in) long and about 3mm (⅛in) across, pointed, glossy green above, with two whitish bands beneath, spreading either side of the shoot. *Bark* Red-brown and flaking. *Flowers* Males and females creamy yellow, on separate plants in spring. *Fruit* Oval, fleshy-coated, purple-brown, 2.5cm (1in) long.
• **NATIVE REGION** C. and E. China.
• **HABITAT** Mountain forests.

male flowers in leaf axils

each fleshy fruit contains a single seed

female flowers at shoot tip

Height 9m (30ft)	Shape Broadly spreading	Leaf persistence Evergreen	Leaf type

| Family CEPHALOTAXACEAE | Species *Cephalotaxus harringtonia* | Author (Forbes) K. Koch |

COW TAIL PINE

Leaves Linear, to 5cm (2in) long and 3mm (⅛in) across, pointed, glossy dark green above, with two bands beneath, spreading either side of the shoot. *Bark* Brown, flaking. *Flowers* Creamy white, males in the leaf axils, females at the tips of the shoots, on separate plants in spring. *Fruit* An oval seed, 2.5cm (1in) long, blue-green ripening to purple-brown.
• **NATIVE REGION** Unknown.
• **HABITAT** Known only in cultivation.
• **REMARK** This species was originally described from a Japanese garden plant.

VAR. DRUPACEA ▷
This wild Japanese form has shorter leaves.

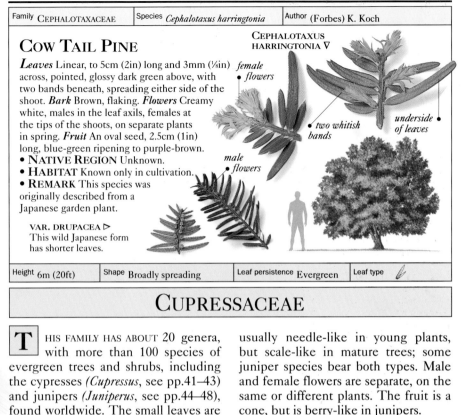

CEPHALOTAXUS HARRINGTONIA ▽

female flowers

two whitish bands

underside of leaves

male flowers

| Height 6m (20ft) | Shape Broadly spreading | Leaf persistence Evergreen | Leaf type |

CUPRESSACEAE

THIS FAMILY HAS ABOUT 20 genera, with more than 100 species of evergreen trees and shrubs, including the cypresses *(Cupressus, see pp.41–43)* and junipers *(Juniperus, see pp.44–48)*, found worldwide. The small leaves are usually needle-like in young plants, but scale-like in mature trees; some juniper species bear both types. Male and female flowers are separate, on the same or different plants. The fruit is a cone, but is berry-like in junipers.

| Family CUPRESSACEAE | Species *Austrocedrus chilensis* | Author (D. Don) Florin & Boutelje |

CHILEAN CEDAR

Leaves Scale-like, to 5mm (³⁄₁₆in) long, flattened, with a blunt point, glossy dark green sometimes marked with white above, with a conspicuous white band beneath, borne in flattened sprays; on upper and lower sides of shoot much smaller. *Bark* Grey-brown, scaly. *Flowers* Males and females both very small, males yellowish, females green, in small clusters at the tips of the shoots in early spring. *Fruit* An oblong cone, 1cm (⅜in) long, green ripening to brown, with four overlapping scales.
• **NATIVE REGION** Argentina, Chile.
• **HABITAT** Mountains.
• **REMARK** Also known as *Libocedrus chilensis*. It is closely related to the incense cedar *(Calocedrus decurrens, see p.36)*.

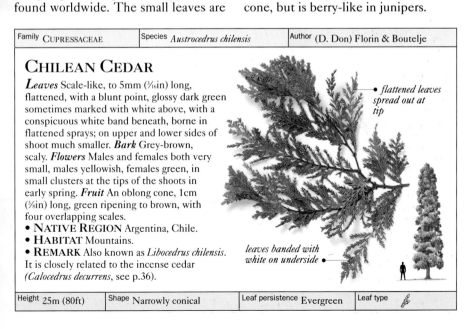

flattened leaves spread out at tip

leaves banded with white on underside

| Height 25m (80ft) | Shape Narrowly conical | Leaf persistence Evergreen | Leaf type |

Family CUPRESSACEAE	Species *Calocedrus decurrens*	Author (Torrey) Florin

INCENSE CEDAR

Leaves Scale-like, to about 3mm (⅛in) long, in sets of two pairs together, with a triangular, sharp-pointed tip, glossy dark green, borne in flattened, aromatic sprays; upper and lower leaves largest. **Bark** Red-brown and scaly. **Flowers** Males and females both very small, males yellow, females green, in small clusters at the tips of the shoots in winter. **Fruit** An oblong, yellow-brown cone, 2.5cm (1in) long, with six overlapping scales.
• **NATIVE REGION**
W. North America.
• **HABITAT** Forests on mountain slopes.
• **REMARK** Also known as *Libocedrus decurrens*. In the wild, old plants eventually become more open in shape. It produces a useful, very aromatic wood.

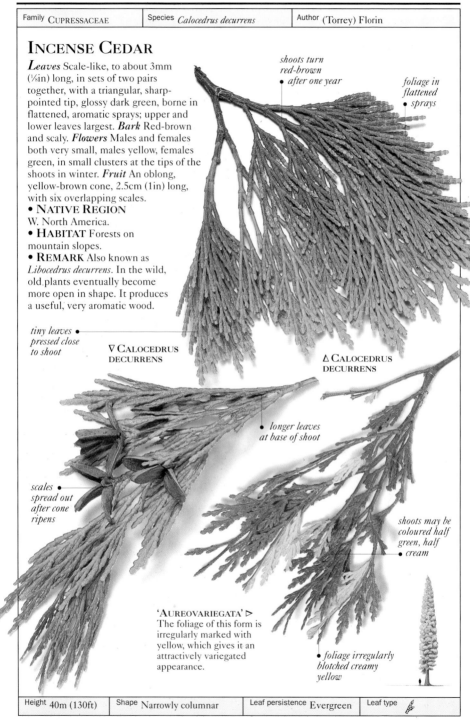

shoots turn red-brown after one year

foliage in flattened sprays

tiny leaves pressed close to shoot

▽ **CALOCEDRUS DECURRENS**

△ **CALOCEDRUS DECURRENS**

longer leaves at base of shoot

scales spread out after cone ripens

shoots may be coloured half green, half cream

'AUREOVARIEGATA' ▷
The foliage of this form is irregularly marked with yellow, which gives it an attractively variegated appearance.

foliage irregularly blotched creamy yellow

Height 40m (130ft)	Shape Narrowly columnar	Leaf persistence Evergreen	Leaf type

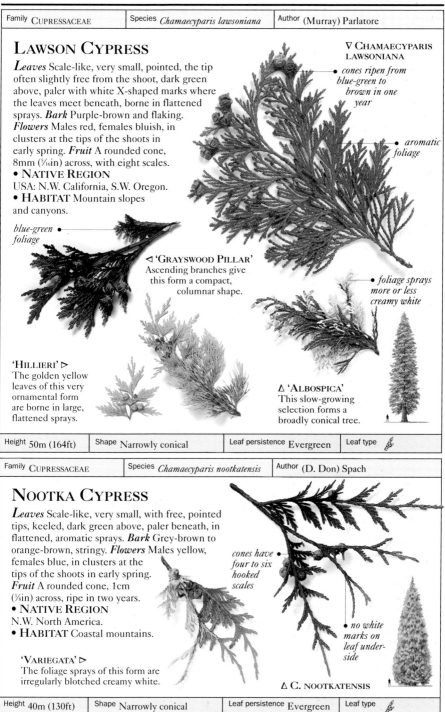

Family CUPRESSACEAE	Species *Chamaecyparis lawsoniana*	Author (Murray) Parlatore

LAWSON CYPRESS

Leaves Scale-like, very small, pointed, the tip often slightly free from the shoot, dark green above, paler with white X-shaped marks where the leaves meet beneath, borne in flattened sprays. **Bark** Purple-brown and flaking. **Flowers** Males red, females bluish, in clusters at the tips of the shoots in early spring. **Fruit** A rounded cone, 8mm (⁵⁄₁₆in) across, with eight scales.
• **NATIVE REGION**
USA: N.W. California, S.W. Oregon.
• **HABITAT** Mountain slopes and canyons.

∇ CHAMAECYPARIS LAWSONIANA

cones ripen from blue-green to brown in one year

aromatic foliage

blue-green foliage

◁ **'GRAYSWOOD PILLAR'**
Ascending branches give this form a compact, columnar shape.

foliage sprays more or less creamy white

'HILLIERI' ▷
The golden yellow leaves of this very ornamental form are borne in large, flattened sprays.

△ **'ALBOSPICA'**
This slow-growing selection forms a broadly conical tree.

Height 50m (164ft)	Shape Narrowly conical	Leaf persistence Evergreen	Leaf type

Family CUPRESSACEAE	Species *Chamaecyparis nootkatensis*	Author (D. Don) Spach

NOOTKA CYPRESS

Leaves Scale-like, very small, with free, pointed tips, keeled, dark green above, paler beneath, in flattened, aromatic sprays. **Bark** Grey-brown to orange-brown, stringy. **Flowers** Males yellow, females blue, in clusters at the tips of the shoots in early spring. **Fruit** A rounded cone, 1cm (⅜in) across, ripe in two years.
• **NATIVE REGION**
N.W. North America.
• **HABITAT** Coastal mountains.

cones have four to six hooked scales

no white marks on leaf underside

'VARIEGATA' ▷
The foliage sprays of this form are irregularly blotched creamy white.

△ C. NOOTKATENSIS

Height 40m (130ft)	Shape Narrowly conical	Leaf persistence Evergreen	Leaf type

| Family CUPRESSACEAE | Species *Chamaecyparis obtusa* | Author (Siebold & Zuccarini) Endlicher |

HINOKI CYPRESS

Leaves Scale-like, very small, blunt at the tip, dark green above, with bright white X- or Y-shaped marks where the leaves meet beneath, in flattened, aromatic sprays. **Bark** Red-brown and soft, peeling in thin strips. **Flowers** Males reddish yellow, females pale brown, in small clusters at the tips of the shoots in spring. **Fruit** A rounded cone, to 1.2cm (½in) across, green ripening to brown.
• **NATIVE REGION** Japan.
• **HABITAT** Usually mountain slopes.
• **REMARK** The cultivated forms include some of dwarf habit.

'CRIPPSII' ▷
The bright golden-yellow coloration of this ornamental form apears only on the outermost branches.

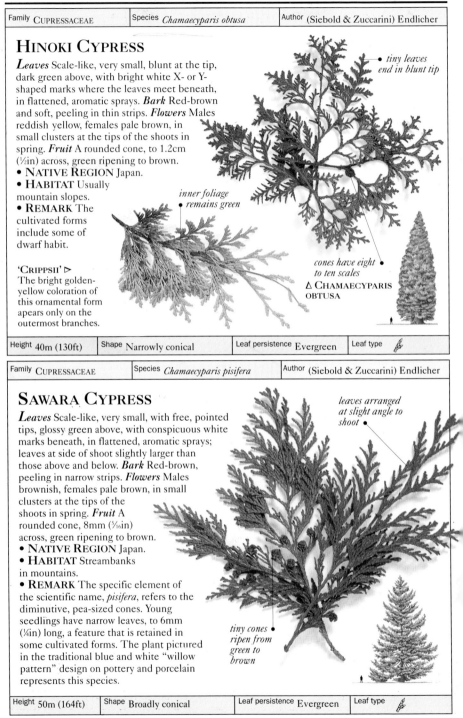

tiny leaves end in blunt tip

inner foliage remains green

cones have eight to ten scales

△ CHAMAECYPARIS OBTUSA

| Height 40m (130ft) | Shape Narrowly conical | Leaf persistence Evergreen | Leaf type |

| Family CUPRESSACEAE | Species *Chamaecyparis pisifera* | Author (Siebold & Zuccarini) Endlicher |

SAWARA CYPRESS

Leaves Scale-like, very small, with free, pointed tips, glossy green above, with conspicuous white marks beneath, in flattened, aromatic sprays; leaves at side of shoot slightly larger than those above and below. **Bark** Red-brown, peeling in narrow strips. **Flowers** Males brownish, females pale brown, in small clusters at the tips of the shoots in spring. **Fruit** A rounded cone, 8mm (5/16in) across, green ripening to brown.
• **NATIVE REGION** Japan.
• **HABITAT** Streambanks in mountains.
• **REMARK** The specific element of the scientific name, *pisifera*, refers to the diminutive, pea-sized cones. Young seedlings have narrow leaves, to 6mm (¼in) long, a feature that is retained in some cultivated forms. The plant pictured in the traditional blue and white "willow pattern" design on pottery and porcelain represents this species.

leaves arranged at slight angle to shoot

tiny cones ripen from green to brown

| Height 50m (164ft) | Shape Broadly conical | Leaf persistence Evergreen | Leaf type |

Family CUPRESSACEAE	Species *Chamaecyparis thyoides*	Author (L.) Britton, Sterns, Poggenberg

WHITE CYPRESS

Leaves Scale-like and very small, pointed at the tip, green to grey-green above, often with a tiny speck of resin, with bright white marks beneath, on small, slender shoots, in small, flattened, aromatic sprays; leaves at side of shoot slightly larger than those above. *Bark* Grey to brown, fibrous, peeling in strips. *Flowers* Males brownish, females green, in small clusters at the tips of the shoots in spring. *Fruit* A rounded cone, 6mm (¼in) across, glaucous ripening to brown, with six pointed scales.

• NATIVE REGION
E. United States.
• HABITAT Usually swamps, wet ground, and moist places.
• REMARK Also known as Atlantic white cedar, swamp cedar.

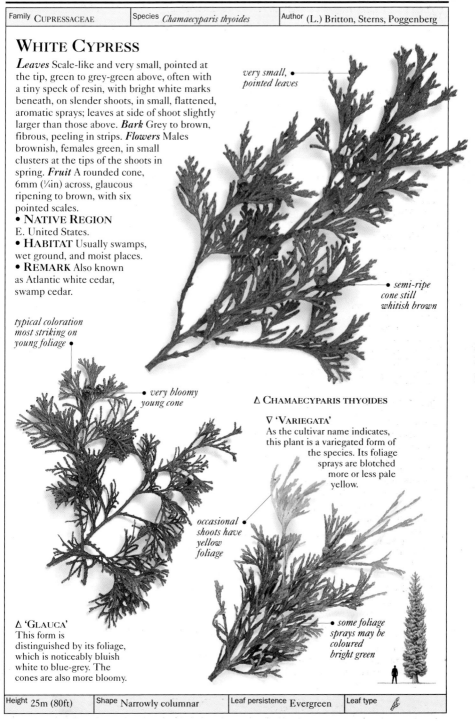

very small, pointed leaves

semi-ripe cone still whitish brown

typical coloration most striking on young foliage

very bloomy young cone

△ CHAMAECYPARIS THYOIDES

▽ 'VARIEGATA'
As the cultivar name indicates, this plant is a variegated form of the species. Its foliage sprays are blotched more or less pale yellow.

occasional shoots have yellow foliage

some foliage sprays may be coloured bright green

△ 'GLAUCA'
This form is distinguished by its foliage, which is noticeably bluish white to blue-grey. The cones are also more bloomy.

Height 25m (80ft)	Shape Narrowly columnar	Leaf persistence Evergreen	Leaf type

Family CUPRESSACEAE	Species x *Cupressocyparis leylandii*	Author (Dallimore & Jackson) Dallimore

LEYLAND CYPRESS

Leaves Scale-like and very small, with pointed tips, dark green above, paler beneath, arranged at various angles to the shoot, borne in flattened sprays; leaves at side of and above shoot similar in size. **Bark** Red-brown, with shallow ridges. **Flowers** Males yellow, females green, in small clusters at the tips of the shoots in early spring. **Fruit** A rounded cone, to 2cm (¾in) across, blue-green ripening to glossy brown.

• **NATIVE REGION** Of garden origin.
• **REMARK** A hybrid between Nootka cypress *(Chamaecyparis nootkatensis,* see p.37) and Monterey cypress *(Cupressus macrocarpa,* see p.42). 'Haggerston Grey', which has dull green foliage, is the form most commonly grown.

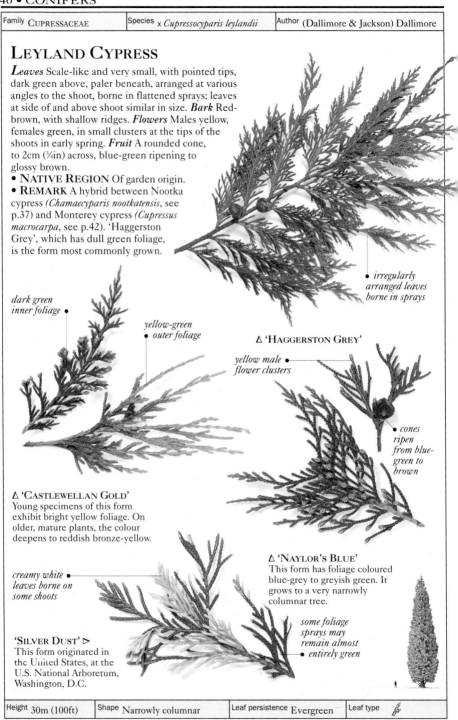

• *irregularly arranged leaves borne in sprays*

△ '**HAGGERSTON GREY**'

yellow male • *flower clusters*

dark green inner foliage •

yellow-green • *outer foliage*

• *cones ripen from blue-green to brown*

△ '**CASTLEWELLAN GOLD**'
Young specimens of this form exhibit bright yellow foliage. On older, mature plants, the colour deepens to reddish bronze-yellow.

△ '**NAYLOR'S BLUE**'
This form has foliage coloured blue-grey to greyish green. It grows to a very narrowly columnar tree.

creamy white • *leaves borne on some shoots*

some foliage sprays may remain almost • *entirely green*

'**SILVER DUST**' ▷
This form originated in the United States, at the U.S. National Arboretum, Washington, D.C.

Height 30m (100ft)	Shape Narrowly columnar	Leaf persistence Evergreen	Leaf type

| Family CUPRESSACEAE | Species *Cupressus cashmeriana* | Author Royle ex Carrière |

KASHMIR CYPRESS

Leaves Scale-like and very small, but with free, spreading tips making the foliage rough to the touch, borne in glaucous, drooping, flattened sprays. **Bark** Red-brown, peeling in vertical strips. **Flowers** Males and females both inconspicuous, in separate clusters on the same plant in early to midwinter. **Fruit** A rounded cone, 1.2cm (½in) across, blue-green becoming greenish yellow ripening to brown, the scales each with a hooked point.
• **NATIVE REGION** Not known; probably Himalayas.
• **HABITAT** Now known only in cultivation.
• **REMARK** A particularly elegant tree, of small to medium height. The habit becomes more spreading as it ages.

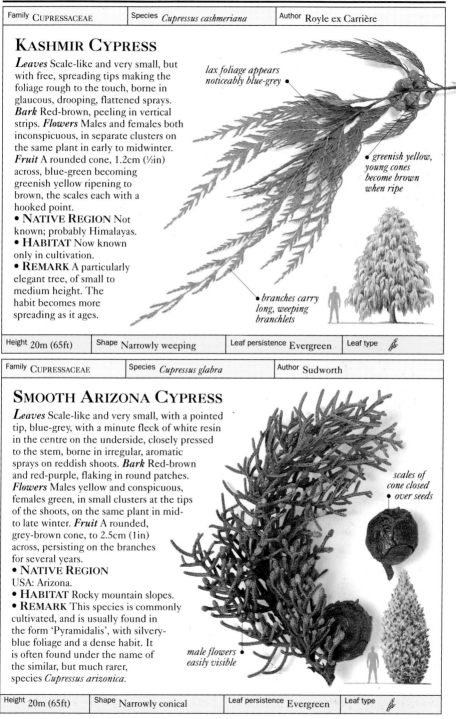

lax foliage appears noticeably blue-grey

greenish yellow, young cones become brown when ripe

branches carry long, weeping branchlets

| Height 20m (65ft) | Shape Narrowly weeping | Leaf persistence Evergreen | Leaf type |

| Family CUPRESSACEAE | Species *Cupressus glabra* | Author Sudworth |

SMOOTH ARIZONA CYPRESS

Leaves Scale-like and very small, with a pointed tip, blue-grey, with a minute fleck of white resin in the centre on the underside, closely pressed to the stem, borne in irregular, aromatic sprays on reddish shoots. **Bark** Red-brown and red-purple, flaking in round patches. **Flowers** Males yellow and conspicuous, females green, in small clusters at the tips of the shoots, on the same plant in mid- to late winter. **Fruit** A rounded, grey-brown cone, to 2.5cm (1in) across, persisting on the branches for several years.
• **NATIVE REGION** USA: Arizona.
• **HABITAT** Rocky mountain slopes.
• **REMARK** This species is commonly cultivated, and is usually found in the form 'Pyramidalis', with silvery-blue foliage and a dense habit. It is often found under the name of the similar, but much rarer, species *Cupressus arizonica.*

scales of cone closed over seeds

male flowers easily visible

| Height 20m (65ft) | Shape Narrowly conical | Leaf persistence Evergreen | Leaf type |

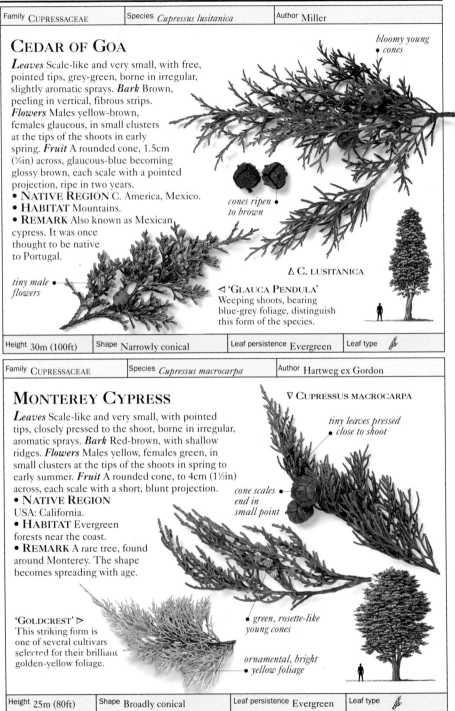

Family CUPRESSACEAE	Species *Cupressus lusitanica*	Author Miller

CEDAR OF GOA

Leaves Scale-like and very small, with free, pointed tips, grey-green, borne in irregular, slightly aromatic sprays. **Bark** Brown, peeling in vertical, fibrous strips. **Flowers** Males yellow-brown, females glaucous, in small clusters at the tips of the shoots in early spring. **Fruit** A rounded cone, 1.5cm (⅝in) across, glaucous-blue becoming glossy brown, each scale with a pointed projection, ripe in two years.
• **NATIVE REGION** C. America, Mexico.
• **HABITAT** Mountains.
• **REMARK** Also known as Mexican cypress. It was once thought to be native to Portugal.

bloomy young cones

cones ripen to brown

tiny male flowers

△ C. LUSITANICA

◁ 'GLAUCA PENDULA'
Weeping shoots, bearing blue-grey foliage, distinguish this form of the species.

Height 30m (100ft)	Shape Narrowly conical	Leaf persistence Evergreen	Leaf type

Family CUPRESSACEAE	Species *Cupressus macrocarpa*	Author Hartweg ex Gordon

MONTEREY CYPRESS

∇ CUPRESSUS MACROCARPA

Leaves Scale-like and very small, with pointed tips, closely pressed to the shoot, borne in irregular, aromatic sprays. **Bark** Red-brown, with shallow ridges. **Flowers** Males yellow, females green, in small clusters at the tips of the shoots in spring to early summer. **Fruit** A rounded cone, to 4cm (1½in) across, each scale with a short, blunt projection.
• **NATIVE REGION** USA: California.
• **HABITAT** Evergreen forests near the coast.
• **REMARK** A rare tree, found around Monterey. The shape becomes spreading with age.

tiny leaves pressed close to shoot

cone scales end in small point

'GOLDCREST' ▷
This striking form is one of several cultivars selected for their brilliant golden-yellow foliage.

green, rosette-like young cones

ornamental, bright yellow foliage

Height 25m (80ft)	Shape Broadly conical	Leaf persistence Evergreen	Leaf type

Family CUPRESSACEAE	Species *Cupressus sempervirens*	Author Linnaeus

ITALIAN CYPRESS

Leaves Scale-like and very small, with blunt tips, very dark green, with no white marks beneath, only slightly aromatic or with no scent, borne in irregular sprays, closely pressed to the shoots. *Bark* Grey-brown, with shallow, spiral ridges. *Flowers* Males yellow-brown, females green, in small clusters at the tips of the shoots in spring. *Fruit* An egg-shaped to rounded cone, to 4cm (1½in) long, green ripening to brown, the scales overlapping, each scale with a small projection.
• **NATIVE REGION** S.W. Asia, E. Mediterranean.
• **HABITAT** Rocky places in mountains.
• **REMARK** The narrow form known as 'Stricta' is so commonly planted in the Mediterranean that it forms a characteristic feature of the landscape.

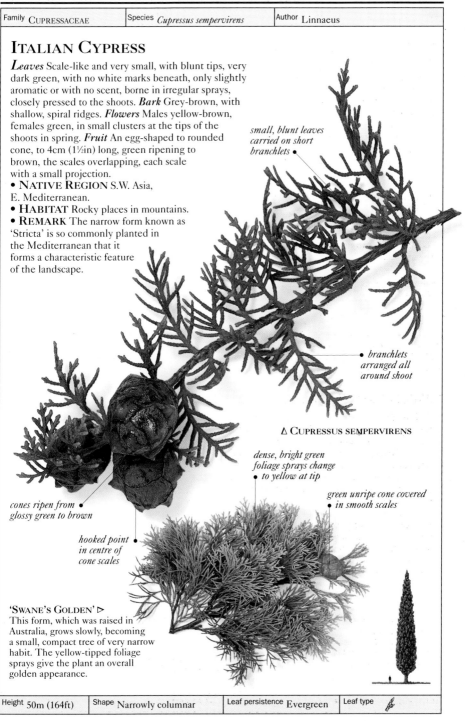

small, blunt leaves carried on short branchlets •

• branchlets arranged all around shoot

△ **CUPRESSUS SEMPERVIRENS**

dense, bright green foliage sprays change • to yellow at tip

green unripe cone covered • in smooth scales

cones ripen from • glossy green to brown

hooked point in centre of cone scales

'SWANE'S GOLDEN' ▷
This form, which was raised in Australia, grows slowly, becoming a small, compact tree of very narrow habit. The yellow-tipped foliage sprays give the plant an overall golden appearance.

Height 50m (164ft)	Shape Narrowly columnar	Leaf persistence Evergreen	Leaf type

| Family CUPRESSACEAE | Species *Fitzroya cupressoides* | Author (Molina) Johnston |

PATAGONIAN CYPRESS

Leaves Oblong and thick, to 3mm (⅛in) long, bluntly pointed, in whorls of three, dark green, with two white bands on each side, on slender, pendulous shoots. **Bark** Red-brown, peeling in long, vertical strips. **Flowers** Males yellow, females yellow-green, borne in small clusters at the tips of the shoots in spring. **Fruit** A rounded, brown cone, 8mm (⁵⁄₁₆in) across.
• **NATIVE REGION** Argentina, Chile.
• **HABITAT** Mountains.
• **REMARK** Also known as alerce. Scientifically named after Captain Fitzroy, in whose ship, the *Beagle*, Charles Darwin voyaged to South America.

leaves in whorls of three

tips of leaves are blunt

leaves persist for several years

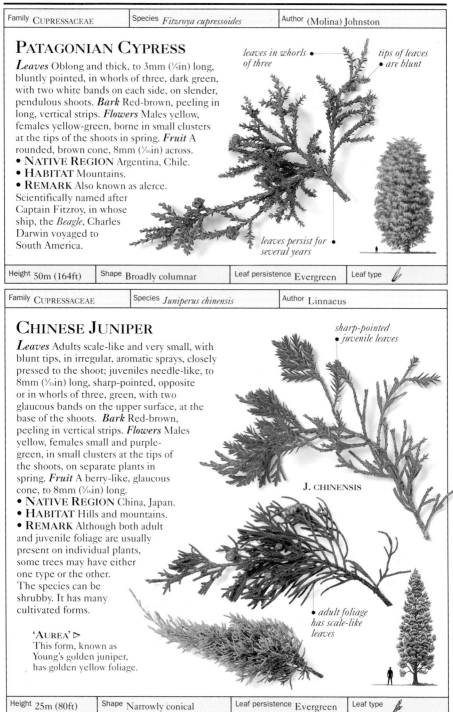

| Height 50m (164ft) | Shape Broadly columnar | Leaf persistence Evergreen | Leaf type |

| Family CUPRESSACEAE | Species *Juniperus chinensis* | Author Linnaeus |

CHINESE JUNIPER

Leaves Adults scale-like and very small, with blunt tips, in irregular, aromatic sprays, closely pressed to the shoot; juveniles needle-like, to 8mm (⁵⁄₁₆in) long, sharp-pointed, opposite or in whorls of three, green, with two glaucous bands on the upper surface, at the base of the shoots. **Bark** Red-brown, peeling in vertical strips. **Flowers** Males yellow, females small and purple-green, in small clusters at the tips of the shoots, on separate plants in spring. **Fruit** A berry-like, glaucous cone, to 8mm (⁵⁄₁₆in) long.
• **NATIVE REGION** China, Japan.
• **HABITAT** Hills and mountains.
• **REMARK** Although both adult and juvenile foliage are usually present on individual plants, some trees may have either one type or the other. The species can be shrubby. It has many cultivated forms.

'AUREA' ▷
This form, known as Young's golden juniper, has golden yellow foliage.

sharp-pointed juvenile leaves

J. CHINENSIS

adult foliage has scale-like leaves

| Height 25m (80ft) | Shape Narrowly conical | Leaf persistence Evergreen | Leaf type |

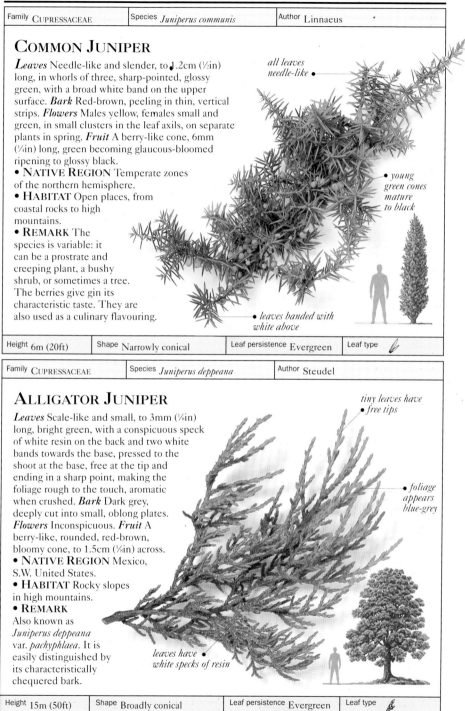

Family CUPRESSACEAE	Species *Juniperus communis*	Author Linnaeus

COMMON JUNIPER

Leaves Needle-like and slender, to 1.2cm (½in) long, in whorls of three, sharp-pointed, glossy green, with a broad white band on the upper surface. *Bark* Red-brown, peeling in thin, vertical strips. *Flowers* Males yellow, females small and green, in small clusters in the leaf axils, on separate plants in spring. *Fruit* A berry-like cone, 6mm (¼in) long, green becoming glaucous-bloomed ripening to glossy black.
• **NATIVE REGION** Temperate zones of the northern hemisphere.
• **HABITAT** Open places, from coastal rocks to high mountains.
• **REMARK** The species is variable: it can be a prostrate and creeping plant, a bushy shrub, or sometimes a tree. The berries give gin its characteristic taste. They are also used as a culinary flavouring.

all leaves needle-like •

• young green cones mature to black

• leaves banded with white above

Height 6m (20ft)	Shape Narrowly conical	Leaf persistence Evergreen	Leaf type

Family CUPRESSACEAE	Species *Juniperus deppeana*	Author Steudel

ALLIGATOR JUNIPER

Leaves Scale-like and small, to 3mm (⅛in) long, bright green, with a conspicuous speck of white resin on the back and two white bands towards the base, pressed to the shoot at the base, free at the tip and ending in a sharp point, making the foliage rough to the touch, aromatic when crushed. *Bark* Dark grey, deeply cut into small, oblong plates. *Flowers* Inconspicuous. *Fruit* A berry-like, rounded, red-brown, bloomy cone, to 1.5cm (⅝in) across.
• **NATIVE REGION** Mexico, S.W. United States.
• **HABITAT** Rocky slopes in high mountains.
• **REMARK** Also known as *Juniperus deppeana* var. *pachyphlaea*. It is easily distinguished by its characteristically chequered bark.

tiny leaves have • free tips

• foliage appears blue-grey

leaves have • white specks of resin

Height 15m (50ft)	Shape Broadly conical	Leaf persistence Evergreen	Leaf type

Family CUPRESSACEAE	Species *Juniperus drupacea*	Author Labillardière

SYRIAN JUNIPER

Leaves Needle-like, rigid, and slender, to 2.5cm (1in) long, in whorls of three, sharp-pointed, marked with two broad, whitish bands above with a green midrib and margin, glossy green and ridged beneath, spreading from three-angled shoots. **Bark** Orange-brown, peeling in thin, vertical strips. **Flowers** Males yellow, females very small and green, borne in small clusters at the tips of short, leafy shoots, on separate plants in spring. **Fruit** A rather large, berry-like, bloomy cone, 2.5cm (1in) long, blue-green at first becoming brown ripening to blackish purple, the triangular scales ending in a pointed tip.
- **NATIVE REGION** S.W. Asia, Greece.
- **HABITAT** Mountain forests.
- **REMARK** The species is easily distinguished by its leaves, which are broader than those of any other juniper. The large cones are seen only rarely in cultivated plants.

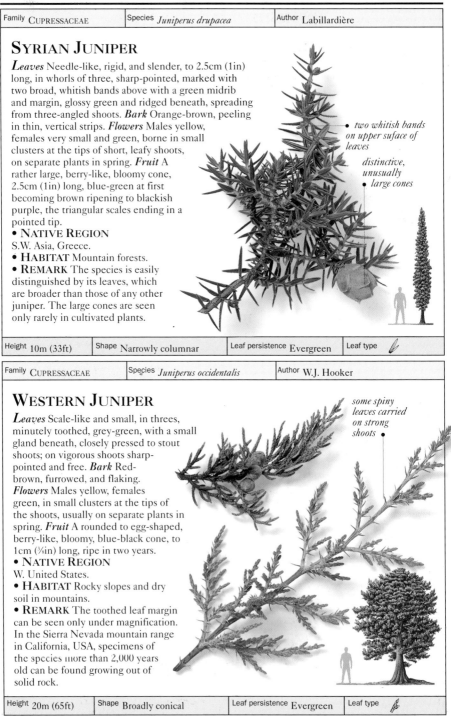

• *two whitish bands on upper suface of leaves*

distinctive, unusually • *large cones*

Height 10m (33ft)	Shape Narrowly columnar	Leaf persistence Evergreen	Leaf type

Family CUPRESSACEAE	Species *Juniperus occidentalis*	Author W.J. Hooker

WESTERN JUNIPER

Leaves Scale-like and small, in threes, minutely toothed, grey-green, with a small gland beneath, closely pressed to stout shoots; on vigorous shoots sharp-pointed and free. **Bark** Red-brown, furrowed, and flaking. **Flowers** Males yellow, females green, in small clusters at the tips of the shoots, usually on separate plants in spring. **Fruit** A rounded to egg-shaped, berry-like, bloomy, blue-black cone, to 1cm (⅜in) long, ripe in two years.
- **NATIVE REGION** W. United States.
- **HABITAT** Rocky slopes and dry soil in mountains.
- **REMARK** The toothed leaf margin can be seen only under magnification. In the Sierra Nevada mountain range in California, USA, specimens of the species more than 2,000 years old can be found growing out of solid rock.

some spiny leaves carried on strong shoots •

Height 20m (65ft)	Shape Broadly conical	Leaf persistence Evergreen	Leaf type

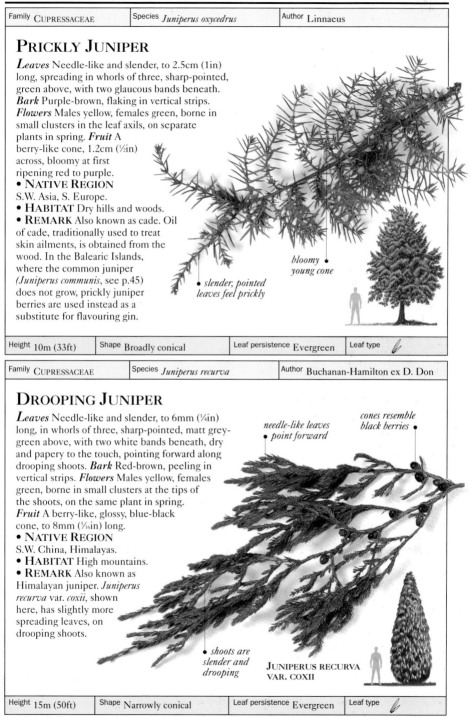

Family CUPRESSACEAE	Species *Juniperus oxycedrus*	Author Linnaeus

PRICKLY JUNIPER

Leaves Needle-like and slender, to 2.5cm (1in) long, spreading in whorls of three, sharp-pointed, green above, with two glaucous bands beneath. **Bark** Purple-brown, flaking in vertical strips. **Flowers** Males yellow, females green, borne in small clusters in the leaf axils, on separate plants in spring. **Fruit** A berry-like cone, 1.2cm (½in) across, bloomy at first ripening red to purple.
• **NATIVE REGION** S.W. Asia, S. Europe.
• **HABITAT** Dry hills and woods.
• **REMARK** Also known as cade. Oil of cade, traditionally used to treat skin ailments, is obtained from the wood. In the Balearic Islands, where the common juniper (*Juniperus communis*, see p.45) does not grow, prickly juniper berries are used instead as a substitute for flavouring gin.

bloomy young cone

slender, pointed leaves feel prickly

Height 10m (33ft)	Shape Broadly conical	Leaf persistence Evergreen	Leaf type

Family CUPRESSACEAE	Species *Juniperus recurva*	Author Buchanan-Hamilton ex D. Don

DROOPING JUNIPER

Leaves Needle-like and slender, to 6mm (¼in) long, in whorls of three, sharp-pointed, matt grey-green above, with two white bands beneath, dry and papery to the touch, pointing forward along drooping shoots. **Bark** Red-brown, peeling in vertical strips. **Flowers** Males yellow, females green, borne in small clusters at the tips of the shoots, on the same plant in spring. **Fruit** A berry-like, glossy, blue-black cone, to 8mm (⁵⁄₁₆in) long.
• **NATIVE REGION** S.W. China, Himalayas.
• **HABITAT** High mountains.
• **REMARK** Also known as Himalayan juniper. *Juniperus recurva* var. *coxii*, shown here, has slightly more spreading leaves, on drooping shoots.

needle-like leaves point forward

cones resemble black berries

shoots are slender and drooping

JUNIPERUS RECURVA VAR. COXII

Height 15m (50ft)	Shape Narrowly conical	Leaf persistence Evergreen	Leaf type

Family CUPRESSACEAE	Species *Juniperus scopulorum*	Author Sargent

ROCKY MOUNTAIN JUNIPER

Leaves Scale-like, very small, green to grey-blue, closely pressed to the shoot. **Bark** Red-brown, peeling in thin strips. **Flowers** Males yellow, females green, in small clusters at the tips of the shoots, usually on the same plant in spring. **Fruit** A berry-like cone, 6mm (¼in) across, blue-black with a glaucous bloom, ripe in two years.
• **NATIVE REGION** W. North America.
• **HABITAT** Woods and rocky soil in mountains.
• **REMARK** Also known as Colorado red cedar, river juniper, Rocky Mountain red cedar. 'Skyrocket', shown here, is the best-known cultivated garden form. This species, which resembles a cypress, gives its name to Cypress Island, in Washington State, USA, where it grows abundantly.

shoots covered in tiny leaves •

• bloomy young cone

JUNIPERUS
SCOPULORUM
'SKYROCKET'

Height 12m (40ft)	Shape Narrowly conical	Leaf persistence Evergreen	Leaf type

Family CUPRESSACEAE	Species *Juniperus virginiana*	Author Linnaeus

PENCIL CEDAR

Leaves Both juvenile and adult foliage usually present; adult leaves scale-like and very small, pointed, usually green to blue-green, closely pressed to the shoot; juvenile leaves needle-like, to 6mm (¼in) long, usually in pairs, sharp-pointed, grey-green above, glaucous beneath, at the tips of the shoots. **Bark** Red-brown, peeling in vertical strips. **Flowers** Males yellow, females green, in small clusters at the tips of the shoots, usually on separate plants in spring. **Fruit** A berry-like, glaucous, bloomy cone, 6mm (¼in) long, ripe in one year.
• **NATIVE REGION** E. North America.
• **HABITAT** Woods and rocky slopes.
• **REMARK** Also known as eastern red cedar, red cedar. Widely distributed and planted. Its wood is used to make pencils.

cones covered in
• white bloom

adult foliage has
• tiny leaves

JUNIPERUS
VIRGINIANA

• blue-grey
leaves

• one-year-old
ripe cones

'GLAUCA' ▷
This form has glaucous-grey foliage.

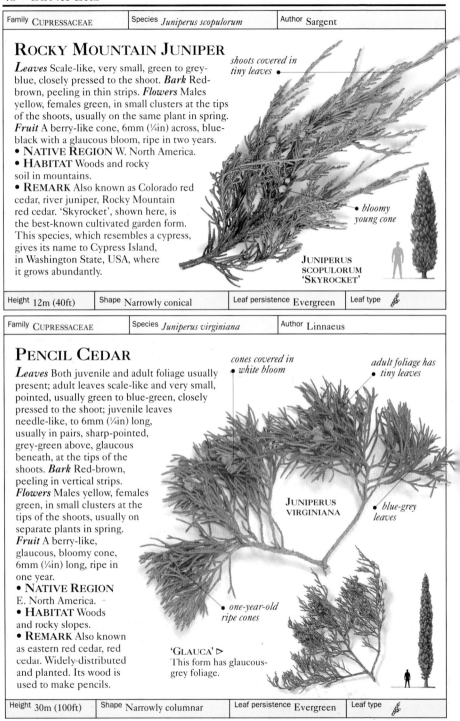

Height 30m (100ft)	Shape Narrowly columnar	Leaf persistence Evergreen	Leaf type

Family CUPRESSACEAE	Species *Thuja koraiensis*	Author Nakai

KOREAN ARBOR-VITAE

Leaves Scale-like and small, bright green above, with bright silvery marks beneath, in flattened sprays, aromatic when crushed. **Bark** Red-brown, peeling in thin scales. **Flowers** Males green, with black tips, females green, in separate clusters at the ends of the shoots, on the same plant in spring. **Fruit** An oblong, upright cone, 1cm (⅜in) long, yellow-green ripening to brown, with eight scales.
• **NATIVE REGION** N.E. China, Korea.
• **HABITAT** Mountain woods.
• **REMARK** This species can be either a small tree or a dense shrub.

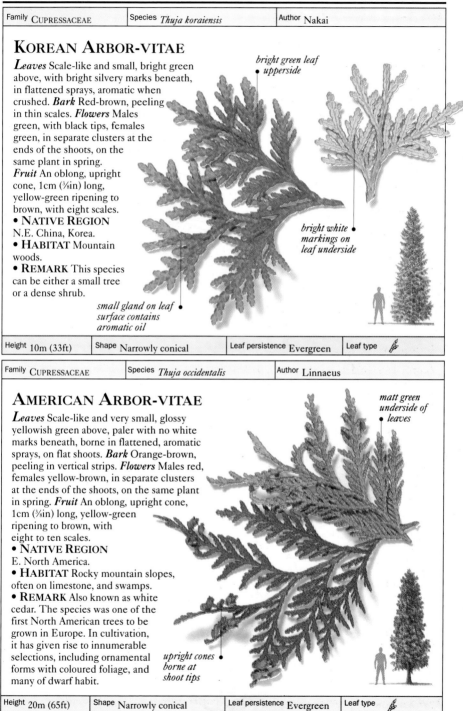

bright green leaf • upperside

bright white • markings on leaf underside

small gland on leaf • surface contains aromatic oil

Height 10m (33ft)	Shape Narrowly conical	Leaf persistence Evergreen	Leaf type

Family CUPRESSACEAE	Species *Thuja occidentalis*	Author Linnaeus

AMERICAN ARBOR-VITAE

Leaves Scale-like and very small, glossy yellowish green above, paler with no white marks beneath, borne in flattened, aromatic sprays, on flat shoots. **Bark** Orange-brown, peeling in vertical strips. **Flowers** Males red, females yellow-brown, in separate clusters at the ends of the shoots, on the same plant in spring. **Fruit** An oblong, upright cone, 1cm (⅜in) long, yellow-green ripening to brown, with eight to ten scales.
• **NATIVE REGION** E. North America.
• **HABITAT** Rocky mountain slopes, often on limestone, and swamps.
• **REMARK** Also known as white cedar. The species was one of the first North American trees to be grown in Europe. In cultivation, it has given rise to innumerable selections, including ornamental forms with coloured foliage, and many of dwarf habit.

matt green underside of • leaves

upright cones borne at shoot tips

Height 20m (65ft)	Shape Narrowly conical	Leaf persistence Evergreen	Leaf type

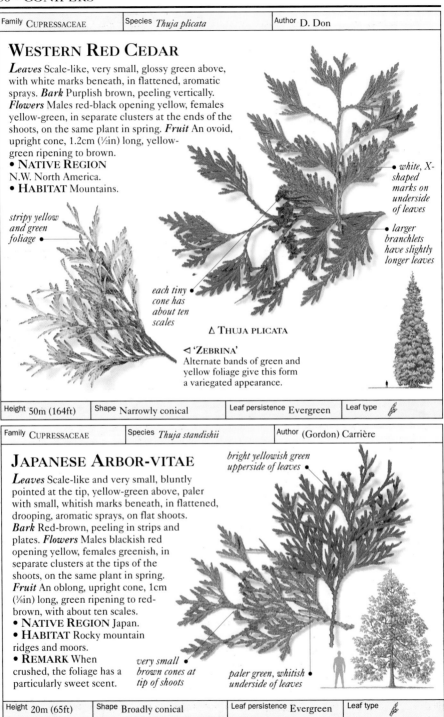

Family CUPRESSACEAE	Species *Thuja plicata*	Author D. Don

WESTERN RED CEDAR

Leaves Scale-like, very small, glossy green above, with white marks beneath, in flattened, aromatic sprays. *Bark* Purplish brown, peeling vertically. *Flowers* Males red-black opening yellow, females yellow-green, in separate clusters at the ends of the shoots, on the same plant in spring. *Fruit* An ovoid, upright cone, 1.2cm (½in) long, yellow-green ripening to brown.
• **NATIVE REGION** N.W. North America.
• **HABITAT** Mountains.

stripy yellow and green foliage •

each tiny • cone has about ten scales

△ THUJA PLICATA

• white, X-shaped marks on underside of leaves

• larger branchlets have slightly longer leaves

◁ 'ZEBRINA'
Alternate bands of green and yellow foliage give this form a variegated appearance.

Height 50m (164ft)	Shape Narrowly conical	Leaf persistence Evergreen	Leaf type

Family CUPRESSACEAE	Species *Thuja standishii*	Author (Gordon) Carrière

JAPANESE ARBOR-VITAE

Leaves Scale-like and very small, bluntly pointed at the tip, yellow-green above, paler with small, whitish marks beneath, in flattened, drooping, aromatic sprays, on flat shoots. *Bark* Red-brown, peeling in strips and plates. *Flowers* Males blackish red opening yellow, females greenish, in separate clusters at the tips of the shoots, on the same plant in spring. *Fruit* An oblong, upright cone, 1cm (⅜in) long, green ripening to red-brown, with about ten scales.
• **NATIVE REGION** Japan.
• **HABITAT** Rocky mountain ridges and moors.
• **REMARK** When crushed, the foliage has a particularly sweet scent.

bright yellowish green upperside of leaves •

very small • brown cones at tip of shoots

paler green, whitish • underside of leaves

Height 20m (65ft)	Shape Broadly conical	Leaf persistence Evergreen	Leaf type

| Family CUPRESSACEAE | Species *Thujopsis dolabrata* | Author (Linnaeus f.) Siebold & Zuccarini |

HIBA

Leaves Scale-like, to 6mm (¼in) long, glossy dark green to yellow-green above, in flattened sprays, on broad, flat shoots. *Bark* Purple-brown, flaking in thin, vertical strips. *Flowers* Males blackish green, females blue-grey, in separate clusters at the ends of the shoots, on the same plant in spring. *Fruit* A brown, bloomy cone, 1.2cm (½in) long.
• NATIVE REGION Japan.
• HABITAT Moist mountain forests.

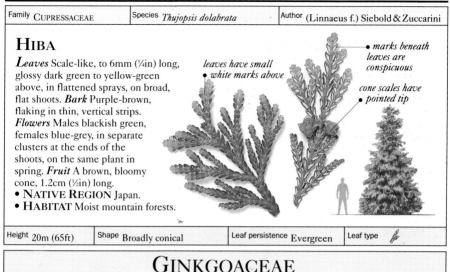

leaves have small white marks above

marks beneath leaves are conspicuous

cone scales have pointed tip

| Height 20m (65ft) | Shape Broadly conical | Leaf persistence Evergreen | Leaf type |

GINKGOACEAE

ALTHOUGH THIS FAMILY HAS only a single member, with no closely related species, fossil records show that similar plants were at one time – between approximately 150 and 200 million years ago – widely distributed in all parts of the world. The species, usually classed as a conifer, is in fact the sole survivor of a group of plants more primitive than the true conifers.

| Family GINKGOACEAE | Species *Ginkgo biloba* | Author Linnaeus |

MAIDENHAIR TREE

Leaves Fan-shaped, about 7.5cm (3in) long, often variously notched and with numerous veins diverging from the base, matt green, turning bright yellow in autumn, carried singly on long shoots, clustered on short side shoots. *Bark* Grey-brown, ridged and fissured. *Flowers* Males and females both small and yellow-green, males in catkin-like clusters, females singly or in pairs on a short stalk, on separate plants in spring. *Fruit* A fleshy, plum-like seed, yellow-green ripening to orange-brown, the kernel edible.
• NATIVE REGION China.
• HABITAT Only in cultivation.
• REMARK The rotting fruit has a particularly unpleasant smell.

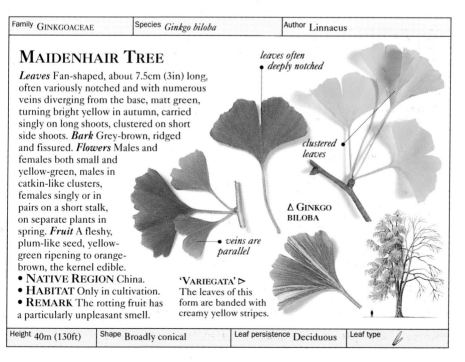

leaves often deeply notched

clustered leaves

△ GINKGO BILOBA

veins are parallel

'VARIEGATA' ▷
The leaves of this form are banded with creamy yellow stripes.

| Height 40m (130ft) | Shape Broadly conical | Leaf persistence Deciduous | Leaf type |

PINACEAE

THIS FAMILY INCLUDES THE silver firs *(Abies, see pp.52–57)*, larches *(Larix, see pp.60–61)*, and pines *(Pinus, see pp.66–75)*. About 200 species of trees and shrubs, in ten genera, grow mainly in northern temperate regions. The species of larch and *Pseudolarix* (see p.76) are deciduous. The flowers are borne separately on the same plant: females develop into a woody cone.

Family PINACEAE	Species *Abies alba*	Author Miller

EUROPEAN SILVER FIR

Leaves Linear, to 3cm (1¼in) long, with a notched tip, glossy dark green above, with two whitish bands beneath, spreading either side of the shoot, shorter and pointing forward above. **Bark** Grey and smooth, cracking into small plates with age. **Flowers** Males yellow, beneath the shoot, females green, upright, borne in separate clusters on the same plant in spring. **Fruit** A cylindrical, upright cone, to 15cm (6in) long, green at first ripening to brown, with protruding, down-turned bracts.
• **NATIVE REGION** Europe.
• **HABITAT** Mountain forests.
• **REMARK** Also known as silver fir. Cones usually grow only high on the tree. This species is widely used as a Christmas tree in many parts of Europe.

notch at tip of leaves
male flowers open to yellow
cone bracts project outwards
white bands on underside of leaves

Height 40m (130ft)	Shape Narrowly conical	Leaf persistence Evergreen	Leaf type

Family PINACEAE	Species *Abies bracteata*	Author (D. Don) Nuttall

SANTA LUCIA FIR

Leaves Needle-like and rigid, to 5cm (2in) long, ending in a very sharp point, glossy dark green above, with two white bands beneath, spreading either side of the shoot. **Bark** Dark grey and smooth. **Flowers** Males yellowish, beneath the shoot, females green, upright, borne in separate clusters on the same plant in spring. **Fruit** An egg-shaped, upright cone, to 10cm (4in) long, green ripening to brown, with conspicuously long, bristly bracts.
• **NATIVE REGION** USA: California.
• **HABITAT** Evergreen forests on mountain slopes.
• **REMARK** Also known as bristlecone fir. It is the rarest native North American fir.

two white bands on underside of leaves
pointed leaf bud

Height 35m (115ft)	Shape Narrowly conical	Leaf persistence Evergreen	Leaf type

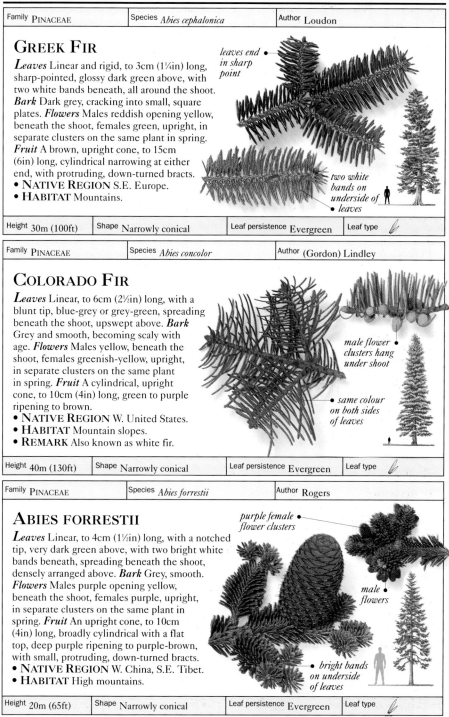

Family PINACEAE	Species *Abies cephalonica*	Author Loudon

GREEK FIR

Leaves Linear and rigid, to 3cm (1¼in) long, sharp-pointed, glossy dark green above, with two white bands beneath, all around the shoot. ***Bark*** Dark grey, cracking into small, square plates. ***Flowers*** Males reddish opening yellow, beneath the shoot, females green, upright, in separate clusters on the same plant in spring. ***Fruit*** A brown, upright cone, to 15cm (6in) long, cylindrical narrowing at either end, with protruding, down-turned bracts.
• **NATIVE REGION** S.E. Europe.
• **HABITAT** Mountains.

leaves end in sharp point

two white bands on underside of leaves

Height 30m (100ft)	Shape Narrowly conical	Leaf persistence Evergreen	Leaf type

Family PINACEAE	Species *Abies concolor*	Author (Gordon) Lindley

COLORADO FIR

Leaves Linear, to 6cm (2½in) long, with a blunt tip, blue-grey or grey-green, spreading beneath the shoot, upswept above. ***Bark*** Grey and smooth, becoming scaly with age. ***Flowers*** Males yellow, beneath the shoot, females greenish-yellow, upright, in separate clusters on the same plant in spring. ***Fruit*** A cylindrical, upright cone, to 10cm (4in) long, green to purple ripening to brown.
• **NATIVE REGION** W. United States.
• **HABITAT** Mountain slopes.
• **REMARK** Also known as white fir.

male flower clusters hang under shoot

same colour on both sides of leaves

Height 40m (130ft)	Shape Narrowly conical	Leaf persistence Evergreen	Leaf type

Family PINACEAE	Species *Abies forrestii*	Author Rogers

ABIES FORRESTII

Leaves Linear, to 4cm (1½in) long, with a notched tip, very dark green above, with two bright white bands beneath, spreading beneath the shoot, densely arranged above. ***Bark*** Grey, smooth. ***Flowers*** Males purple opening yellow, beneath the shoot, females purple, upright, in separate clusters on the same plant in spring. ***Fruit*** An upright cone, to 10cm (4in) long, broadly cylindrical with a flat top, deep purple ripening to purple-brown, with small, protruding, down-turned bracts.
• **NATIVE REGION** W. China, S.E. Tibet.
• **HABITAT** High mountains.

purple female flower clusters

male flowers

bright bands on underside of leaves

Height 20m (65ft)	Shape Narrowly conical	Leaf persistence Evergreen	Leaf type

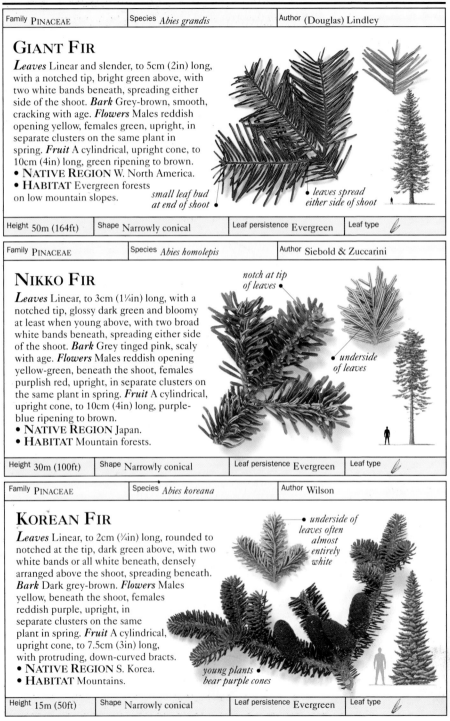

Family PINACEAE	Species *Abies grandis*	Author (Douglas) Lindley

GIANT FIR

Leaves Linear and slender, to 5cm (2in) long, with a notched tip, bright green above, with two white bands beneath, spreading either side of the shoot. **Bark** Grey-brown, smooth, cracking with age. **Flowers** Males reddish opening yellow, females green, upright, in separate clusters on the same plant in spring. **Fruit** A cylindrical, upright cone, to 10cm (4in) long, green ripening to brown.
• **NATIVE REGION** W. North America.
• **HABITAT** Evergreen forests on low mountain slopes.

small leaf bud at end of shoot •

• *leaves spread either side of shoot*

Height 50m (164ft)	Shape Narrowly conical	Leaf persistence Evergreen	Leaf type

Family PINACEAE	Species *Abies homolepis*	Author Siebold & Zuccarini

NIKKO FIR

notch at tip of leaves •

Leaves Linear, to 3cm (1¼in) long, with a notched tip, glossy dark green and bloomy at least when young above, with two broad white bands beneath, spreading either side of the shoot. **Bark** Grey tinged pink, scaly with age. **Flowers** Males reddish opening yellow-green, beneath the shoot, females purplish red, upright, in separate clusters on the same plant in spring. **Fruit** A cylindrical, upright cone, to 10cm (4in) long, purple-blue ripening to brown.
• **NATIVE REGION** Japan.
• **HABITAT** Mountain forests.

• *underside of leaves*

Height 30m (100ft)	Shape Narrowly conical	Leaf persistence Evergreen	Leaf type

Family PINACEAE	Species *Abies koreana*	Author Wilson

KOREAN FIR

• *underside of leaves often almost entirely white*

Leaves Linear, to 2cm (¾in) long, rounded to notched at the tip, dark green above, with two white bands or all white beneath, densely arranged above the shoot, spreading beneath. **Bark** Dark grey-brown. **Flowers** Males yellow, beneath the shoot, females reddish purple, upright, in separate clusters on the same plant in spring. **Fruit** A cylindrical, upright cone, to 7.5cm (3in) long, with protruding, down-curved bracts.
• **NATIVE REGION** S. Korea.
• **HABITAT** Mountains.

young plants bear purple cones •

Height 15m (50ft)	Shape Narrowly conical	Leaf persistence Evergreen	Leaf type

Family PINACEAE	Species *Abies lasiocarpa*	Author (W.J. Hooker) Nuttall

SUBALPINE FIR

Leaves Linear, to 4cm (1½in) long, with a notched tip, grey-green above, with two white bands beneath, arranged upright above the shoot, the central leaves pointing forward, spreading beneath. **Bark** Grey-white, smooth, with resin blisters. **Flowers** Males tinged red opening yellow, beneath the shoot, females purple, upright, in separate clusters on the same plant in spring. **Fruit** A cylindrical, upright cone, to 10cm (4in) long, deep purple ripening to brown.
• **NATIVE REGION** W. North America.
• **HABITAT** From sea level to the mountains.

ABIES LASIOCARPA ▷

VAR. ARIZONICA ▷
This form, commonly known as the corkbark fir, comes from the south of the region. It is distinguished by its bluer leaves and corky bark.

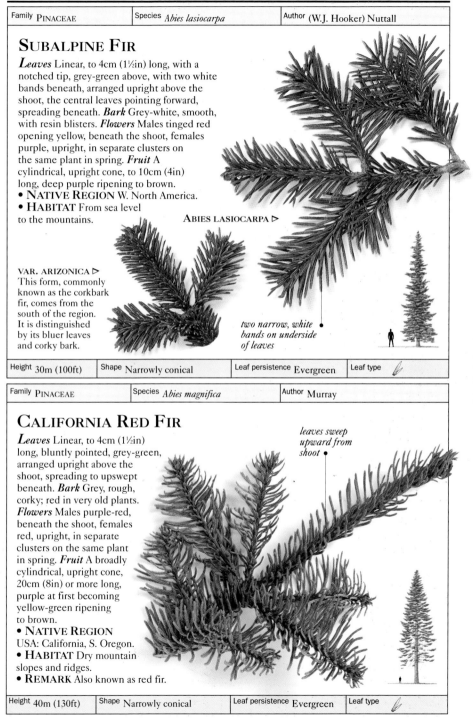

two narrow, white bands on underside of leaves

Height 30m (100ft)	Shape Narrowly conical	Leaf persistence Evergreen	Leaf type

Family PINACEAE	Species *Abies magnifica*	Author Murray

CALIFORNIA RED FIR

Leaves Linear, to 4cm (1½in) long, bluntly pointed, grey-green, arranged upright above the shoot, spreading to upswept beneath. **Bark** Grey, rough, corky; red in very old plants. **Flowers** Males purple-red, beneath the shoot, females red, upright, in separate clusters on the same plant in spring. **Fruit** A broadly cylindrical, upright cone, 20cm (8in) or more long, purple at first becoming yellow-green ripening to brown.
• **NATIVE REGION** USA: California, S. Oregon.
• **HABITAT** Dry mountain slopes and ridges.
• **REMARK** Also known as red fir.

leaves sweep upward from shoot •

Height 40m (130ft)	Shape Narrowly conical	Leaf persistence Evergreen	Leaf type

Family PINACEAE	Species *Abies nordmanniana*	Author (Steven) Spach

CAUCASIAN FIR

Leaves Linear, to 4cm (1½in) long, with a notched tip, glossy bright green above, with two white bands beneath, dense above the shoot, spreading beneath. **Bark** Grey and smooth, cracking into small, square plates with age. **Flowers** Males reddish, beneath the shoot, females green, upright, in separate clusters on the same plant in spring. **Fruit** A broadly cylindrical, upright cone, to 15cm (6in) long, green ripening to purple-brown, with protruding, down-curved bracts.
• **NATIVE REGION** Caucasus, N.E. Turkey.
• **HABITAT** Mountain forests.

male flower clusters open yellow •

Height 50m (164ft)	Shape Broadly conical	Leaf persistence Evergreen	Leaf type

Family PINACEAE	Species *Abies numidica*	Author Carrière

ALGERIAN FIR

Leaves Linear and rigid, to 2cm (¾in) long, rounded or notched at the tip, dark grey-green above, with a small whitish patch towards the tip, with two white bands beneath, densely arranged all around the shoot, upright above, spreading beneath. **Bark** Grey-purple, smooth, flaking with age. **Flowers** Males tinged red opening yellow, beneath the shoot, females green, upright, in separate clusters on the same plant in spring. **Fruit** A cylindrical, upright cone, to 18cm (7¼in) long, purple-green ripening to brown, ending in an abrupt point.
• **NATIVE REGION** Algeria.
• **HABITAT** Mountains near the coast.
• **REMARK** A rare species in the wild. It is closely related to the Spanish fir *(Abies pinsapo, see p.57).*

• green female flower clusters

cones end in • blunt tip

purplish green • young cones ripen to brown

short, stubby, blunt-pointed leaves •

conspicuous white • bands on underside of leaves

• upper leaf surface is marked white towards tip

Height 25m (80ft)	Shape Narrowly conical	Leaf persistence Evergreen	Leaf type

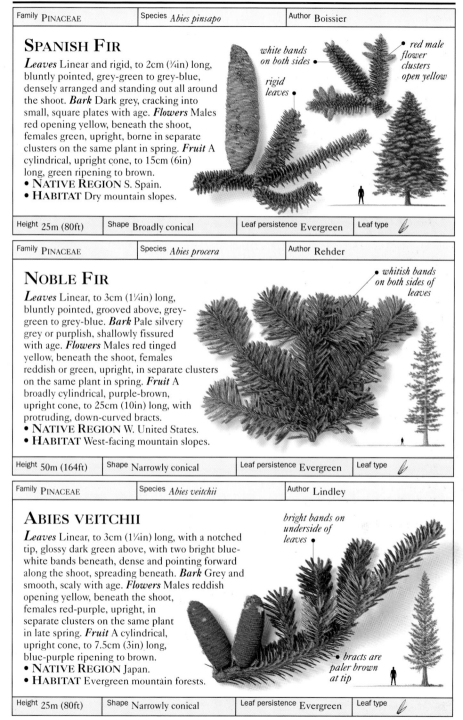

Family PINACEAE	Species *Abies pinsapo*	Author Boissier

SPANISH FIR

Leaves Linear and rigid, to 2cm (¾in) long, bluntly pointed, grey-green to grey-blue, densely arranged and standing out all around the shoot. **Bark** Dark grey, cracking into small, square plates with age. **Flowers** Males red opening yellow, beneath the shoot, females green, upright, borne in separate clusters on the same plant in spring. **Fruit** A cylindrical, upright cone, to 15cm (6in) long, green ripening to brown.
• **NATIVE REGION** S. Spain.
• **HABITAT** Dry mountain slopes.

white bands on both sides •

rigid leaves •

• *red male flower clusters open yellow*

Height 25m (80ft)	Shape Broadly conical	Leaf persistence Evergreen	Leaf type

Family PINACEAE	Species *Abies procera*	Author Rehder

NOBLE FIR

Leaves Linear, to 3cm (1¼in) long, bluntly pointed, grooved above, grey-green to grey-blue. **Bark** Pale silvery grey or purplish, shallowly fissured with age. **Flowers** Males red tinged yellow, beneath the shoot, females reddish or green, upright, in separate clusters on the same plant in spring. **Fruit** A broadly cylindrical, purple-brown, upright cone, to 25cm (10in) long, with protruding, down-curved bracts.
• **NATIVE REGION** W. United States.
• **HABITAT** West-facing mountain slopes.

• *whitish bands on both sides of leaves*

Height 50m (164ft)	Shape Narrowly conical	Leaf persistence Evergreen	Leaf type

Family PINACEAE	Species *Abies veitchii*	Author Lindley

ABIES VEITCHII

Leaves Linear, to 3cm (1¼in) long, with a notched tip, glossy dark green above, with two bright blue-white bands beneath, dense and pointing forward along the shoot, spreading beneath. **Bark** Grey and smooth, scaly with age. **Flowers** Males reddish opening yellow, beneath the shoot, females red-purple, upright, in separate clusters on the same plant in late spring. **Fruit** A cylindrical, upright cone, to 7.5cm (3in) long, blue-purple ripening to brown.
• **NATIVE REGION** Japan.
• **HABITAT** Evergreen mountain forests.

bright bands on underside of leaves •

• *bracts are paler brown at tip*

Height 25m (80ft)	Shape Narrowly conical	Leaf persistence Evergreen	Leaf type

Family PINACEAE	Species *Cedrus atlantica*	Author Manetti

ATLAS CEDAR

Leaves Needle-like and slender, to 2cm (¾in) long, borne singly on long shoots, in dense whorls on very slow-growing, shorter side shoots, sharp-pointed, grey-green to dark green, on hairy shoots. **Bark** Dark grey on old trees fissured into scaly plates. **Flowers** Males yellow, females green, both carried upright, in separate clusters on the same plant in autumn. **Fruit** A barrel-shaped, upright cone, to 7.5cm (3in) long, green-purple when young becoming purple-brown ripening to brown, ripe in two to three years, breaking up before falling.
• **NATIVE REGION** Algeria, Morocco.
• **HABITAT** Forests.
• **REMARK** The species is sometimes listed as a geographical subspecies of the cedar of Lebanon *(Cedrus libani,* see p.59), from which it is usually most easily distinguished by its habit. In the wild, it is found only in the North African Atlas Mountains, a mountain range that lies between the Mediterranean and the Sahara.

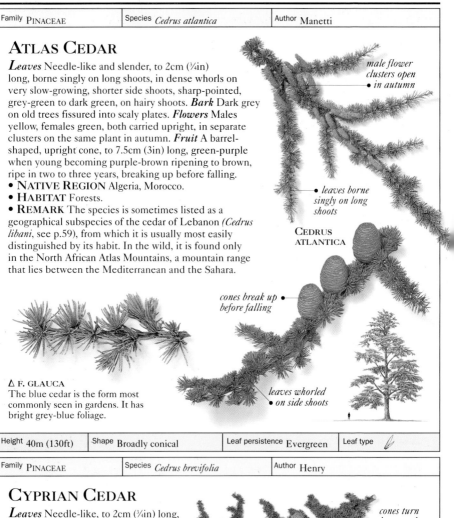

male flower clusters open • in autumn

• leaves borne singly on long shoots

CEDRUS ATLANTICA

cones break up • before falling

leaves whorled • on side shoots

△ F. GLAUCA
The blue cedar is the form most commonly seen in gardens. It has bright grey-blue foliage.

Height 40m (130ft)	Shape Broadly conical	Leaf persistence Evergreen	Leaf type

Family PINACEAE	Species *Cedrus brevifolia*	Author Henry

CYPRIAN CEDAR

Leaves Needle-like, to 2cm (¾in) long, borne singly on long shoots, in dense whorls on slow-growing side shoots, dark green. **Bark** Dark grey, cracking into vertical plates. **Flowers** Males blue-green, females green, both carried upright, in separate clusters on the same plant in autumn. **Fruit** A cylindrical, upright cone, to 7cm (2¾in) long, purple-green at first ripening to brown.
• **NATIVE REGION** Cyprus.
• **HABITAT** Mountains.
• **REMARK** Short leaves distinguish this species from the closely related cedar of Lebanon *(Cedrus libani,* see p.59).

cones turn brown when • ripe

whorled leaves • are very short

Height 20m (65ft)	Shape Broadly conical	Leaf persistence Evergreen	Leaf type

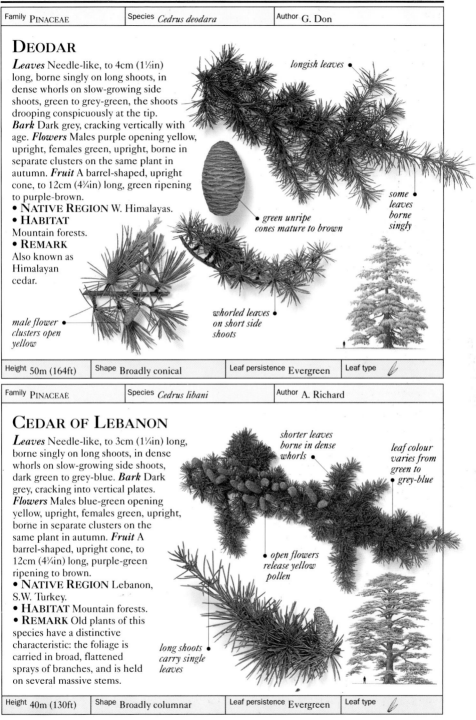

Family PINACEAE		Species *Cedrus deodara*		Author G. Don

DEODAR

Leaves Needle-like, to 4cm (1½in) long, borne singly on long shoots, in dense whorls on slow-growing side shoots, green to grey-green, the shoots drooping conspicuously at the tip.
Bark Dark grey, cracking vertically with age. **Flowers** Males purple opening yellow, upright, females green, upright, borne in separate clusters on the same plant in autumn. **Fruit** A barrel-shaped, upright cone, to 12cm (4¾in) long, green ripening to purple-brown.
• **NATIVE REGION** W. Himalayas.
• **HABITAT** Mountain forests.
• **REMARK** Also known as Himalayan cedar.

longish leaves

some leaves borne singly

green unripe cones mature to brown

male flower clusters open yellow

whorled leaves on short side shoots

Height 50m (164ft)	Shape Broadly conical	Leaf persistence Evergreen	Leaf type

Family PINACEAE		Species *Cedrus libani*		Author A. Richard

CEDAR OF LEBANON

Leaves Needle-like, to 3cm (1¼in) long, borne singly on long shoots, in dense whorls on slow-growing side shoots, dark green to grey-blue. **Bark** Dark grey, cracking into vertical plates.
Flowers Males blue-green opening yellow, upright, females green, upright, borne in separate clusters on the same plant in autumn. **Fruit** A barrel-shaped, upright cone, to 12cm (4¾in) long, purple-green ripening to brown.
• **NATIVE REGION** Lebanon, S.W. Turkey.
• **HABITAT** Mountain forests.
• **REMARK** Old plants of this species have a distinctive characteristic: the foliage is carried in broad, flattened sprays of branches, and is held on several massive stems.

shorter leaves borne in dense whorls

leaf colour varies from green to grey-blue

open flowers release yellow pollen

long shoots carry single leaves

Height 40m (130ft)	Shape Broadly columnar	Leaf persistence Evergreen	Leaf type

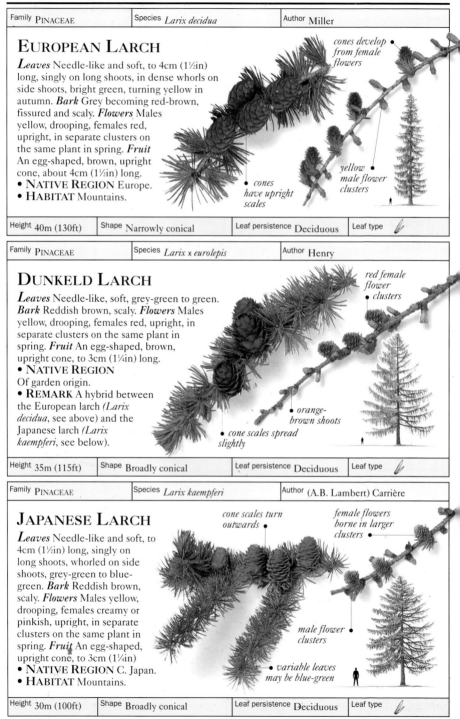

Family PINACEAE	Species *Larix decidua*	Author Miller

EUROPEAN LARCH

Leaves Needle-like and soft, to 4cm (1½in) long, singly on long shoots, in dense whorls on side shoots, bright green, turning yellow in autumn. ***Bark*** Grey becoming red-brown, fissured and scaly. ***Flowers*** Males yellow, drooping, females red, upright, in separate clusters on the same plant in spring. ***Fruit*** An egg-shaped, brown, upright cone, about 4cm (1½in) long.
• **NATIVE REGION** Europe.
• **HABITAT** Mountains.

cones develop from female flowers

yellow male flower clusters

cones have upright scales

Height 40m (130ft)	Shape Narrowly conical	Leaf persistence Deciduous	Leaf type

Family PINACEAE	Species *Larix x eurolepis*	Author Henry

DUNKELD LARCH

Leaves Needle-like, soft, grey-green to green. ***Bark*** Reddish brown, scaly. ***Flowers*** Males yellow, drooping, females red, upright, in separate clusters on the same plant in spring. ***Fruit*** An egg-shaped, brown, upright cone, to 3cm (1¼in) long.
• **NATIVE REGION** Of garden origin.
• **REMARK** A hybrid between the European larch *(Larix decidua,* see above) and the Japanese larch *(Larix kaempferi,* see below).

red female flower clusters

orange-brown shoots

cone scales spread slightly

Height 35m (115ft)	Shape Broadly conical	Leaf persistence Deciduous	Leaf type

Family PINACEAE	Species *Larix kaempferi*	Author (A.B. Lambert) Carrière

JAPANESE LARCH

Leaves Needle-like and soft, to 4cm (1½in) long, singly on long shoots, whorled on side shoots, grey-green to blue-green. ***Bark*** Reddish brown, scaly. ***Flowers*** Males yellow, drooping, females creamy or pinkish, upright, in separate clusters on the same plant in spring. ***Fruit*** An egg-shaped, upright cone, to 3cm (1¼in)
• **NATIVE REGION** C. Japan.
• **HABITAT** Mountains.

cone scales turn outwards

female flowers borne in larger clusters

male flower clusters

variable leaves may be blue-green

Height 30m (100ft)	Shape Broadly conical	Leaf persistence Deciduous	Leaf type

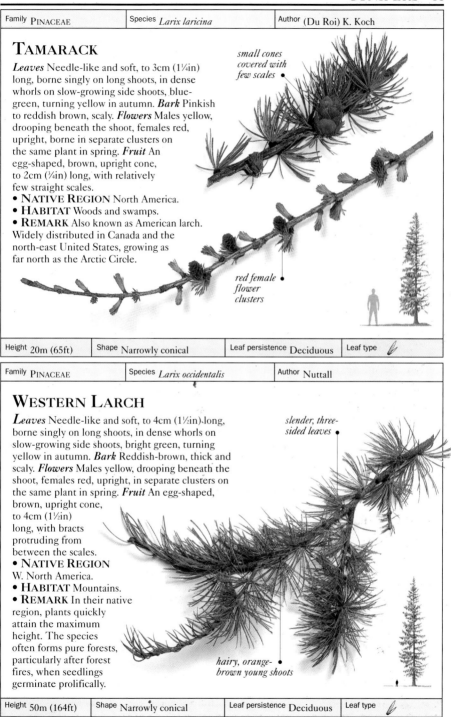

Family PINACEAE	Species *Larix laricina*	Author (Du Roi) K. Koch

TAMARACK

Leaves Needle-like and soft, to 3cm (1¼in) long, borne singly on long shoots, in dense whorls on slow-growing side shoots, blue-green, turning yellow in autumn. **Bark** Pinkish to reddish brown, scaly. **Flowers** Males yellow, drooping beneath the shoot, females red, upright, borne in separate clusters on the same plant in spring. **Fruit** An egg-shaped, brown, upright cone, to 2cm (¾in) long, with relatively few straight scales.
• **NATIVE REGION** North America.
• **HABITAT** Woods and swamps.
• **REMARK** Also known as American larch. Widely distributed in Canada and the north-east United States, growing as far north as the Arctic Circle.

small cones covered with few scales •

red female • flower clusters

Height 20m (65ft)	Shape Narrowly conical	Leaf persistence Deciduous	Leaf type

Family PINACEAE	Species *Larix occidentalis*	Author Nuttall

WESTERN LARCH

Leaves Needle-like and soft, to 4cm (1½in) long, borne singly on long shoots, in dense whorls on slow-growing side shoots, bright green, turning yellow in autumn. **Bark** Reddish-brown, thick and scaly. **Flowers** Males yellow, drooping beneath the shoot, females red, upright, in separate clusters on the same plant in spring. **Fruit** An egg-shaped, brown, upright cone, to 4cm (1½in) long, with bracts protruding from between the scales.
• **NATIVE REGION** W. North America.
• **HABITAT** Mountains.
• **REMARK** In their native region, plants quickly attain the maximum height. The species often forms pure forests, particularly after forest fires, when seedlings germinate prolifically.

slender, three-sided leaves •

hairy, orange-brown young shoots •

Height 50m (164ft)	Shape Narrowly conical	Leaf persistence Deciduous	Leaf type

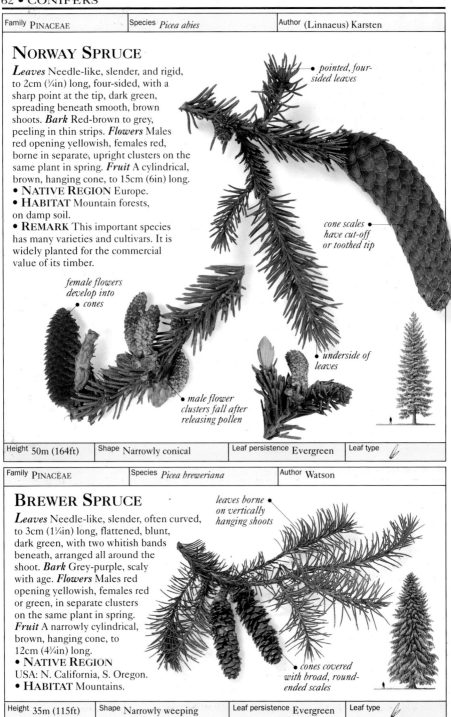

Family PINACEAE	Species *Picea abies*	Author (Linnaeus) Karsten

NORWAY SPRUCE

Leaves Needle-like, slender, and rigid, to 2cm (¾in) long, four-sided, with a sharp point at the tip, dark green, spreading beneath smooth, brown shoots. **Bark** Red-brown to grey, peeling in thin strips. **Flowers** Males red opening yellowish, females red, borne in separate, upright clusters on the same plant in spring. **Fruit** A cylindrical, brown, hanging cone, to 15cm (6in) long.
• **NATIVE REGION** Europe.
• **HABITAT** Mountain forests, on damp soil.
• **REMARK** This important species has many varieties and cultivars. It is widely planted for the commercial value of its timber.

pointed, four-sided leaves

cone scales have cut-off or toothed tip

female flowers develop into cones

underside of leaves

male flower clusters fall after releasing pollen

Height 50m (164ft)	Shape Narrowly conical	Leaf persistence Evergreen	Leaf type

Family PINACEAE	Species *Picea breweriana*	Author Watson

BREWER SPRUCE

Leaves Needle-like, slender, often curved, to 3cm (1¼in) long, flattened, blunt, dark green, with two whitish bands beneath, arranged all around the shoot. **Bark** Grey-purple, scaly with age. **Flowers** Males red opening yellowish, females red or green, in separate clusters on the same plant in spring. **Fruit** A narrowly cylindrical, brown, hanging cone, to 12cm (4¾in) long.
• **NATIVE REGION** USA: N. California, S. Oregon.
• **HABITAT** Mountains.

leaves borne on vertically hanging shoots

cones covered with broad, round-ended scales

Height 35m (115ft)	Shape Narrowly weeping	Leaf persistence Evergreen	Leaf type

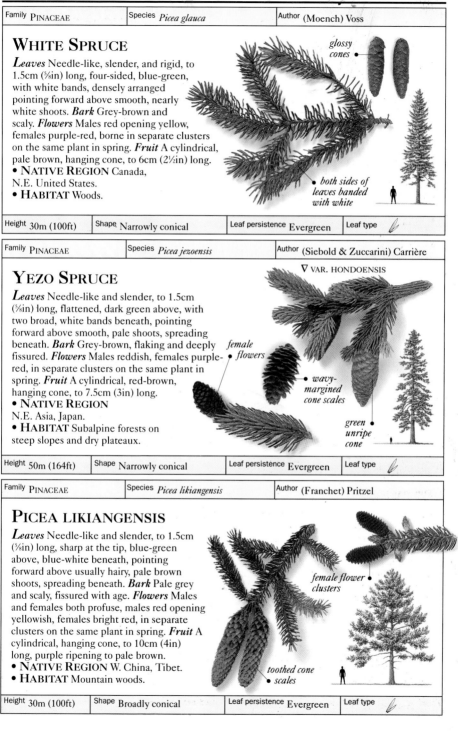

Family PINACEAE	Species *Picea glauca*	Author (Moench) Voss

WHITE SPRUCE

Leaves Needle-like, slender, and rigid, to 1.5cm (⅝in) long, four-sided, blue-green, with white bands, densely arranged pointing forward above smooth, nearly white shoots. *Bark* Grey-brown and scaly. *Flowers* Males red opening yellow, females purple-red, borne in separate clusters on the same plant in spring. *Fruit* A cylindrical, pale brown, hanging cone, to 6cm (2½in) long.
• **NATIVE REGION** Canada, N.E. United States.
• **HABITAT** Woods.

glossy cones

both sides of leaves banded with white

Height 30m (100ft)	Shape Narrowly conical	Leaf persistence Evergreen	Leaf type

Family PINACEAE	Species *Picea jezoensis*	Author (Siebold & Zuccarini) Carrière

YEZO SPRUCE

∇ VAR. HONDOENSIS

Leaves Needle-like and slender, to 1.5cm (⅝in) long, flattened, dark green above, with two broad, white bands beneath, pointing forward above smooth, pale shoots, spreading beneath. *Bark* Grey-brown, flaking and deeply fissured. *Flowers* Males reddish, females purple-red, in separate clusters on the same plant in spring. *Fruit* A cylindrical, red-brown, hanging cone, to 7.5cm (3in) long.
• **NATIVE REGION** N.E. Asia, Japan.
• **HABITAT** Subalpine forests on steep slopes and dry plateaux.

female flowers

wavy-margined cone scales

green unripe cone

Height 50m (164ft)	Shape Narrowly conical	Leaf persistence Evergreen	Leaf type

Family PINACEAE	Species *Picea likiangensis*	Author (Franchet) Pritzel

PICEA LIKIANGENSIS

Leaves Needle-like and slender, to 1.5cm (⅝in) long, sharp at the tip, blue-green above, blue-white beneath, pointing forward above usually hairy, pale brown shoots, spreading beneath. *Bark* Pale grey and scaly, fissured with age. *Flowers* Males and females both profuse, males red opening yellowish, females bright red, in separate clusters on the same plant in spring. *Fruit* A cylindrical, hanging cone, to 10cm (4in) long, purple ripening to pale brown.
• **NATIVE REGION** W. China, Tibet.
• **HABITAT** Mountain woods.

female flower clusters

toothed cone scales

Height 30m (100ft)	Shape Broadly conical	Leaf persistence Evergreen	Leaf type

| Family PINACEAE | Species *Picea mariana* | Author (Miller) B.S.P. |

BLACK SPRUCE

Leaves Needle-like, slender, to 1.5cm (⅝in) long, four-sided, bluntly pointed, blue-green above, blue-white beneath, borne all around hairy, yellow-brown shoots. *Bark* Grey-brown and flaking. *Flowers* Males and females both red, in separate clusters on the same plant in spring. *Fruit* An egg-shaped, red-brown, hanging cone, to 4cm (1½in) long.
• **NATIVE REGION** Canada, N.E. United States.
HABITAT Mountain slopes and bogs.

rigid leaves are four-sided

unusually short cones

| Height 30m (100ft) | Shape Narrowly conical | Leaf persistence Evergreen | Leaf type |

| Family PINACEAE | Species *Picea omorika* | Author (Pančić) Purkyně |

SERBIAN SPRUCE

Leaves Needle-like and slender, to 2cm (¾in) long, flattened, glossy dark green above, most lying above but some all around hairy, pale brown shoots. *Bark* Purple-brown, cracking into square plates. *Flowers* Males and females both red, borne in separate clusters on the same plant in spring. *Fruit* A narrowly egg-shaped, purple-brown, hanging cone, to 6cm (2½in) long.
• **NATIVE REGION** Bosnia-Herzegovina/Yugoslavia.
• **HABITAT** Near River Drina, on limestone.

leaves spread out from shoots

bluish white bands on underside of leaves

| Height 30m (100ft) | Shape Narrowly conical | Leaf persistence Evergreen | Leaf type |

| Family PINACEAE | Species *Picea orientalis* | Author (Linnaeus) Link |

ORIENTAL SPRUCE

Leaves Needle-like, to 8mm (⁵⁄₁₆in) long, four-sided, bluntly pointed at the tip, glossy dark green, pointing forward all around hairy, whitish to pale brown shoots. *Bark* Pinkish brown, flaking in small plates. *Flowers* Males red opening yellow, females red, in separate clusters on the same plant in spring. *Fruit* A cylindrical, hanging cone, to 10cm (4in) long, purple ripening to brown.
• **NATIVE REGION** Caucasus, N.E. Turkey.
• **HABITAT** Mountain forests.

rigid, blunt-pointed leaves

PICEA ▷
ORIENTALIS

cone marked with resin

◁ 'AUREA'
A form with bright yellow young foliage.

| Height 50m (164ft) | Shape Narrowly conical | Leaf persistence Evergreen | Leaf type |

| Family PINACEAE | Species *Picea pungens* | Author Engelmann |

COLORADO SPRUCE

PICEA ▷
PUNGENS

four-sided,
• rigid leaves

Leaves Needle-like, to 3cm (1¼in) long,
spine-tipped, grey-green to blue-grey,
arranged all around pale brown shoots.
Bark Purple-grey, scaly. **Flowers** Males
reddish, females green, in separate
clusters on the same plant in late
spring. **Fruit** A pale brown, hanging cone, to 10cm (4in) long.
• **NATIVE REGION**
W. United States.
• **HABITAT** High mountains,
on dry slopes and streambanks.

△ 'KOSTER'
This form has
bright silvery
blue foliage.

• tooth-tipped
cone scales

| Height 35m (115ft) | Shape Narrowly conical | Leaf persistence Evergreen | Leaf type |

| Family PINACEAE | Species *Picea sitchensis* | Author (Bongard) Carrière |

SITKA SPRUCE

Leaves Needle-like and slender, to 3cm (1¼in)
long, sharp-pointed, bright green above, with
two white bands beneath, arranged all around
whitish to pale brown shoots, parted beneath.
Bark Grey and purple-grey, flaking in large
scales. **Flowers** Males reddish, females
green, borne in separate clusters on
the same plant in spring. **Fruit** A
cylindrical, pale brown, hanging
cone, to 10cm (4in) long.
• **NATIVE REGION**
W. North America.
• **HABITAT** Coastal, moist lowland.

• leaves borne on
smooth shoots

two white bands
on underside
• of leaves

• tooth-tipped
cone scales

| Height 50m (164ft) | Shape Narrowly conical | Leaf persistence Evergreen | Leaf type |

| Family PINACEAE | Species *Picea smithiana* | Author (Wallich) Boissier |

WEST HIMALAYAN SPRUCE

long, slender,
• curved leaves

Leaves Needle-like, long, and slender, to
4cm (1½in) long, four-sided, dark green,
arranged all around smooth, glossy, pale
brown, hanging shoots. **Bark** Purple-
grey, flaking in scales. **Flowers** Males
yellow-green, hanging, at the tips of the
shoots, females green, upright, in separate
clusters on the same plant in late spring
to early summer. **Fruit** A hanging cone,
to 20cm (8in) long, green ripening to
glossy brown.
• **NATIVE REGION** W. Himalayas.
• **HABITAT** High evergreen forests.

• very pale-
coloured
shoots

| Height 40m (130ft) | Shape Narrowly weeping | Leaf persistence Evergreen | Leaf type |

Family PINACEAE	Species *Pinus ayacahuite*	Author Ehrenberg

MEXICAN WHITE PINE

◁ VAR. VEITCHII

Leaves Needle-like and slender, to 15cm (6in) long, in clusters of five, blue-green, borne on finely hairy, yellow-brown shoots. **Bark** Grey, rough and coarsely fissured. **Flowers** Males yellow, females red, in separate clusters on the young shoots in early summer. **Fruit** A cylindrical, yellow-brown, resinous, hanging cone, to 45cm (18in) long, with purple-tipped scales.
• **NATIVE REGION** N. Guatemala, Mexico.
• **HABITAT** Mountain slopes.

long, often curved leaves droop on shoots

Height 35m (115ft)	Shape Broadly conical	Leaf persistence Evergreen	Leaf type

Family PINACEAE	Species *Pinus bungeana*	Author Zuccarini

LACE-BARK PINE

Leaves Needle-like and rigid, to 7.5cm (3in) long, in clusters of three, with a sharp point at the tip, yellow-green, borne on smooth, grey-green shoots. **Bark** Grey-green and creamy white, flaking in small patches. **Flowers** Males yellow, females green, borne in separate clusters on the young shoots in early summer. **Fruit** An egg-shaped, yellow-brown cone, to 7cm (2¾in) long, with spine-tipped scales.
• **NATIVE REGION** N. China.
• **HABITAT** Mainly steep mountain slopes, on shale.

sparsely arranged clusters of three leaves

small, squat cones

Height 20m (65ft)	Shape Broadly conical	Leaf persistence Evergreen	Leaf type

Family PINACEAE	Species *Pinus cembra*	Author Linnaeus

AROLLA PINE

Leaves Needle-like, to 9cm (3½in) long, in clusters of three, glossy green on the outer surface, blue-grey on the inner, on greenish shoots, the shoots covered in orange-brown hairs. **Bark** Grey-brown and scaly. **Flowers** Males purple opening yellow, females red, in separate clusters on the young shoots in late spring. **Fruit** An egg-shaped cone, to 7.5cm (3in) long, blue-purple ripening to red-brown, never opening fully.
• **NATIVE REGION** N. Asia, Europe.
• **HABITAT** Mountains.
• **REMARK** Also known as Swiss stone pine.

densely bunched leaf clusters

Height 20m (65ft)	Shape Narrowly columnar	Leaf persistence Evergreen	Leaf type

Family PINACEAE	Species *Pinus contorta*	Author Loudon

BEACH PINE

Leaves Needle-like and twisted, to 5cm (2in) long, in pairs, densely arranged, dark green or yellow-green, on smooth, green-brown shoots. *Bark* Red-brown, fissured into small squares. *Flowers* Males yellow, females red, in separate clusters on the young shoots in late spring. *Fruit* An egg-shaped, pale brown cone, pointing backward along the shoot, to 5cm (2in) long, the scales with slender spines.
• **NATIVE REGION** W. North America.
• **HABITAT** Coastal dunes and bogs.
• **REMARK** Also known as shore pine. Widely distributed from Alaska to Mexico. The lodgepole pine, var. *latifolia*, can reach 30m (100ft) in mountain habitats.

cone scales tipped with spines •

P. CONTORTA

female • flower clusters

▽ PINUS CONTORTA

shorter • cone

one-year cones still green •

male flower • clusters

longer leaves •

◁ VAR. LATIFOLIA

Height 10m (33ft)	Shape Broadly conical	Leaf persistence Evergreen	Leaf type

Family PINACEAE	Species *Pinus coulteri*	Author D. Don

BIG-CONE PINE

Leaves Needle-like and stiff, to 30cm (12in) long, in clusters of three, grey-green, on very stout, bloomy shoots. *Bark* Purple-brown, scaly, deeply fissured. *Flowers* Males purple opening yellow, females red, borne in separate clusters on the young shoots in late spring to early summer. *Fruit* An egg-shaped, yellow-brown, resinous cone, to 30cm (12in) long, the scales ending in hooked spines, usually remaining closed for many years.
• **NATIVE REGION** USA: California.
• **HABITAT** Dry, rocky slopes in the mountains.

cone scales end in stout, hooked point •

long, stiff needles in clusters of • three

Height 25m (80ft)	Shape Broadly spreading	Leaf persistence Evergreen	Leaf type

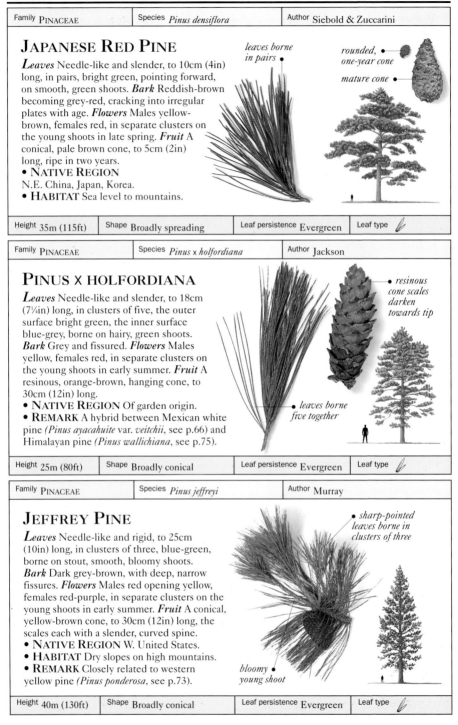

| Family PINACEAE | Species *Pinus densiflora* | Author Siebold & Zuccarini |

JAPANESE RED PINE

Leaves Needle-like and slender, to 10cm (4in) long, in pairs, bright green, pointing forward, on smooth, green shoots. **Bark** Reddish-brown becoming grey-red, cracking into irregular plates with age. **Flowers** Males yellow-brown, females red, in separate clusters on the young shoots in late spring. **Fruit** A conical, pale brown cone, to 5cm (2in) long, ripe in two years.
• **NATIVE REGION** N.E. China, Japan, Korea.
• **HABITAT** Sea level to mountains.

leaves borne in pairs

rounded, one-year cone

mature cone

| Height 35m (115ft) | Shape Broadly spreading | Leaf persistence Evergreen | Leaf type |

| Family PINACEAE | Species *Pinus x holfordiana* | Author Jackson |

PINUS X HOLFORDIANA

Leaves Needle-like and slender, to 18cm (7¼in) long, in clusters of five, the outer surface bright green, the inner surface blue-grey, borne on hairy, green shoots. **Bark** Grey and fissured. **Flowers** Males yellow, females red, in separate clusters on the young shoots in early summer. **Fruit** A resinous, orange-brown, hanging cone, to 30cm (12in) long.
• **NATIVE REGION** Of garden origin.
• **REMARK** A hybrid between Mexican white pine *(Pinus ayacahuite* var. *veitchii*, see p.66) and Himalayan pine *(Pinus wallichiana*, see p.75).

resinous cone scales darken towards tip

leaves borne five together

| Height 25m (80ft) | Shape Broadly conical | Leaf persistence Evergreen | Leaf type |

| Family PINACEAE | Species *Pinus jeffreyi* | Author Murray |

JEFFREY PINE

Leaves Needle-like and rigid, to 25cm (10in) long, in clusters of three, blue-green, borne on stout, smooth, bloomy shoots. **Bark** Dark grey-brown, with deep, narrow fissures. **Flowers** Males red opening yellow, females red-purple, in separate clusters on the young shoots in early summer. **Fruit** A conical, yellow-brown cone, to 30cm (12in) long, the scales each with a slender, curved spine.
• **NATIVE REGION** W. United States.
• **HABITAT** Dry slopes on high mountains.
• **REMARK** Closely related to western yellow pine *(Pinus ponderosa*, see p.73).

sharp-pointed leaves borne in clusters of three

bloomy young shoot

| Height 40m (130ft) | Shape Broadly conical | Leaf persistence Evergreen | Leaf type |

Family PINACEAE	Species *Pinus koraiensis*	Author Siebold & Zuccarini

KOREAN PINE

Leaves Needle-like and slender, to 12cm (4¾in) long, in dense clusters of five, glossy green on the outer surface, blue-white on the inner. **Bark** Dark grey, thick, flaking. **Flowers** Males red opening yellow, females red, in separate clusters on the young shoots in early summer. **Fruit** A conical, purple-brown cone, to 12cm (4¾in) long.
• **NATIVE REGION** N.E. Asia, Japan, Korea.
• **HABITAT** River valleys and low mountain slopes.

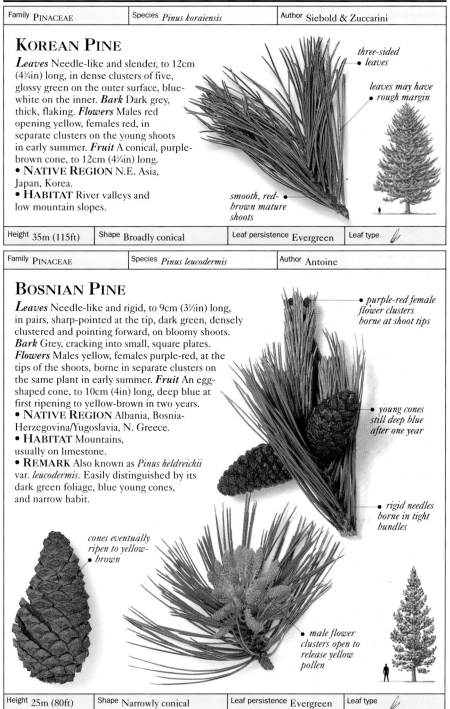

three-sided leaves

leaves may have rough margin

smooth, red-brown mature shoots

Height 35m (115ft)	Shape Broadly conical	Leaf persistence Evergreen	Leaf type

Family PINACEAE	Species *Pinus leucodermis*	Author Antoine

BOSNIAN PINE

Leaves Needle-like and rigid, to 9cm (3½in) long, in pairs, sharp-pointed at the tip, dark green, densely clustered and pointing forward, on bloomy shoots. **Bark** Grey, cracking into small, square plates. **Flowers** Males yellow, females purple-red, at the tips of the shoots, borne in separate clusters on the same plant in early summer. **Fruit** An egg-shaped cone, to 10cm (4in) long, deep blue at first ripening to yellow-brown in two years.
• **NATIVE REGION** Albania, Bosnia-Herzegovina/Yugoslavia, N. Greece.
• **HABITAT** Mountains, usually on limestone.
• **REMARK** Also known as *Pinus heldreichii* var. *leucodermis*. Easily distinguished by its dark green foliage, blue young cones, and narrow habit.

purple-red female flower clusters borne at shoot tips

young cones still deep blue after one year

rigid needles borne in tight bundles

cones eventually ripen to yellow-brown

male flower clusters open to release yellow pollen

Height 25m (80ft)	Shape Narrowly conical	Leaf persistence Evergreen	Leaf type

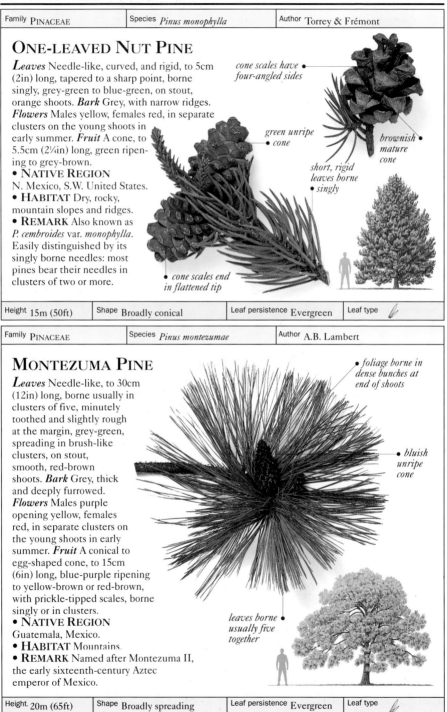

Family PINACEAE	Species *Pinus monophylla*	Author Torrey & Frémont

ONE-LEAVED NUT PINE

Leaves Needle-like, curved, and rigid, to 5cm (2in) long, tapered to a sharp point, borne singly, grey-green to blue-green, on stout, orange shoots. **Bark** Grey, with narrow ridges. **Flowers** Males yellow, females red, in separate clusters on the young shoots in early summer. **Fruit** A cone, to 5.5cm (2¼in) long, green ripening to grey-brown.
• **NATIVE REGION** N. Mexico, S.W. United States.
• **HABITAT** Dry, rocky, mountain slopes and ridges.
• **REMARK** Also known as *P. cembroides* var. *monophylla*. Easily distinguished by its singly borne needles: most pines bear their needles in clusters of two or more.

cone scales have four-angled sides

green unripe cone

brownish mature cone

short, rigid leaves borne singly

cone scales end in flattened tip

Height 15m (50ft)	Shape Broadly conical	Leaf persistence Evergreen	Leaf type

Family PINACEAE	Species *Pinus montezumae*	Author A.B. Lambert

MONTEZUMA PINE

Leaves Needle-like, to 30cm (12in) long, borne usually in clusters of five, minutely toothed and slightly rough at the margin, grey-green, spreading in brush-like clusters, on stout, smooth, red-brown shoots. **Bark** Grey, thick and deeply furrowed. **Flowers** Males purple opening yellow, females red, in separate clusters on the young shoots in early summer. **Fruit** A conical to egg-shaped cone, to 15cm (6in) long, blue-purple ripening to yellow-brown or red-brown, with prickle-tipped scales, borne singly or in clusters.
• **NATIVE REGION** Guatemala, Mexico.
• **HABITAT** Mountains.
• **REMARK** Named after Montezuma II, the early sixteenth-century Aztec emperor of Mexico.

foliage borne in dense bunches at end of shoots

bluish unripe cone

leaves borne usually five together

Height 20m (65ft)	Shape Broadly spreading	Leaf persistence Evergreen	Leaf type

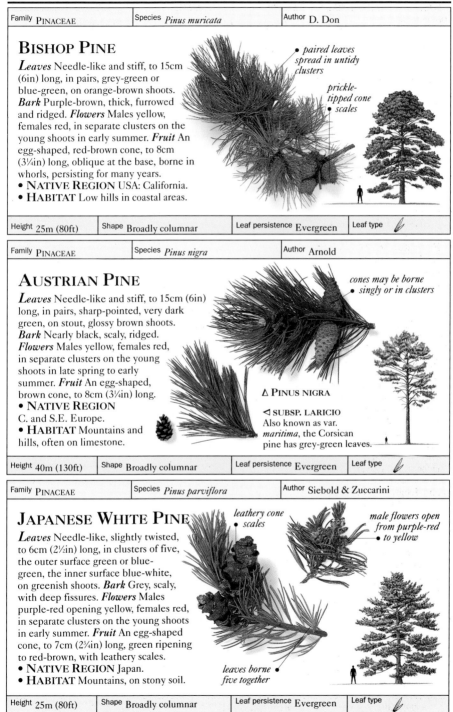

Family PINACEAE	Species *Pinus muricata*	Author D. Don

BISHOP PINE

Leaves Needle-like and stiff, to 15cm (6in) long, in pairs, grey-green or blue-green, on orange-brown shoots. *Bark* Purple-brown, thick, furrowed and ridged. *Flowers* Males yellow, females red, in separate clusters on the young shoots in early summer. *Fruit* An egg-shaped, red-brown cone, to 8cm (3¼in) long, oblique at the base, borne in whorls, persisting for many years.
• **NATIVE REGION** USA: California.
• **HABITAT** Low hills in coastal areas.

paired leaves spread in untidy clusters

prickle-tipped cone scales

Height 25m (80ft)	Shape Broadly columnar	Leaf persistence Evergreen	Leaf type

Family PINACEAE	Species *Pinus nigra*	Author Arnold

AUSTRIAN PINE

Leaves Needle-like and stiff, to 15cm (6in) long, in pairs, sharp-pointed, very dark green, on stout, glossy brown shoots. *Bark* Nearly black, scaly, ridged. *Flowers* Males yellow, females red, in separate clusters on the young shoots in late spring to early summer. *Fruit* An egg-shaped, brown cone, to 8cm (3¼in) long.
• **NATIVE REGION** C. and S.E. Europe.
• **HABITAT** Mountains and hills, often on limestone.

cones may be borne singly or in clusters

△ PINUS NIGRA

◁ SUBSP. LARICIO
Also known as var. *maritima*, the Corsican pine has grey-green leaves.

Height 40m (130ft)	Shape Broadly columnar	Leaf persistence Evergreen	Leaf type

Family PINACEAE	Species *Pinus parviflora*	Author Siebold & Zuccarini

JAPANESE WHITE PINE

Leaves Needle-like, slightly twisted, to 6cm (2½in) long, in clusters of five, the outer surface green or blue-green, the inner surface blue-white, on greenish shoots. *Bark* Grey, scaly, with deep fissures. *Flowers* Males purple-red opening yellow, females red, in separate clusters on the young shoots in early summer. *Fruit* An egg-shaped cone, to 7cm (2¾in) long, green ripening to red-brown, with leathery scales.
• **NATIVE REGION** Japan.
• **HABITAT** Mountains, on stony soil.

leathery cone scales

male flowers open from purple-red to yellow

leaves borne five together

Height 25m (80ft)	Shape Broadly columnar	Leaf persistence Evergreen	Leaf type

Family PINACEAE	Species *Pinus peuce*	Author Grisebach

MACEDONIAN PINE

Leaves Needle-like and stiff, to 10cm (4in) long, in dense clusters of five, blue-green, pointing forward on smooth, bloomy, green shoots. **Bark** Purple-brown, fissured and cracked into plates. **Flowers** Males yellow, females red, in separate clusters on the young shoots in early summer. **Fruit** A cylindrical to conical, resinous, drooping cone, to 15cm (6in) long, green at first ripening to brown.
• **NATIVE REGION** S.E. Europe.
• **HABITAT** Mountains.

female flowers

slender leaves in clusters of five

Height 30m (100ft)	Shape Narrowly columnar	Leaf persistence Evergreen	Leaf type

Family PINACEAE	Species *Pinus pinaster*	Author Aiton

MARITIME PINE

Leaves Needle-like and stiff, to 20cm (8in) long, in pairs, sharp-pointed, grey-green becoming dark green, borne on stout shoots. **Bark** Purple-brown, ridged, deeply fissured. **Flowers** Males yellow, females red, in separate clusters on the young shoots in early summer. **Fruit** A conical, glossy brown cone, to 20cm (8in) long, the scales with sharp prickles, persisting for many years.
• **NATIVE REGION** N. Africa, S.W. Europe.
• **HABITAT** Sandy soil.

all leaves point forward on shoot

Height 35m (115ft)	Shape Broadly columnar	Leaf persistence Evergreen	Leaf type

Family PINACEAE	Species *Pinus pinea*	Author Linnaeus

STONE PINE

Leaves Needle-like and stout, to 12cm (4¾in) long, in pairs, grey-green, on smooth, orange-brown shoots; on young plants, singly, bright blue-grey. **Bark** Orange-brown, deeply fissured. **Flowers** Males yellow, females green, borne in separate clusters on the young shoots in early summer. **Fruit** A nearly rounded, heavy, glossy brown cone, to 12cm (4¾in) long.
• **NATIVE REGION** Mediterranean.
• **HABITAT** Sandy soil near the coast.

cones contain edible seeds

thick leaves borne in pairs

Height 20m (65ft)	Shape Broadly spreading	Leaf persistence Evergreen	Leaf type

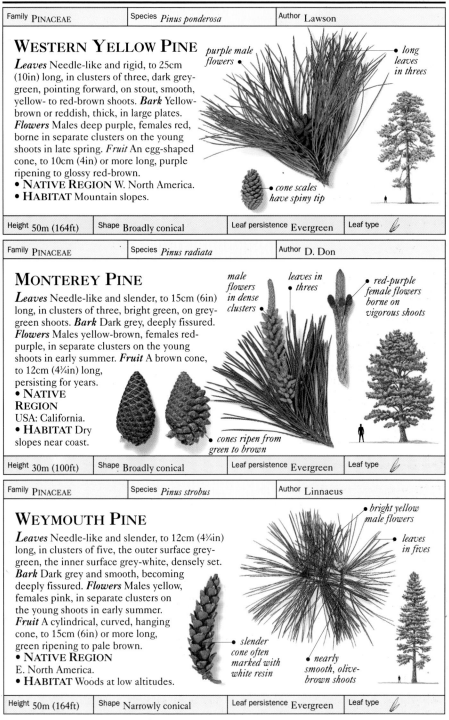

Family PINACEAE		Species *Pinus ponderosa*		Author Lawson

WESTERN YELLOW PINE

purple male flowers

long leaves in threes

Leaves Needle-like and rigid, to 25cm (10in) long, in clusters of three, dark grey-green, pointing forward, on stout, smooth, yellow- to red-brown shoots. **Bark** Yellow-brown or reddish, thick, in large plates. **Flowers** Males deep purple, females red, borne in separate clusters on the young shoots in late spring. **Fruit** An egg-shaped cone, to 10cm (4in) or more long, purple ripening to glossy red-brown.
• **NATIVE REGION** W. North America.
• **HABITAT** Mountain slopes.

cone scales have spiny tip

Height 50m (164ft)	Shape Broadly conical	Leaf persistence Evergreen	Leaf type

Family PINACEAE		Species *Pinus radiata*		Author D. Don

MONTEREY PINE

male flowers in dense clusters

leaves in threes

red-purple female flowers borne on vigorous shoots

Leaves Needle-like and slender, to 15cm (6in) long, in clusters of three, bright green, on grey-green shoots. **Bark** Dark grey, deeply fissured. **Flowers** Males yellow-brown, females red-purple, in separate clusters on the young shoots in early summer. **Fruit** A brown cone, to 12cm (4¾in) long, persisting for years.
• **NATIVE REGION** USA: California.
• **HABITAT** Dry slopes near coast.

cones ripen from green to brown

Height 30m (100ft)	Shape Broadly conical	Leaf persistence Evergreen	Leaf type

Family PINACEAE		Species *Pinus strobus*		Author Linnaeus

WEYMOUTH PINE

bright yellow male flowers

leaves in fives

Leaves Needle-like and slender, to 12cm (4¾in) long, in clusters of five, the outer surface grey-green, the inner surface grey-white, densely set. **Bark** Dark grey and smooth, becoming deeply fissured. **Flowers** Males yellow, females pink, in separate clusters on the young shoots in early summer. **Fruit** A cylindrical, curved, hanging cone, to 15cm (6in) or more long, green ripening to pale brown.
• **NATIVE REGION** E. North America.
• **HABITAT** Woods at low altitudes.

slender cone often marked with white resin

nearly smooth, olive-brown shoots

Height 50m (164ft)	Shape Narrowly conical	Leaf persistence Evergreen	Leaf type

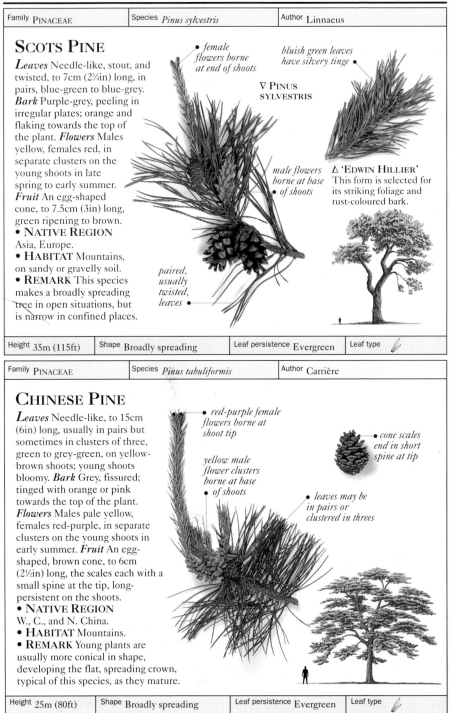

Family PINACEAE	Species *Pinus sylvestris*	Author Linnaeus

SCOTS PINE

Leaves Needle-like, stout, and twisted, to 7cm (2¾in) long, in pairs, blue-green to blue-grey. **Bark** Purple-grey, peeling in irregular plates; orange and flaking towards the top of the plant. **Flowers** Males yellow, females red, in separate clusters on the young shoots in late spring to early summer. **Fruit** An egg-shaped cone, to 7.5cm (3in) long, green ripening to brown.
• **NATIVE REGION** Asia, Europe.
• **HABITAT** Mountains, on sandy or gravelly soil.
• **REMARK** This species makes a broadly spreading tree in open situations, but is narrow in confined places.

female flowers borne at end of shoots

∇ PINUS SYLVESTRIS

bluish green leaves have silvery tinge

male flowers borne at base of shoots

△ 'EDWIN HILLIER' This form is selected for its striking foliage and rust-coloured bark.

paired, usually twisted, leaves

Height 35m (115ft)	Shape Broadly spreading	Leaf persistence Evergreen	Leaf type

Family PINACEAE	Species *Pinus tabuliformis*	Author Carrière

CHINESE PINE

Leaves Needle-like, to 15cm (6in) long, usually in pairs but sometimes in clusters of three, green to grey-green, on yellow-brown shoots; young shoots bloomy. **Bark** Grey, fissured; tinged with orange or pink towards the top of the plant. **Flowers** Males pale yellow, females red-purple, in separate clusters on the young shoots in early summer. **Fruit** An egg-shaped, brown cone, to 6cm (2½in) long, the scales each with a small spine at the tip, long-persistent on the shoots.
• **NATIVE REGION** W., C., and N. China.
• **HABITAT** Mountains.
• **REMARK** Young plants are usually more conical in shape, developing the flat, spreading crown, typical of this species, as they mature.

red-purple female flowers borne at shoot tip

yellow male flower clusters borne at base of shoots

cone scales end in short spine at tip

leaves may be in pairs or clustered in threes

Height 25m (80ft)	Shape Broadly spreading	Leaf persistence Evergreen	Leaf type

Family PINACEAE	Species *Pinus thunbergii*	Author Parlatore

JAPANESE BLACK PINE

Leaves Needle-like and rigid, to 10cm (4in) long, in pairs, sharp-pointed, densely set, pointing forward, on smooth, yellow-brown shoots. **Bark** Grey, cracking into irregular plates. **Flowers** Males yellowish, females purple-red, in separate clusters on the young shoots in early summer. **Fruit** An egg-shaped cone, to 7cm (2¾in) long, purple or green ripening to grey-brown.
• **NATIVE REGION** N.E. China, Japan, Korea.
• **HABITAT** Near coastline.
• **REMARK** This species is related to the Austrian pine *(Pinus nigra*, see p.71). In winter, it is easily distinguished by its white-hairy leaf buds.

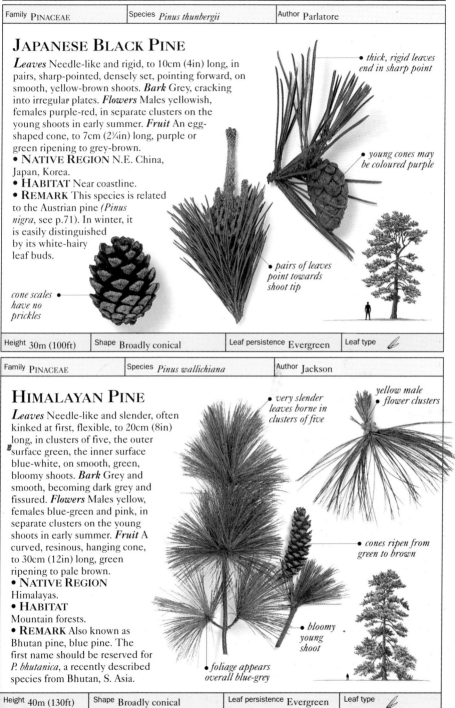

• *thick, rigid leaves end in sharp point*

• *young cones may be coloured purple*

• *pairs of leaves point towards shoot tip*

cone scales • *have no prickles*

Height 30m (100ft)	Shape Broadly conical	Leaf persistence Evergreen	Leaf type

Family PINACEAE	Species *Pinus wallichiana*	Author Jackson

HIMALAYAN PINE

Leaves Needle-like and slender, often kinked at first, flexible, to 20cm (8in) long, in clusters of five, the outer surface green, the inner surface blue-white, on smooth, green, bloomy shoots. **Bark** Grey and smooth, becoming dark grey and fissured. **Flowers** Males yellow, females blue-green and pink, in separate clusters on the young shoots in early summer. **Fruit** A curved, resinous, hanging cone, to 30cm (12in) long, green ripening to pale brown.
• **NATIVE REGION** Himalayas.
• **HABITAT** Mountain forests.
• **REMARK** Also known as Bhutan pine, blue pine. The first name should be reserved for *P. bhutanica*, a recently described species from Bhutan, S. Asia.

• *very slender leaves borne in clusters of five*

yellow male • *flower clusters*

• *cones ripen from green to brown*

• *bloomy young shoot*

• *foliage appears overall blue-grey*

Height 40m (130ft)	Shape Broadly conical	Leaf persistence Evergreen	Leaf type

Family PINACEAE	Species *Pseudolarix amabilis*	Author (Nelson) Rehder

GOLDEN LARCH

Leaves Linear and slender, to 5cm (2in) long, borne singly on long shoots, in dense whorls on upcurved, short shoots, turning golden yellow in autumn. **Bark** Grey-brown, cracking into small, square plates. **Flowers** Males and females both yellow, in separate clusters at the ends of short shoots, on the same plant in late spring or early summer. **Fruit** An egg-shaped cone, to 5cm (2in) long, green ripening to brown, breaking up before falling.
• **NATIVE REGION** E. China.
• **HABITAT** Mountain forests.
• **REMARK** A relative of the larches *(Larix*, see pp.60–61).

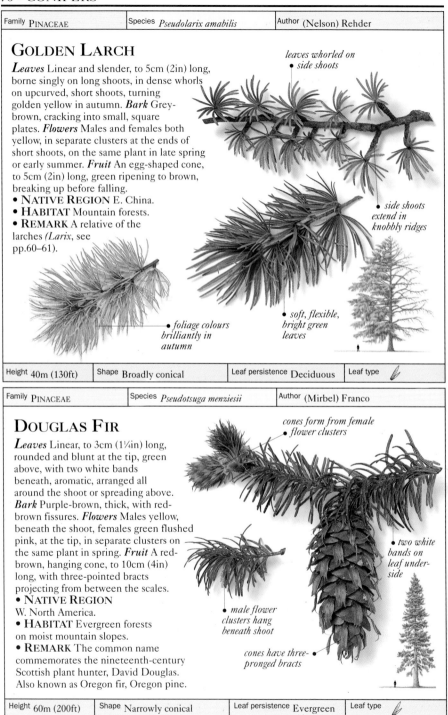

leaves whorled on side shoots

side shoots extend in knobbly ridges

foliage colours brilliantly in autumn

soft, flexible, bright green leaves

Height 40m (130ft)	Shape Broadly conical	Leaf persistence Deciduous	Leaf type

Family PINACEAE	Species *Pseudotsuga menziesii*	Author (Mirbel) Franco

DOUGLAS FIR

Leaves Linear, to 3cm (1¼in) long, rounded and blunt at the tip, green above, with two white bands beneath, aromatic, arranged all around the shoot or spreading above. **Bark** Purple-brown, thick, with red-brown fissures. **Flowers** Males yellow, beneath the shoot, females green flushed pink, at the tip, in separate clusters on the same plant in spring. **Fruit** A red-brown, hanging cone, to 10cm (4in) long, with three-pointed bracts projecting from between the scales.
• **NATIVE REGION** W. North America.
• **HABITAT** Evergreen forests on moist mountain slopes.
• **REMARK** The common name commemorates the nineteenth-century Scottish plant hunter, David Douglas. Also known as Oregon fir, Oregon pine.

cones form from female flower clusters

two white bands on leaf under-side

male flower clusters hang beneath shoot

cones have three-pronged bracts

Height 60m (200ft)	Shape Narrowly conical	Leaf persistence Evergreen	Leaf type

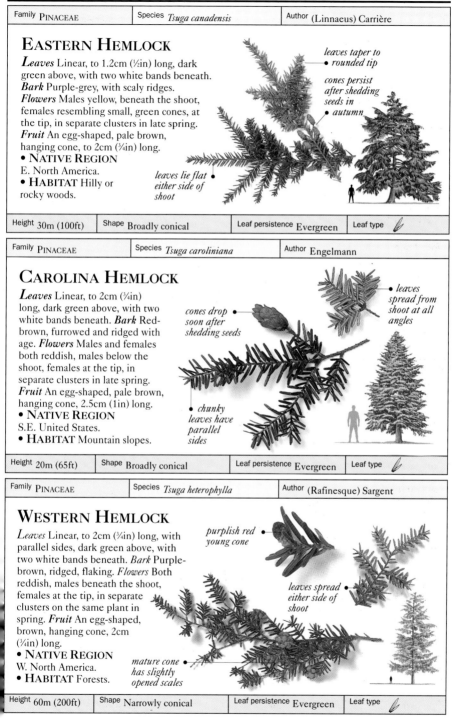

Family PINACEAE	Species *Tsuga canadensis*	Author (Linnaeus) Carrière

EASTERN HEMLOCK

Leaves Linear, to 1.2cm (½in) long, dark green above, with two white bands beneath. **Bark** Purple-grey, with scaly ridges. **Flowers** Males yellow, beneath the shoot, females resembling small, green cones, at the tip, in separate clusters in late spring. **Fruit** An egg-shaped, pale brown, hanging cone, to 2cm (¾in) long.
• **NATIVE REGION** E. North America.
• **HABITAT** Hilly or rocky woods.

leaves taper to rounded tip

cones persist after shedding seeds in autumn

leaves lie flat either side of shoot

Height 30m (100ft)	Shape Broadly conical	Leaf persistence Evergreen	Leaf type

Family PINACEAE	Species *Tsuga caroliniana*	Author Engelmann

CAROLINA HEMLOCK

Leaves Linear, to 2cm (¾in) long, dark green above, with two white bands beneath. **Bark** Red-brown, furrowed and ridged with age. **Flowers** Males and females both reddish, males below the shoot, females at the tip, in separate clusters in late spring. **Fruit** An egg-shaped, pale brown, hanging cone, 2.5cm (1in) long.
• **NATIVE REGION** S.E. United States.
• **HABITAT** Mountain slopes.

cones drop soon after shedding seeds

leaves spread from shoot at all angles

chunky leaves have parallel sides

Height 20m (65ft)	Shape Broadly conical	Leaf persistence Evergreen	Leaf type

Family PINACEAE	Species *Tsuga heterophylla*	Author (Rafinesque) Sargent

WESTERN HEMLOCK

Leaves Linear, to 2cm (¾in) long, with parallel sides, dark green above, with two white bands beneath. **Bark** Purple-brown, ridged, flaking. **Flowers** Both reddish, males beneath the shoot, females at the tip, in separate clusters on the same plant in spring. **Fruit** An egg-shaped, brown, hanging cone, 2cm (¾in) long.
• **NATIVE REGION** W. North America.
• **HABITAT** Forests.

purplish red young cone

leaves spread either side of shoot

mature cone has slightly opened scales

Height 60m (200ft)	Shape Narrowly conical	Leaf persistence Evergreen	Leaf type

PODOCARPACEAE

O VER 100 SPECIES OF evergreen trees and shrubs, mainly in the genus *Podocarpus*, belong to this family; most grow in warm regions of the southern hemisphere. Male and female flowers are usually on separate plants, the males in catkin-like clusters. Females develop into a fleshy cone or seed.

Family PODOCARPACEAE	Species *Podocarpus andinus*	Author Endlicher

PLUM-FRUITED YEW

Leaves Linear, to 2.5cm (1in) long, abruptly short-pointed, deep blue-green above, with two whitish bands beneath, all around the shoot. **Bark** Dark grey and smooth. **Flowers** Males yellow, in branched clusters 2.5cm (1in) long, females small, green, on separate plants in early summer. **Fruit** Fleshy, plum-like, edible, green ripening to yellow, with a single seed.
• **NATIVE REGION** Argentina, S. Chile.
• **HABITAT** Mountains.

• *flattened leaves*

• *two paler bands on underside of leaves*

fruit matures to yellow •

Height 15m (50ft)	Shape Broadly conical	Leaf persistence Evergreen	Leaf type

Family PODOCARPACEAE	Species *Saxegothaea conspicua*	Author Lindley

PRINCE ALBERT'S YEW

Leaves Linear, usually curved, to 3cm (1¼in) long, with a fine, sharp point at the tip, dark green above, with two whitish bands beneath, loosely arranged in two ranks either side of the shoot or spreading all around it. **Bark** Purple-brown, smooth, peeling in strips. **Flowers** Males purplish, in the leaf axils, beneath the shoot, females blue-green, at the tip of the shoot, in separate clusters on the same plant in late spring to early summer. **Fruit** A rounded, fleshy cone, to 2cm (¾in) across, with prickly, blue-green scales.
• **NATIVE REGION** Chile.
• **HABITAT** Forests.

• *tiny, purplish male flower clusters*

leaves end in small, sharp point at tip •

• *prickle-pointed cone scales*

Height 12m (40ft)	Shape Broadly conical	Leaf persistence Evergreen	Leaf type

TAXACEAE

T HIS FAMILY IS OFTEN classed apart from the true conifers because its members do not bear their seeds in cones. The six genera contain about 18 species of evergreen trees and shrubs. Male and female flowers are usually on separate plants. Females mature to a single seed surrounded by a fleshy aril.

Family TAXACEAE	Species *Taxus baccata*	Author Linnaeus

COMMON YEW

Leaves Linear, to 3cm (1¼in) long, pointed at the tip, dark green above, with two paler green bands beneath, mainly spreading in two ranks either side of the shoot. **Bark** Purple-brown, smooth and flaking. **Flowers** Males and females both small, males pale yellow, in clusters in the leaf axils, beneath the shoot, females singly, at the end of the shoot, on separate plants in spring. **Fruit** A single seed, enclosed in a fleshy, usually red, aril, the whole 1cm (⅜in) long, open at the top, exposing the green seed.
• **NATIVE REGION** N. Africa, S.W. Asia, Europe.
• **HABITAT** Limey soil.
• **REMARK** All parts are poisonous, except the aril.

'LUTEA' ▷
The yellow-berried yew is named for the colour of its fruits.

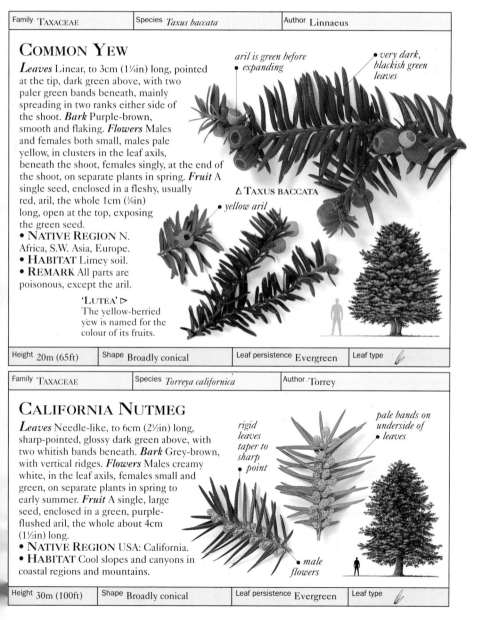

aril is green before
• expanding

• very dark,
blackish green
leaves

△ TAXUS BACCATA

• yellow aril

Height 20m (65ft)	Shape Broadly conical	Leaf persistence Evergreen	Leaf type

Family TAXACEAE	Species *Torreya californica*	Author Torrey

CALIFORNIA NUTMEG

Leaves Needle-like, to 6cm (2½in) long, sharp-pointed, glossy dark green above, with two whitish bands beneath. **Bark** Grey-brown, with vertical ridges. **Flowers** Males creamy white, in the leaf axils, females small and green, on separate plants in spring to early summer. **Fruit** A single, large seed, enclosed in a green, purple-flushed aril, the whole about 4cm (1½in) long.
• **NATIVE REGION** USA: California.
• **HABITAT** Cool slopes and canyons in coastal regions and mountains.

rigid
leaves
taper to
sharp
• point

pale bands on
underside of
• leaves

• male
flowers

Height 30m (100ft)	Shape Broadly conical	Leaf persistence Evergreen	Leaf type

TAXODIACEAE

THE SWAMP CYPRESS family contains about ten genera and 15 species of deciduous and evergreen trees, found in North America, east Asia, and Tasmania. The leaves may be needle- or scale-like. Male and female flowers are borne separately on the same plant; females develop into woody cones.

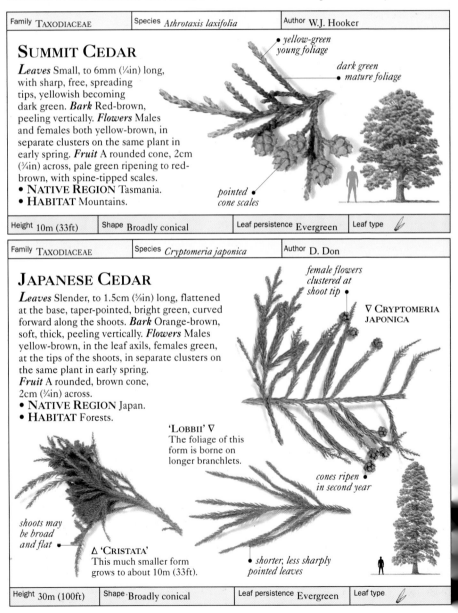

Family TAXODIACEAE	Species *Athrotaxis laxifolia*	Author W.J. Hooker

SUMMIT CEDAR

Leaves Small, to 6mm (¼in) long, with sharp, free, spreading tips, yellowish becoming dark green. **Bark** Red-brown, peeling vertically. **Flowers** Males and females both yellow-brown, in separate clusters on the same plant in early spring. **Fruit** A rounded cone, 2cm (¾in) across, pale green ripening to red-brown, with spine-tipped scales.
• **NATIVE REGION** Tasmania.
• **HABITAT** Mountains.

yellow-green young foliage

dark green mature foliage

pointed cone scales

Height 10m (33ft)	Shape Broadly conical	Leaf persistence Evergreen	Leaf type

Family TAXODIACEAE	Species *Cryptomeria japonica*	Author D. Don

JAPANESE CEDAR

Leaves Slender, to 1.5cm (⅝in) long, flattened at the base, taper-pointed, bright green, curved forward along the shoots. **Bark** Orange-brown, soft, thick, peeling vertically. **Flowers** Males yellow-brown, in the leaf axils, females green, at the tips of the shoots, in separate clusters on the same plant in early spring. **Fruit** A rounded, brown cone, 2cm (¾in) across.
• **NATIVE REGION** Japan.
• **HABITAT** Forests.

female flowers clustered at shoot tip

▽ **CRYPTOMERIA JAPONICA**

'LOBBII' ▽
The foliage of this form is borne on longer branchlets.

cones ripen in second year

shoots may be broad and flat

△ **'CRISTATA'**
This much smaller form grows to about 10m (33ft).

shorter, less sharply pointed leaves

Height 30m (100ft)	Shape Broadly conical	Leaf persistence Evergreen	Leaf type

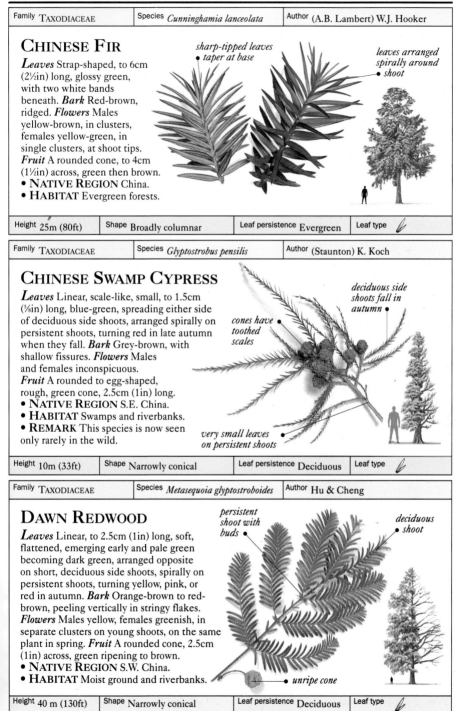

Family TAXODIACEAE	Species *Cunninghamia lanceolata*	Author (A.B. Lambert) W.J. Hooker

CHINESE FIR

sharp-tipped leaves • taper at base

leaves arranged spirally around • shoot

Leaves Strap-shaped, to 6cm (2½in) long, glossy green, with two white bands beneath. **Bark** Red-brown, ridged. **Flowers** Males yellow-brown, in clusters, females yellow-green, in single clusters, at shoot tips. **Fruit** A rounded cone, to 4cm (1½in) across, green then brown.
• **NATIVE REGION** China.
• **HABITAT** Evergreen forests.

Height 25m (80ft)	Shape Broadly columnar	Leaf persistence Evergreen	Leaf type

Family TAXODIACEAE	Species *Glyptostrobus pensilis*	Author (Staunton) K. Koch

CHINESE SWAMP CYPRESS

deciduous side shoots fall in autumn •

Leaves Linear, scale-like, small, to 1.5cm (⅝in) long, blue-green, spreading either side of deciduous side shoots, arranged spirally on persistent shoots, turning red in late autumn when they fall. **Bark** Grey-brown, with shallow fissures. **Flowers** Males and females inconspicuous. **Fruit** A rounded to egg-shaped, rough, green cone, 2.5cm (1in) long.
• **NATIVE REGION** S.E. China.
• **HABITAT** Swamps and riverbanks.
• **REMARK** This species is now seen only rarely in the wild.

cones have • toothed scales

very small leaves • on persistent shoots

Height 10m (33ft)	Shape Narrowly conical	Leaf persistence Deciduous	Leaf type

Family TAXODIACEAE	Species *Metasequoia glyptostroboides*	Author Hu & Cheng

DAWN REDWOOD

persistent shoot with buds •

deciduous • shoot

Leaves Linear, to 2.5cm (1in) long, soft, flattened, emerging early and pale green becoming dark green, arranged opposite on short, deciduous side shoots, spirally on persistent shoots, turning yellow, pink, or red in autumn. **Bark** Orange-brown to red-brown, peeling vertically in stringy flakes. **Flowers** Males yellow, females greenish, in separate clusters on young shoots, on the same plant in spring. **Fruit** A rounded cone, 2.5cm (1in) across, green ripening to brown.
• **NATIVE REGION** S.W. China.
• **HABITAT** Moist ground and riverbanks.

• unripe cone

Height 40 m (130ft)	Shape Narrowly conical	Leaf persistence Deciduous	Leaf type

Family TAXODIACEAE	Species *Sciadopitys verticillata*	Author Siebold & Zuccarini

UMBRELLA PINE

Leaves Needle-like, to 12cm (4¾in) long, deeply grooved on both sides, deep green above, yellow-green beneath. **Bark** Red-brown, peeling in long, vertical strips. **Flowers** Males yellow, in many clusters, females green, at the ends of the shoots, on the same plant in spring. **Fruit** An egg-shaped cone, to 7.5cm (3in) long, green ripening to red-brown in two years.
• **NATIVE REGION** Japan.
• **HABITAT** Mountains.

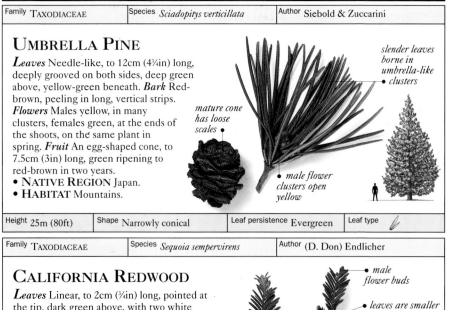

mature cone has loose scales •

slender leaves borne in umbrella-like • clusters

• *male flower clusters open yellow*

Height 25m (80ft)	Shape Narrowly conical	Leaf persistence Evergreen	Leaf type

Family TAXODIACEAE	Species *Sequoia sempervirens*	Author (D. Don) Endlicher

CALIFORNIA REDWOOD

Leaves Linear, to 2cm (¾in) long, pointed at the tip, dark green above, with two white bands beneath, spreading either side of the shoot. **Bark** Red-brown, soft and fibrous, very thick, with broad ridges. **Flowers** Males yellow-brown, females green, in separate clusters on the same plant in late winter to early spring. **Fruit** A barrel-shaped to rounded, red-brown cone, to 3cm (1¼in) long, ripe in one year.
• **NATIVE REGION** USA: S. Oregon, California.
• **HABITAT** Low slopes in coastal regions.

• *male flower buds*

• *leaves are smaller on coning shoots*

Height 100m (330ft)	Shape Narrowly conical	Leaf persistence Evergreen	Leaf type

Family TAXODIACEAE	Species *Sequoiadendron giganteum*	Author (Lindley) Buchholz

WELLINGTONIA

one-year-old cone still green •

tiny, pointed leaves make foliage rough • to the touch

Leaves To 8mm (⁵⁄₁₆in) long, sharp-pointed, with spreading tips, deep blue-green, all around the shoot. **Bark** Red-brown, soft, fibrous, very thick. **Flowers** Males yellow, at the ends of the shoots, females green, in separate clusters in early spring. **Fruit** A barrel-shaped cone, to 7.5cm (3in) long, green ripening to brown in two years, often persisting for years.
• **NATIVE REGION** USA: California.
• **HABITAT** West-facing mountain slopes.

• *male flower buds open in early spring*

Height 80m (260ft)	Shape Narrowly conical	Leaf persistence Evergreen	Leaf type

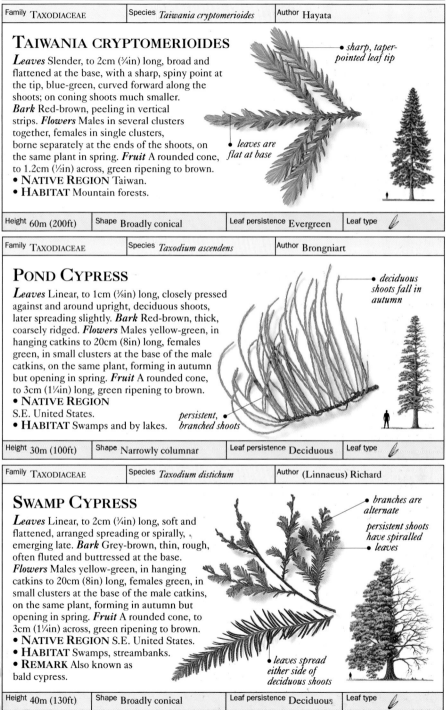

Family TAXODIACEAE	Species *Taiwania cryptomerioides*	Author Hayata

TAIWANIA CRYPTOMERIOIDES

Leaves Slender, to 2cm (¾in) long, broad and flattened at the base, with a sharp, spiny point at the tip, blue-green, curved forward along the shoots; on coning shoots much smaller. **Bark** Red-brown, peeling in vertical strips. **Flowers** Males in several clusters together, females in single clusters, borne separately at the ends of the shoots, on the same plant in spring. **Fruit** A rounded cone, to 1.2cm (½in) across, green ripening to brown.
• **NATIVE REGION** Taiwan.
• **HABITAT** Mountain forests.

sharp, taper-pointed leaf tip

leaves are flat at base

Height 60m (200ft)	Shape Broadly conical	Leaf persistence Evergreen	Leaf type

Family TAXODIACEAE	Species *Taxodium ascendens*	Author Brongniart

POND CYPRESS

Leaves Linear, to 1cm (⅜in) long, closely pressed against and around upright, deciduous shoots, later spreading slightly. **Bark** Red-brown, thick, coarsely ridged. **Flowers** Males yellow-green, in hanging catkins to 20cm (8in) long, females green, in small clusters at the base of the male catkins, on the same plant, forming in autumn but opening in spring. **Fruit** A rounded cone, to 3cm (1¼in) long, green ripening to brown.
• **NATIVE REGION** S.E. United States.
• **HABITAT** Swamps and by lakes.

deciduous shoots fall in autumn

persistent, branched shoots

Height 30m (100ft)	Shape Narrowly columnar	Leaf persistence Deciduous	Leaf type

Family TAXODIACEAE	Species *Taxodium distichum*	Author (Linnaeus) Richard

SWAMP CYPRESS

Leaves Linear, to 2cm (¾in) long, soft and flattened, arranged spreading or spirally, emerging late. **Bark** Grey-brown, thin, rough, often fluted and buttressed at the base. **Flowers** Males yellow-green, in hanging catkins to 20cm (8in) long, females green, in small clusters at the base of the male catkins, on the same plant, forming in autumn but opening in spring. **Fruit** A rounded cone, to 3cm (1¼in) across, green ripening to brown.
• **NATIVE REGION** S.E. United States.
• **HABITAT** Swamps, streambanks.
• **REMARK** Also known as bald cypress.

branches are alternate

persistent shoots have spiralled leaves

leaves spread either side of deciduous shoots

Height 40m (130ft)	Shape Broadly conical	Leaf persistence Deciduous	Leaf type

BROADLEAVES

ACERACEAE

T HE MAPLE FAMILY has two genera and over 100 species of evergreen and deciduous trees and shrubs. Some extend to the tropics, but most occur in northern temperate regions.

The opposite leaves are often lobed, sometimes merely toothed, or may be divided into several leaflets. The small male and female flowers vary from cream to yellow, green, red, or purple. They are borne, sometimes separately, on the same or different plants, usually opening as the young foliage unfolds. The winged fruits are in two halves. In maples *(Acer)*, one side of each half has an elongated wing; in *Dipteronia*, each half is winged all the way around.

Family ACERACEAE	Species *Acer buergerianum*	Author Miquel

TRIDENT MAPLE

Leaves Palmate, to 10cm (4in) long and across, narrowed at the base, with three forward-pointing lobes, usually untoothed or sparsely toothed at the margin, dark green above, bluish beneath, becoming smooth on both sides, turning red in autumn. **Bark** Grey-brown, peeling in scaly plates with age. **Flowers** Small and yellow-green, in broadly conical, upright clusters in spring with the young leaves. **Fruit** With parallel, upright wings, to 2.5cm (1in) long, green or reddish at first ripening to brown.
• **NATIVE REGION** China, Japan.
• **HABITAT** Mountain woods.

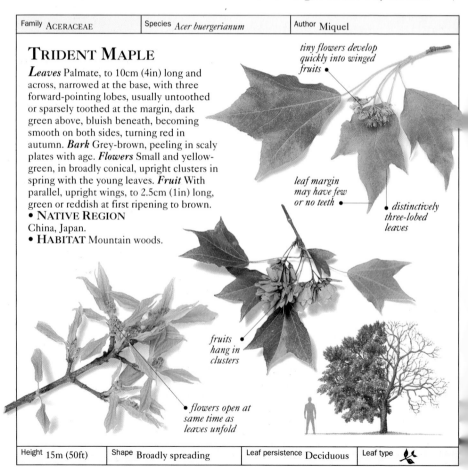

tiny flowers develop quickly into winged fruits •

leaf margin may have few or no teeth •

• distinctively three-lobed leaves

fruits hang in clusters

• flowers open at same time as leaves unfold

Height 15m (50ft)	Shape Broadly spreading	Leaf persistence Deciduous	Leaf type

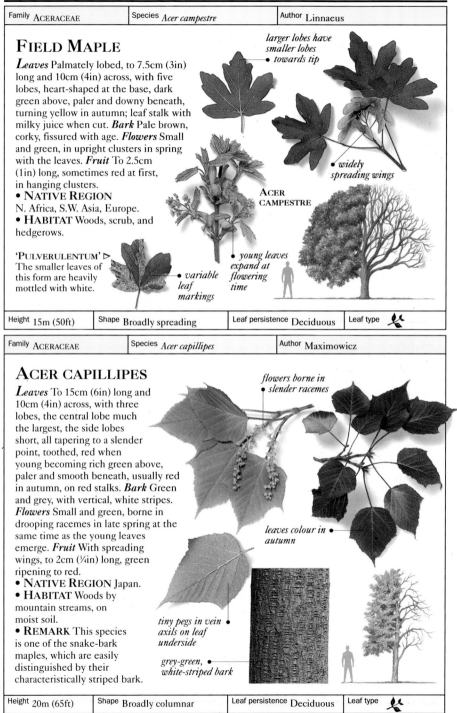

| Family ACERACEAE | Species *Acer campestre* | Author Linnaeus |

FIELD MAPLE

Leaves Palmately lobed, to 7.5cm (3in) long and 10cm (4in) across, with five lobes, heart-shaped at the base, dark green above, paler and downy beneath, turning yellow in autumn; leaf stalk with milky juice when cut. ***Bark*** Pale brown, corky, fissured with age. ***Flowers*** Small and green, in upright clusters in spring with the leaves. ***Fruit*** To 2.5cm (1in) long, sometimes red at first, in hanging clusters.
• **NATIVE REGION** N. Africa, S.W. Asia, Europe.
• **HABITAT** Woods, scrub, and hedgerows.

'PULVERULENTUM' ▷ The smaller leaves of this form are heavily mottled with white.

larger lobes have smaller lobes
• *towards tip*

ACER CAMPESTRE

• *widely spreading wings*

• *variable leaf markings*

• *young leaves expand at flowering time*

| Height 15m (50ft) | Shape Broadly spreading | Leaf persistence Deciduous | Leaf type |

| Family ACERACEAE | Species *Acer capillipes* | Author Maximowicz |

ACER CAPILLIPES

Leaves To 15cm (6in) long and 10cm (4in) across, with three lobes, the central lobe much the largest, the side lobes short, all tapering to a slender point, toothed, red when young becoming rich green above, paler and smooth beneath, usually red in autumn, on red stalks. ***Bark*** Green and grey, with vertical, white stripes. ***Flowers*** Small and green, borne in drooping racemes in late spring at the same time as the young leaves emerge. ***Fruit*** With spreading wings, to 2cm (¾in) long, green ripening to red.
• **NATIVE REGION** Japan.
• **HABITAT** Woods by mountain streams, on moist soil.
• **REMARK** This species is one of the snake-bark maples, which are easily distinguished by their characteristically striped bark.

flowers borne in • *slender racemes*

leaves colour in • *autumn*

tiny pegs in vein • *axils on leaf underside*

grey-green, • *white-striped bark*

| Height 20m (65ft) | Shape Broadly columnar | Leaf persistence Deciduous | Leaf type |

Family ACERACEAE	Species *Acer cappadocicum*	Author Gleditsch

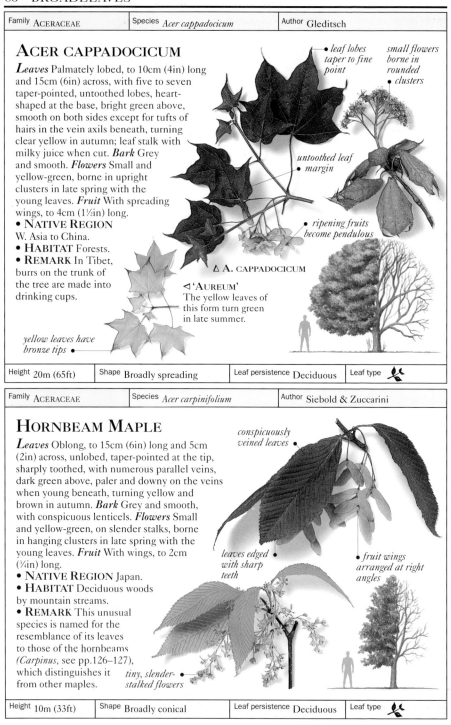

ACER CAPPADOCICUM

Leaves Palmately lobed, to 10cm (4in) long and 15cm (6in) across, with five to seven taper-pointed, untoothed lobes, heart-shaped at the base, bright green above, smooth on both sides except for tufts of hairs in the vein axils beneath, turning clear yellow in autumn; leaf stalk with milky juice when cut. **Bark** Grey and smooth. **Flowers** Small and yellow-green, borne in upright clusters in late spring with the young leaves. **Fruit** With spreading wings, to 4cm (1½in) long.
• **NATIVE REGION** W. Asia to China.
• **HABITAT** Forests.
• **REMARK** In Tibet, burrs on the trunk of the tree are made into drinking cups.

leaf lobes taper to fine point

small flowers borne in rounded clusters

untoothed leaf margin

ripening fruits become pendulous

△ **A. CAPPADOCICUM**

◁ **'AUREUM'**
The yellow leaves of this form turn green in late summer.

yellow leaves have bronze tips

Height 20m (65ft)	Shape Broadly spreading	Leaf persistence Deciduous	Leaf type

Family ACERACEAE	Species *Acer carpinifolium*	Author Siebold & Zuccarini

HORNBEAM MAPLE

Leaves Oblong, to 15cm (6in) long and 5cm (2in) across, unlobed, taper-pointed at the tip, sharply toothed, with numerous parallel veins, dark green above, paler and downy on the veins when young beneath, turning yellow and brown in autumn. **Bark** Grey and smooth, with conspicuous lenticels. **Flowers** Small and yellow-green, on slender stalks, borne in hanging clusters in late spring with the young leaves. **Fruit** With wings, to 2cm (¾in) long.
• **NATIVE REGION** Japan.
• **HABITAT** Deciduous woods by mountain streams.
• **REMARK** This unusual species is named for the resemblance of its leaves to those of the hornbeams *(Carpinus,* see pp.126–127), which distinguishes it from other maples.

conspicuously veined leaves

leaves edged with sharp teeth

fruit wings arranged at right angles

tiny, slender-stalked flowers

Height 10m (33ft)	Shape Broadly conical	Leaf persistence Deciduous	Leaf type

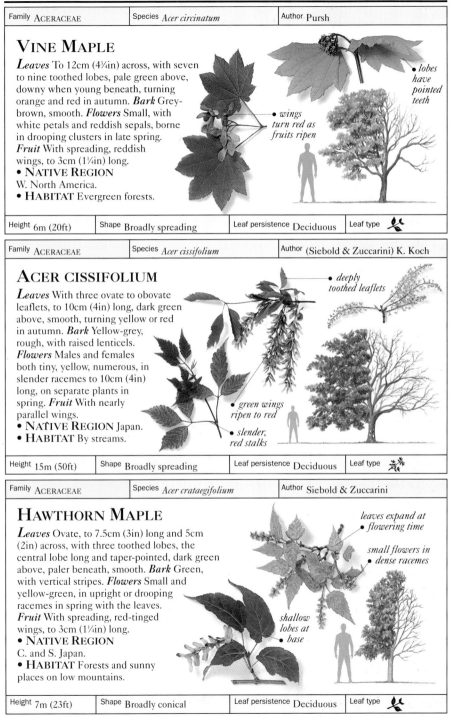

Family ACERACEAE	Species *Acer circinatum*	Author Pursh

VINE MAPLE

Leaves To 12cm (4¾in) across, with seven to nine toothed lobes, pale green above, downy when young beneath, turning orange and red in autumn. **Bark** Grey-brown, smooth. **Flowers** Small, with white petals and reddish sepals, borne in drooping clusters in late spring. **Fruit** With spreading, reddish wings, to 3cm (1¼in) long.
• **NATIVE REGION** W. North America.
• **HABITAT** Evergreen forests.

lobes have pointed teeth

wings turn red as fruits ripen

Height 6m (20ft)	Shape Broadly spreading	Leaf persistence Deciduous	Leaf type

Family ACERACEAE	Species *Acer cissifolium*	Author (Siebold & Zuccarini) K. Koch

ACER CISSIFOLIUM

Leaves With three ovate to obovate leaflets, to 10cm (4in) long, dark green above, smooth, turning yellow or red in autumn. **Bark** Yellow-grey, rough, with raised lenticels. **Flowers** Males and females both tiny, yellow, numerous, in slender racemes to 10cm (4in) long, on separate plants in spring. **Fruit** With nearly parallel wings.
• **NATIVE REGION** Japan.
• **HABITAT** By streams.

deeply toothed leaflets

green wings ripen to red

slender, red stalks

Height 15m (50ft)	Shape Broadly spreading	Leaf persistence Deciduous	Leaf type

Family ACERACEAE	Species *Acer crataegifolium*	Author Siebold & Zuccarini

HAWTHORN MAPLE

Leaves Ovate, to 7.5cm (3in) long and 5cm (2in) across, with three toothed lobes, the central lobe long and taper-pointed, dark green above, paler beneath, smooth. **Bark** Green, with vertical stripes. **Flowers** Small and yellow-green, in upright or drooping racemes in spring with the leaves. **Fruit** With spreading, red-tinged wings, to 3cm (1¼in) long.
• **NATIVE REGION** C. and S. Japan.
• **HABITAT** Forests and sunny places on low mountains.

leaves expand at flowering time

small flowers in dense racemes

shallow lobes at base

Height 7m (23ft)	Shape Broadly conical	Leaf persistence Deciduous	Leaf type

Family ACERACEAE	Species *Acer davidii*	Author Franchet

ACER DAVIDII

Leaves Ovate, to 15cm (6in) long and 10cm (4in) across, with or without small lobes, heart-shaped at the base, toothed, glossy dark green above, downy when young beneath, some forms turning orange in autumn. *Bark* Green, with vertical, white stripes, becoming grey and cracking with age. *Flowers* Small and green, in drooping racemes in late spring with the young leaves. *Fruit* With spreading wings, to 3cm (1¼in) long.
• NATIVE REGION China.
• HABITAT Mountain thickets and woods.
• REMARK The species is one of the snake-bark maples, and is variable in size and shape of leaf. Several cultivated forms are grown in gardens.

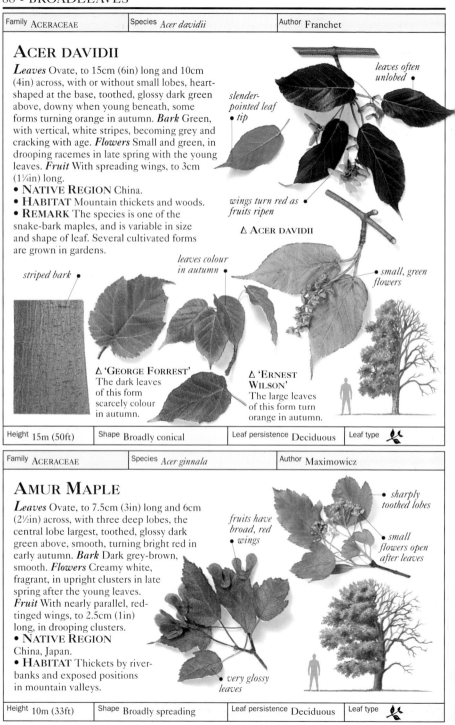

leaves often unlobed •

slender-pointed leaf • tip

wings turn red as fruits ripen •

△ ACER DAVIDII

leaves colour in autumn •

striped bark •

• small, green flowers

△ 'GEORGE FORREST' The dark leaves of this form scarcely colour in autumn.

△ 'ERNEST WILSON' The large leaves of this form turn orange in autumn.

Height 15m (50ft)	Shape Broadly conical	Leaf persistence Deciduous	Leaf type

Family ACERACEAE	Species *Acer ginnala*	Author Maximowicz

AMUR MAPLE

Leaves Ovate, to 7.5cm (3in) long and 6cm (2½in) across, with three deep lobes, the central lobe largest, toothed, glossy dark green above, smooth, turning bright red in early autumn. *Bark* Dark grey-brown, smooth. *Flowers* Creamy white, fragrant, in upright clusters in late spring after the young leaves. *Fruit* With nearly parallel, red-tinged wings, to 2.5cm (1in) long, in drooping clusters.
• NATIVE REGION China, Japan.
• HABITAT Thickets by river-banks and exposed positions in mountain valleys.

• sharply toothed lobes

fruits have broad, red • wings

• small flowers open after leaves

• very glossy leaves

Height 10m (33ft)	Shape Broadly spreading	Leaf persistence Deciduous	Leaf type

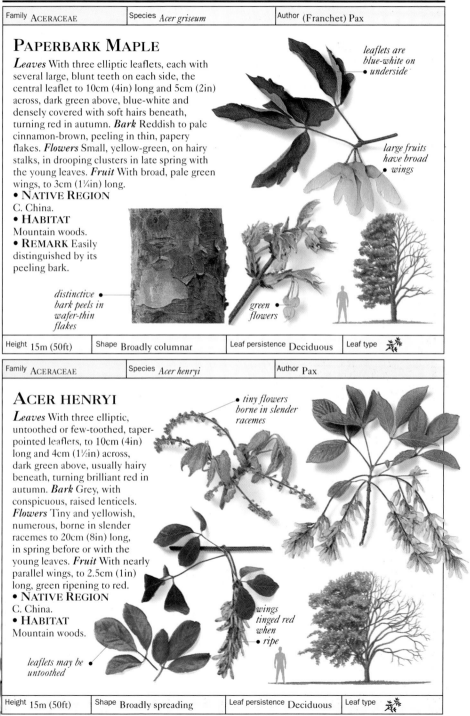

Family ACERACEAE	Species *Acer griseum*	Author (Franchet) Pax

PAPERBARK MAPLE

Leaves With three elliptic leaflets, each with several large, blunt teeth on each side, the central leaflet to 10cm (4in) long and 5cm (2in) across, dark green above, blue-white and densely covered with soft hairs beneath, turning red in autumn. ***Bark*** Reddish to pale cinnamon-brown, peeling in thin, papery flakes. ***Flowers*** Small, yellow-green, on hairy stalks, in drooping clusters in late spring with the young leaves. ***Fruit*** With broad, pale green wings, to 3cm (1¼in) long.
• **NATIVE REGION**
C. China.
• **HABITAT**
Mountain woods.
• **REMARK** Easily distinguished by its peeling bark.

leaflets are blue-white on • underside

large fruits have broad • wings

distinctive • bark peels in wafer-thin flakes

green • flowers

Height 15m (50ft)	Shape Broadly columnar	Leaf persistence Deciduous	Leaf type

Family ACERACEAE	Species *Acer henryi*	Author Pax

ACER HENRYI

Leaves With three elliptic, untoothed or few-toothed, taper-pointed leaflets, to 10cm (4in) long and 4cm (1½in) across, dark green above, usually hairy beneath, turning brilliant red in autumn. ***Bark*** Grey, with conspicuous, raised lenticels. ***Flowers*** Tiny and yellowish, numerous, borne in slender racemes to 20cm (8in) long, in spring before or with the young leaves. ***Fruit*** With nearly parallel wings, to 2.5cm (1in) long, green ripening to red.
• **NATIVE REGION**
C. China.
• **HABITAT**
Mountain woods.

• tiny flowers borne in slender racemes

wings tinged red when • ripe

leaflets may be • untoothed

Height 15m (50ft)	Shape Broadly spreading	Leaf persistence Deciduous	Leaf type

Family ACERACEAE	Species *Acer japonicum*	Author Thunberg

FULLMOON MAPLE

Leaves Rounded in outline, with 7 to 11 taper-pointed, sharply toothed, ovate to lanceolate lobes, to 13cm (5in) long and across, silky-hairy on both sides when young, becoming dark green above, nearly smooth on both sides, turning red in autumn, carried on downy stalks. **Bark** Grey-brown and smooth. **Flowers** Small and red-purple, with yellow anthers, borne in long-stalked, drooping clusters in spring as the young leaves emerge. **Fruit** With spreading wings, green or green tinged red, to 2.5cm (1in) long.
• **NATIVE REGION** Japan.
• **HABITAT** Mountain woods, usually in dry, sunny situations.
• **REMARK** The form shown, 'Vitifolium', has somewhat larger leaves, with 10 to 12 lobes, and bronzy young foliage.

'VITIFOLIUM' ▷

numerously lobed leaves

heart-shaped leaf base

leaves turn deep red in autumn

△ 'VITIFOLIUM'

◁ 'VITIFOLIUM'

△ 'VITIFOLIUM'

flower clusters droop on long stalks

red-purple flower petals

◁ 'ACONITIFOLIUM'
The leaves of this form are deeply lobed and toothed.

◁ 'VITIFOLIUM'

leaves cut to base in slender lobes

spreading fruit wings

Height 10m (33ft)	Shape Broadly spreading	Leaf persistence Deciduous	Leaf type

Family ACERACEAE	Species *Acer lobelii*	Author Tenore

ACER LOBELII

Leaves Palmately lobed, to 15cm (6in) long and slightly more across, with five usually wavy-edged, untoothed, pointed lobes, glossy deep green and smooth above, with tufts of hairs in the vein axils beneath, on blue-white, bloomy shoots. **Bark** Pale grey and smooth, with shallow, vertical fissures. **Flowers** Small and yellow-green, in upright clusters in late spring with the leaves. **Fruit** With spreading, green wings, to 3cm (1¼in) long, in upright clusters.
• **NATIVE REGION** S. Italy.
• **HABITAT** Mountain woods.

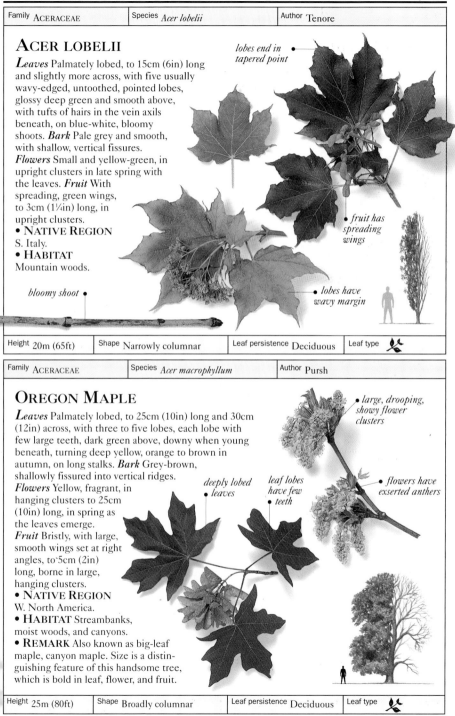

lobes end in tapered point

fruit has spreading wings

bloomy shoot

lobes have wavy margin

Height 20m (65ft)	Shape Narrowly columnar	Leaf persistence Deciduous	Leaf type

Family ACERACEAE	Species *Acer macrophyllum*	Author Pursh

OREGON MAPLE

Leaves Palmately lobed, to 25cm (10in) long and 30cm (12in) across, with three to five lobes, each lobe with few large teeth, dark green above, downy when young beneath, turning deep yellow, orange to brown in autumn, on long stalks. **Bark** Grey-brown, shallowly fissured into vertical ridges. **Flowers** Yellow, fragrant, in hanging clusters to 25cm (10in) long, in spring as the leaves emerge. **Fruit** Bristly, with large, smooth wings set at right angles, to 5cm (2in) long, borne in large, hanging clusters.
• **NATIVE REGION** W. North America.
• **HABITAT** Streambanks, moist woods, and canyons.
• **REMARK** Also known as big-leaf maple, canyon maple. Size is a distinguishing feature of this handsome tree, which is bold in leaf, flower, and fruit.

large, drooping, showy flower clusters

deeply lobed leaves

leaf lobes have few teeth

flowers have exserted anthers

Height 25m (80ft)	Shape Broadly columnar	Leaf persistence Deciduous	Leaf type

Family ACERACEAE	Species *Acer maximowiczianum*	Author Miquel

NIKKO MAPLE

Leaves With three untoothed or slightly toothed leaflets, the central leaflet to 10cm (4in) long and 6cm (2½in) across, the lateral leaflets smaller and unequal-sided at the base, dark green and smooth above, blue-white and softly hairy beneath, turning red in autumn. **Bark** Grey-brown and smooth. **Flowers** Small and yellow, borne drooping in clusters of three, on downy stalks, in late spring at the same time as the young leaves emerge. **Fruit** With broad, spreading, green wings, to 5cm (2in) long.
• **NATIVE REGION** Japan.
• **HABITAT** By streams.
• **REMARK** Also known as *Acer nikoense*. The most notable feature of this species is its autumn colour. The fruits, though attractive, rarely contain good seed.

underside of leaflets covered • in soft hairs

brilliant • autumn colour

leaflets edged with shallow • teeth

Height 20m (65ft)	Shape Broadly spreading	Leaf persistence Deciduous	Leaf type

Family ACERACEAE	Species *Acer miyabei*	Author Maximowicz

ACER MIYABEI

Leaves Palmately lobed, to 13cm (5in) long, with three to five lobes, the larger lobes taper-pointed at the tip, each with few large, blunt teeth at the margin, heart-shaped at the base, bright green above, paler beneath, downy on both sides, more densely so beneath, turning yellow in autumn, carried on slender, red stalks; leaf stalk with milky juice when cut. **Bark** Grey-brown, corky, with shallow, orange-brown fissures, peeling in thin scales on old plants. **Flowers** Individually either male or male and female, small and yellow, borne drooping in slender-stalked clusters at the ends of short, leafy shoots, in spring at the same time as the young leaves emerge. **Fruit** With spreading or sometimes slightly curved wings, to 2.5cm (1in) long.
• **NATIVE REGION** Japan.
• **HABITAT** Woods.

green flowers borne in rounded clusters •

deeply lobed leaves •

fruit wings • spread widely

• leaf lobes have rounded teeth

Height 12m (40ft)	Shape Broadly columnar	Leaf persistence Deciduous	Leaf type

Family ACERACEAE	Species *Acer negundo*	Author Linnaeus

BOX ELDER

Leaves Pinnate, with three to five or seven toothed, sometimes lobed leaflets, each borne on a slender rachis and ending in a long, tapered point, the terminal leaflet to 10cm (4in) long and 6cm (2½in) across, dark green and smooth above, smooth or downy beneath.
Bark Grey-brown and smooth.
Flowers Males and females both small, yellow-green, or pink in some forms, without petals, the females soon showing small, developing fruit wings, in hanging, tassel-like clusters, on separate plants in spring before or with the leaves. *Fruit* With down-pointing, curved wings, to 4cm (1½in) long, persisting on the plant during winter.
• NATIVE REGION North America.
• HABITAT Riverbanks, on moist soil.
• REMARK Also known as ash-leaved maple. The species is variable, and has several cultivated, ornamental forms.

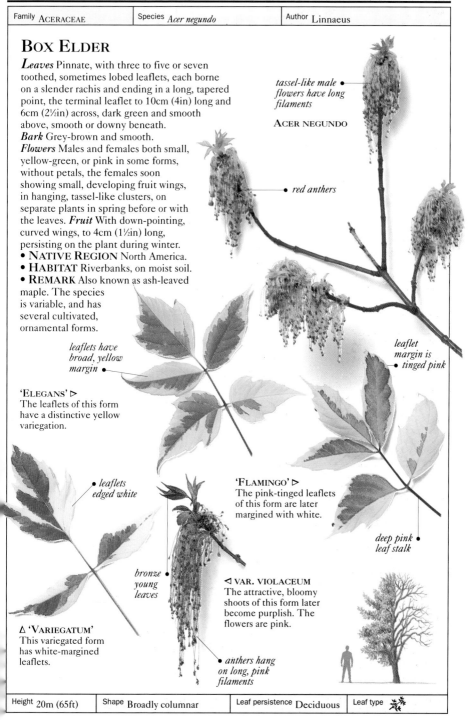

tassel-like male flowers have long filaments

ACER NEGUNDO

• red anthers

leaflet margin is • tinged pink

leaflets have broad, yellow margin •

'ELEGANS' ▷
The leaflets of this form have a distinctive yellow variegation.

• leaflets edged white

'FLAMINGO' ▷
The pink-tinged leaflets of this form are later margined with white.

deep pink • leaf stalk

bronze young leaves

◁ VAR. VIOLACEUM
The attractive, bloomy shoots of this form later become purplish. The flowers are pink.

Δ 'VARIEGATUM'
This variegated form has white-margined leaflets.

• anthers hang on long, pink filaments

Height 20m (65ft)	Shape Broadly columnar	Leaf persistence Deciduous	Leaf type

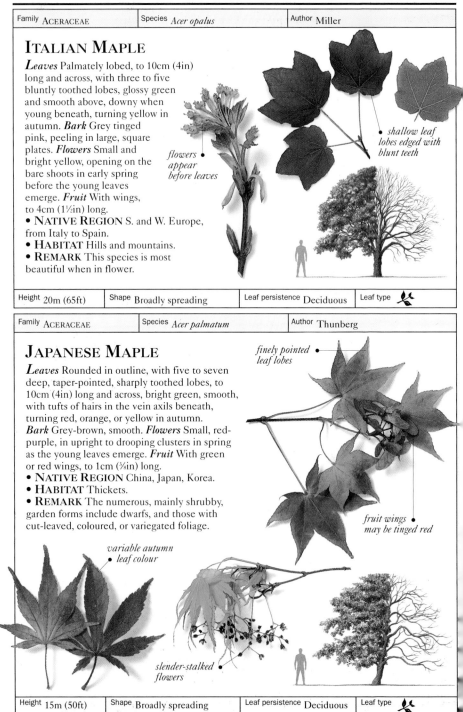

Family ACERACEAE	Species *Acer opalus*	Author Miller

ITALIAN MAPLE

Leaves Palmately lobed, to 10cm (4in) long and across, with three to five bluntly toothed lobes, glossy green and smooth above, downy when young beneath, turning yellow in autumn. *Bark* Grey tinged pink, peeling in large, square plates. *Flowers* Small and bright yellow, opening on the bare shoots in early spring before the young leaves emerge. *Fruit* With wings, to 4cm (1½in) long.
• **NATIVE REGION** S. and W. Europe, from Italy to Spain.
• **HABITAT** Hills and mountains.
• **REMARK** This species is most beautiful when in flower.

flowers appear before leaves

shallow leaf lobes edged with blunt teeth

Height 20m (65ft)	Shape Broadly spreading	Leaf persistence Deciduous	Leaf type

Family ACERACEAE	Species *Acer palmatum*	Author Thunberg

JAPANESE MAPLE

finely pointed leaf lobes

Leaves Rounded in outline, with five to seven deep, taper-pointed, sharply toothed lobes, to 10cm (4in) long and across, bright green, smooth, with tufts of hairs in the vein axils beneath, turning red, orange, or yellow in autumn. *Bark* Grey-brown, smooth. *Flowers* Small, red-purple, in upright to drooping clusters in spring as the young leaves emerge. *Fruit* With green or red wings, to 1cm (⅜in) long.
• **NATIVE REGION** China, Japan, Korea.
• **HABITAT** Thickets.
• **REMARK** The numerous, mainly shrubby, garden forms include dwarfs, and those with cut-leaved, coloured, or variegated foliage.

fruit wings may be tinged red

variable autumn leaf colour

slender-stalked flowers

Height 15m (50ft)	Shape Broadly spreading	Leaf persistence Deciduous	Leaf type

Family ACERACEAE	Species *Acer palmatum*	Author Thunberg

• *leaf lobes taper to fine point*

• *leaves unfold in spring from slender buds*

• *bright pink winter shoots*

△ '**ATROPURPUREUM**'
This form is selected for its deep red-purple foliage, which turns brilliant red in autumn. It usually makes a smaller tree.

autumn coloration varies from yellow to shades of orange and brown •

△ '**SENKAKI**'

◁ '**SENKAKI**'
Commonly known as coral-bark maple, this form has small leaves, which mature from orange-yellow to pale green, and turn bronzy yellow in autumn.

smaller, sharply lobed leaves crowded in dense masses •

purplish leaves very deeply cut into long, slender lobes •

▷ '**LINEARILOBUM ATROPURPUREUM**'
Spidery, red-purple leaves characterize this form. Its winged autumn fruits are tinged red, and hang in small clusters.

△'**RIBESIFOLIUM**'
This smaller form makes a compact plant, reaching about 5m (16ft).

Height 15m (50ft)	Shape Broadly spreading	Leaf persistence Deciduous	Leaf type

Family ACERACEAE	Species *Acer pensylvanicum*	Author Linnaeus

MOOSEWOOD

Leaves To 15cm (6in) or more long and nearly the same across, with three triangular, taper-pointed, toothed, forward-pointing lobes towards the end, deep yellow-green and smooth above, with red-brown hairs when young beneath, turning yellow in autumn. **Bark** Green, vertically striped red-brown and white, becoming grey with age. **Flowers** Small, yellow-green, borne in drooping racemes in late spring at the same time as the young leaves emerge. **Fruit** With green, down-curved wings, to 2.5cm (1in) long.

- **NATIVE REGION** E. North America.
- **HABITAT** Moist woods.
- **REMARK** Also known as striped maple. This species is the only North American snake-bark maple. The common name, moosewood, is given because moose eat the bark in winter.

leaves cut into three pointed lobes

green flower petals

◁ △ ACER PENSYLVANICUM

striking winter shoots

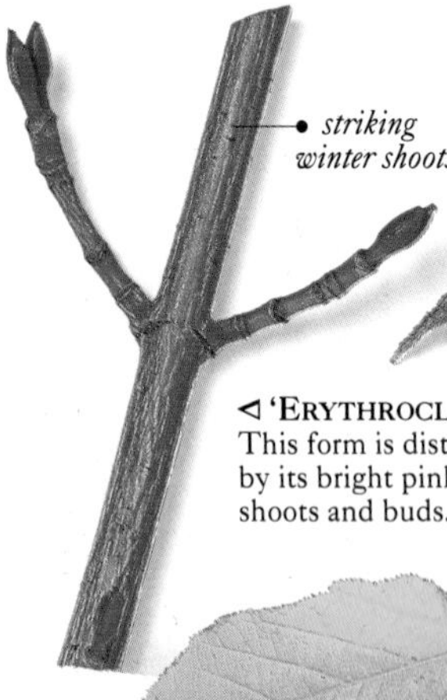

◁ 'ERYTHROCLADUM'
This form is distinguished by its bright pink young shoots and buds.

short side lobes

typically striped bark

larger central lobe

△ ACER PENSYLVANICUM

Height 8m (26ft)	Shape Broadly columnar	Leaf persistence Deciduous	Leaf type

Family ACERACEAE	Species *Acer platanoides*	Author Linnaeus

NORWAY MAPLE

Leaves Palmately lobed, to 15cm (6in) long and 17.5cm (7in) across, with five lobes, each lobe ending in several teeth with long, slender points, bright green, smooth when mature on both sides, turning yellow or sometimes red in autumn; the long, slender leaf stalk exudes milky juice when cut. *Bark* Grey and smooth. *Flowers* Small and bright yellow-green, borne in conspicuous clusters in spring before and with the young leaves. *Fruit* With large, spreading wings, to 5cm (2in) long.
• **NATIVE REGION** S.W. Asia, Europe.
• **HABITAT** Mountain woods.
• **REMARK** A fast-growing species, which quickly reaches its maximum height. In cultivation, it has many ornamental forms, selected for both foliage and habit.

lobes end in slender teeth

fruits have large wings

◁ **ACER PLATANOIDES**

△ **ACER PLATANOIDES**

flowers open before leaves

▽ **'CRIMSON KING'**
This form has deep red-purple leaves, and red bud scales and flower stalks.

▽ **'CRIMSON SENTRY'**
The bright red young leaves of this form mature to deep purple-green. The tree has an upright habit.

red bud scales

red flower stalks

leaf stalks are deep purple

mature leaves are deep purple

young leaves are reddish

Height 25m (80ft)	Shape Broadly columnar	Leaf persistence Deciduous	Leaf type

Family ACERACEAE	Species *Acer platanoides*	Author Linnaeus

∇ 'CUCULLATUM'
This form is selected for its unusual foliage. The leaves are fan-shaped, but end in down-turned, twisted, claw-like lobes, which make the leaves appear almost distorted.

young leaves are purplish red •

lobe ends • *turn under*

mature leaves • *are deep green*

△ 'DEBORAH'
The leaves of this form are coloured red as they emerge and unfold, and later mature to dark green.

• *shallow leaf lobes*

broad, creamy • *leaf margin*

∇ 'LORBERGII'
This smaller form reaches up to 15m (50ft). The pale green leaves are deeply cut into five lobes, which are smooth at the margin and long-pointed at the tip.

△ 'DRUMMONDII'
A strikingly variegated form in which the broad, creamy yellow leaf margin matures to creamy white. Reverting shoots with all green leaves are occasionally produced.

leaves are • *divided to the base*

Height 25m (80ft)	Shape Broadly columnar	Leaf persistence Deciduous	Leaf type

| Family ACERACEAE | Species *Acer pseudoplatanus* | Author Linnaeus |

SYCAMORE

Leaves Palmately lobed, to 12cm (4¾in) long and 15cm (6in) across, with five coarsely toothed lobes, dark green and smooth above, rather blue-grey beneath. ***Bark*** Pinkish to yellowish grey, peeling in irregular plates. ***Flowers*** Small and yellow-green, without petals, in dense, hanging clusters in spring with the young leaves. ***Fruit*** With somewhat down-pointing wings, to 2.5cm (1in) long.
• **NATIVE REGION** S.W. Asia, Europe.
• **HABITAT** Deciduous mountain woods.
• **REMARK** In Scotland, also known as plane.
The species is widely naturalized in North America and Great Britain. In open sites, it may tend towards a spreading shape.

• *heart-shaped leaf base*

leaves are deep • *green above*

△ **ACER PSEUDOPLATANUS**

• *pendulous flower clusters*

• *fruit wings are bright red*

△ F. ERYTHROCARPUM
The young fruits of this form have spectacular bright red wings.

△ 'ATROPURPUREUM'
The special feature of this cultivar is the underside of the leaves, which is coloured purple.

attractively coloured young foliage •

• *variegation is striking*

'BRILLIANTISSIMUM' △
The young leaves of this form are bright pink as they unfold, becoming whitish with green veins, maturing to yellow-green.

• *leaf under-side is tinged purple*

◁ 'NIZETII'
The leaves of this selection have bold blotches of pinkish white on the upper surface. The underside is purplish green.

| Height 30m (100ft) | Shape Broadly columnar | Leaf persistence Deciduous | Leaf type |

Family ACERACEAE	Species *Acer rubrum*	Author Linnaeus

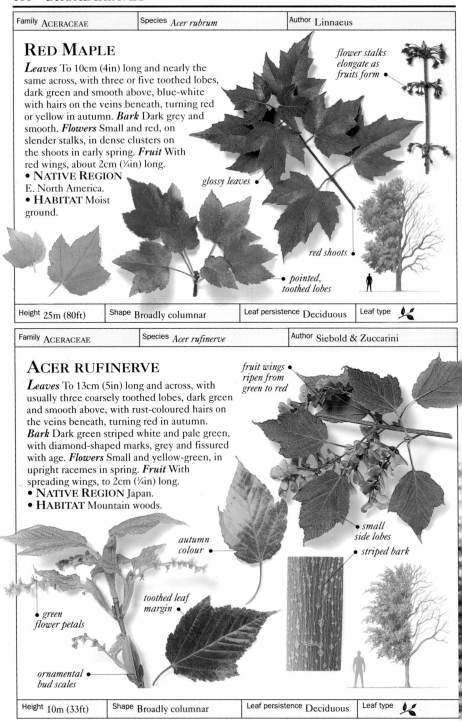

RED MAPLE

Leaves To 10cm (4in) long and nearly the same across, with three or five toothed lobes, dark green and smooth above, blue-white with hairs on the veins beneath, turning red or yellow in autumn. ***Bark*** Dark grey and smooth. ***Flowers*** Small and red, on slender stalks, in dense clusters on the shoots in early spring. ***Fruit*** With red wings, about 2cm (¾in) long.
• **NATIVE REGION** E. North America.
• **HABITAT** Moist ground.

flower stalks elongate as fruits form

glossy leaves

red shoots

pointed, toothed lobes

Height 25m (80ft)	Shape Broadly columnar	Leaf persistence Deciduous	Leaf type

Family ACERACEAE	Species *Acer rufinerve*	Author Siebold & Zuccarini

ACER RUFINERVE

Leaves To 13cm (5in) long and across, with usually three coarsely toothed lobes, dark green and smooth above, with rust-coloured hairs on the veins beneath, turning red in autumn. ***Bark*** Dark green striped white and pale green, with diamond-shaped marks, grey and fissured with age. ***Flowers*** Small and yellow-green, in upright racemes in spring. ***Fruit*** With spreading wings, to 2cm (¾in) long.
• **NATIVE REGION** Japan.
• **HABITAT** Mountain woods.

fruit wings ripen from green to red

small side lobes

striped bark

autumn colour

toothed leaf margin

green flower petals

ornamental bud scales

Height 10m (33ft)	Shape Broadly columnar	Leaf persistence Deciduous	Leaf type

Family ACERACEAE	Species *Acer saccharinum*	Author Linnaeus

SILVER MAPLE

Leaves Palmately lobed, to 15cm (6in) long and across, with five lobes, each itself lobed and sharply toothed, light green and smooth above, blue-white and thinly hairy beneath, usually turning yellow in autumn. *Bark* Grey, smooth, flaking with age. *Flowers* Males and females both small and greenish yellow, without petals, in clusters on the shoots in early spring. *Fruit* With spreading wings, to 2cm (¾in) long.
• **NATIVE REGION** E. North America.
• **HABITAT** Moist soil and riverbanks.

blue-white underside of leaf

leaves turn yellow in autumn

lobes narrow towards leaf base

Height 30m (100ft)	Shape Broadly columnar	Leaf persistence Deciduous	Leaf type

Family ACERACEAE	Species *Acer saccharum*	Author Marshall

SUGAR MAPLE

Leaves Palmately lobed, to 13cm (5in) long and slightly more across, with five lobes, the three largest with few prominent teeth, heart-shaped at the base, mid- to dark green above, with hairs in the vein axils beneath, turning yellow to orange or red in autumn. *Bark* Grey-brown, smooth, becoming furrowed and scaly with age. *Flowers* Small, yellow-green, without petals, drooping on slender stalks, in open clusters in spring with the young leaves. *Fruit* With nearly parallel wings, to 2.5cm (1in) long.
• **NATIVE REGION** E. North America.
• **HABITAT** Rich woods.
• **REMARK** Also known as rock maple. The sap is processed into maple syrup.

tapered lobes edged with few teeth

variable autumn leaf colour

Height 30m (100ft)	Shape Broadly columnar	Leaf persistence Deciduous	Leaf type

Family ACERACEAE	Species *Acer shirasawanum*	Author Koidzumi

ACER SHIRASAWANUM

Leaves Rounded in outline, to 12cm (4¾in) long and across, with about 11 sharply toothed lobes, bright green above, smooth on both sides, turning orange and red in autumn. **Bark** Grey-brown and smooth. **Flowers** Small, with a pink calyx and cream sepals, in spreading to upright clusters in spring with the leaves. **Fruit** With widely spreading wings, in upright clusters.
• **NATIVE REGION** Japan.
• **HABITAT** Mountain slopes and valleys.
• **REMARK** This species is often confused with the full-moon maple *(Acer japonicum,* see p.90), to which it is related.

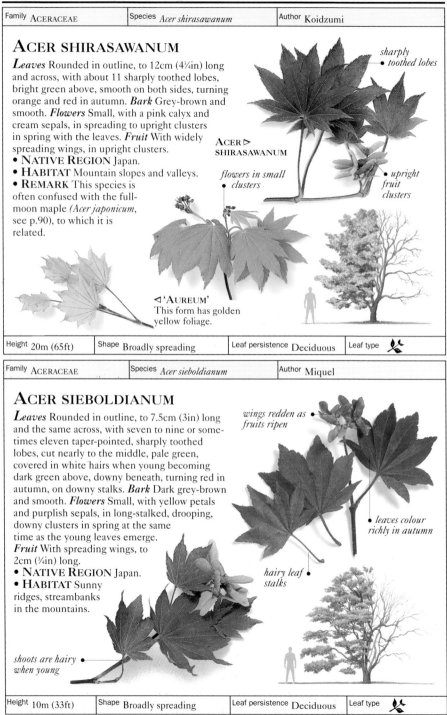

sharply toothed lobes

ACER ▷
SHIRASAWANUM

flowers in small clusters

upright fruit clusters

◁ **'AUREUM'**
This form has golden yellow foliage.

Height 20m (65ft)	Shape Broadly spreading	Leaf persistence Deciduous	Leaf type

Family ACERACEAE	Species *Acer sieboldianum*	Author Miquel

ACER SIEBOLDIANUM

Leaves Rounded in outline, to 7.5cm (3in) long and the same across, with seven to nine or sometimes eleven taper-pointed, sharply toothed lobes, cut nearly to the middle, pale green, covered in white hairs when young becoming dark green above, downy beneath, turning red in autumn, on downy stalks. **Bark** Dark grey-brown and smooth. **Flowers** Small, with yellow petals and purplish sepals, in long-stalked, drooping, downy clusters in spring at the same time as the young leaves emerge. **Fruit** With spreading wings, to 2cm (¾in) long.
• **NATIVE REGION** Japan.
• **HABITAT** Sunny ridges, streambanks in the mountains.

wings redden as fruits ripen

leaves colour richly in autumn

hairy leaf stalks

shoots are hairy when young

Height 10m (33ft)	Shape Broadly spreading	Leaf persistence Deciduous	Leaf type

Family ACERACEAE	Species *Acer spicatum*	Author Lamarck

MOUNTAIN MAPLE

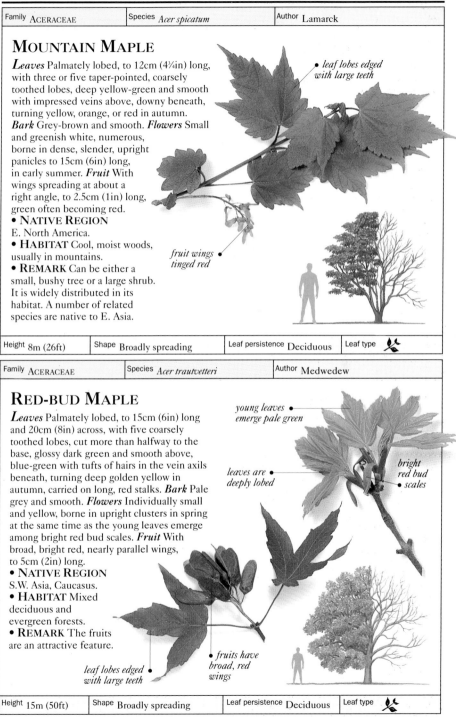

leaf lobes edged with large teeth

Leaves Palmately lobed, to 12cm (4¾in) long, with three or five taper-pointed, coarsely toothed lobes, deep yellow-green and smooth with impressed veins above, downy beneath, turning yellow, orange, or red in autumn. **Bark** Grey-brown and smooth. **Flowers** Small and greenish white, numerous, borne in dense, slender, upright panicles to 15cm (6in) long, in early summer. **Fruit** With wings spreading at about a right angle, to 2.5cm (1in) long, green often becoming red.
• **NATIVE REGION**
E. North America.
• **HABITAT** Cool, moist woods, usually in mountains.
• **REMARK** Can be either a small, bushy tree or a large shrub. It is widely distributed in its habitat. A number of related species are native to E. Asia.

fruit wings tinged red

Height 8m (26ft)	Shape Broadly spreading	Leaf persistence Deciduous	Leaf type

Family ACERACEAE	Species *Acer trautvetteri*	Author Medwedew

RED-BUD MAPLE

young leaves emerge pale green

Leaves Palmately lobed, to 15cm (6in) long and 20cm (8in) across, with five coarsely toothed lobes, cut more than halfway to the base, glossy dark green and smooth above, blue-green with tufts of hairs in the vein axils beneath, turning deep golden yellow in autumn, carried on long, red stalks. **Bark** Pale grey and smooth. **Flowers** Individually small and yellow, borne in upright clusters in spring at the same time as the young leaves emerge among bright red bud scales. **Fruit** With broad, bright red, nearly parallel wings, to 5cm (2in) long.
• **NATIVE REGION**
S.W. Asia, Caucasus.
• **HABITAT** Mixed deciduous and evergreen forests.
• **REMARK** The fruits are an attractive feature.

leaves are deeply lobed

bright red bud scales

leaf lobes edged with large teeth

fruits have broad, red wings

Height 15m (50ft)	Shape Broadly spreading	Leaf persistence Deciduous	Leaf type

Family ACERACEAE	Species *Acer triflorum*	Author Komarov

ACER TRIFLORUM

Leaves With three few-toothed leaflets, the central leaflet to 10cm (4in) long and 4cm (1½in) across, rather pale green above, with bristly hairs on both sides, turning bright orange or red in autumn. **Bark** Pale brown to grey-brown, peeling vertically. **Flowers** Small and yellow, in drooping clusters of three in spring with the young leaves. **Fruit** With nearly parallel wings, to 3cm (1¼in) long.
- **NATIVE REGION** N.E. China, Korea.
- **HABITAT** Mountain woods and ravines.

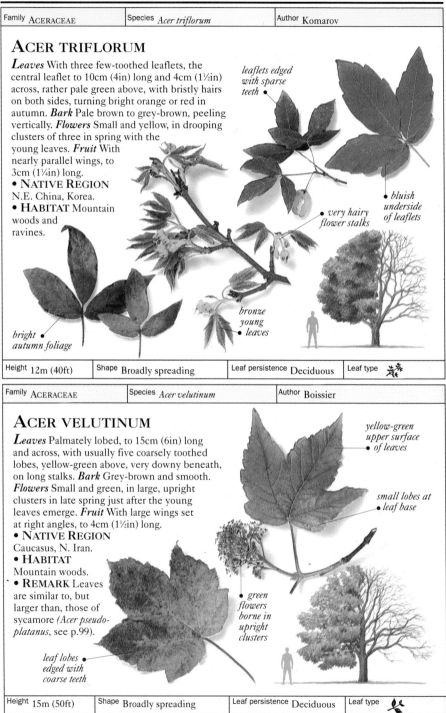

leaflets edged with sparse teeth

bluish underside of leaflets

very hairy flower stalks

bronze young leaves

bright autumn foliage

Height 12m (40ft)	Shape Broadly spreading	Leaf persistence Deciduous	Leaf type

Family ACERACEAE	Species *Acer velutinum*	Author Boissier

ACER VELUTINUM

Leaves Palmately lobed, to 15cm (6in) long and across, with usually five coarsely toothed lobes, yellow-green above, very downy beneath, on long stalks. **Bark** Grey-brown and smooth. **Flowers** Small and green, in large, upright clusters in late spring just after the young leaves emerge. **Fruit** With large wings set at right angles, to 4cm (1½in) long.
- **NATIVE REGION** Caucasus, N. Iran.
- **HABITAT** Mountain woods.
- **REMARK** Leaves are similar to, but larger than, those of sycamore (*Acer pseudoplatanus*, see p.99).

yellow-green upper surface of leaves

small lobes at leaf base

green flowers borne in upright clusters

leaf lobes edged with coarse teeth

Height 15m (50ft)	Shape Broadly spreading	Leaf persistence Deciduous	Leaf type

ANACARDIACEAE

W ITH A WIDE DISTRIBUTION in the warm regions of the world, this family contains over 800 species of evergreen and deciduous trees, shrubs, and climbing plants, collected in 80 genera. The leaves are nearly always alternate, and are pinnate or simple.

Small male and female flowers are sometimes borne on separate plants. The foliage often contains a skin-irritating resin. Other family members include the cashew nut *(Anacardium occidentale)*, mango *(Mangifera indica)*, and poison ivy *(Rhus radicans)*.

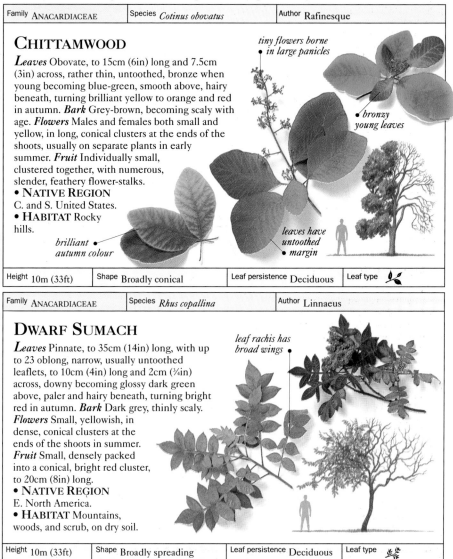

Family ANACARDIACEAE	Species *Cotinus obovatus*	Author Rafinesque

CHITTAMWOOD

Leaves Obovate, to 15cm (6in) long and 7.5cm (3in) across, rather thin, untoothed, bronze when young becoming blue-green, smooth above, hairy beneath, turning brilliant yellow to orange and red in autumn. **Bark** Grey-brown, becoming scaly with age. **Flowers** Males and females both small and yellow, in long, conical clusters at the ends of the shoots, usually on separate plants in early summer. **Fruit** Individually small, clustered together, with numerous, slender, feathery flower-stalks.
• **NATIVE REGION** C. and S. United States.
• **HABITAT** Rocky hills.

tiny flowers borne in large panicles

bronzy young leaves

brilliant autumn colour

leaves have untoothed margin

Height 10m (33ft)	Shape Broadly conical	Leaf persistence Deciduous	Leaf type

Family ANACARDIACEAE	Species *Rhus copallina*	Author Linnaeus

DWARF SUMACH

Leaves Pinnate, to 35cm (14in) long, with up to 23 oblong, narrow, usually untoothed leaflets, to 10cm (4in) long and 2cm (¾in) across, downy becoming glossy dark green above, paler and hairy beneath, turning bright red in autumn. **Bark** Dark grey, thinly scaly. **Flowers** Small, yellowish, in dense, conical clusters at the ends of the shoots in summer. **Fruit** Small, densely packed into a conical, bright red cluster, to 20cm (8in) long.
• **NATIVE REGION** E. North America.
• **HABITAT** Mountains, woods, and scrub, on dry soil.

leaf rachis has broad wings

Height 10m (33ft)	Shape Broadly spreading	Leaf persistence Deciduous	Leaf type

Family ANACARDIACEAE	Species *Rhus trichocarpa*	Author Miquel

RHUS TRICHOCARPA

Leaves To 50cm (20in) long, with up to 17 ovate, taper-pointed leaflets, to 10cm (4in) long and 4cm (1½in) across, reddish at first becoming matt dark green, downy, turning orange-red in autumn. *Bark* Pale grey-brown, with conspicuous lenticels. *Flowers* Very small, yellowish, in conical panicles in the leaf axils in summer. *Fruit* Small, brownish yellow.
• NATIVE REGION China, Japan, Korea.
• HABITAT Mountain and roadside thickets.

• *small, bristly fruits*

leaflets usually
• *untoothed*

Height 8m (26ft)	Shape Broadly spreading	Leaf persistence Deciduous	Leaf type

Family ANACARDIACEAE	Species *Rhus typhina*	Author Linnaeus

STAG'S-HORN SUMACH

Leaves To 60cm (24in) long, with up to 27 lanceolate to oblong, sharply toothed leaflets, to 12cm (4¾in) long and 5cm (2in) across, dark green above, blue-green beneath, downy on both sides when young becoming nearly smooth, turning bright orange and red in autumn, on stout, velvety shoots. *Bark* Dark brown and smooth. *Flowers* Males and females both small and green, in dense, conical clusters at the ends of the shoots, on the same plant or on separate plants in summer. *Fruit* Small, bright red, in a dense, conical cluster, to 20cm (8in) long.
• NATIVE REGION E. North America.
• HABITAT Meadows, scrub, and wood margins, often on dry, rocky soil.

◁ RHUS TYPHINA

• *leaves colour brilliantly in autumn*

RHUS TYPHINA ▷

lobed leaflets •

flowers are green •

◁ 'DISSECTA'
This ornamental form has finely cut leaflets.

Height 10m (33ft)	Shape Broadly spreading	Leaf persistence Deciduous	Leaf type

ANNONACEAE

A MAINLY TROPICAL FAMILY, with more than 2,000 species, related to the magnolias *(Magnolia,* see pp.202–215). The trees typically have simple, alternate leaves, and flowers with the petals arranged in whorls of three. The custard apples *(Annona)* are well-known members of the family.

Family ANNONACEAE	Species *Asimina triloba*	Author (Linnaeus) Dunal

PAWPAW

Leaves Oblong to obovate, to 25cm (10in) long, taper-pointed at the tip, untoothed, rather pale green, downy when young becoming smooth beneath, turning yellow in autumn. **Bark** Grey-brown, becoming somewhat rough and scaly with age. **Flowers** To 4cm (1½in) across, green at first becoming purple-brown, with six petals, the inner three upright, the outer three larger and spreading, borne singly on short, stout stalks on the old shoots in late spring as the young leaves emerge. **Fruit** Fleshy and edible, to 15cm (6in) long, green at first becoming yellow-brown when ripe.
• **NATIVE REGION** E. North America.
• **HABITAT** Rich, moist woods.
• **REMARK** The flavour of the unusual fruits may be likened to that of bananas. This species is often confused with *Carica papaya*, a tropical tree grown for its edible fruits, and also known by the common name, pawpaw.

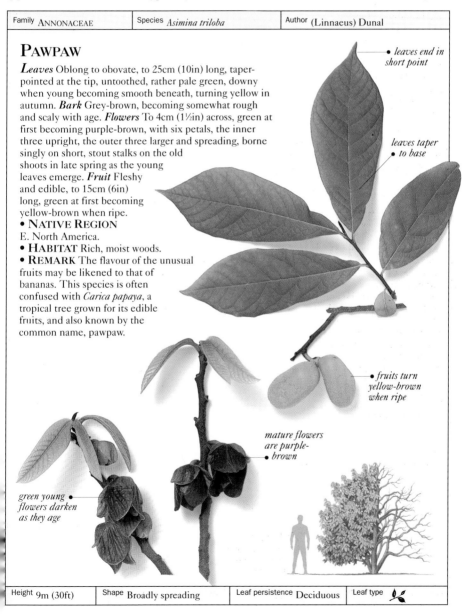

leaves end in short point

leaves taper to base

fruits turn yellow-brown when ripe

mature flowers are purple-brown

green young flowers darken as they age

Height 9m (30ft)	Shape Broadly spreading	Leaf persistence Deciduous	Leaf type

AQUIFOLIACEAE

A FAMILY OF WIDE DISTRIBUTION in temperate and tropical regions, comprising over 400 evergreen and deciduous species, almost all of which are hollies *(Ilex)*. The trees and shrubs usually have alternate leaves. Male and female flowers are small, white or pink, borne on separate plants; females develop in autumn into yellow, red, orange, or black berries. The leaves of *Ilex paraguariensis*, a South American species, are used for yerba maté tea.

Family AQUIFOLIACEAE	Species *Ilex x altaclerensis*	Author (hort. ex Loudon) Dallimore

HIGHCLERE HOLLY

Leaves Variable in size and shape, oblong to ovate or nearly rounded, to 13cm (5in) or more long and 7.5cm (3in) across, spine-tipped and often with a spiny margin, glossy dark green above. **Bark** Grey and smooth. **Flowers** Males and females both small and white, usually tinged purple, fragrant, in clusters in the leaf axils, borne on separate plants in spring. **Fruit** A large, fleshy, red berry.
• **NATIVE REGION** Of garden origin.
• **REMARK** A hybrid between the common holly *(Ilex aquifolium,* see p.109) and *Ilex perado,* a species native to the Canary Islands, Madeira, and the Azores. This hybrid is recognized mainly as named cultivars, and is represented in gardens by many ornamental forms.

◁ 'BELGICA AUREA'
The long leaves of this female plant have few spines.

reddish purple • leaf stalks

creamy yellow • leaf margin

△ 'CAMELLIIFOLIA'
A female plant, with nearly spineless leaves, purple when young.

• deeply veined leaves

'GOLDEN KING' △
The broad, thick leaves of this female plant have a bold, yellow margin.

red-tinged buds open into white flowers •

'LAWSONIANA' ▷
The yellow-splashed leaves of this female plant have a nearly spineless margin.

glossy, dark leaves •

△ 'HODGINSII'
A male plant, with large, few-spined, dark green leaves and purple shoots.

irregularly blotched yellow and green marks on leaves

◁ 'WILSONII'
This female plant has large leaves.

Height 20m (65ft)	Shape Broadly columnar	Leaf persistence Evergreen	Leaf type

Family AQUIFOLIACEAE	Species *Ilex aquifolium*	Author Linnaeus

COMMON HOLLY

Leaves Variable, elliptic to ovate, to 10cm (4in) long and 5cm (2in) across, spine-tipped, juveniles on lower part of plant with a very spiny margin, adults with a more or less spineless margin, glossy dark green above. *Bark* Pale grey and smooth. *Flowers* Males and females both small and white or purple-tinged, fragrant, borne in clusters in the leaf axils, usually on separate plants in late spring. *Fruit* A usually red berry, to 1cm (⅜in) across.
• **NATIVE REGION**
W. Asia, Europe.
• **HABITAT** Woods, particularly those of beech and oak.
• **REMARK** This species has given rise to numerous variations in both leaf and fruit.

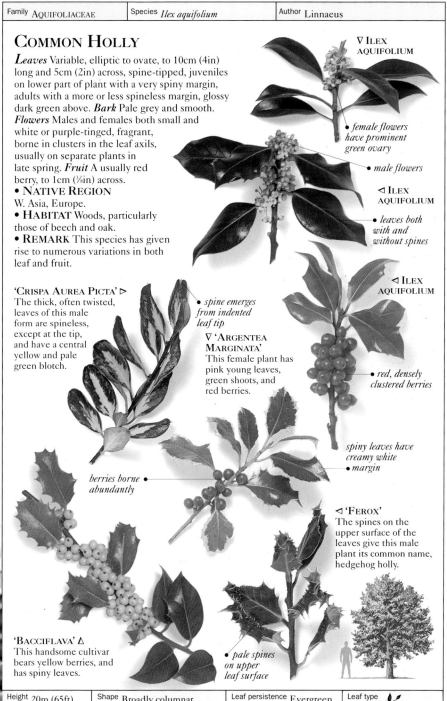

▽ **ILEX AQUIFOLIUM**

• *female flowers have prominent green ovary*

• *male flowers*

◁ **ILEX AQUIFOLIUM**

• *leaves both with and without spines*

◁ **ILEX AQUIFOLIUM**

• *red, densely clustered berries*

'CRISPA AUREA PICTA' ▷
The thick, often twisted, leaves of this male form are spineless, except at the tip, and have a central yellow and pale green blotch.

• *spine emerges from indented leaf tip*

▽ **'ARGENTEA MARGINATA'**
This female plant has pink young leaves, green shoots, and red berries.

spiny leaves have creamy white margin

• *berries borne abundantly*

◁ **'FEROX'**
The spines on the upper surface of the leaves give this male plant its common name, hedgehog holly.

'BACCIFLAVA' △
This handsome cultivar bears yellow berries, and has spiny leaves.

• *pale spines on upper leaf surface*

Height 20m (65ft)	Shape Broadly columnar	Leaf persistence Evergreen	Leaf type

Family AQUIFOLIACEAE	Species *Ilex aquifolium*	Author Linnaeus

∇ 'FLAVESCENS'
The moonlight holly, a female plant, has leaves flushed yellow. The leaf stalk and midrib are also yellow.

creamy spines on leaf surface and • *at margin*

• *leaves may be irregularly spined*

• *glossy green surface either side of leaf midrib*

△ 'FEROX ARGENTEA'
The leaves of this male cultivar have a creamy yellow to white margin. The tree is commonly known as silver hedgehog holly.

• *leaves may have smooth margin*

leaf margin may be tinged pink •

• *red berries borne in abundance*

△ 'HANDSWORTH NEW SILVER'
Purple stems, white-margined leaves, and small red berries characterize this female form.

• *deeply impressed leaf veins*

◁ 'J.C. VAN TOL'
This plant is both male and female. Its thick leaves are glossy dark green and smooth above, and have few spines or none at all.

Height 20m (65ft)	Shape Broadly columnar	Leaf persistence Evergreen	Leaf type

Family AQUIFOLIACEAE	Species *Ilex aquifolium*	Author Linnaeus

'MADAME BRIOT' ▷
The leaves of this bushy
female form are broad,
and have a dark
yellow margin. The
tree bears scarlet
berries in autumn.

*stems and
leaf stalks
flushed
purple* •

*older stems
become
• green*

• *large, strongly
spined
leaves*

*berries grow •
in tight
clusters*

△ **'PYRAMIDALIS
FRUCTU LUTEO'**
The oval, glossy
green, often spineless,
leaves of this female
plant contrast well
with the abundant
yellow berries.

• *leaves may
be spined at
tip only*

*some spines •
point up,
some down*

*berries carried •
close to the stem
on short stalks*

*flower
buds in
• leaf axils*

△ **'SILVER MILKMAID'**
The leaves of this old cultivar
are dark green, with a creamy
white blotch in the centre. It
has red berries. In spite of the
inappropriate name, plants
that were once called 'Silver
Milkboy' are also female.

• *faint grey-
green marbling
on leaves*

△ **'SILVER QUEEN'**
This male clone has
broad, white-margined
leaves, which are pale
orange-pink when young.
The shoots are coloured
deep purple.

Height 20m (65ft)	Shape Broadly columnar	Leaf persistence Evergreen	Leaf type

Family AQUIFOLIACEAE	Species *Ilex x koehneana*	Author Loesener

ILEX X KOEHNEANA

Leaves Elliptic to oblong, to 15cm (6in) long, very spiny at the margin, often bronze when young becoming glossy dark green, the young shoots flushed purple. **Bark** Grey and smooth. **Flowers** Males and females both small and greenish white, borne in clusters in the leaf axils, on separate plants in spring. **Fruit** A red berry, 8mm (⁵⁄₁₆in) across.
• **NATIVE REGION** Of garden origin.
• **REMARK** A hybrid, first reported in Florence, Italy, between common holly *(I. aquifolium*, see p.109) and tarajo holly *(I. latifolia*, see below). The large leaves show the influence of the latter parent.

'CHESTNUT LEAF' ▷ This form originated in France. It has strongly spined leaves, and bears small, brilliant red berries.

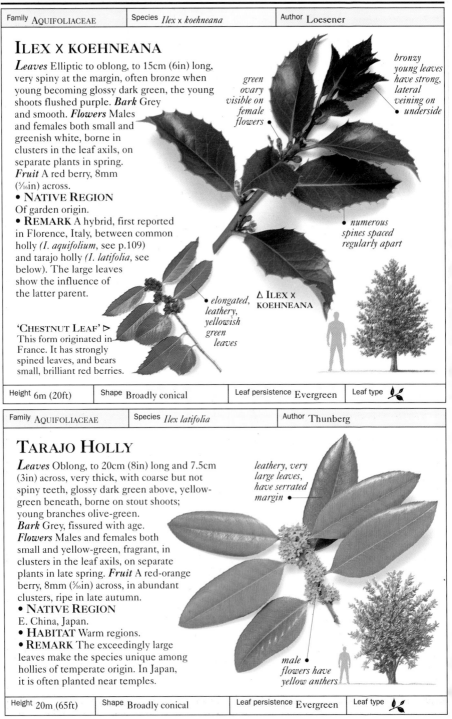

green ovary visible on female flowers

bronzy young leaves have strong, lateral veining on underside

numerous spines spaced regularly apart

elongated, leathery, yellowish green leaves

△ ILEX X KOEHNEANA

Height 6m (20ft)	Shape Broadly conical	Leaf persistence Evergreen	Leaf type

Family AQUIFOLIACEAE	Species *Ilex latifolia*	Author Thunberg

TARAJO HOLLY

Leaves Oblong, to 20cm (8in) long and 7.5cm (3in) across, very thick, with coarse but not spiny teeth, glossy dark green above, yellow-green beneath, borne on stout shoots; young branches olive-green. **Bark** Grey, fissured with age. **Flowers** Males and females both small and yellow-green, fragrant, in clusters in the leaf axils, on separate plants in late spring. **Fruit** A red-orange berry, 8mm (⁵⁄₁₆in) across, in abundant clusters, ripe in late autumn.
• **NATIVE REGION** E. China, Japan.
• **HABITAT** Warm regions.
• **REMARK** The exceedingly large leaves make the species unique among hollies of temperate origin. In Japan, it is often planted near temples.

leathery, very large leaves, have serrated margin

male flowers have yellow anthers

Height 20m (65ft)	Shape Broadly conical	Leaf persistence Evergreen	Leaf type

| Family AQUIFOLIACEAE | Species *Ilex opaca* | Author Aiton |

AMERICAN HOLLY

Leaves Elliptic, to 10cm (4in) long and 5cm (2in) across, spiny at the tip and margin, matt dark green or yellow-green above, yellow-green beneath. *Bark* Grey and smooth. *Flowers* Males and females small, dull white, in the leaf axils, usually on separate plants in late spring. *Fruit* A usually red berry, to 1cm (⅜in) across.
• **NATIVE REGION** E. United States.
• **HABITAT** Sandy soil near the coast and moist woods.

• *smooth, matt upper leaf surface*

• *female flowers*

| Height 15m (50ft) | Shape Broadly conical | Leaf persistence Evergreen | Leaf type |

| Family AQUIFOLIACEAE | Species *Ilex pedunculosa* | Author Miquel |

ILEX PEDUNCULOSA

Leaves Ovate to elliptic, to 7.5cm (3in) long and 3cm (1¼in) across, taper-pointed, untoothed, glossy dark green above. *Bark* Grey-green, smooth. *Flowers* Males and females small, white, in the leaf axils and on the shoots, on separate plants in summer. *Fruit* A bright red berry, to 8mm (⁵⁄₁₆in) across.
• **NATIVE REGION** China, Japan, Taiwan.
• **HABITAT** Woods and thickets.

• *leaf margin turns bronze*

• *male flowers borne in clusters*

• *long fruit stalks*

| Height 10m (33ft) | Shape Broadly conical | Leaf persistence Evergreen | Leaf type |

| Family AQUIFOLIACEAE | Species *Ilex purpurea* | Author Hasskarl |

ILEX PURPUREA

Leaves Elliptic-lanceolate, to 12cm (4¾in) long and 4cm (1½in) across, tapered, toothed, glossy dark green above, paler beneath, smooth. *Bark* Grey, smooth. *Flowers* Males and females deep reddish lilac, the corona with four reflexed lobes, in the leaf axils and on the shoots, on separate plants in early to mid-summer. *Fruit* A red berry, 8mm (⁵⁄₁₆in) long.
• **NATIVE REGION** China, Japan.
• **HABITAT** Mountain woods.

numerous male flowers clustered
• *together*

• *bronzy young foliage*

| Height 13m (42ft) | Shape Broadly conical | Leaf persistence Evergreen | Leaf type |

ARALIACEAE

W ITH MORE THAN 50 GENERA and some 800 species, this family of evergreen and deciduous trees, shrubs, and herbaceous plants is found all over the world, particularly in the tropics. The leaves are usually compound or lobed, and the small, greenish white or white flowers are borne in clusters.

Family ARALIACEAE	Species *Aralia spinosa*	Author Linnaeus

DEVIL'S WALKING STICK

Leaves Bipinnate and very large, to 1m (39in) or more long, with numerous ovate, taper-pointed, toothed leaflets, to 7.5cm (3in) long and 4cm (1½in) across, bronze when young becoming dark green above, paler beneath, hairy on both sides, turning yellow to purple in autumn, with a prickly stalk, carried on very stout, spiny shoots. **Bark** Grey, with stout prickles. **Flowers** Small and white, in small, rounded clusters, the clusters forming large heads, borne on a single main axis in late summer. **Fruit** Rounded and purple-black, 6mm (¼in) long.
• **NATIVE REGION** E. United States.
• **HABITAT** Riverbanks and moist woods.
• **REMARK** Also known as angelica tree, Hercules' club.

small, blackish fruits carried • on red stalks

ARALIA △ ▽ SPINOSA

large leaves composed of numerous leaflets •

▽ ARALIA ELATA
This similar species, from north-east Asia and Japan, flowers in autumn, when *Aralia spinosa* is in fruit.

• flower clusters have one central stalk

flowers have • exserted, yellow anthers

• flower clusters branch from base of stem

Height 10m (33ft)	Shape Broadly spreading	Leaf persistence Deciduous	Leaf type

Family ARALIACEAE	Species *Kalopanax pictus*	Author (Thunberg) Nakai

CASTOR ARALIA

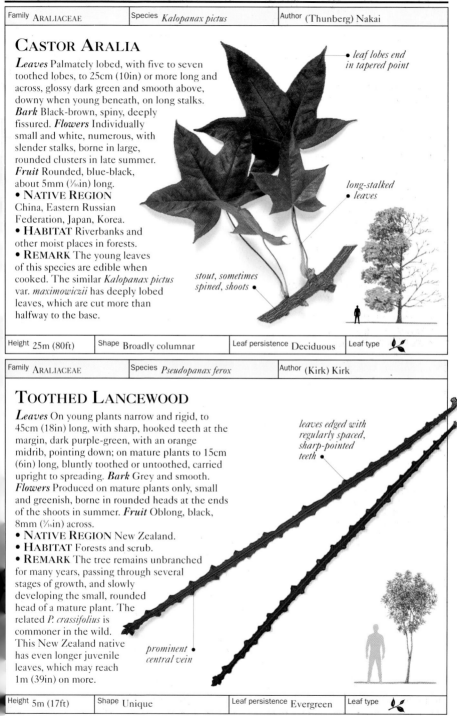

Leaves Palmately lobed, with five to seven toothed lobes, to 25cm (10in) or more long and across, glossy dark green and smooth above, downy when young beneath, on long stalks. **Bark** Black-brown, spiny, deeply fissured. **Flowers** Individually small and white, numerous, with slender stalks, borne in large, rounded clusters in late summer. **Fruit** Rounded, blue-black, about 5mm (³⁄₁₆in) long.
• **NATIVE REGION** China, Eastern Russian Federation, Japan, Korea.
• **HABITAT** Riverbanks and other moist places in forests.
• **REMARK** The young leaves of this species are edible when cooked. The similar *Kalopanax pictus* var. *maximowiczii* has deeply lobed leaves, which are cut more than halfway to the base.

leaf lobes end in tapered point

long-stalked leaves

stout, sometimes spined, shoots

Height 25m (80ft)	Shape Broadly columnar	Leaf persistence Deciduous	Leaf type

Family ARALIACEAE	Species *Pseudopanax ferox*	Author (Kirk) Kirk

TOOTHED LANCEWOOD

Leaves On young plants narrow and rigid, to 45cm (18in) long, with sharp, hooked teeth at the margin, dark purple-green, with an orange midrib, pointing down; on mature plants to 15cm (6in) long, bluntly toothed or untoothed, carried upright to spreading. **Bark** Grey and smooth. **Flowers** Produced on mature plants only, small and greenish, borne in rounded heads at the ends of the shoots in summer. **Fruit** Oblong, black, 8mm (⁵⁄₁₆in) across.
• **NATIVE REGION** New Zealand.
• **HABITAT** Forests and scrub.
• **REMARK** The tree remains unbranched for many years, passing through several stages of growth, and slowly developing the small, rounded head of a mature plant. The related *P. crassifolius* is commoner in the wild. This New Zealand native has even longer juvenile leaves, which may reach 1m (39in) on more.

leaves edged with regularly spaced, sharp-pointed teeth

prominent central vein

Height 5m (17ft)	Shape Unique	Leaf persistence Evergreen	Leaf type

BETULACEAE

S OME OF THE most well-known catkin-bearing plants belong to the birch family, which also includes the hazels *(Corylus, see p.127)*. Its six genera and more than 150 species of deciduous trees and shrubs grow wild mainly in northern temperate regions; alders *(Alnus, see pp.116–117)* extend to the Andes. The leaves are alternate. Male and female flowers are borne in separate catkins on the same plant, but only the males are conspicuous.

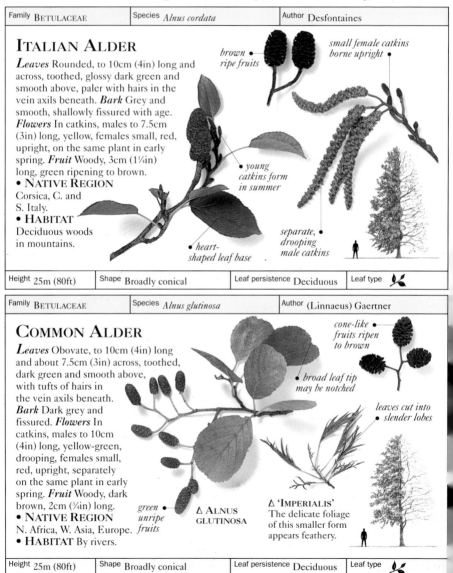

Family BETULACEAE	Species *Alnus cordata*	Author Desfontaines

ITALIAN ALDER

Leaves Rounded, to 10cm (4in) long and across, toothed, glossy dark green and smooth above, paler with hairs in the vein axils beneath. *Bark* Grey and smooth, shallowly fissured with age. *Flowers* In catkins, males to 7.5cm (3in) long, yellow, females small, red, upright, on the same plant in early spring. *Fruit* Woody, 3cm (1¼in) long, green ripening to brown.
• NATIVE REGION Corsica, C. and S. Italy.
• HABITAT Deciduous woods in mountains.

brown • ripe fruits

small female catkins borne upright •

• young catkins form in summer

separate, • drooping male catkins

• heart-shaped leaf base

Height 25m (80ft)	Shape Broadly conical	Leaf persistence Deciduous	Leaf type

Family BETULACEAE	Species *Alnus glutinosa*	Author (Linnaeus) Gaertner

COMMON ALDER

Leaves Obovate, to 10cm (4in) long and about 7.5cm (3in) across, toothed, dark green and smooth above, with tufts of hairs in the vein axils beneath. *Bark* Dark grey and fissured. *Flowers* In catkins, males to 10cm (4in) long, yellow-green, drooping, females small, red, upright, separately on the same plant in early spring. *Fruit* Woody, dark brown, 2cm (¾in) long.
• NATIVE REGION N. Africa, W. Asia, Europe.
• HABITAT By rivers.

cone-like • fruits ripen to brown

• broad leaf tip may be notched

leaves cut into • slender lobes

green • unripe fruits

△ ALNUS GLUTINOSA

△ 'IMPERIALIS' The delicate foliage of this smaller form appears feathery.

Height 25m (80ft)	Shape Broadly conical	Leaf persistence Deciduous	Leaf type

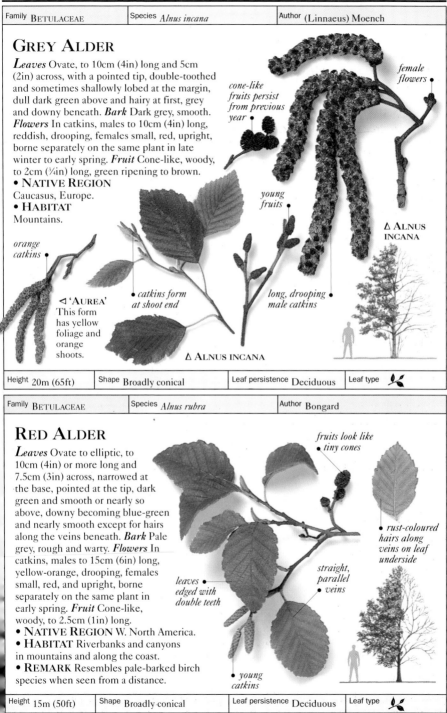

Family BETULACEAE	Species *Alnus incana*	Author (Linnaeus) Moench

GREY ALDER

Leaves Ovate, to 10cm (4in) long and 5cm (2in) across, with a pointed tip, double-toothed and sometimes shallowly lobed at the margin, dull dark green above and hairy at first, grey and downy beneath. **Bark** Dark grey, smooth. **Flowers** In catkins, males to 10cm (4in) long, reddish, drooping, females small, red, upright, borne separately on the same plant in late winter to early spring. **Fruit** Cone-like, woody, to 2cm (¾in) long, green ripening to brown.
• **NATIVE REGION** Caucasus, Europe.
• **HABITAT** Mountains.

cone-like fruits persist from previous year

female flowers

young fruits

△ ALNUS INCANA

long, drooping male catkins

orange catkins

◁ 'AUREA' This form has yellow foliage and orange shoots.

catkins form at shoot end

△ ALNUS INCANA

Height 20m (65ft)	Shape Broadly conical	Leaf persistence Deciduous	Leaf type

Family BETULACEAE	Species *Alnus rubra*	Author Bongard

RED ALDER

Leaves Ovate to elliptic, to 10cm (4in) or more long and 7.5cm (3in) across, narrowed at the base, pointed at the tip, dark green and smooth or nearly so above, downy becoming blue-green and nearly smooth except for hairs along the veins beneath. **Bark** Pale grey, rough and warty. **Flowers** In catkins, males to 15cm (6in) long, yellow-orange, drooping, females small, red, and upright, borne separately on the same plant in early spring. **Fruit** Cone-like, woody, to 2.5cm (1in) long.
• **NATIVE REGION** W. North America.
• **HABITAT** Riverbanks and canyons in mountains and along the coast.
• **REMARK** Resembles pale-barked birch species when seen from a distance.

fruits look like tiny cones

rust-coloured hairs along veins on leaf underside

straight, parallel veins

leaves edged with double teeth

young catkins

Height 15m (50ft)	Shape Broadly conical	Leaf persistence Deciduous	Leaf type

Family BETULACEAE	Species *Betula albo-sinensis*	Author Burkill

BETULA ALBO-SINENSIS

Leaves Ovate, to 7.5cm (3in) long and 4cm (1½in) across, taper-pointed, toothed, downy when young becoming smooth and glossy green, turning yellow in autumn, carried on slightly rough shoots; young shoots sticky. ***Bark*** Orange-red to coppery red, peeling in thin, papery, horizontal strips; cream when freshly exposed. ***Flowers*** In catkins, males to 6cm (2½in), yellow, drooping, females green, upright, borne separately on the same plant in spring. ***Fruit*** A catkin, breaking up when ripe.
• **NATIVE REGION** W. China.
• **HABITAT** High woods in mountains.
• **REMARK** The coloured, peeling bark makes this species one of the most striking of all the birches.

glossy, sharply toothed leaves

catkins form in summer and open next spring

upright female catkins

drooping male catkins

△ **BETULA ALBO-SINENSIS**

reddish bark marked with pale lenticels

▽ **VAR. SEPTENTRIONALIS**
This form is distinguished by its matt, rather than glossy, green leaves, and coppery to grey-pink bark.

matt green leaves

grey-pink bark peels in thin strips

leaves carried on roughish shoots

male catkins borne at end of shoots

fruiting female catkins borne upright

Height 25m (80ft)	Shape Broadly conical	Leaf persistence Deciduous	Leaf type

Family BETULACEAE	Species *Betula alleghaniensis*	Author Britton

YELLOW BIRCH

Leaves Ovate-oblong, to 10cm (4in) or more long and 5cm (2in) across, pointed, toothed, becoming matt deep green above, paler beneath, turning yellow in autumn, on aromatic shoots. **Bark** Yellow-brown, peeling horizontally. **Flowers** In catkins, males to 10cm (4in) long, yellow, females reddish green, on the same plant in spring. **Fruit** A stout, erect catkin, breaking up when ripe.
• **NATIVE REGION** E. North America.
• **HABITAT** Moist woods.

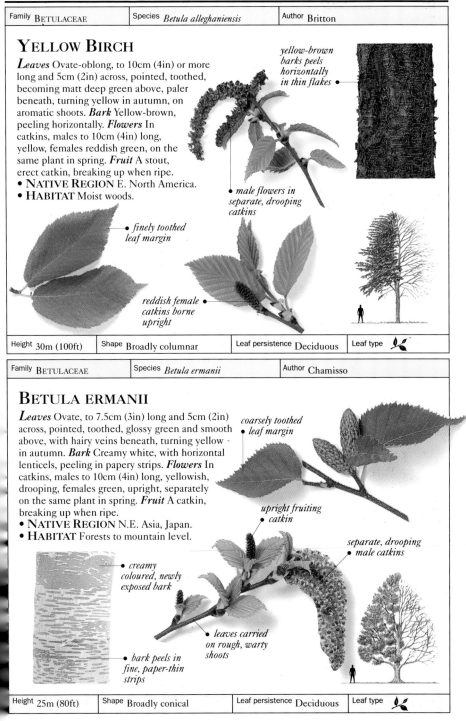

yellow-brown barks peels horizontally in thin flakes

male flowers in separate, drooping catkins

finely toothed leaf margin

reddish female catkins borne upright

Height 30m (100ft)	Shape Broadly columnar	Leaf persistence Deciduous	Leaf type

Family BETULACEAE	Species *Betula ermanii*	Author Chamisso

BETULA ERMANII

Leaves Ovate, to 7.5cm (3in) long and 5cm (2in) across, pointed, toothed, glossy green and smooth above, with hairy veins beneath, turning yellow in autumn. **Bark** Creamy white, with horizontal lenticels, peeling in papery strips. **Flowers** In catkins, males to 10cm (4in) long, yellowish, drooping, females green, upright, separately on the same plant in spring. **Fruit** A catkin, breaking up when ripe.
• **NATIVE REGION** N.E. Asia, Japan.
• **HABITAT** Forests to mountain level.

coarsely toothed leaf margin

upright fruiting catkin

separate, drooping male catkins

creamy coloured, newly exposed bark

leaves carried on rough, warty shoots

bark peels in fine, paper-thin strips

Height 25m (80ft)	Shape Broadly conical	Leaf persistence Deciduous	Leaf type

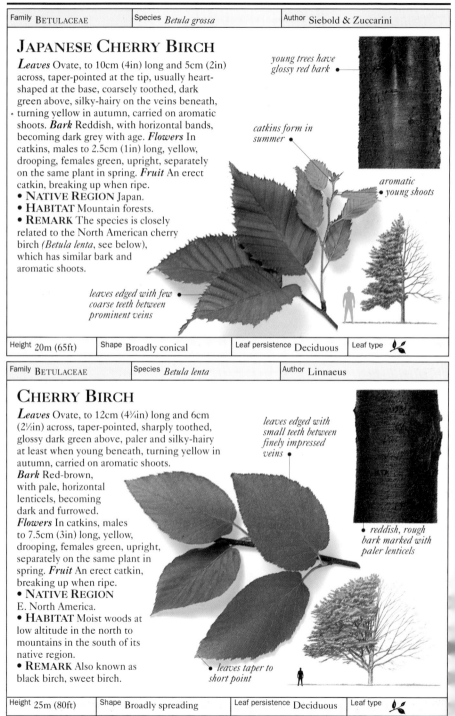

Family BETULACEAE	Species *Betula grossa*	Author Siebold & Zuccarini

JAPANESE CHERRY BIRCH

Leaves Ovate, to 10cm (4in) long and 5cm (2in) across, taper-pointed at the tip, usually heart-shaped at the base, coarsely toothed, dark green above, silky-hairy on the veins beneath, turning yellow in autumn, carried on aromatic shoots. **Bark** Reddish, with horizontal bands, becoming dark grey with age. **Flowers** In catkins, males to 2.5cm (1in) long, yellow, drooping, females green, upright, separately on the same plant in spring. **Fruit** An erect catkin, breaking up when ripe.
• **NATIVE REGION** Japan.
• **HABITAT** Mountain forests.
• **REMARK** The species is closely related to the North American cherry birch *(Betula lenta,* see below), which has similar bark and aromatic shoots.

young trees have glossy red bark •

catkins form in summer •

aromatic • young shoots

leaves edged with few • coarse teeth between prominent veins

Height 20m (65ft)	Shape Broadly conical	Leaf persistence Deciduous	Leaf type

Family BETULACEAE	Species *Betula lenta*	Author Linnaeus

CHERRY BIRCH

Leaves Ovate, to 12cm (4¾in) long and 6cm (2½in) across, taper-pointed, sharply toothed, glossy dark green above, paler and silky-hairy at least when young beneath, turning yellow in autumn, carried on aromatic shoots.
Bark Red-brown, with pale, horizontal lenticels, becoming dark and furrowed.
Flowers In catkins, males to 7.5cm (3in) long, yellow, drooping, females green, upright, separately on the same plant in spring. **Fruit** An erect catkin, breaking up when ripe.
• **NATIVE REGION** E. North America.
• **HABITAT** Moist woods at low altitude in the north to mountains in the south of its native region.
• **REMARK** Also known as black birch, sweet birch.

leaves edged with small teeth between finely impressed veins •

• reddish, rough bark marked with paler lenticels

• leaves taper to short point

Height 25m (80ft)	Shape Broadly spreading	Leaf persistence Deciduous	Leaf type

Family BETULACEAE	Species *Betula maximowicziana*	Author Regel

MONARCH BIRCH

Leaves Broadly ovate, to 15cm (6in) long and 12cm (4¾in) across, deeply heart-shaped at the base, taper-pointed at the tip, sharply and doubly toothed, dark green and smooth above, turning yellow in autumn, carried on warty shoots. **Bark** Reddish brown at first becoming greyish white tinged orange-yellow and pink, with horizontal lenticels, peeling in papery strips. **Flowers** In catkins, males to 10cm (4in) long, yellow-brown, drooping, females green, clustered together, spreading to drooping, borne separately on the same plant in late winter. **Fruit** A pendulous catkin, breaking up when ripe.
• **NATIVE REGION** C. and N. Japan.
• **HABITAT** Woods.
• **REMARK** Also known as Japanese red birch. The leaves are larger than those of any other birch.

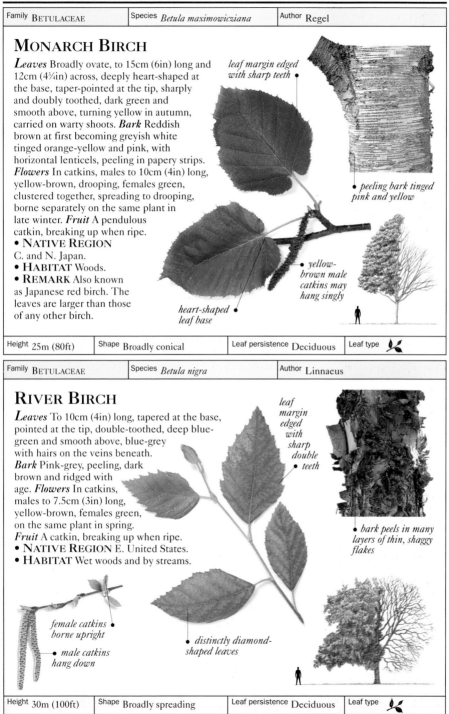

leaf margin edged with sharp teeth •

• peeling bark tinged pink and yellow

• yellow-brown male catkins may hang singly

heart-shaped • leaf base

Height 25m (80ft)	Shape Broadly conical	Leaf persistence Deciduous	Leaf type

Family BETULACEAE	Species *Betula nigra*	Author Linnaeus

RIVER BIRCH

Leaves To 10cm (4in) long, tapered at the base, pointed at the tip, double-toothed, deep blue-green and smooth above, blue-grey with hairs on the veins beneath. **Bark** Pink-grey, peeling, dark brown and ridged with age. **Flowers** In catkins, males to 7.5cm (3in) long, yellow-brown, females green, on the same plant in spring. **Fruit** A catkin, breaking up when ripe.
• **NATIVE REGION** E. United States.
• **HABITAT** Wet woods and by streams.

leaf margin edged with sharp double • teeth

• bark peels in many layers of thin, shaggy flakes

female catkins • borne upright

• male catkins hang down

• distinctly diamond-shaped leaves

Height 30m (100ft)	Shape Broadly spreading	Leaf persistence Deciduous	Leaf type

Family BETULACEAE	Species *Betula papyrifera*	Author Marshall

PAPER BIRCH

Leaves Ovate, to 10cm (4in) long and 7.5cm (3in) across, taper-pointed, toothed, dark green above, paler and with hairs on the veins at least when young beneath, turning yellow to orange in autumn. *Bark* White, with conspicuous dark lenticels, peeling in thin layers; pale pinkish orange when freshly exposed. *Flowers* In catkins, males to 10cm (4in) long, yellow, drooping, females slender, green, spreading or drooping, borne separately on the same plant in spring. *Fruit* A catkin, breaking up when ripe.
• **NATIVE REGION** North America.
• **HABITAT** Woods in northerly latitudes and on mountains.
• **REMARK** Also known as canoe birch. The bark was used by Native Americans to make canoes, which gives the alternative common name. This most widespread of the American birches occurs from Labrador to Alaska and in the northern United States.

smooth leaf upperside •

• *green fruiting catkins droop*

leaf margin edged with • *small teeth*

• *male catkins hang down from shoot tip*

• *leaves turn from green to yellow and orange in autumn*

bark spotted with dark, horizontal lenticels •

female catkins • *hang at an angle*

• *paler leaf underside has hairy veins*

peeling bark reveals • *orange-pink layer beneath*

Height 30m (100ft)	Shape Broadly conical	Leaf persistence Deciduous	Leaf type

Family BETULACEAE	Species *Betula pendula*	Author Roth

SILVER BIRCH

Leaves Ovate to triangular, to 6cm (2⅓in) long and 4cm (1½in) across, taper-pointed, coarsely double-toothed, glossy dark green above, turning yellow in autumn, carried on slender, hairless, warty, pendulous shoots. *Bark* White, developing dark, rugged cracks at the base with age. *Flowers* In catkins, males to 6cm (2⅓in) long, yellow, drooping, females green, upright or drooping, borne separately on the same plant in early spring. *Fruit* A catkin, breaking up when ripe.
• **NATIVE REGION** N. Asia, Europe.
• **HABITAT** Light, especially sandy, soil.
• **REMARK** Also known as European white birch. Forms extensive woods in its habitat.

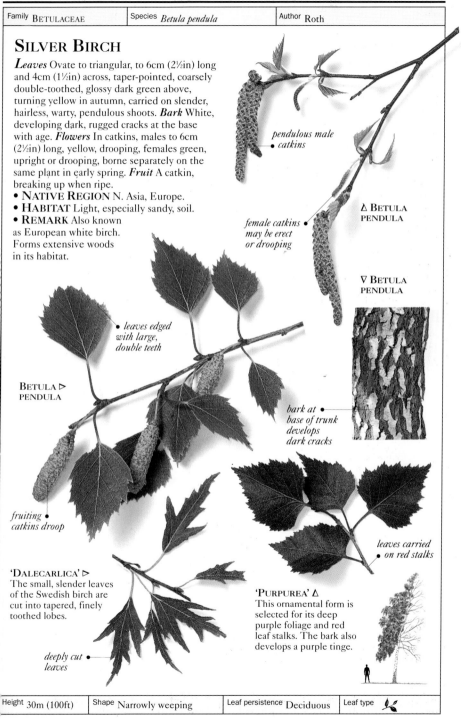

pendulous male catkins

△ **BETULA PENDULA**

female catkins may be erect or drooping

▽ **BETULA PENDULA**

leaves edged with large, double teeth

BETULA ▷ PENDULA

bark at base of trunk develops dark cracks

fruiting catkins droop

'DALECARLICA' ▷
The small, slender leaves of the Swedish birch are cut into tapered, finely toothed lobes.

deeply cut leaves

leaves carried on red stalks

'PURPUREA' △
This ornamental form is selected for its deep purple foliage and red leaf stalks. The bark also develops a purple tinge.

Height 30m (100ft)	Shape Narrowly weeping	Leaf persistence Deciduous	Leaf type

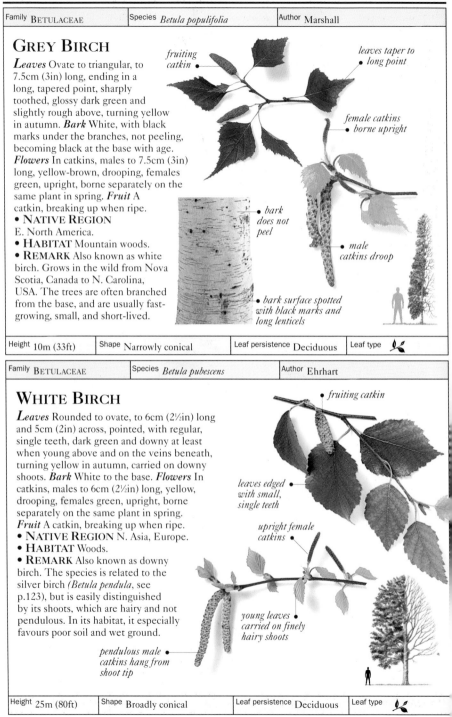

| Family BETULACEAE | Species *Betula populifolia* | Author Marshall |

GREY BIRCH

Leaves Ovate to triangular, to 7.5cm (3in) long, ending in a long, tapered point, sharply toothed, glossy dark green and slightly rough above, turning yellow in autumn. **Bark** White, with black marks under the branches, not peeling, becoming black at the base with age. **Flowers** In catkins, males to 7.5cm (3in) long, yellow-brown, drooping, females green, upright, borne separately on the same plant in spring. **Fruit** A catkin, breaking up when ripe.
• **NATIVE REGION** E. North America.
• **HABITAT** Mountain woods.
• **REMARK** Also known as white birch. Grows in the wild from Nova Scotia, Canada to N. Carolina, USA. The trees are often branched from the base, and are usually fast-growing, small, and short-lived.

fruiting catkin

leaves taper to long point

female catkins borne upright

bark does not peel

male catkins droop

bark surface spotted with black marks and long lenticels

| Height 10m (33ft) | Shape Narrowly conical | Leaf persistence Deciduous | Leaf type |

| Family BETULACEAE | Species *Betula pubescens* | Author Ehrhart |

WHITE BIRCH

Leaves Rounded to ovate, to 6cm (2½in) long and 5cm (2in) across, pointed, with regular, single teeth, dark green and downy at least when young above and on the veins beneath, turning yellow in autumn, carried on downy shoots. **Bark** White to the base. **Flowers** In catkins, males to 6cm (2½in) long, yellow, drooping, females green, upright, borne separately on the same plant in spring. **Fruit** A catkin, breaking up when ripe.
• **NATIVE REGION** N. Asia, Europe.
• **HABITAT** Woods.
• **REMARK** Also known as downy birch. The species is related to the silver birch *(Betula pendula*, see p.123), but is easily distinguished by its shoots, which are hairy and not pendulous. In its habitat, it especially favours poor soil and wet ground.

fruiting catkin

leaves edged with small, single teeth

upright female catkins

young leaves carried on finely hairy shoots

pendulous male catkins hang from shoot tip

| Height 25m (80ft) | Shape Broadly conical | Leaf persistence Deciduous | Leaf type |

Family BETULACEAE	Species *Betula utilis*	Author D. Don

HIMALAYAN BIRCH

Leaves Ovate, to 10cm (4in) long and 6cm (2½in) across, taper-pointed, toothed, dark sometimes glossy green above, downy on the veins beneath, turning a rich, golden yellow in autumn, on downy shoots. **Bark** Very variable, glossy orange-brown or dark copper-brown to pinkish or pure white, paper-thin and peeling. **Flowers** In catkins, males yellow and drooping, to 12cm (4¾in) or more long, females green and upright, in spring. **Fruit** A catkin, green ripening to brown, breaking up when ripe.
• **NATIVE REGION** China, Himalayas.
• **HABITAT** High mountain forests.
• **REMARK** This widely distributed species includes some fine white-barked birches. In the Himalayas, the bark is used for making paper, and for roofing.

• *fruits ripen from female catkins*

△ BETULA UTILIS

▽ BETULA UTILIS

• *female catkins borne upright*

• *raised, brown lenticels clearly visible on smooth, white bark*

• *male catkins may be as long as18cm (7¼in)*

• *bark peels in horizontal strips*

△ VAR. JACQUEMONTII
This variety, characterized by its white bark, is variable in leaf. Three different forms are shown.

VAR. JACQUEMONTII ▽
'SILVER SHADOW'
A form with large and drooping, dark green leaves.

VAR. JACQUEMONTII △
'GRAYSWOOD GHOST'
Very glossy leaves distinguish this attractive form.

◁ VAR. JACQUEMONTII
'JERMYNS'
This vigorous variety has broad leaves.

Height 25m (80ft)	Shape Broadly conical	Leaf persistence Deciduous	Leaf type

| Family BETULACEAE | Species *Carpinus betulus* | Author Linnaeus |

HORNBEAM

Leaves Ovate-oblong, to 10cm (4in) long and 6cm (2½in) across, pointed, double-toothed, with conspicuous veins, dark green and smooth above, downy on the veins beneath, turning yellow in autumn. ***Bark*** Pale grey, fluted, fissured with age. ***Flowers*** In catkins, males to 5cm (2in) long, yellowish, drooping, females small, green, at the tips of the shoots, borne separately on the same plant in spring. ***Fruit*** A nut, with three-lobed bracts, the bracts green turning yellowish brown, clustered in pendulous catkins, to 7.5cm (3in) long.
• **NATIVE REGION** S.W. Asia, Europe.
• **HABITAT** Hedgerows and broadleaf woods.
• **REMARK** A common hedging plant.

leaf margin edged with double teeth

three-lobed, usually untoothed, bract surrounds each fruit

fruit bracts coloured green in summer

female catkins at shoot tip

male catkins hang down

fruits ripen in autumn

| Height 30m (100ft) | Shape Broadly spreading | Leaf persistence Deciduous | Leaf type |

| Family BETULACEAE | Species *Carpinus caroliniana* | Author Walter |

AMERICAN HORNBEAM

Leaves Ovate, to 10cm (4in) long, taper-pointed at the tip, double-toothed, dark green, turning orange to red in autumn, on slender shoots. ***Bark*** Grey, smooth, and fluted. ***Flowers*** In catkins, males to 4cm (1½in) long, yellowish, drooping, females small, green, at the tips of the shoots, borne separately on the same plant in spring. ***Fruit*** A nut, with two- or three-lobed, green bracts, clustered in pendulous catkins, to 7.5cm (3in) long.
• **NATIVE REGION** Mexico, E. North America.
• **HABITAT** Moist woods, riverbanks, and swamps.
• **REMARK** Also known as blue beech, water beech. Similar to beech *(Fagus,* see pp.151–153), but distinguished by its fruit.

leaves edged with coarse double teeth

toothed fruit bracts

| Height 10m (33ft) | Shape Broadly spreading | Leaf persistence Deciduous | Leaf type |

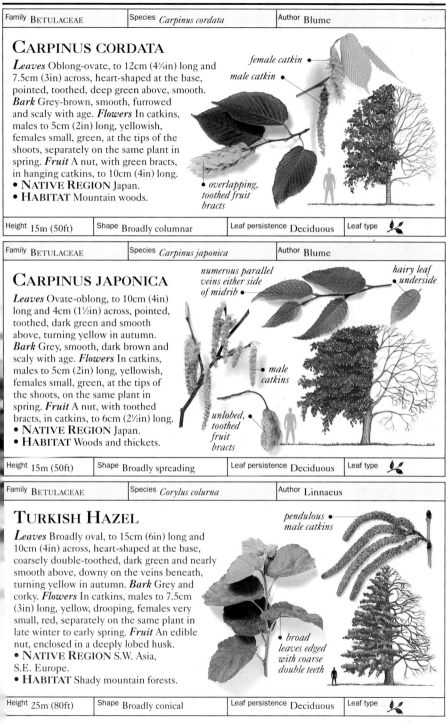

Family BETULACEAE	Species *Carpinus cordata*	Author Blume

CARPINUS CORDATA

Leaves Oblong-ovate, to 12cm (4¾in) long and 7.5cm (3in) across, heart-shaped at the base, pointed, toothed, deep green above, smooth. *Bark* Grey-brown, smooth, furrowed and scaly with age. *Flowers* In catkins, males to 5cm (2in) long, yellowish, females small, green, at the tips of the shoots, separately on the same plant in spring. *Fruit* A nut, with green bracts, in hanging catkins, to 10cm (4in) long.
• **NATIVE REGION** Japan.
• **HABITAT** Mountain woods.

female catkin •
male catkin •

• *overlapping, toothed fruit bracts*

Height 15m (50ft)	Shape Broadly columnar	Leaf persistence Deciduous	Leaf type

Family BETULACEAE	Species *Carpinus japonica*	Author Blume

CARPINUS JAPONICA

Leaves Ovate-oblong, to 10cm (4in) long and 4cm (1½in) across, pointed, toothed, dark green and smooth above, turning yellow in autumn. *Bark* Grey, smooth, dark brown and scaly with age. *Flowers* In catkins, males to 5cm (2in) long, yellowish, females small, green, at the tips of the shoots, on the same plant in spring. *Fruit* A nut, with toothed bracts, in catkins, to 6cm (2½in) long.
• **NATIVE REGION** Japan.
• **HABITAT** Woods and thickets.

numerous parallel veins either side of midrib •

hairy leaf • underside

• *male catkins*

unlobed, • toothed fruit bracts

Height 15m (50ft)	Shape Broadly spreading	Leaf persistence Deciduous	Leaf type

Family BETULACEAE	Species *Corylus colurna*	Author Linnaeus

TURKISH HAZEL

Leaves Broadly oval, to 15cm (6in) long and 10cm (4in) across, heart-shaped at the base, coarsely double-toothed, dark green and nearly smooth above, downy on the veins beneath, turning yellow in autumn. *Bark* Grey and corky. *Flowers* In catkins, males to 7.5cm (3in) long, yellow, drooping, females very small, red, separately on the same plant in late winter to early spring. *Fruit* An edible nut, enclosed in a deeply lobed husk.
• **NATIVE REGION** S.W. Asia, S.E. Europe.
• **HABITAT** Shady mountain forests.

pendulous • male catkins

• *broad leaves edged with coarse double teeth*

Height 25m (80ft)	Shape Broadly conical	Leaf persistence Deciduous	Leaf type

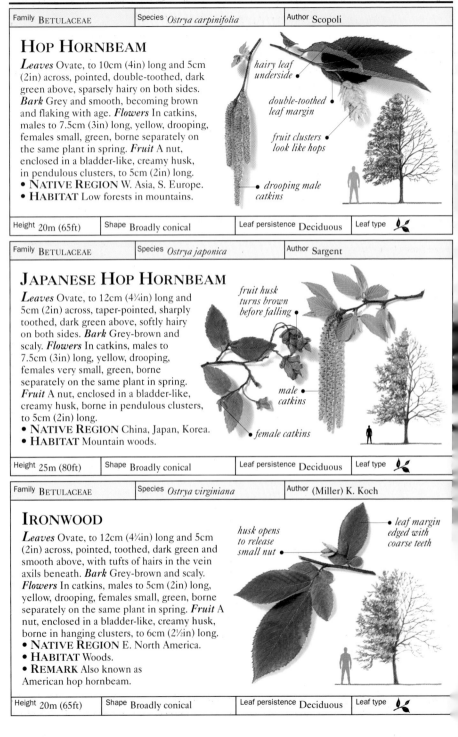

Family BETULACEAE	Species *Ostrya carpinifolia*	Author Scopoli

HOP HORNBEAM

Leaves Ovate, to 10cm (4in) long and 5cm (2in) across, pointed, double-toothed, dark green above, sparsely hairy on both sides. *Bark* Grey and smooth, becoming brown and flaking with age. *Flowers* In catkins, males to 7.5cm (3in) long, yellow, drooping, females small, green, borne separately on the same plant in spring. *Fruit* A nut, enclosed in a bladder-like, creamy husk, in pendulous clusters, to 5cm (2in) long.
• **NATIVE REGION** W. Asia, S. Europe.
• **HABITAT** Low forests in mountains.

hairy leaf underside •

double-toothed leaf margin •

fruit clusters look like hops •

• drooping male catkins

Height 20m (65ft)	Shape Broadly conical	Leaf persistence Deciduous	Leaf type

Family BETULACEAE	Species *Ostrya japonica*	Author Sargent

JAPANESE HOP HORNBEAM

Leaves Ovate, to 12cm (4¾in) long and 5cm (2in) across, taper-pointed, sharply toothed, dark green above, softly hairy on both sides. *Bark* Grey-brown and scaly. *Flowers* In catkins, males to 7.5cm (3in) long, yellow, drooping, females very small, green, borne separately on the same plant in spring. *Fruit* A nut, enclosed in a bladder-like, creamy husk, borne in pendulous clusters, to 5cm (2in) long.
• **NATIVE REGION** China, Japan, Korea.
• **HABITAT** Mountain woods.

fruit husk turns brown before falling •

male • catkins

• female catkins

Height 25m (80ft)	Shape Broadly conical	Leaf persistence Deciduous	Leaf type

Family BETULACEAE	Species *Ostrya virginiana*	Author (Miller) K. Koch

IRONWOOD

Leaves Ovate, to 12cm (4¾in) long and 5cm (2in) across, pointed, toothed, dark green and smooth above, with tufts of hairs in the vein axils beneath. *Bark* Grey-brown and scaly. *Flowers* In catkins, males to 5cm (2in) long, yellow, drooping, females small, green, borne separately on the same plant in spring. *Fruit* A nut, enclosed in a bladder-like, creamy husk, borne in hanging clusters, to 6cm (2½in) long.
• **NATIVE REGION** E. North America.
• **HABITAT** Woods.
• **REMARK** Also known as American hop hornbeam.

husk opens to release small nut •

• leaf margin edged with coarse teeth

Height 20m (65ft)	Shape Broadly conical	Leaf persistence Deciduous	Leaf type

BIGNONIACEAE

T HIS IS A LARGELY TROPICAL family, with evergreen and deciduous trees, shrubs, a few herbaceous plants, and many climbers. It comprises more than 100 genera and some 700 species, widely distributed, found particularly in South America. The leaves are often compound, and are arranged in whorls or opposite. The tubular flowers end in an often frilly-petalled, flared bell.

Family BIGNONIACEAE	Species *Catalpa bignonioides*	Author Walter

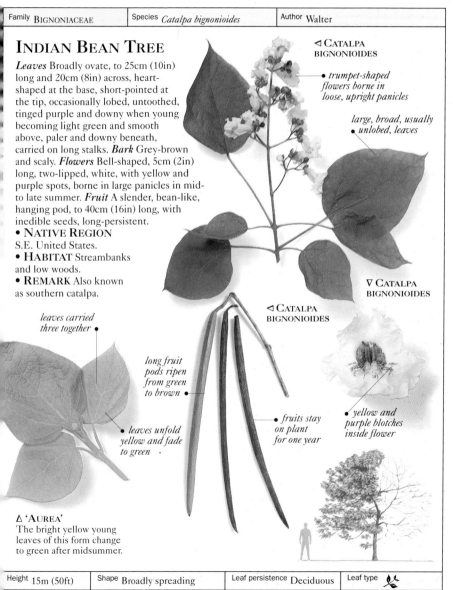

INDIAN BEAN TREE

Leaves Broadly ovate, to 25cm (10in) long and 20cm (8in) across, heart-shaped at the base, short-pointed at the tip, occasionally lobed, untoothed, tinged purple and downy when young becoming light green and smooth above, paler and downy beneath, carried on long stalks. *Bark* Grey-brown and scaly. *Flowers* Bell-shaped, 5cm (2in) long, two-lipped, white, with yellow and purple spots, borne in large panicles in mid- to late summer. *Fruit* A slender, bean-like, hanging pod, to 40cm (16in) long, with inedible seeds, long-persistent.
• **NATIVE REGION** S.E. United States.
• **HABITAT** Streambanks and low woods.
• **REMARK** Also known as southern catalpa.

◁ CATALPA BIGNONIOIDES

• *trumpet-shaped flowers borne in loose, upright panicles*

large, broad, usually • unlobed, leaves

▽ CATALPA BIGNONIOIDES

◁ CATALPA BIGNONIOIDES

leaves carried three together •

long fruit pods ripen from green to brown •

• leaves unfold yellow and fade to green ·

• fruits stay on plant for one year

• yellow and purple blotches inside flower

△ 'AUREA'
The bright yellow young leaves of this form change to green after midsummer.

Height 15m (50ft)	Shape Broadly spreading	Leaf persistence Deciduous	Leaf type

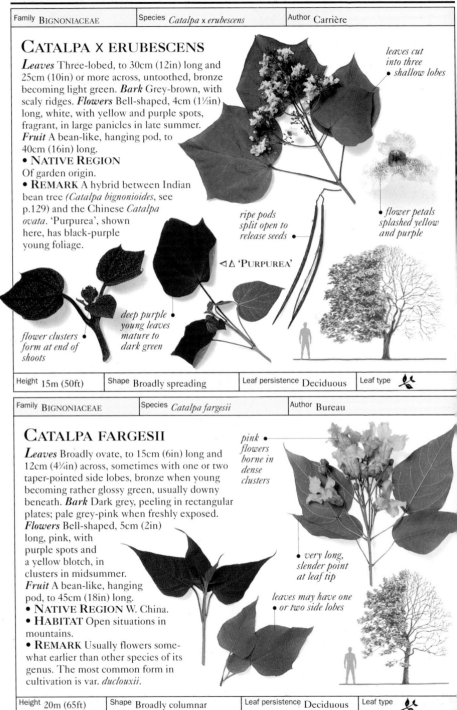

Family	BIGNONIACEAE	Species	*Catalpa* x *erubescens*	Author	Carrière

CATALPA X ERUBESCENS

Leaves Three-lobed, to 30cm (12in) long and 25cm (10in) or more across, untoothed, bronze becoming light green. **Bark** Grey-brown, with scaly ridges. **Flowers** Bell-shaped, 4cm (1½in) long, white, with yellow and purple spots, fragrant, in large panicles in late summer. **Fruit** A bean-like, hanging pod, to 40cm (16in) long.

• **NATIVE REGION**
Of garden origin.
• **REMARK** A hybrid between Indian bean tree *(Catalpa bignonioides*, see p.129) and the Chinese *Catalpa ovata*. 'Purpurea', shown here, has black-purple young foliage.

leaves cut into three shallow lobes

flower petals splashed yellow and purple

ripe pods split open to release seeds

◁△ 'PURPUREA'

deep purple young leaves mature to dark green

flower clusters form at end of shoots

Height 15m (50ft)	Shape Broadly spreading	Leaf persistence Deciduous	Leaf type

Family	BIGNONIACEAE	Species	*Catalpa fargesii*	Author	Bureau

CATALPA FARGESII

Leaves Broadly ovate, to 15cm (6in) long and 12cm (4¾in) across, sometimes with one or two taper-pointed side lobes, bronze when young becoming rather glossy green, usually downy beneath. **Bark** Dark grey, peeling in rectangular plates; pale grey-pink when freshly exposed. **Flowers** Bell-shaped, 5cm (2in) long, pink, with purple spots and a yellow blotch, in clusters in midsummer. **Fruit** A bean-like, hanging pod, to 45cm (18in) long.

• **NATIVE REGION** W. China.
• **HABITAT** Open situations in mountains.
• **REMARK** Usually flowers somewhat earlier than other species of its genus. The most common form in cultivation is var. *duclouxii*.

pink flowers borne in dense clusters

very long, slender point at leaf tip

leaves may have one or two side lobes

Height 20m (65ft)	Shape Broadly columnar	Leaf persistence Deciduous	Leaf type

| Family BIGNONIACEAE | Species *Catalpa speciosa* | Author (Warder ex Barney) Engelmann |

WESTERN CATALPA

Leaves Broadly ovate, to 30cm (12in) long and 20cm (8in) across, with a long, tapering point at the tip, glossy dark green and downy when young becoming smooth above, downy beneath, carried on long stalks. **Bark** Grey, scaly and fissured. **Flowers** Bell-shaped, 5cm (2in) long, white, spotted with yellow and some purple, borne in large panicles in summer. **Fruit** Slender, bean-like, and hanging, to 45cm (18in) long, persisting on the plant until the following year.
• **NATIVE REGION** United States.
• **HABITAT** Riverbanks, damp woods, and swamps.

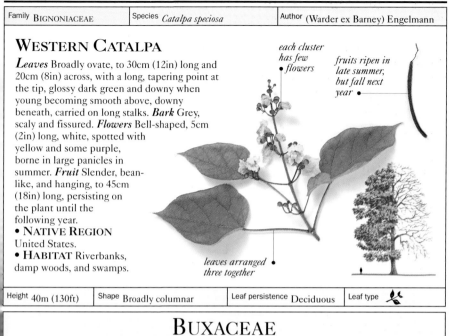

each cluster has few • flowers

fruits ripen in late summer, but fall next year •

• leaves arranged three together

| Height 40m (130ft) | Shape Broadly columnar | Leaf persistence Deciduous | Leaf type |

BUXACEAE

T HE PLANT KNOWN AS THE common box *(Buxus sempervirens)* is the most familiar tree in this family, which contains four or five genera, with some 60 species of evergreen trees, shrubs, and the occasional herbaceous plant. They have usually opposite leaves, and small flowers borne in clusters.

| Family BUXACEAE | Species *Buxus sempervirens* | Author Linnaeus |

COMMON BOX

Leaves Ovate to oblong, to 2.5cm (1in) long and 1cm (⅜in) across, notched at the tip, glossy dark green above, paler beneath, on four-angled shoots. **Bark** Grey and smooth, cracking into small squares with age. **Flowers** Males and females both small and green, males with conspicuous, yellow anthers, separate but in the same cluster, in the leaf axils in early spring. **Fruit** A small, woody, green capsule, to 8mm (⁵⁄₁₆in) long.
• **NATIVE REGION** N. Africa, S.W. Asia, Europe.
• **HABITAT** Usually alkaline soil.
• **REMARK** Can be either a small tree or a large shrub, producing a very hard, close-grained, yellow wood. In cultivation, it is traditionally used as a hedging plant, and for topiary.

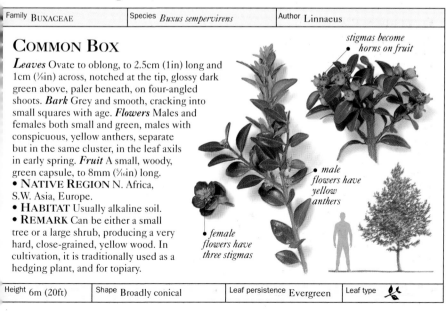

stigmas become • horns on fruit

• male flowers have yellow anthers

• female flowers have three stigmas

| Height 6m (20ft) | Shape Broadly conical | Leaf persistence Evergreen | Leaf type |

CELASTRACEAE

T HIS WIDESPREAD FAMILY contains nearly 100 genera and over 1,000 species of evergreen and deciduous trees, shrubs, and climbing plants. The leaves are opposite or alternate, and the flowers usually small and greenish.

Family CELASTRACEAE	Species *Euonymus europaeus*	Author Linnaeus

SPINDLE TREE

Leaves Elliptic to ovate or lanceolate, to 8cm (3¼in) long and 3cm (1¼in) across, taper-pointed, finely toothed, usually turning red in autumn. *Bark* Grey and smooth. *Flowers* Males and females both small and greenish white, with four petals, borne in clusters of up to ten in the leaf axils, sometimes on separate plants in late spring to early summer. *Fruit* Bright pink, about 1.2cm (½in) across, the four lobes opening to reveal bright orange-coated seeds.
• NATIVE REGION W. Asia, Europe.
• HABITAT Woods, thickets, and hedgerows.

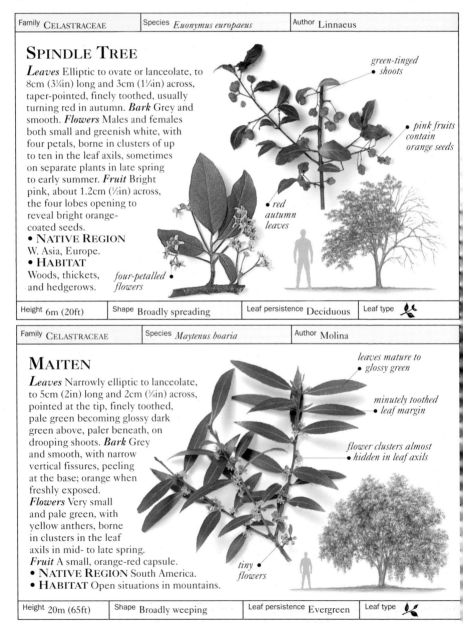

green-tinged • shoots

• pink fruits contain orange seeds

• red autumn leaves

four-petalled • flowers

Height 6m (20ft)	Shape Broadly spreading	Leaf persistence Deciduous	Leaf type

Family CELASTRACEAE	Species *Maytenus boaria*	Author Molina

MAITEN

Leaves Narrowly elliptic to lanceolate, to 5cm (2in) long and 2cm (¾in) across, pointed at the tip, finely toothed, pale green becoming glossy dark green above, paler beneath, on drooping shoots. *Bark* Grey and smooth, with narrow vertical fissures, peeling at the base; orange when freshly exposed.
Flowers Very small and pale green, with yellow anthers, borne in clusters in the leaf axils in mid- to late spring.
Fruit A small, orange-red capsule.
• NATIVE REGION South America.
• HABITAT Open situations in mountains.

leaves mature to • glossy green

minutely toothed • leaf margin

flower clusters almost • hidden in leaf axils

tiny • flowers

Height 20m (65ft)	Shape Broadly weeping	Leaf persistence Evergreen	Leaf type

CERCIDIPHYLLACEAE

T HE SPECIES DESCRIBED here is the only member of this family. It was once thought to be related to the magnolias *(Magnolia,* see pp.202–215), and was classified with them, but is now regarded as a plant of primitive origin, and more closely related to the planes *(Platanus,* see pp.234–235).

Family CERCIDIPHYLLACEAE	Species *Cercidiphyllum japonicum*	Author Siebold & Zuccarini

KATSURA TREE

Leaves Rounded, to 7.5cm (3in) long and across, heart-shaped at the base, with rounded teeth, bronzy becoming blue-green and smooth, turning yellow, pink, or purple in autumn. *Bark* Grey-brown, furrowed, flaking. *Flowers* Small and without petals, males with numerous red stamens, females with four to six red styles, in the leaf axils, on separate plants in early spring. *Fruit* A small, curved, green pod.
• NATIVE REGION Himalayas to Japan.
• HABITAT Mountain forests.

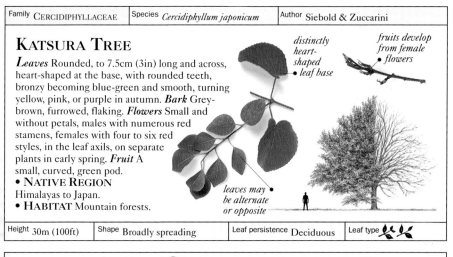

distinctly heart-shaped • leaf base

fruits develop from female • flowers

leaves may • be alternate or opposite

Height 30m (100ft)	Shape Broadly spreading	Leaf persistence Deciduous	Leaf type

CORNACEAE

T HIS FAMILY HAS about 12 genera and 100 species of evergreen and deciduous trees and shrubs, and includes the dogwoods *(Cornus,* see pp.133–138); most grow in northern temperate regions. Leaves are usually opposite. The small flowers may be surrounded by conspicuous bracts.

Family CORNACEAE	Species *Cornus alternifolia*	Author Linnaeus f.

CORNUS ALTERNIFOLIA

Leaves Elliptic to ovate, to 12cm (4¾in) long and 6cm (2½in) across, bright green and smooth above, bluish and hairy beneath. *Bark* Grey to brown, ridged with age. *Flowers* Creamy, in flattened heads to 6cm (2½in) across, in early summer. *Fruit* Berry-like, blue-black, to 6mm (¼in) across.
• NATIVE REGION E. North America.
• HABITAT Woods, thickets, by streams.

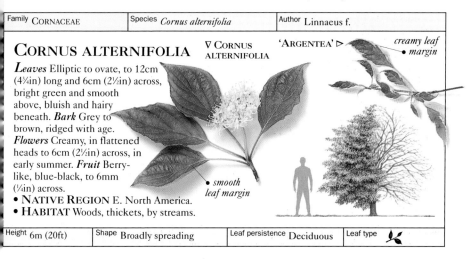

▽ CORNUS ALTERNIFOLIA

'ARGENTEA' ▷

creamy leaf • margin

smooth leaf margin

Height 6m (20ft)	Shape Broadly spreading	Leaf persistence Deciduous	Leaf type

Family CORNACEAE	Species *Cornus controversa*	Author Hemsley

CORNUS CONTROVERSA

Leaves Ovate to elliptic, to 15cm (6in) long and 7.5cm (3in) across, taper-pointed, untoothed, glossy dark green and smooth above, blue-green beneath, turning purple in autumn, carried on long, slender stalks, clustered at the tips of the shoots. **Bark** Smooth, grey, becoming fissured with age. **Flowers** Small and creamy white, with four petals, borne in flattened heads to 15cm (6in) across, along distinctly layered branches in early to midsummer. **Fruit** A small, rounded, blue-black berry.
• **NATIVE REGION** E. Asia.
• **HABITAT** Woods and thickets.
• **REMARK** This species and the much smaller *Cornus alternifolia* (see p.133) are the only two dogwoods that bear their leaves alternately, rather than opposite. In Japan, wooden dolls are often made from the wood of this tree.

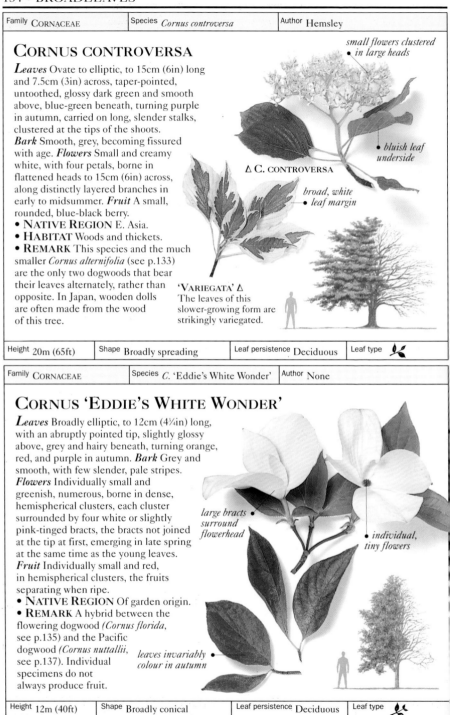

small flowers clustered in large heads

△ C. CONTROVERSA

bluish leaf underside

broad, white leaf margin

'VARIEGATA' △
The leaves of this slower-growing form are strikingly variegated.

Height 20m (65ft)	Shape Broadly spreading	Leaf persistence Deciduous	Leaf type

Family CORNACEAE	Species *C.* 'Eddie's White Wonder'	Author None

CORNUS 'EDDIE'S WHITE WONDER'

Leaves Broadly elliptic, to 12cm (4¾in) long, with an abruptly pointed tip, slightly glossy above, grey and hairy beneath, turning orange, red, and purple in autumn. **Bark** Grey and smooth, with few slender, pale stripes. **Flowers** Individually small and greenish, numerous, borne in dense, hemispherical clusters, each cluster surrounded by four white or slightly pink-tinged bracts, the bracts not joined at the tip at first, emerging in late spring at the same time as the young leaves. **Fruit** Individually small and red, in hemispherical clusters, the fruits separating when ripe.
• **NATIVE REGION** Of garden origin.
• **REMARK** A hybrid between the flowering dogwood (*Cornus florida*, see p.135) and the Pacific dogwood (*Cornus nuttallii*, see p.137). Individual specimens do not always produce fruit.

large bracts surround flowerhead

individual, tiny flowers

leaves invariably colour in autumn

Height 12m (40ft)	Shape Broadly conical	Leaf persistence Deciduous	Leaf type

Family CORNACEAE	Species *Cornus florida*	Author Linnaeus

FLOWERING DOGWOOD

Leaves Ovate to elliptic, to 10cm (4in) long and 6cm (2½in) across, taper-pointed, untoothed, dark green and smooth above, whitish and softly hairy beneath, turning red in autumn, carried on bloomy shoots. *Bark* Red-brown to blackish, deeply cracked into small, square plates. *Flowers* Small and greenish, numerous, in dense, hemispherical clusters, each cluster surrounded by four white to deep pink bracts, each bract notched at the tip, visible in bud during winter, opening in late spring before or with the young leaves. *Fruit* Individually small, red, in clusters, the fruits separating when ripe.
• **NATIVE REGION**
E. North America.
• **HABITAT** Acid soil in woods.

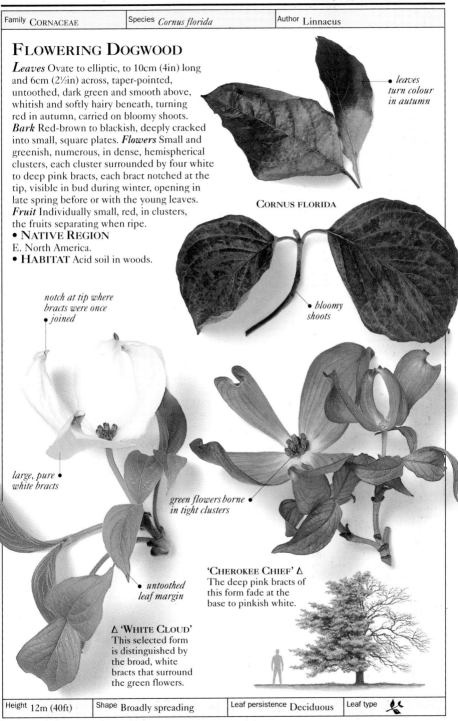

leaves
turn colour
in autumn

CORNUS FLORIDA

notch at tip where
bracts were once
• joined

• bloomy
shoots

large, pure •
white bracts

green flowers borne •
in tight clusters

• *untoothed
leaf margin*

'CHEROKEE CHIEF' △
The deep pink bracts of
this form fade at the
base to pinkish white.

△ **'WHITE CLOUD'**
This selected form
is distinguished by
the broad, white
bracts that surround
the green flowers.

Height 12m (40ft)	Shape Broadly spreading	Leaf persistence Deciduous	Leaf type

| Family CORNACEAE | Species *Cornus kousa* | Author Hance |

JAPANESE STRAWBERRY TREE

Leaves Ovate, to 7.5cm (3in) long and 5cm (2in) across, taper-pointed, with a wavy margin, untoothed, dark green and smooth above, smooth with tufts of brown hairs in the vein axils beneath. *Bark* Red-brown, peeling in irregular plates with age. *Flowers* Tiny, yellow-white or greenish, numerous, in dense, hemispherical, long-stalked, upright clusters, each cluster surrounded by four creamy white or pink-tinged, taper-pointed bracts, in early summer. *Fruit* Individually small, clustered together in a fleshy, strawberry-like, edible, red, pendulous head.
• **NATIVE REGION** Japan.
• **HABITAT** Mountain woods.

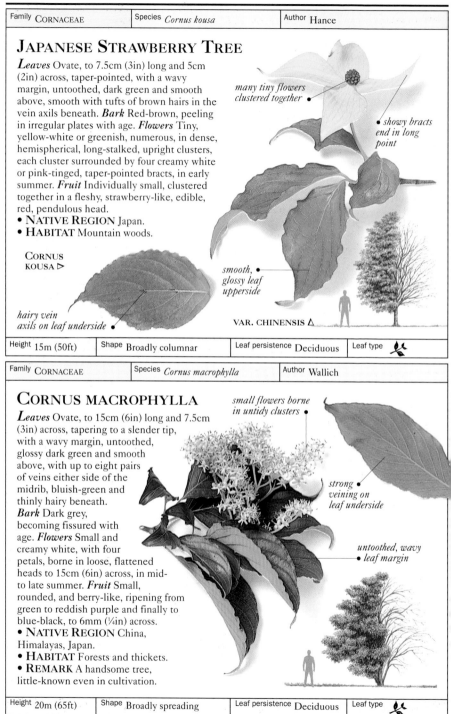

many tiny flowers clustered together •

• showy bracts end in long point

CORNUS
KOUSA ▷

hairy vein axils on leaf underside •

smooth, • glossy leaf upperside

VAR. CHINENSIS △

| Height 15m (50ft) | Shape Broadly columnar | Leaf persistence Deciduous | Leaf type |

| Family CORNACEAE | Species *Cornus macrophylla* | Author Wallich |

CORNUS MACROPHYLLA

Leaves Ovate, to 15cm (6in) long and 7.5cm (3in) across, tapering to a slender tip, with a wavy margin, untoothed, glossy dark green and smooth above, with up to eight pairs of veins either side of the midrib, bluish-green and thinly hairy beneath. *Bark* Dark grey, becoming fissured with age. *Flowers* Small and creamy white, with four petals, borne in loose, flattened heads to 15cm (6in) across, in mid- to late summer. *Fruit* Small, rounded, and berry-like, ripening from green to reddish purple and finally to blue-black, to 6mm (¼in) across.
• **NATIVE REGION** China, Himalayas, Japan.
• **HABITAT** Forests and thickets.
• **REMARK** A handsome tree, little-known even in cultivation.

small flowers borne in untidy clusters •

strong • veining on leaf underside

untoothed, wavy • leaf margin

| Height 20m (65ft) | Shape Broadly spreading | Leaf persistence Deciduous | Leaf type |

Family CORNACEAE	Species *Cornus nuttallii*	Author Audubon

PACIFIC DOGWOOD

Leaves Elliptic to obovate, to 15cm (6in) long and 7.5cm (3in) across, pointed, untoothed, dark green and nearly smooth above, hairy when young beneath, often turning yellow and occasionally red in autumn. *Bark* Grey and smooth, with few slender, pale stripes, slightly fluted at the base. *Flowers* Tiny and greenish, numerous, borne in dense, hemispherical, upright clusters, each cluster surrounded by four to seven large bracts to 7.5cm (3in) long, creamy white at first becoming white or white flushed pink, in late spring. *Fruit* Small, red, in hemispherical clusters, the fruits separating when ripe.
• **NATIVE REGION** W. North America.
• **HABITAT** Lowland forests, and on mountains in the south of its native region.

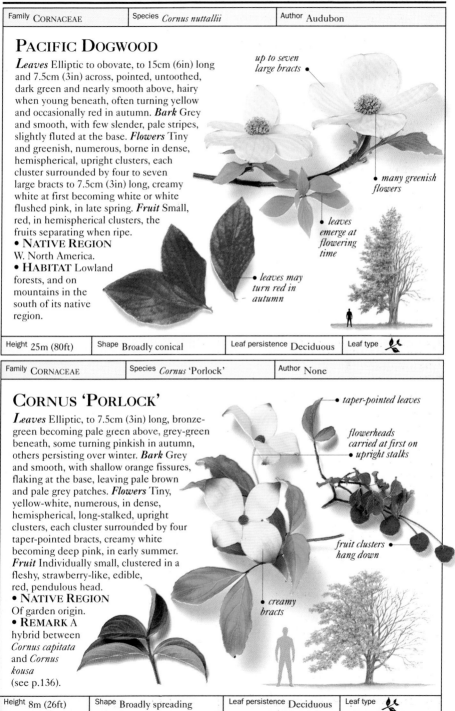

up to seven large bracts

many greenish flowers

leaves emerge at flowering time

leaves may turn red in autumn

Height 25m (80ft)	Shape Broadly conical	Leaf persistence Deciduous	Leaf type

Family CORNACEAE	Species *Cornus* 'Porlock'	Author None

CORNUS 'PORLOCK'

Leaves Elliptic, to 7.5cm (3in) long, bronze-green becoming pale green above, grey-green beneath, some turning pinkish in autumn, others persisting over winter. *Bark* Grey and smooth, with shallow orange fissures, flaking at the base, leaving pale brown and pale grey patches. *Flowers* Tiny, yellow-white, numerous, in dense, hemispherical, long-stalked, upright clusters, each cluster surrounded by four taper-pointed bracts, creamy white becoming deep pink, in early summer. *Fruit* Individually small, clustered in a fleshy, strawberry-like, edible, red, pendulous head.
• **NATIVE REGION** Of garden origin.
• **REMARK** A hybrid between *Cornus capitata* and *Cornus kousa* (see p.136).

taper-pointed leaves

flowerheads carried at first on upright stalks

fruit clusters hang down

creamy bracts

Height 8m (26ft)	Shape Broadly spreading	Leaf persistence Deciduous	Leaf type

Family CORNACEAE	Species *Cornus walteri*	Author Wangerin

CORNUS WALTERI

Leaves Elliptic, to 10cm (4in) long and 5cm (2in) across, tapered at the tip, untoothed, slightly glossy dark green above, thinly hairy beneath. **Bark** Pale grey-brown, deeply fissured, with narrow, rather corky, ridges. **Flowers** Individually small and creamy white, with four petals, borne in flattened heads 7.5cm (3in) across, in mid-summer. **Fruit** Small, rounded, and black.
• **NATIVE REGION** China.
• **HABITAT** Mountain woods.
• **REMARK** The species can be either a shrub or a small tree. It is uncommon in the wild, and little-known even in cultivation. In winter, the upperside of shoots exposed to the sun is purplish pink.

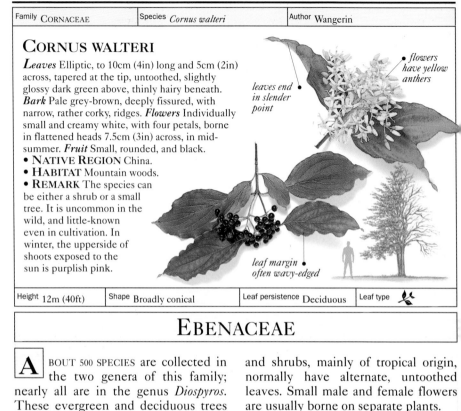

flowers have yellow anthers

leaves end in slender point

leaf margin often wavy-edged

Height 12m (40ft)	Shape Broadly conical	Leaf persistence Deciduous	Leaf type

EBENACEAE

ABOUT 500 SPECIES are collected in the two genera of this family; nearly all are in the genus *Diospyros*. These evergreen and deciduous trees and shrubs, mainly of tropical origin, normally have alternate, untoothed leaves. Small male and female flowers are usually borne on separate plants.

Family EBENACEAE	Species *Diospyros kaki*	Author Linnaeus f.

CHINESE PERSIMMON

Leaves Ovate to obovate, to 15cm (6in) or more long and 7.5cm (3in) across, pointed at the tip, untoothed, glossy dark green and smooth or nearly so above, paler and usually hairy beneath, turning red or orange in autumn. **Bark** Pale grey and scaly, peeling to furrowed. **Flowers** Males and females both small and bell-shaped, about 1.5cm (⅝in) long, yellow, males in clusters together, females singly, on young shoots, on separate plants in midsummer. **Fruit** A large, juicy, yellow to orange or red berry, to 7.5cm (3in) across, edible when ripe.
• **NATIVE REGION** Unknown.
• **HABITAT** Known only in cultivation.
• **REMARK** Fruits are also known as kaki.

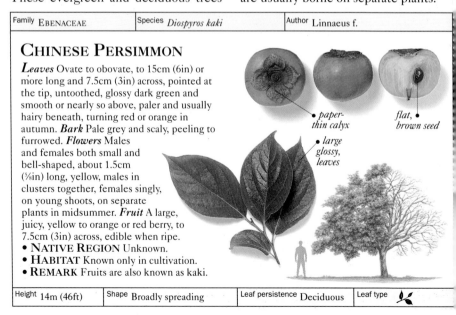

paper-thin calyx

flat, brown seed

large glossy, leaves

Height 14m (46ft)	Shape Broadly spreading	Leaf persistence Deciduous	Leaf type

Family EBENACEAE	Species *Diospyros lotus*	Author Linnaeus

DATE PLUM

Leaves Ovate to lanceolate, to 15cm (6in) long, pointed, untoothed, glossy dark green above, grey-green beneath, smooth or hairy on both sides. **Bark** Grey, smooth, fissured into square plates with age. **Flowers** Males and females both bell-shaped, about 5mm (³⁄₁₆in) long, deep pink or orange-yellow, males in clusters, females singly, on the underside of the young shoots, on separate plants in mid-summer. **Fruit** An edible berry, 2cm (¾in) across, green ripening to yellow-brown to blue-black, sometimes bloomy.
• **NATIVE REGION** S.W. Asia and N. Iran.
• **HABITAT** Woods.
• **REMARK** In its native region, the species is widely cultivated for its edible fruits.

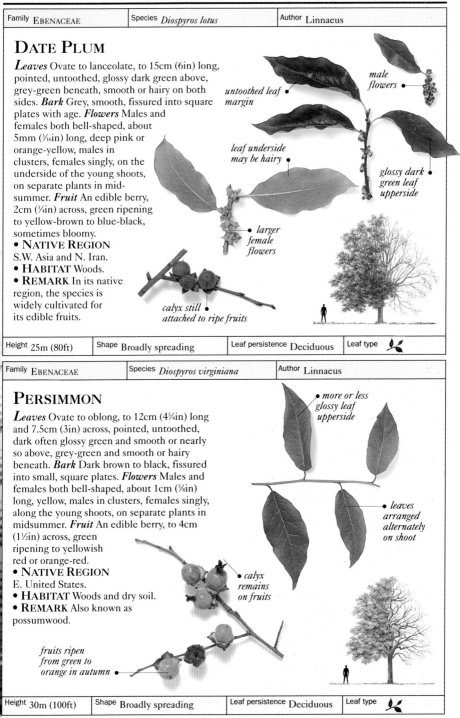

untoothed leaf margin

male flowers

leaf underside may be hairy

glossy dark green leaf upperside

larger female flowers

calyx still attached to ripe fruits

Height 25m (80ft)	Shape Broadly spreading	Leaf persistence Deciduous	Leaf type

Family EBENACEAE	Species *Diospyros virginiana*	Author Linnaeus

PERSIMMON

Leaves Ovate to oblong, to 12cm (4¾in) long and 7.5cm (3in) across, pointed, untoothed, dark often glossy green and smooth or nearly so above, grey-green and smooth or hairy beneath. **Bark** Dark brown to black, fissured into small, square plates. **Flowers** Males and females both bell-shaped, about 1cm (³⁄₈in) long, yellow, males in clusters, females singly, along the young shoots, on separate plants in midsummer. **Fruit** An edible berry, to 4cm (1½in) across, green ripening to yellowish red or orange-red.
• **NATIVE REGION** E. United States.
• **HABITAT** Woods and dry soil.
• **REMARK** Also known as possumwood.

more or less glossy leaf upperside

leaves arranged alternately on shoot

calyx remains on fruits

fruits ripen from green to orange in autumn

Height 30m (100ft)	Shape Broadly spreading	Leaf persistence Deciduous	Leaf type

ELAEAGNACEAE

T HE OLEASTER FAMILY has three genera, with some 50 species of evergreen and deciduous small trees and shrubs spreading to all temperate northern regions. The plants are often spiny. The untoothed, usually scaly, leaves are opposite or alternate. Small, petalless male and female flowers may be borne on separate plants; in several species they develop into edible fruits.

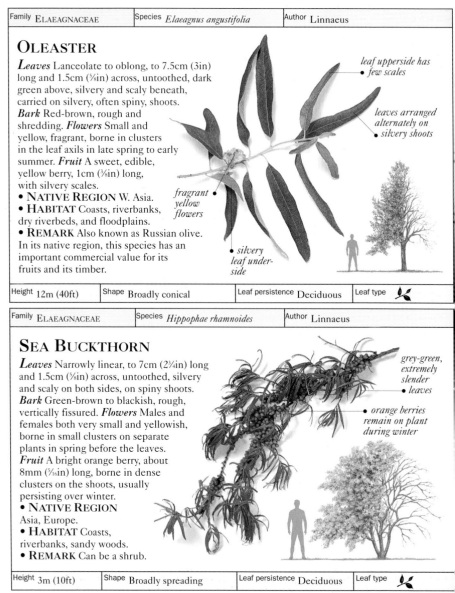

Family ELAEAGNACEAE	Species *Elaeagnus angustifolia*	Author Linnaeus

OLEASTER

Leaves Lanceolate to oblong, to 7.5cm (3in) long and 1.5cm (⅝in) across, untoothed, dark green above, silvery and scaly beneath, carried on silvery, often spiny, shoots. **Bark** Red-brown, rough and shredding. **Flowers** Small and yellow, fragrant, borne in clusters in the leaf axils in late spring to early summer. **Fruit** A sweet, edible, yellow berry, 1cm (⅜in) long, with silvery scales.
• **NATIVE REGION** W. Asia.
• **HABITAT** Coasts, riverbanks, dry riverbeds, and floodplains.
• **REMARK** Also known as Russian olive. In its native region, this species has an important commercial value for its fruits and its timber.

leaf upperside has few scales

leaves arranged alternately on silvery shoots

fragrant yellow flowers

silvery leaf underside

Height 12m (40ft)	Shape Broadly conical	Leaf persistence Deciduous	Leaf type

Family ELAEAGNACEAE	Species *Hippophae rhamnoides*	Author Linnaeus

SEA BUCKTHORN

Leaves Narrowly linear, to 7cm (2¾in) long and 1.5cm (⅝in) across, untoothed, silvery and scaly on both sides, on spiny shoots. **Bark** Green-brown to blackish, rough, vertically fissured. **Flowers** Males and females both very small and yellowish, borne in small clusters on separate plants in spring before the leaves. **Fruit** A bright orange berry, about 8mm (⁵⁄₁₆in) long, borne in dense clusters on the shoots, usually persisting over winter.
• **NATIVE REGION** Asia, Europe.
• **HABITAT** Coasts, riverbanks, sandy woods.
• **REMARK** Can be a shrub.

grey-green, extremely slender leaves

orange berries remain on plant during winter

Height 3m (10ft)	Shape Broadly spreading	Leaf persistence Deciduous	Leaf type

ERICACEAE

T HE HEATHER FAMILY, with about 100 genera and some 3,000 species, occurs almost worldwide: it is of restricted distribution only in Australia. The plants are in the main evergreen and deciduous trees and shrubs, with usually alternate leaves. The flowers vary in shape and size, but normally have five petals, joined at least at the base. In all members of the family, a root-associated fungus assists the plant in absorbing nutrients.

Family ERICACEAE	Species *Arbutus andrachne*	Author Linnaeus

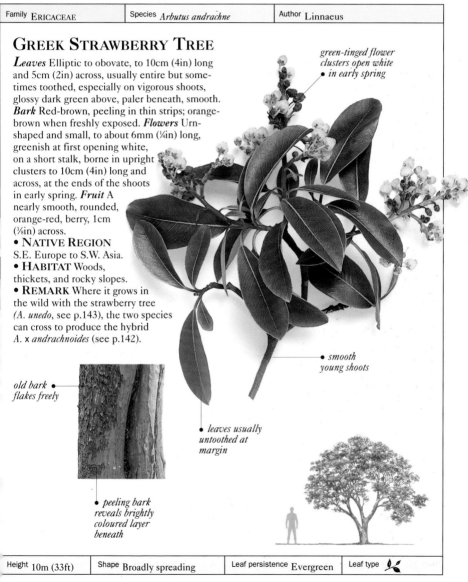

GREEK STRAWBERRY TREE

Leaves Elliptic to obovate, to 10cm (4in) long and 5cm (2in) across, usually entire but sometimes toothed, especially on vigorous shoots, glossy dark green above, paler beneath, smooth. **Bark** Red-brown, peeling in thin strips; orange-brown when freshly exposed. **Flowers** Urn-shaped and small, to about 6mm (¼in) long, greenish at first opening white, on a short stalk, borne in upright clusters to 10cm (4in) long and across, at the ends of the shoots in early spring. **Fruit** A nearly smooth, rounded, orange-red, berry, 1cm (⅜in) across.

• **NATIVE REGION** S.E. Europe to S.W. Asia.
• **HABITAT** Woods, thickets, and rocky slopes.
• **REMARK** Where it grows in the wild with the strawberry tree (*A. unedo*, see p.143), the two species can cross to produce the hybrid *A.* × *andrachnoides* (see p.142).

green-tinged flower clusters open white • in early spring

• smooth young shoots

old bark • flakes freely

• leaves usually untoothed at margin

• peeling bark reveals brightly coloured layer beneath

Height 10m (33ft)	Shape Broadly spreading	Leaf persistence Evergreen	Leaf type

Family ERICACEAE	Species *Arbutus x andrachnoides*	Author Link

ARBUTUS X ANDRACHNOIDES

Leaves Ovate to elliptic, to 10cm (4in) long and 5cm (2in) across, toothed, glossy dark green above, paler beneath, smooth on both sides. *Bark* Red-brown, peeling vertically in long, thin strips. *Flowers* Urn-shaped, small, and white, in drooping clusters at the ends of the shoots, over a long period between autumn and spring. *Fruit* A strawberry-like, warty, red berry, 1.5cm (⅝in) across.
• **NATIVE REGION** Greece.
• **HABITAT** Woods and thickets.
• **REMARK** A naturally occurring hybrid between the Greek strawberry tree *(Arbutus andrachne,* see p.141), whose attractive, peeling bark it inherits, and the strawberry tree *(Arbutus unedo,* see p.143), found in the wild where the parent plants grow together.

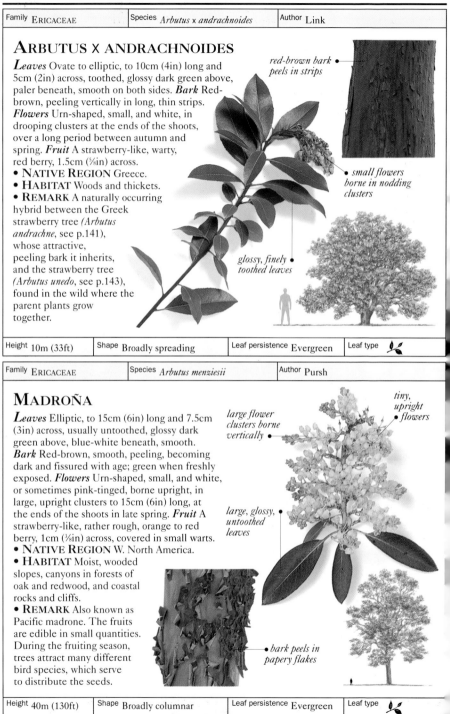

red-brown bark peels in strips

small flowers borne in nodding clusters

glossy, finely toothed leaves

Height 10m (33ft)	Shape Broadly spreading	Leaf persistence Evergreen	Leaf type

Family ERICACEAE	Species *Arbutus menziesii*	Author Pursh

MADROÑA

Leaves Elliptic, to 15cm (6in) long and 7.5cm (3in) across, usually untoothed, glossy dark green above, blue-white beneath, smooth. *Bark* Red-brown, smooth, peeling, becoming dark and fissured with age; green when freshly exposed. *Flowers* Urn-shaped, small, and white, or sometimes pink-tinged, borne upright, in large, upright clusters to 15cm (6in) long, at the ends of the shoots in late spring. *Fruit* A strawberry-like, rather rough, orange to red berry, 1cm (⅜in) across, covered in small warts.
• **NATIVE REGION** W. North America.
• **HABITAT** Moist, wooded slopes, canyons in forests of oak and redwood, and coastal rocks and cliffs.
• **REMARK** Also known as Pacific madrone. The fruits are edible in small quantities. During the fruiting season, trees attract many different bird species, which serve to distribute the seeds.

large flower clusters borne vertically

tiny, upright flowers

large, glossy, untoothed leaves

bark peels in papery flakes

Height 40m (130ft)	Shape Broadly columnar	Leaf persistence Evergreen	Leaf type

Family ERICACEAE	Species *Arbutus unedo*	Author Linnaeus

STRAWBERRY TREE

Leaves Elliptic to oblong or obovate, to 10cm (4in) long and 5cm (2in) across, toothed, very glossy dark green above, paler beneath, smooth on both sides. *Bark* Red-brown, rough and fissured, not peeling. *Flowers* Urn-shaped, small, and white, or sometimes pink, borne in drooping clusters about 5cm (2in) long, at the ends of the shoots in autumn. *Fruit* A strawberry-like, roughly warty, red berry, 2cm (¾in) across, ripening in autumn from flowers borne the previous year.
• **NATIVE REGION** S.W. Ireland, Mediterranean.
• **HABITAT** Rocky places and thickets.
• **REMARK** One of the few members of the family that grows on limey soil. With flowers and fruits borne at the same time, it is a particularly ornamental species.

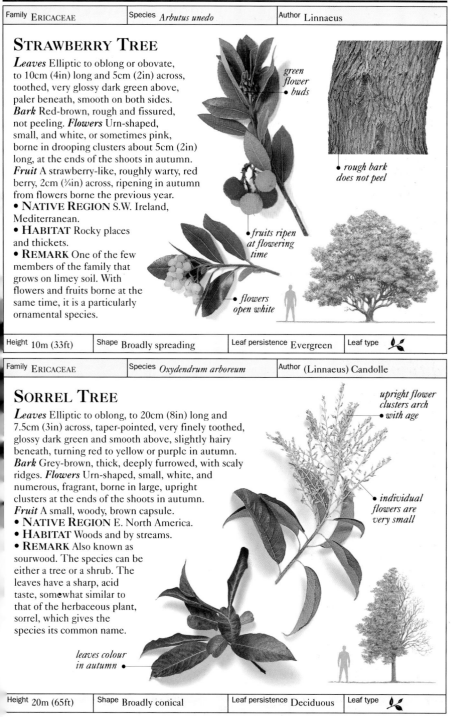

green flower buds

rough bark does not peel

fruits ripen at flowering time

flowers open white

Height 10m (33ft)	Shape Broadly spreading	Leaf persistence Evergreen	Leaf type

Family ERICACEAE	Species *Oxydendrum arboreum*	Author (Linnaeus) Candolle

SORREL TREE

Leaves Elliptic to oblong, to 20cm (8in) long and 7.5cm (3in) across, taper-pointed, very finely toothed, glossy dark green and smooth above, slightly hairy beneath, turning red to yellow or purple in autumn. *Bark* Grey-brown, thick, deeply furrowed, with scaly ridges. *Flowers* Urn-shaped, small, white, and numerous, fragrant, borne in large, upright clusters at the ends of the shoots in autumn. *Fruit* A small, woody, brown capsule.
• **NATIVE REGION** E. North America.
• **HABITAT** Woods and by streams.
• **REMARK** Also known as sourwood. The species can be either a tree or a shrub. The leaves have a sharp, acid taste, somewhat similar to that of the herbaceous plant, sorrel, which gives the species its common name.

upright flower clusters arch with age

individual flowers are very small

leaves colour in autumn

Height 20m (65ft)	Shape Broadly conical	Leaf persistence Deciduous	Leaf type

Family ERICACEAE	Species *Rhododendron arboreum*	Author W.W. Smith

RHODODENDRON ARBOREUM

Leaves Oblong to lanceolate, to 20cm (8in) long and 5cm (2in) across, thick and leathery, tapering to a pointed tip, glossy dark green and smooth with deeply impressed midrib and veins above, variably hairy from silvery to rusty and often shining beneath. **Bark** Red-brown, rough and shredding. **Flowers** Bell-shaped, to 5cm (2in) long, red, pink, or sometimes white, in dense clusters of up to 20 in late winter to mid-spring. **Fruit** A woody, brown capsule, splitting open to release numerous tiny seeds.
• **NATIVE REGION** Himalayas, with forms extending to S.W. China and Sri Lanka.
• **HABITAT** Forests and thickets in hills and mountains.
• **REMARK** In its native region and habitat, this species is a tree; in less favourable situations it may be only a large shrub. It was the first rhododendron to be introduced to Europe from the Himalayas. The young leaves are poisonous.

parallel veins run either side of prominent midrib

flowers vary in colour from white through pink to deep red

thinly hairy, shining leaf underside

deep red anthers tipped with creamy pollen

flower petals marked with darker spots on inner surface

thick, leathery leaves have smooth, glossy upper surface

up to 20 flowers clustered together in each rounded head

Height 15m (50ft)	Shape Broadly columnar	Leaf persistence Evergreen	Leaf type

EUCOMMIACEAE

THE ONLY MEMBER of this family, *Eucommia ulmoides* is a vigorous and decorative plant when mature. It is thought to be related most closely to the elms *(Ulmus, see pp.308–309)*. If in doubt about its identity, the rubbery latex, which forms an integral part of the leaf structure, provides instant identification. However, the latex is present in quantities that are too small to make commercial extraction an economic proposition. This unique species is the only tree from temperate regions known to produce rubber.

Family EUCOMMIACEAE	Species *Eucommia ulmoides*	Author Oliver

EUCOMMIA ULMOIDES

Leaves Ovate to elliptic, to 20cm (8in) long and 9cm (3½in) across, leathery, taper-pointed at the tip, toothed, glossy dark green, with prominent lateral veining, drooping on thin shoots. **Bark** Pale dove-grey, deeply fissured. **Flowers** Males and females both very small, without petals, opening on the old shoots, on separate plants in late spring just before or as the young leaves emerge. **Fruit** Winged, green keys, 4cm (1½in) long, in clusters, each key containing a seed.
• **NATIVE REGION** Not known; probably S.W. China.
• **HABITAT** Not established.
• **REMARK** This hardy tree was introduced to the West in about 1896, from plants propagated in China, and is now known only in cultivation. In China, the bark is used for medicinal purposes.

INVISIBLE RUBBER ▷
When a leaf is gently torn apart, and is held upside-down by its stalk, the two separate parts remain hanging together, connected almost invisibly by a network of gossamer-like latex fibres.

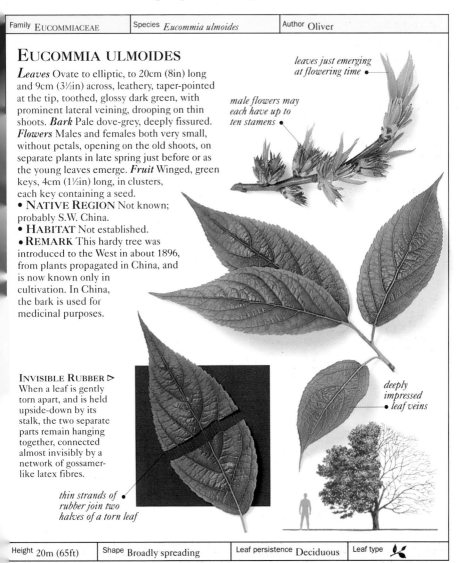

leaves just emerging at flowering time

male flowers may each have up to ten stamens

deeply impressed leaf veins

thin strands of rubber join two halves of a torn leaf

Height 20m (65ft)	Shape Broadly spreading	Leaf persistence Deciduous	Leaf type

EUCRYPHIACEAE

A FAMILY OF A SINGLE GENUS, with five species of evergreen trees or shrubs native to Chile and south-east Australia, including Tasmania. The leaves are opposite, and either simple or pinnate, toothed or untoothed. The white flowers have usually four petals and numerous stamens.

Family EUCRYPHIACEAE	Species *Eucryphia cordifolia*	Author Cavanilles

ULMO

Leaves Oblong, to 7.5cm (3in) long and 5cm (2in) across, heart-shaped at the base, toothed, dark green above, grey and hairy beneath. **Bark** Grey and smooth. **Flowers** 5cm (2in) across, white, with four petals, the numerous stamens turning from pink to orange, fragrant, borne singly in the leaf axils in late summer. **Fruit** A small, woody capsule.
• **NATIVE REGION** Chile.
• **HABITAT** Rain forests.
• **REMARK** At high altitudes, this species is a large shrub.

fine network of veins on underside of leaves

stamens have orange anthers

flower stalks are pink on exposed side

Height 40m (130ft)	Shape Narrowly columnar	Leaf persistence Evergreen	Leaf type

Family EUCRYPHIACEAE	Species *Eucryphia glutinosa*	Author (Poeppig & Endlicher) Baillon

EUCRYPHIA GLUTINOSA

Leaves Pinnate, with three to five leaflets, to 6cm (2½in) long and 3cm (1¼in) across, toothed, glossy dark green above, paler beneath, hairy at least when young on both sides. **Bark** Grey and smooth. **Flowers** 5cm (2in) across, white, with four petals and numerous pink-tipped stamens, fragrant, borne singly in the leaf axils in late summer. **Fruit** A small, woody capsule.
• **NATIVE REGION** Chile.
• **HABITAT** Forests and riverbanks.
• **REMARK** Cultivated plants of the species are semi-evergreen or deciduous, with most leaves turning orange-red in autumn before falling.

'PLENA' ▷
This selected form has double flowers.

▽ EUCRYPHIA GLUTINOSA

flowers have eight or more petals

prominently toothed, glossy leaflets

anthers coloured deep pink at first

Height 10m (33ft)	Shape Narrowly columnar	Leaf persistence Evergreen	Leaf type

Family EUCRYPHIACEAE	Species *Eucryphia x intermedia*	Author Bausch

EUCRYPHIA X INTERMEDIA

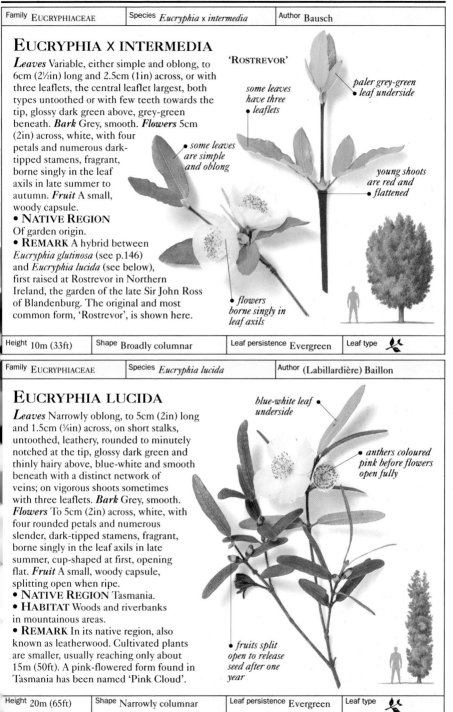

Leaves Variable, either simple and oblong, to 6cm (2½in) long and 2.5cm (1in) across, or with three leaflets, the central leaflet largest, both types untoothed or with few teeth towards the tip, glossy dark green above, grey-green beneath. **Bark** Grey, smooth. **Flowers** 5cm (2in) across, white, with four petals and numerous dark-tipped stamens, fragrant, borne singly in the leaf axils in late summer to autumn. **Fruit** A small, woody capsule.
• **NATIVE REGION** Of garden origin.
• **REMARK** A hybrid between *Eucryphia glutinosa* (see p.146) and *Eucryphia lucida* (see below), first raised at Rostrevor in Northern Ireland, the garden of the late Sir John Ross of Blandenburg. The original and most common form, 'Rostrevor', is shown here.

'ROSTREVOR'

some leaves have three leaflets

paler grey-green leaf underside

some leaves are simple and oblong

young shoots are red and flattened

flowers borne singly in leaf axils

Height 10m (33ft)	Shape Broadly columnar	Leaf persistence Evergreen	Leaf type

Family EUCRYPHIACEAE	Species *Eucryphia lucida*	Author (Labillardière) Baillon

EUCRYPHIA LUCIDA

Leaves Narrowly oblong, to 5cm (2in) long and 1.5cm (⅝in) across, on short stalks, untoothed, leathery, rounded to minutely notched at the tip, glossy dark green and thinly hairy above, blue-white and smooth beneath with a distinct network of veins; on vigorous shoots sometimes with three leaflets. **Bark** Grey, smooth. **Flowers** To 5cm (2in) across, white, with four rounded petals and numerous slender, dark-tipped stamens, fragrant, borne singly in the leaf axils in late summer, cup-shaped at first, opening flat. **Fruit** A small, woody capsule, splitting open when ripe.
• **NATIVE REGION** Tasmania.
• **HABITAT** Woods and riverbanks in mountainous areas.
• **REMARK** In its native region, also known as leatherwood. Cultivated plants are smaller, usually reaching only about 15m (50ft). A pink-flowered form found in Tasmania has been named 'Pink Cloud'.

blue-white leaf underside

anthers coloured pink before flowers open fully

fruits split open to release seed after one year

Height 20m (65ft)	Shape Narrowly columnar	Leaf persistence Evergreen	Leaf type

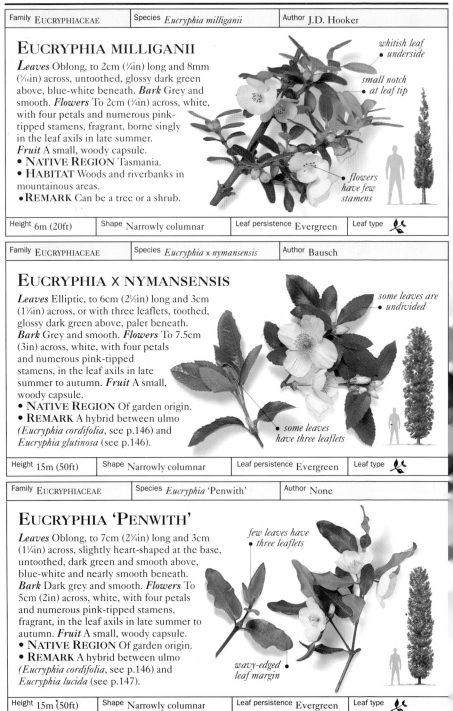

Family EUCRYPHIACEAE	Species *Eucryphia milliganii*	Author J.D. Hooker

EUCRYPHIA MILLIGANII

Leaves Oblong, to 2cm (¾in) long and 8mm (⁵⁄₁₆in) across, untoothed, glossy dark green above, blue-white beneath. *Bark* Grey and smooth. *Flowers* To 2cm (¾in) across, white, with four petals and numerous pink-tipped stamens, fragrant, borne singly in the leaf axils in late summer.
Fruit A small, woody capsule.
• **NATIVE REGION** Tasmania.
• **HABITAT** Woods and riverbanks in mountainous areas.
• **REMARK** Can be a tree or a shrub.

whitish leaf
• underside

small notch
• at leaf tip

• flowers
have few
stamens

Height 6m (20ft)	Shape Narrowly columnar	Leaf persistence Evergreen	Leaf type

Family EUCRYPHIACEAE	Species *Eucryphia x nymansensis*	Author Bausch

EUCRYPHIA X NYMANSENSIS

Leaves Elliptic, to 6cm (2½in) long and 3cm (1¼in) across, or with three leaflets, toothed, glossy dark green above, paler beneath. *Bark* Grey and smooth. *Flowers* To 7.5cm (3in) across, white, with four petals and numerous pink-tipped stamens, in the leaf axils in late summer to autumn. *Fruit* A small, woody capsule.
• **NATIVE REGION** Of garden origin.
• **REMARK** A hybrid between ulmo (*Eucryphia cordifolia*, see p.146) and *Eucryphia glutinosa* (see p.146).

some leaves are
• undivided

• some leaves
have three leaflets

Height 15m (50ft)	Shape Narrowly columnar	Leaf persistence Evergreen	Leaf type

Family EUCRYPHIACEAE	Species *Eucryphia* 'Penwith'	Author None

EUCRYPHIA 'PENWITH'

Leaves Oblong, to 7cm (2¾in) long and 3cm (1¼in) across, slightly heart-shaped at the base, untoothed, dark green and smooth above, blue-white and nearly smooth beneath. *Bark* Dark grey and smooth. *Flowers* To 5cm (2in) across, white, with four petals and numerous pink-tipped stamens, fragrant, in the leaf axils in late summer to autumn. *Fruit* A small, woody capsule.
• **NATIVE REGION** Of garden origin.
• **REMARK** A hybrid between ulmo (*Eucryphia cordifolia*, see p.146) and *Eucryphia lucida* (see p.147).

few leaves have
• three leaflets

wavy-edged •
leaf margin

Height 15m (50ft)	Shape Narrowly columnar	Leaf persistence Evergreen	Leaf type

FAGACEAE

SOME VERY FAMILIAR deciduous and evergreen trees belong to this family, which includes the chestnuts *(Castanea, see pp.149–150)*, beeches *(Fagus, see pp.151–153)*, and oaks *(Quercus, see pp.158–173)*. Eight genera with over 1,000 species extend from northern temperate regions to parts of the southern hemisphere. The leaves are simple, lobed, or toothed. The small male or female flowers are often in separate catkins, on the same plant. The fruit is a nut, surrounded by, or enclosed in, a cupule.

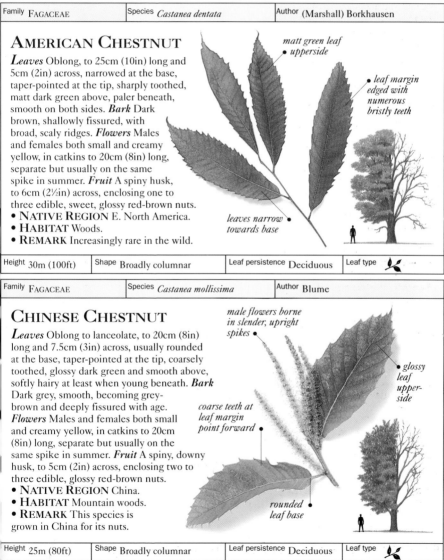

Family FAGACEAE	Species *Castanea dentata*	Author (Marshall) Borkhausen

AMERICAN CHESTNUT

Leaves Oblong, to 25cm (10in) long and 5cm (2in) across, narrowed at the base, taper-pointed at the tip, sharply toothed, matt dark green above, paler beneath, smooth on both sides. *Bark* Dark brown, shallowly fissured, with broad, scaly ridges. *Flowers* Males and females both small and creamy yellow, in catkins to 20cm (8in) long, separate but usually on the same spike in summer. *Fruit* A spiny husk, to 6cm (2½in) across, enclosing one to three edible, sweet, glossy red-brown nuts.
• **NATIVE REGION** E. North America.
• **HABITAT** Woods.
• **REMARK** Increasingly rare in the wild.

matt green leaf upperside

leaf margin edged with numerous bristly teeth

leaves narrow towards base

Height 30m (100ft)	Shape Broadly columnar	Leaf persistence Deciduous	Leaf type

Family FAGACEAE	Species *Castanea mollissima*	Author Blume

CHINESE CHESTNUT

Leaves Oblong to lanceolate, to 20cm (8in) long and 7.5cm (3in) across, usually rounded at the base, taper-pointed at the tip, coarsely toothed, glossy dark green and smooth above, softly hairy at least when young beneath. *Bark* Dark grey, smooth, becoming grey-brown and deeply fissured with age. *Flowers* Males and females both small and creamy yellow, in catkins to 20cm (8in) long, separate but usually on the same spike in summer. *Fruit* A spiny, downy husk, to 5cm (2in) across, enclosing two to three edible, glossy red-brown nuts.
• **NATIVE REGION** China.
• **HABITAT** Mountain woods.
• **REMARK** This species is grown in China for its nuts.

male flowers borne in slender, upright spikes

glossy leaf upperside

coarse teeth at leaf margin point forward

rounded leaf base

Height 25m (80ft)	Shape Broadly columnar	Leaf persistence Deciduous	Leaf type

Family FAGACEAE	Species *Castanea sativa*	Author Miller

SWEET CHESTNUT

Leaves Oblong, to 20cm (8in) long and 7.5cm (3in) across, usually rounded or heart-shaped at the base, taper-pointed at the tip, toothed, glossy dark green and smooth above, paler becoming smooth beneath. *Bark* Grey and smooth, becoming brown and usually spirally ridged with age. *Flowers* Males and females both small and creamy yellow, in catkins to 25cm (10in) long, separate but usually on the same spike in summer. *Fruit* A spiny husk, to 6cm (2½in) across, enclosing one to three edible, glossy red-brown nuts.
• NATIVE REGION N. Africa, S.W. Asia, S. Europe.
• HABITAT Woods.

leaves edged with coarse, bristly teeth

green fruit husks

male and female flowers clustered on same spike

each prickly fruit husk contains up to three nuts

Height 30m (100ft)	Shape Broadly columnar	Leaf persistence Deciduous	Leaf type

Family FAGACEAE	Species *Chrysolepis chrysophylla*	Author (W.J. Hooker) Hjelmqvist

GOLDEN CHINKAPIN

Leaves Oblong to lanceolate, to 10cm (4in) or more long and 2.5cm (1in) across, rigid, leathery, untoothed, glossy dark green above, hairy beneath. *Bark* Grey, furrowed. *Flowers* Males and females both creamy white, fragrant, in catkins to 4cm (1½in) long, separate but usually on the same spike in summer. *Fruit* A spiny husk, to 4cm (1½in) across, enclosing one to three edible, glossy brown nuts.
• NATIVE REGION W. United States.
• HABITAT Woods and thickets in coastal mountains.

leaves taper to very long, slender point

nuts inside densely prickly husk ripen in two years

leaf underside covered in golden hairs

Height 30m (100ft)	Shape Broadly conical	Leaf persistence Evergreen	Leaf type

Family FAGACEAE	Species *Fagus grandifolia*	Author Ehrhart

AMERICAN BEECH

Leaves Ovate to elliptic, to 12cm (4¾in) long and 6cm (2½in) across, taper-pointed, toothed, with 11 to 15 pairs of veins, silky-hairy becoming smooth or nearly so, glossy dark green above, paler beneath, turning yellow in autumn. ***Bark*** Grey, smooth. ***Flowers*** Males and females both small, males yellow, females green, in separate clusters on the same plant in mid-spring. ***Fruit*** A husk, to 2cm (¾in) long, enclosing one to three small, edible nuts.
• **NATIVE REGION** E. North America.
• **HABITAT** Rich woods.

• *leaves edged with sharp teeth*

up to 15 pairs of parallel • *veins*

glossy dark green • *leaf upperside*

bristly • *fruit husk matures from green to brown*

Height 25m (80ft)	Shape Broadly spreading	Leaf persistence Deciduous	Leaf type

Family FAGACEAE	Species *Fagus orientalis*	Author Lipsky

ORIENTAL BEECH

Leaves Elliptic to obovate, to 12cm (4¾in) long and 6cm (2½in) across, usually with a wavy margin, untoothed or slightly toothed, with up to 12 pairs of veins, dark green and smooth above, silky-hairy on the veins beneath, turning yellow in autumn. ***Bark*** Grey and smooth, sometimes furrowed. ***Flowers*** Males and females both small, males yellow, females green, in separate clusters on the same plant in mid-spring. ***Fruit*** A bristly husk, to 2.5cm (1in) long, enclosing one to three small, edible nuts.
• **NATIVE REGION** S.W. Asia, S.E. Europe.
• **HABITAT** Hills and mountains.

• *fruit husk splits open into four lobes*

leaves turn colour in • *autumn*

up to • *12 pairs of parallel veins*

wavy leaf • *margin may be untoothed or sparsely toothed*

Height 30m (100ft)	Shape Broadly spreading	Leaf persistence Deciduous	Leaf type

Family FAGACEAE	Species *Fagus sylvatica*	Author Linnaeus

COMMON BEECH

Leaves Ovate to obovate, to 10cm (4in) long and 6cm (2½in) across, abruptly short-pointed, with a wavy margin, untoothed or edged with small teeth, with fewer than ten pairs of veins, silky-hairy when unfolding becoming smooth, glossy dark green above, paler beneath, turning yellow in autumn. *Bark* Grey, smooth. *Flowers* Small, males yellow, females green, borne in separate clusters on the same plant in mid-spring as the young, pale green leaves emerge. *Fruit* A bristly husk, to 2.5cm (1in) long, enclosing one to three small, edible nuts.
• **NATIVE REGION** Europe.
• **HABITAT** Woods, particularly on chalk.

fruit husk covered in dense bristles •

◁ △ FAGUS SYLVATICA

• *wavy, untoothed or slightly toothed leaf margin*

no more than ten pairs of parallel veins •

▽ 'ASPLENIIFOLIA'
The slender leaves of the fern-leaved beech are deeply cut into long, narrow lobes.

• *leaves taper to long, fine point*

△ 'AUREA PENDULA'
This slender tree has hanging branches, clothed from spring to autumn with foliage that matures from golden yellow to green.

• *curiously contorted leaves*

'CRISTATA' ▷
Clustered and seemingly misshapen leaves are a feature of this very unusual form.

Height 40m (130ft)	Shape Broadly spreading	Leaf persistence Deciduous	Leaf type

- *short-pointed, glossy dark green leaves*

▽ 'DAWYCK PURPLE'
The copper beeches are charaterized by their deep red-purple foliage. 'Dawyck Purple', one such form, grows into a narrowly columnar tree. It is a seedling of 'Dawyck', which is similar, but has green foliage.

broad, taper-pointed leaves coloured very deep purple

unequal-sided • leaf base

△ 'PRINCE GEORGE OF CRETE'
This form is selected for its particularly large, broad leaves. Other forms with large leaves also occur. This group is known as *Fagus sylvatica* f. *latifolia*.

▷ 'ROTUNDIFOLIA'
The cultivar name of this distinct form describes the small, rounded leaves that characterize this tree. They are carried on strongly upswept branches.

rounded • leaves

deep red-purple • leaves tinged green

smaller leaves have fewer pairs of • parallel veins

leaf margin cut into • triangular teeth

◁ 'ROHANII'
This cultivar resembles the fern-leaved beech *(Fagus sylvatica* 'Aspleniifolia', see p.152). Its has somewhat broader leaves coloured greenish purple.

red leaf veins • and stalks

Family FAGACEAE	Species *Lithocarpus edulis*	Author (Makino) Nakai

LITHOCARPUS EDULIS

Leaves Narrowly elliptic, to 15cm (6in) long and 5cm (2in) across, gradually tapered from the centre of the leaf to the base, with a short, blunt point at the tip, untoothed, rigid and leathery, glossy pale green above, grey-green beneath, smooth. *Bark* Grey-brown, smooth. *Flowers* Males and females both very small and creamy white, in slender, upright catkins, males at the tip of the catkin, females at the base, in the leaf axils in late summer. *Fruit* A pointed acorn, to 2.5cm (1in) long, about one-third enclosed in a cup, in stalkless clusters, ripe in two years.
• **NATIVE REGION** Japan.
• **HABITAT** Woods.
• **REMARK** *Lithocarpus* species are closely related to the oaks *(Quercus,* see pp.158–173), but differ in their upright catkins.

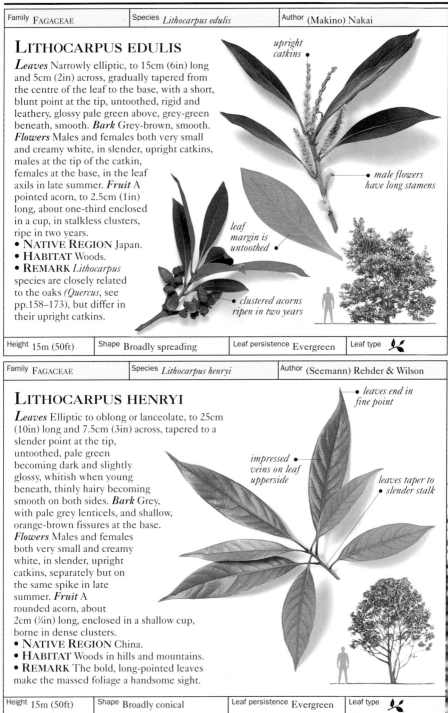

upright catkins

male flowers have long stamens

leaf margin is untoothed

clustered acorns ripen in two years

Height 15m (50ft)	Shape Broadly spreading	Leaf persistence Evergreen	Leaf type

Family FAGACEAE	Species *Lithocarpus henryi*	Author (Seemann) Rehder & Wilson

LITHOCARPUS HENRYI

Leaves Elliptic to oblong or lanceolate, to 25cm (10in) long and 7.5cm (3in) across, tapered to a slender point at the tip, untoothed, pale green becoming dark and slightly glossy, whitish when young beneath, thinly hairy becoming smooth on both sides. *Bark* Grey, with pale grey lenticels, and shallow, orange-brown fissures at the base. *Flowers* Males and females both very small and creamy white, in slender, upright catkins, separately but on the same spike in late summer. *Fruit* A rounded acorn, about 2cm (¾in) long, enclosed in a shallow cup, borne in dense clusters.
• **NATIVE REGION** China.
• **HABITAT** Woods in hills and mountains.
• **REMARK** The bold, long-pointed leaves make the massed foliage a handsome sight.

leaves end in fine point

impressed veins on leaf upperside

leaves taper to slender stalk

Height 15m (50ft)	Shape Broadly conical	Leaf persistence Evergreen	Leaf type

Family FAGACEAE	Species *Nothofagus antarctica*	Author (J.G. Forster) Oersted

ANTARCTIC BEECH

Leaves Ovate, to 3cm (1¼in) long and 2cm (¾in) across, finely toothed, with usually four pairs of veins, glossy dark green above, more or less smooth on both sides. **Bark** Dark grey, cracking into plates and flaking with age. **Flowers** Males and females both very small, males with red anthers, in clusters of one to three, females with red stigmas, in clusters of two to three, in the leaf axils in late spring. **Fruit** A smooth husk, to 6mm (¼in) long, enclosing three small nuts.
• **NATIVE REGION** S. Argentina. S. Chile.
• **HABITAT** Deciduous woods and scrub in mountains.
• **REMARK** Also known as nirre. In its native region and habitat, the species is usually a medium-sized tree, but it can also form a large shrub.

• *usually four pairs of parallel veins*

leaf margin edged with numerous • *fine teeth*

husked • *fruits in short clusters*

Height 15m (50ft)	Shape Broadly columnar	Leaf persistence Deciduous	Leaf type

Family FAGACEAE	Species *Nothofagus betuloides*	Author (Mirbel) Blume

NOTHOFAGUS BETULOIDES

Leaves Ovate to elliptic, to 2.5cm (1in) long and 2cm (¾in) across, broadly tapered to the often unequal base, bluntly toothed, glossy dark blackish green above, paler and glossy with a fine network of veins beneath, smooth on both sides; older leaves often with small, dark spots beneath. **Bark** Very dark grey, cracking into plates and flaking with age. **Flowers** Males and females both very small, males with red anthers, singly, females with red stigmas, in clusters of three, in the leaf axils in late spring. **Fruit** A bristly husk, to 6mm (¼in) long, enclosing three small nuts.
• **NATIVE REGION** Argentina, Chile.
• **HABITAT** Evergreen forests.
• **REMARK** Sometimes shrubby.

• *fine network of veins on paler leaf underside*

leaf margin edged with many blunt teeth •

• *young shoots have small red stipules*

Height 25m (80ft)	Shape Broadly columnar	Leaf persistence Evergreen	Leaf type

Family FAGACEAE	Species *Nothofagus dombeyi*	Author (Mirbel) Blume

NOTHOFAGUS DOMBEYI

Leaves Narrowly ovate, to 4cm (1½in) long and 1.5cm (⅝in) across, rounded at the often unequal base, finely and sharply toothed, glossy dark green above, paler and glossy with a fine network of veins beneath, smooth, with small, black spots. ***Bark*** Dark grey, cracking into plates and flaking with age. ***Flowers*** Males and females both very small, males with red anthers, in clusters of three, females with red stigmas, in clusters of three, in the leaf axils in late spring. ***Fruit*** A bristly husk, to 6mm (¼in) long, enclosing three small nuts.
• **NATIVE REGION**
Argentina, Chile.
• **HABITAT**
Mountain forests.
• **REMARK** This species is similar to *Nothofagus betuloides* (see p.155), but differs in its larger leaves and taller growing habit.

tiny fruit husks split open when ripe

lightly impressed veins

leaf margin edged with fine, sharp teeth

Height 40m (130ft)	Shape Broadly columnar	Leaf persistence Evergreen	Leaf type

Family FAGACEAE	Species *Nothofagus nervosa*	Author (Poeppig & Endlicher) Oersted

RAULI

Leaves Oblong, to 10cm (4in) long and 4cm (1½in) across, finely toothed, with 15 to 18 pairs of veins, bronze becoming matt deep green above, hairy on both sides, turning yellow in autumn. ***Bark*** Dark grey, fissured with age. ***Flowers*** Very small, greenish, males singly, females in clusters of three, in the leaf axils in late spring. ***Fruit*** A bristly husk, to 1cm (⅜in) long, enclosing three small nuts.
• **NATIVE REGION**
Argentina, Chile.
• **HABITAT** Forests.
• **REMARK** Also known as *Nothofagus procera*.

regularly spaced, fine teeth at leaf margin

dark green mature leaves

bronzy young leaves

between 15 and 18 pairs of prominent veins

hairy leaf underside

Height 25m (80ft)	Shape Broadly conical	Leaf persistence Deciduous	Leaf type

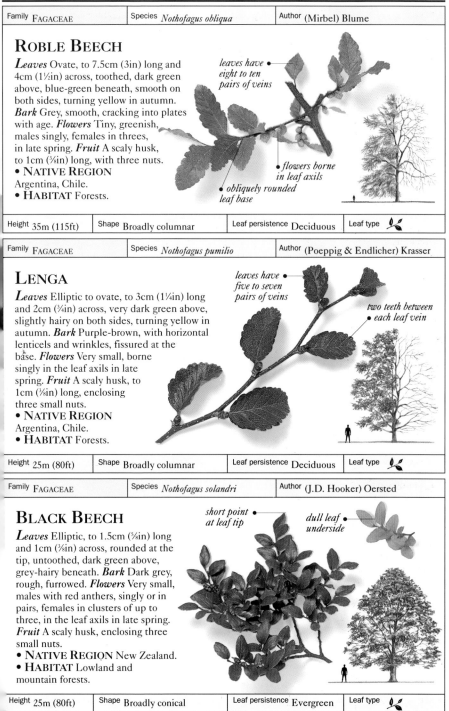

| Family FAGACEAE | Species *Nothofagus obliqua* | Author (Mirbel) Blume |

ROBLE BEECH

Leaves Ovate, to 7.5cm (3in) long and 4cm (1½in) across, toothed, dark green above, blue-green beneath, smooth on both sides, turning yellow in autumn. **Bark** Grey, smooth, cracking into plates with age. **Flowers** Tiny, greenish, males singly, females in threes, in late spring. **Fruit** A scaly husk, to 1cm (⅜in) long, with three nuts.
• **NATIVE REGION** Argentina, Chile.
• **HABITAT** Forests.

leaves have • eight to ten pairs of veins

flowers borne in leaf axils

obliquely rounded leaf base

| Height 35m (115ft) | Shape Broadly columnar | Leaf persistence Deciduous | Leaf type |

| Family FAGACEAE | Species *Nothofagus pumilio* | Author (Poeppig & Endlicher) Krasser |

LENGA

Leaves Elliptic to ovate, to 3cm (1¼in) long and 2cm (¾in) across, very dark green above, slightly hairy on both sides, turning yellow in autumn. **Bark** Purple-brown, with horizontal lenticels and wrinkles, fissured at the base. **Flowers** Very small, borne singly in the leaf axils in late spring. **Fruit** A scaly husk, to 1cm (⅜in) long, enclosing three small nuts.
• **NATIVE REGION** Argentina, Chile.
• **HABITAT** Forests.

leaves have • five to seven pairs of veins

two teeth between • each leaf vein

| Height 25m (80ft) | Shape Broadly columnar | Leaf persistence Deciduous | Leaf type |

| Family FAGACEAE | Species *Nothofagus solandri* | Author (J.D. Hooker) Oersted |

BLACK BEECH

Leaves Elliptic, to 1.5cm (⅝in) long and 1cm (⅜in) across, rounded at the tip, untoothed, dark green above, grey-hairy beneath. **Bark** Dark grey, rough, furrowed. **Flowers** Very small, males with red anthers, singly or in pairs, females in clusters of up to three, in the leaf axils in late spring. **Fruit** A scaly husk, enclosing three small nuts.
• **NATIVE REGION** New Zealand.
• **HABITAT** Lowland and mountain forests.

short point • at leaf tip

dull leaf • underside

| Height 25m (80ft) | Shape Broadly conical | Leaf persistence Evergreen | Leaf type |

Family FAGACEAE	Species *Quercus acutissima*	Author Carruthers

QUERCUS ACUTISSIMA

Leaves Oblong, to 20cm (8in) long and 6cm (2½in) across, with numerous veins ending in slender-tipped teeth, glossy green above, paler beneath, smooth on both sides. *Bark* Grey-brown, with deep fissures. *Flowers* Males in yellow-green, drooping catkins, females inconspicuous, separately on the same plant in late spring. *Fruit* A rounded acorn, to 2.5cm (1in) long, about two-thirds enclosed in a cup.
• **NATIVE REGION**
Himalayas to Japan.
• **HABITAT** Woods.

acorn cup loosely covered with long, slender scales •

• *leaves edged with bristle-like teeth*

Height 15m (50ft)	Shape Broadly spreading	Leaf persistence Deciduous	Leaf type

Family FAGACEAE	Species *Quercus alba*	Author Linnaeus

WHITE OAK

Leaves Obovate, to 20cm (8in) long and 10cm (4in) across, tapered at the base, deeply cut into two to four lobes on each side, pink-tinged and white-hairy becoming bright green above, blue-green beneath, turning purple-red in autumn. *Bark* Pale grey and scaly, fissured with age. *Flowers* Males in yellow-green, drooping catkins, females inconspicuous, borne separately on the same plant in late spring. *Fruit* An acorn, to 2.5cm (1in) long, one-quarter enclosed in a roughened cup.
• **NATIVE REGION** E. North America.
• **HABITAT** Dry woods.
• **REMARK** In the USA, the State tree of Connecticut, Illinois, and Maryland.

rough-textured, scaly acorn cup •

untoothed • *leaf lobes*

• *leaves colour brilliantly in autumn*

Height 35m (115ft)	Shape Broadly spreading	Leaf persistence Deciduous	Leaf type

Family FAGACEAE	Species *Quercus alnifolia*	Author Poech

GOLDEN OAK OF CYPRUS

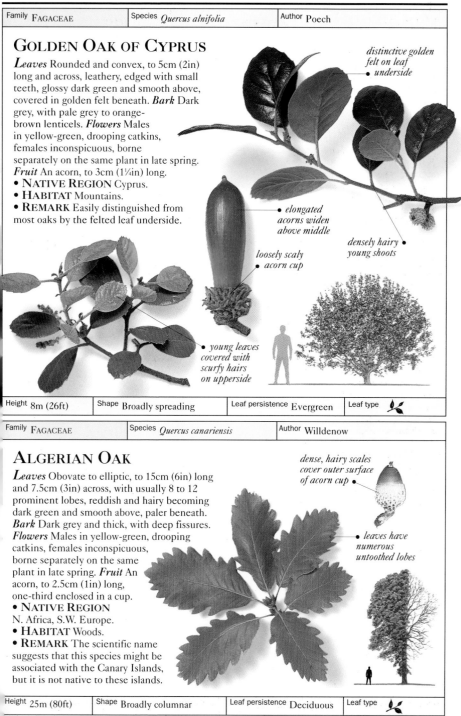

Leaves Rounded and convex, to 5cm (2in) long and across, leathery, edged with small teeth, glossy dark green and smooth above, covered in golden felt beneath. **Bark** Dark grey, with pale grey to orange-brown lenticels. **Flowers** Males in yellow-green, drooping catkins, females inconspicuous, borne separately on the same plant in late spring. **Fruit** An acorn, to 3cm (1¼in) long.
• **NATIVE REGION** Cyprus.
• **HABITAT** Mountains.
• **REMARK** Easily distinguished from most oaks by the felted leaf underside.

distinctive golden felt on leaf underside

elongated acorns widen above middle

densely hairy young shoots

loosely scaly acorn cup

young leaves covered with scurfy hairs on upperside

Height 8m (26ft)	Shape Broadly spreading	Leaf persistence Evergreen	Leaf type

Family FAGACEAE	Species *Quercus canariensis*	Author Willdenow

ALGERIAN OAK

Leaves Obovate to elliptic, to 15cm (6in) long and 7.5cm (3in) across, with usually 8 to 12 prominent lobes, reddish and hairy becoming dark green and smooth above, paler beneath. **Bark** Dark grey and thick, with deep fissures. **Flowers** Males in yellow-green, drooping catkins, females inconspicuous, borne separately on the same plant in late spring. **Fruit** An acorn, to 2.5cm (1in) long, one-third enclosed in a cup.
• **NATIVE REGION** N. Africa, S.W. Europe.
• **HABITAT** Woods.
• **REMARK** The scientific name suggests that this species might be associated with the Canary Islands, but it is not native to these islands.

dense, hairy scales cover outer surface of acorn cup

leaves have numerous untoothed lobes

Height 25m (80ft)	Shape Broadly columnar	Leaf persistence Deciduous	Leaf type

Family FAGACEAE	Species *Quercus castaneifolia*	Author C.A. Meyer

CHESTNUT-LEAVED OAK

Leaves Oblong, to 20cm (8in) long and
7.5cm (3in) across, with 10 to 12 teeth on
each side, glossy dark green and smooth
above, blue-grey and thinly hairy beneath.
Bark Grey and smooth.
Flowers Males in yellow-
green, drooping catkins,
females inconspicuous, borne
separately on the same plant in
late spring. *Fruit* An acorn, to
2.5cm (1in) long, one-half
enclosed in a cup, the cup
covered in long scales.
• NATIVE REGION
Caucasus, N. Iran.
• HABITAT Forests.

*veins end in
triangular teeth •*

*• leaf
underside*

*• glossy
upper
leaf
surface*

Height 30m (100ft)	Shape Broadly spreading	Leaf persistence Deciduous	Leaf type 🍂

Family FAGACEAE	Species *Quercus cerris*	Author Linnaeus

TURKEY OAK

Leaves Elliptic to oblong, to 12cm (4¾in) long
and 7.5cm (3in) across, deeply lobed, toothed,
glossy dark green above, downy when young
becoming smooth beneath. *Bark* Dark grey-
brown, thick, rough, and deeply ridged.
Flowers Males in yellow-green, drooping
catkins, females inconspicuous, borne
separately on the same plant in early
summer. *Fruit* An acorn, to
2.5cm (1in) long, one-half
enclosed in a cup, the cup
covered in long, slender scales.
• NATIVE REGION
C. and S. Europe.
• HABITAT Woods.

*variable
leaf lobing •*

*slender
stipules
clustered
around
leaf bud •*

QUERCUS CERRIS

*strikingly
variegated,
ornamental
foliage •*

'VARIEGATA' ▷
The leaves of
this form are
margined yellow
when they unfold,
and creamy white
as they mature.

Height 35m (115ft)	Shape Broadly spreading	Leaf persistence Deciduous	Leaf type 🍂

Family FAGACEAE	Species *Quercus coccinea*	Author Münchhausen

SCARLET OAK

Leaves Elliptic, to 15cm (6in) long and 10cm (4in) across, deeply lobed, toothed, glossy dark green and smooth above, paler and glossy with small tufts of hairs in the vein axils beneath, turning bright red in autumn. **Bark** Dark grey-brown, smooth, shallowly ridged with age. **Flowers** Males in yellow-green, drooping catkins, females inconspicuous, separately on the same plant in late spring. **Fruit** An acorn, to 2.5cm (1in) long, up to one-half enclosed in a glossy cup.
• **NATIVE REGION** E. North America.
• **HABITAT** Woods and sandy soil.

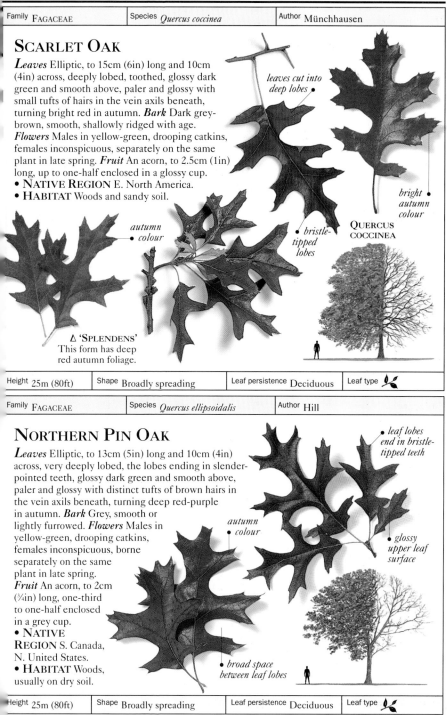

leaves cut into deep lobes

bright autumn colour

autumn colour

bristle-tipped lobes

QUERCUS COCCINEA

△ 'SPLENDENS'
This form has deep red autumn foliage.

Height 25m (80ft)	Shape Broadly spreading	Leaf persistence Deciduous	Leaf type

Family FAGACEAE	Species *Quercus ellipsoidalis*	Author Hill

NORTHERN PIN OAK

Leaves Elliptic, to 13cm (5in) long and 10cm (4in) across, very deeply lobed, the lobes ending in slender-pointed teeth, glossy dark green and smooth above, paler and glossy with distinct tufts of brown hairs in the vein axils beneath, turning deep red-purple in autumn. **Bark** Grey, smooth or lightly furrowed. **Flowers** Males in yellow-green, drooping catkins, females inconspicuous, borne separately on the same plant in late spring. **Fruit** An acorn, to 2cm (¾in) long, one-third to one-half enclosed in a grey cup.
• **NATIVE REGION** S. Canada, N. United States.
• **HABITAT** Woods, usually on dry soil.

leaf lobes end in bristle-tipped teeth

autumn colour

glossy upper leaf surface

broad space between leaf lobes

Height 25m (80ft)	Shape Broadly spreading	Leaf persistence Deciduous	Leaf type

Family FAGACEAE	Species *Quercus falcata*	Author Michaux

SPANISH OAK

Leaves Elliptic to ovate, to 20cm (8in) long and 15cm (6in) across, deeply cut into bristle-tipped lobes, the terminal lobe often long and narrow, glossy dark green and smooth above, covered in brown or greyish hairs beneath. **Bark** Dark grey-brown, fissured into narrow ridges. **Flowers** Males in yellow-green, drooping catkins, females inconspicuous, borne separately on the same plant in late spring. **Fruit** An acorn, to 2cm (¾in) long, one-third to one-half enclosed in a broad, shallow cup.
• **NATIVE REGION** S.E. United States.
• **HABITAT** Dry woods from coast to mountains.

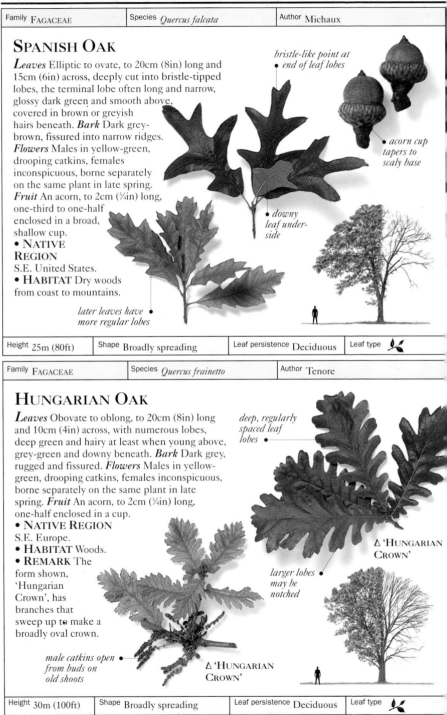

bristle-like point at • end of leaf lobes

• acorn cup tapers to scaly base

• downy leaf underside

later leaves have • more regular lobes

Height 25m (80ft)	Shape Broadly spreading	Leaf persistence Deciduous	Leaf type

Family FAGACEAE	Species *Quercus frainetto*	Author Tenore

HUNGARIAN OAK

Leaves Obovate to oblong, to 20cm (8in) long and 10cm (4in) across, with numerous lobes, deep green and hairy at least when young above, grey-green and downy beneath. **Bark** Dark grey, rugged and fissured. **Flowers** Males in yellow-green, drooping catkins, females inconspicuous, borne separately on the same plant in late spring. **Fruit** An acorn, to 2cm (¾in) long, one-half enclosed in a cup.
• **NATIVE REGION** S.E. Europe.
• **HABITAT** Woods.
• **REMARK** The form shown, 'Hungarian Crown', has branches that sweep up to make a broadly oval crown.

deep, regularly spaced leaf lobes •

△ 'HUNGARIAN CROWN'

larger lobes • may be notched

male catkins open • from buds on old shoots

△ 'HUNGARIAN CROWN'

Height 30m (100ft)	Shape Broadly spreading	Leaf persistence Deciduous	Leaf type

| Family FAGACEAE | Species *Quercus x hispanica* | Author Lamarck |

QUERCUS X HISPANICA

'LUCOMBEANA'

Leaves Ovate to elliptic or oblong,
to 13cm (5in) long and 5cm (2in)
across, toothed, glossy dark
green above, grey and downy
beneath. **Bark** Grey, corky.
Flowers Males in yellow-green,
drooping catkins, females
inconspicuous, separately
on the same plant in late
spring. **Fruit** An acorn, to
2.5cm (1in) long, about one-
third enclosed in a cup.
• **NATIVE REGION** S.W. Europe.
• **HABITAT** Woods, usually with both parents.
• **REMARK** A hybrid between turkey oak
(Q. cerris, see p.160) and cork oak *(Q. suber, see
p.172).* 'Lucombeana' is the most familiar form.

downy under-side

glossy upper surface

| Height 30m (100ft) | Shape Broadly spreading | Leaf persistence Deciduous | Leaf type |

| Family FAGACEAE | Species *Quercus ilex* | Author Linnaeus |

HOLM OAK

Leaves Elliptic to narrowly ovate, to 7.5cm
(3in) long and 5cm (2in) across, rigid and
leathery, taper-pointed, untoothed or with few
small teeth, white-hairy when young
becoming glossy dark green above, grey
and hairy beneath; on young plants,
variable in shape, with a spiny margin.
Bark Nearly black, rough, cracking into
small squares. **Flowers** Males in yellow,
drooping catkins, females inconspicuous,
separately on the same plant in early summer.
Fruit An acorn, to 2cm (¾in) long, one-third
enclosed in a cup.
• **NATIVE REGION** Mediterranean.
• **HABITAT** Hills, woods,
scrub, and dry places.

hairy young leaves

white-hairy young shoots

tiny, pointed acorns

male catkins open on young shoots

upper leaf surface becomes smooth

hairy leaf underside

| Height 30m (100ft) | Shape Broadly spreading | Leaf persistence Evergreen | Leaf type |

| Family FAGACEAE | Species *Quercus imbricaria* | Author A. Michaux |

SHINGLE OAK

Leaves Oblong to lanceolate, to 15cm (6in) long and 7.5cm (3in) across, ending in a fine point, untoothed, yellow when young becoming glossy dark green and smooth above, grey-hairy beneath, often persisting far into winter. *Bark* Grey-brown, smooth at first becoming fissured with age. *Flowers* Males in yellow-green, drooping catkins, females inconspicuous, borne separately on the same plant in early summer. *Fruit* An acorn, to 2cm (¾in) long, one-third to one-half enclosed in a cup, the cup covered in broad, hairy scales.
• **NATIVE REGION** C. and E. United States.
• **HABITAT** Rich woods and riverbanks.
• **REMARK** Early settlers made roof shingles from the wood, giving this species its common name.

untoothed leaves end in small, bristle-like tip

overlapping scales cover outer surface of acorn cup

| Height 25m (80ft) | Shape Broadly spreading | Leaf persistence Deciduous | Leaf type |

| Family FAGACEAE | Species *Quercus laurifolia* | Author A. Michaux |

LAUREL OAK

Leaves Oblanceolate to oblong, to 10cm (4in) long and 4cm (1½in) across, sometimes shallowly lobed, untoothed, glossy green, smooth on both sides. *Bark* Grey and scaly. *Flowers* Males in yellow-green, drooping catkins, females inconspicuous, borne separately on the same plant in early summer. *Fruit* An acorn, to 1.5cm (⅝in) long, one-third enclosed in a cup.
• **NATIVE REGION** S.E. United States.
• **HABITAT** Woods, sandy soil, and swamp margins on the coastal plain.
• **REMARK** Also known as Darlington oak. The leaves look rather like those of the bay laurel (*Laurus nobilis*, see p.188). They persist through autumn into winter, giving the tree a semi-evergreen appearance.

shallowly lobed leaves may appear almost unlobed

acorns are nearly rounded in shape

tapered leaf base

| Height 20m (65ft) | Shape Broadly conical | Leaf persistence Deciduous | Leaf type |

Family FAGACEAE	Species *Quercus macranthera*	Author Fischer & C.A. Meyer

QUERCUS MACRANTHERA

Leaves Obovate, to 15cm (6in) long and 10cm (4in) across, with 6 to 11 rounded lobes on each side, dark green above, paler and hairy beneath, carried on stout, densely hairy shoots. *Bark* Grey-brown, thick and fissured. *Flowers* Males in yellow-green, drooping catkins, females inconspicuous, borne separately on the same plant in early summer. *Fruit* An acorn, to 2.5cm (1in) long, one-half enclosed in a cup, the cup covered in hairy scales.
• **NATIVE REGION** Caucasus, N. Iran.
• **HABITAT** Forests on dry mountain slopes.

hairy scales pressed close to outer surface of acorn cup

leaves divided into 6 to 11 lobes on each side

lobes become smaller towards tip of leaf

Height 20m (65ft)	Shape Broadly spreading	Leaf persistence Deciduous	Leaf type

Family FAGACEAE	Species *Quercus macrocarpa*	Author A. Michaux

BURR OAK

Leaves Obovate, to 25cm (10in) long and 12cm (4¾in) across, deeply cut into round-ended lobes, with a distinct, broad sinus towards the base, glossy green and smooth above, paler and hairy beneath. *Bark* Grey, rough and deeply furrowed. *Flowers* Males in yellow, drooping catkins, females inconspicuous, borne separately on the same plant in early summer. *Fruit* An acorn, to 5cm (2in) long, one-half or more enclosed in a cup, the cup rimmed with a fringe of scales.
• **NATIVE REGION** E. North America.
• **HABITAT** Rich woods.
• **REMARK** Also known as blue oak, mossy cup oak. The acorns are larger than those of any other North American oak.

shallower lobes between middle and tip of leaf

wide space between lobes towards base of leaf

Height 40m (130ft)	Shape Broadly spreading	Leaf persistence Deciduous	Leaf type

Family FAGACEAE	Species *Quercus marilandica*	Author Münchhausen

BLACK JACK OAK

Leaves Triangular-obovate, to 25cm (10in) long and nearly the same across at the tip, tapered at the base, usually with three bristle-pointed lobes at the tip, glossy dark green above, paler beneath, thinly hairy becoming nearly smooth on both sides. **Bark** Blackish, cracking into small, square plates. **Flowers** Males in yellow-green, drooping catkins, females inconspicuous, borne separately on the same plant in early summer. **Fruit** An acorn, to 2cm (¾in) long, about one-half enclosed in a cup.
• **NATIVE REGION** E. United States.
• **HABITAT** Woods and poor, often sandy, soil.

deep acorn cup covered in broad, hairy scales •

• lobes end in slender bristles

broad, three-lobed • leaf tip

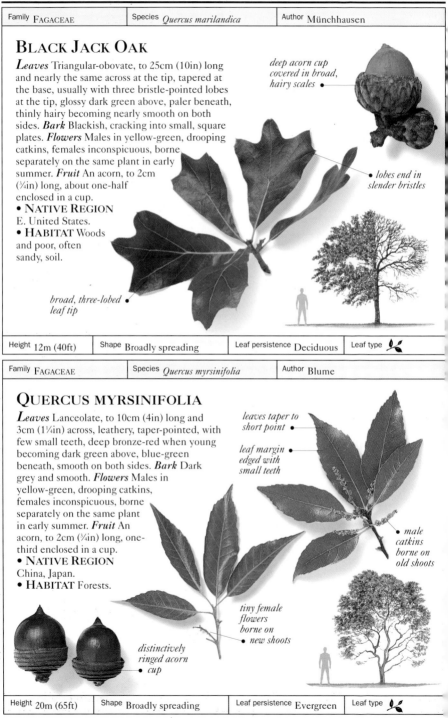

Height 12m (40ft)	Shape Broadly spreading	Leaf persistence Deciduous	Leaf type

Family FAGACEAE	Species *Quercus myrsinifolia*	Author Blume

QUERCUS MYRSINIFOLIA

Leaves Lanceolate, to 10cm (4in) long and 3cm (1¼in) across, leathery, taper-pointed, with few small teeth, deep bronze-red when young becoming dark green above, blue-green beneath, smooth on both sides. **Bark** Dark grey and smooth. **Flowers** Males in yellow-green, drooping catkins, females inconspicuous, borne separately on the same plant in early summer. **Fruit** An acorn, to 2cm (¾in) long, one-third enclosed in a cup.
• **NATIVE REGION** China, Japan.
• **HABITAT** Forests.

leaves taper to short point •

leaf margin • edged with small teeth

• male catkins borne on old shoots

tiny female flowers borne on • new shoots

distinctively ringed acorn • cup

Height 20m (65ft)	Shape Broadly spreading	Leaf persistence Evergreen	Leaf type

| Family FAGACEAE | Species *Quercus palustris* | Author Münchhausen |

PIN OAK

Leaves Elliptic to obovate, to 15cm (6in) long and 12cm (4¾in) across, deeply lobed, glossy green on both sides, paler with tufts of brown hairs in the vein axils beneath. ***Bark*** Grey-brown, smooth. ***Flowers*** Males in yellow-green, drooping catkins, females inconspicuous, borne separately on the same plant in late spring. ***Fruit*** An acorn, to 1.5cm (⅝in) long, one-quarter to one-third enclosed in a broad cup.
• **NATIVE REGION** S.E. Canada, E. United States.
• **HABITAT** Swampy woods.

hairy tufts in vein axils on underside of leaves

bristle-tipped teeth at end of leaf lobes

shallow, saucer-like acorn cup

| Height 30m (100ft) | Shape Broadly conical | Leaf persistence Deciduous | Leaf type |

| Family FAGACEAE | Species *Quercus petraea* | Author (Mattuschka) Lieblein |

SESSILE OAK

Leaves Elliptic, to 12cm (4¾in) long and 7.5cm (3in) across, with rounded lobes, usually tapered at the base, without auricles, slightly glossy dark green and smooth above, paler and thinly hairy beneath, the stalk to 1cm (⅜in) or more long. ***Bark*** Grey, with vertical ridges. ***Flowers*** Males in yellow-green, drooping catkins, females inconspicuous, borne separately on the same plant in late spring. ***Fruit*** An acorn, to 3cm (1¼in) long, about one-third enclosed in a cup.
• **NATIVE REGION** Europe.
• **HABITAT** Woods.
• **REMARK** Also known as durmast oak.

rounded, untoothed leaf lobes

yellow-green leaf stalk

unstalked or very short-stalked acorns

small scales pressed close to acorn cup

| Height 40m (130ft) | Shape Broadly spreading | Leaf persistence Deciduous | Leaf type |

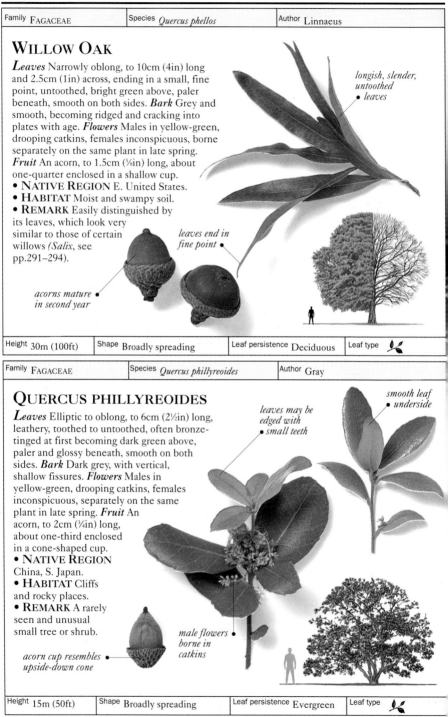

Family FAGACEAE	Species *Quercus phellos*	Author Linnaeus

WILLOW OAK

Leaves Narrowly oblong, to 10cm (4in) long and 2.5cm (1in) across, ending in a small, fine point, untoothed, bright green above, paler beneath, smooth on both sides. **Bark** Grey and smooth, becoming ridged and cracking into plates with age. **Flowers** Males in yellow-green, drooping catkins, females inconspicuous, borne separately on the same plant in late spring. **Fruit** An acorn, to 1.5cm (⅝in) long, about one-quarter enclosed in a shallow cup.
• **NATIVE REGION** E. United States.
• **HABITAT** Moist and swampy soil.
• **REMARK** Easily distinguished by its leaves, which look very similar to those of certain willows *(Salix,* see pp.291–294).

longish, slender, untoothed • leaves

leaves end in fine point •

acorns mature • in second year

Height 30m (100ft)	Shape Broadly spreading	Leaf persistence Deciduous	Leaf type

Family FAGACEAE	Species *Quercus phillyreoides*	Author Gray

QUERCUS PHILLYREOIDES

Leaves Elliptic to oblong, to 6cm (2½in) long, leathery, toothed to untoothed, often bronze-tinged at first becoming dark green above, paler and glossy beneath, smooth on both sides. **Bark** Dark grey, with vertical, shallow fissures. **Flowers** Males in yellow-green, drooping catkins, females inconspicuous, separately on the same plant in late spring. **Fruit** An acorn, to 2cm (¾in) long, about one-third enclosed in a cone-shaped cup.
• **NATIVE REGION** China, S. Japan.
• **HABITAT** Cliffs and rocky places.
• **REMARK** A rarely seen and unusual small tree or shrub.

smooth leaf • underside

leaves may be edged with • small teeth

acorn cup resembles • upside-down cone

male flowers • borne in catkins

Height 15m (50ft)	Shape Broadly spreading	Leaf persistence Evergreen	Leaf type

Family FAGACEAE	Species *Quercus pontica*	Author K. Koch

ARMENIAN OAK

Leaves Obovate to broadly elliptic, to 15cm (6in) long and 10cm (4in) across, tapered at the base, the numerous parallel veins ending in small, pointed teeth, hairy when young becoming bright green and smooth above, blue-green beneath, turning yellow-brown in autumn, carried on stout shoots. *Bark* Grey to purple-brown and thinly scaly, becoming rugged with age. *Flowers* Males in yellow-green, long, slender, drooping catkins, females inconspicuous, borne separately on the same plant in late spring. *Fruit* An acorn, to 2cm (¾in) long, one-half enclosed in a cup.
• **NATIVE REGION** Caucasus, N.E. Turkey.
• **HABITAT** Mountain woods.
• **REMARK** This species can be either a very small tree or a bushy shrub.

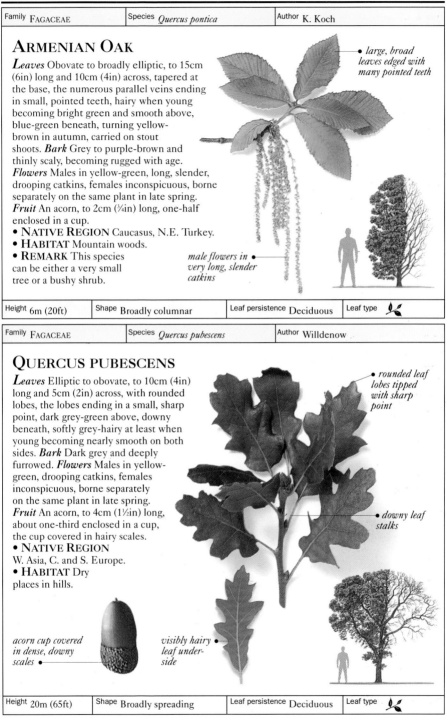

• *large, broad leaves edged with many pointed teeth*

male flowers in very long, slender catkins •

Height 6m (20ft)	Shape Broadly columnar	Leaf persistence Deciduous	Leaf type

Family FAGACEAE	Species *Quercus pubescens*	Author Willdenow

QUERCUS PUBESCENS

Leaves Elliptic to obovate, to 10cm (4in) long and 5cm (2in) across, with rounded lobes, the lobes ending in a small, sharp point, dark grey-green above, downy beneath, softly grey-hairy at least when young becoming nearly smooth on both sides. *Bark* Dark grey and deeply furrowed. *Flowers* Males in yellow-green, drooping catkins, females inconspicuous, borne separately on the same plant in late spring. *Fruit* An acorn, to 4cm (1½in) long, about one-third enclosed in a cup, the cup covered in hairy scales.
• **NATIVE REGION** W. Asia, C. and S. Europe.
• **HABITAT** Dry places in hills.

• *rounded leaf lobes tipped with sharp point*

• *downy leaf stalks*

acorn cup covered in dense, downy scales •

visibly hairy leaf underside •

Height 20m (65ft)	Shape Broadly spreading	Leaf persistence Deciduous	Leaf type

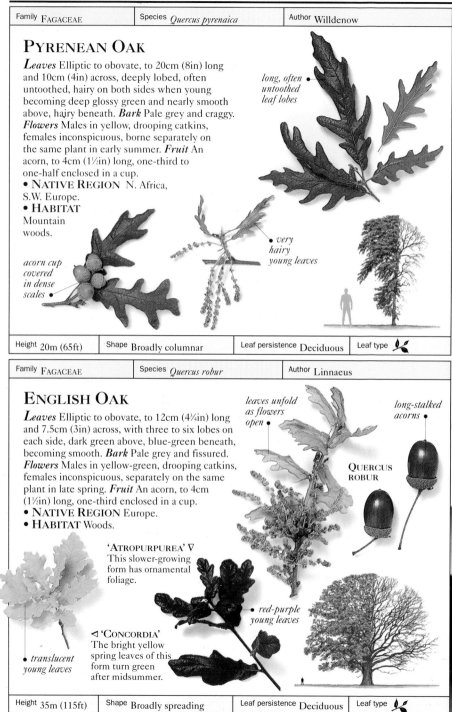

Family FAGACEAE	Species *Quercus pyrenaica*	Author Willdenow

PYRENEAN OAK

Leaves Elliptic to obovate, to 20cm (8in) long and 10cm (4in) across, deeply lobed, often untoothed, hairy on both sides when young becoming deep glossy green and nearly smooth above, hairy beneath. **Bark** Pale grey and craggy. **Flowers** Males in yellow, drooping catkins, females inconspicuous, borne separately on the same plant in early summer. **Fruit** An acorn, to 4cm (1½in) long, one-third to one-half enclosed in a cup.
• NATIVE REGION N. Africa, S.W. Europe.
• HABITAT Mountain woods.

long, often untoothed leaf lobes

very hairy young leaves

acorn cup covered in dense scales •

Height 20m (65ft)	Shape Broadly columnar	Leaf persistence Deciduous	Leaf type

Family FAGACEAE	Species *Quercus robur*	Author Linnaeus

ENGLISH OAK

Leaves Elliptic to obovate, to 12cm (4¾in) long and 7.5cm (3in) across, with three to six lobes on each side, dark green above, blue-green beneath, becoming smooth. **Bark** Pale grey and fissured. **Flowers** Males in yellow-green, drooping catkins, females inconspicuous, separately on the same plant in late spring. **Fruit** An acorn, to 4cm (1½in) long, one-third enclosed in a cup.
• NATIVE REGION Europe.
• HABITAT Woods.

leaves unfold as flowers open •

long-stalked acorns •

QUERCUS ROBUR

'ATROPURPUREA' ▽
This slower-growing form has ornamental foliage.

red-purple young leaves

◁ 'CONCORDIA'
The bright yellow spring leaves of this form turn green after midsummer.

• translucent young leaves

Height 35m (115ft)	Shape Broadly spreading	Leaf persistence Deciduous	Leaf type

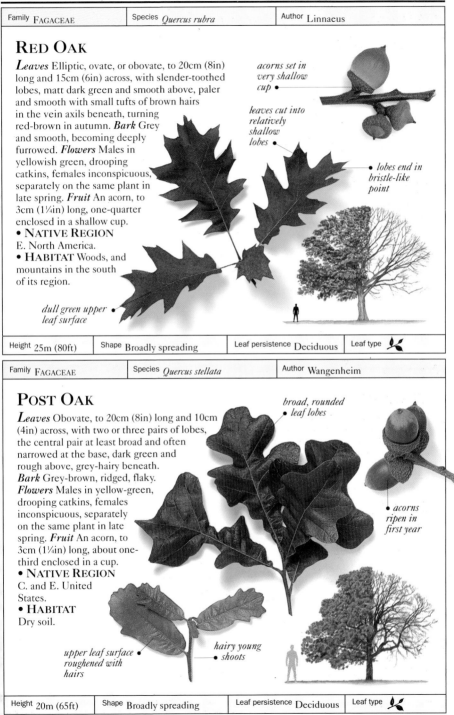

| Family FAGACEAE | Species *Quercus rubra* | Author Linnaeus |

RED OAK

Leaves Elliptic, ovate, or obovate, to 20cm (8in) long and 15cm (6in) across, with slender-toothed lobes, matt dark green and smooth above, paler and smooth with small tufts of brown hairs in the vein axils beneath, turning red-brown in autumn. *Bark* Grey and smooth, becoming deeply furrowed. *Flowers* Males in yellowish green, drooping catkins, females inconspicuous, separately on the same plant in late spring. *Fruit* An acorn, to 3cm (1¼in) long, one-quarter enclosed in a shallow cup.
• **NATIVE REGION** E. North America.
• **HABITAT** Woods, and mountains in the south of its region.

acorns set in very shallow cup

leaves cut into relatively shallow lobes

lobes end in bristle-like point

dull green upper leaf surface

| Height 25m (80ft) | Shape Broadly spreading | Leaf persistence Deciduous | Leaf type |

| Family FAGACEAE | Species *Quercus stellata* | Author Wangenheim |

POST OAK

Leaves Obovate, to 20cm (8in) long and 10cm (4in) across, with two or three pairs of lobes, the central pair at least broad and often narrowed at the base, dark green and rough above, grey-hairy beneath. *Bark* Grey-brown, ridged, flaky. *Flowers* Males in yellow-green, drooping catkins, females inconspicuous, separately on the same plant in late spring. *Fruit* An acorn, to 3cm (1¼in) long, about one-third enclosed in a cup.
• **NATIVE REGION** C. and E. United States.
• **HABITAT** Dry soil.

broad, rounded leaf lobes

acorns ripen in first year

upper leaf surface roughened with hairs

hairy young shoots

| Height 20m (65ft) | Shape Broadly spreading | Leaf persistence Deciduous | Leaf type |

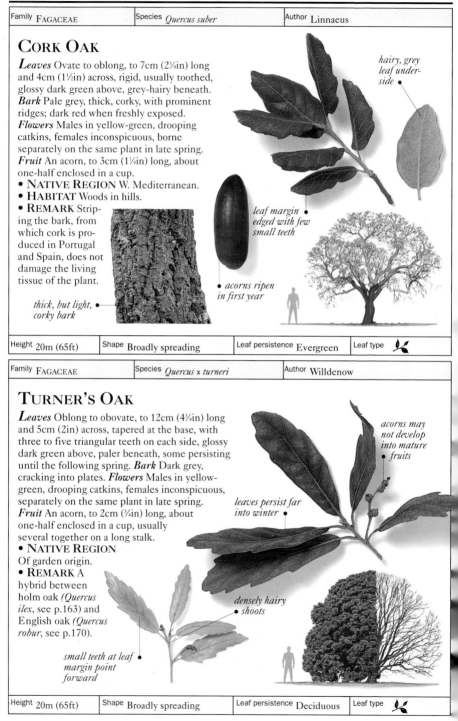

Family FAGACEAE	Species *Quercus suber*	Author Linnaeus

CORK OAK

Leaves Ovate to oblong, to 7cm (2¾in) long and 4cm (1½in) across, rigid, usually toothed, glossy dark green above, grey-hairy beneath. *Bark* Pale grey, thick, corky, with prominent ridges; dark red when freshly exposed. *Flowers* Males in yellow-green, drooping catkins, females inconspicuous, borne separately on the same plant in late spring. *Fruit* An acorn, to 3cm (1¼in) long, about one-half enclosed in a cup.
• **NATIVE REGION** W. Mediterranean.
• **HABITAT** Woods in hills.
• **REMARK** Stripping the bark, from which cork is produced in Portugal and Spain, does not damage the living tissue of the plant.

hairy, grey leaf underside

leaf margin edged with few small teeth

thick, but light, corky bark

acorns ripen in first year

Height 20m (65ft)	Shape Broadly spreading	Leaf persistence Evergreen	Leaf type

Family FAGACEAE	Species *Quercus x turneri*	Author Willdenow

TURNER'S OAK

Leaves Oblong to obovate, to 12cm (4¾in) long and 5cm (2in) across, tapered at the base, with three to five triangular teeth on each side, glossy dark green above, paler beneath, some persisting until the following spring. *Bark* Dark grey, cracking into plates. *Flowers* Males in yellow-green, drooping catkins, females inconspicuous, separately on the same plant in late spring. *Fruit* An acorn, to 2cm (¾in) long, about one-half enclosed in a cup, usually several together on a long stalk.
• **NATIVE REGION** Of garden origin.
• **REMARK** A hybrid between holm oak *(Quercus ilex,* see p.163) and English oak *(Quercus robur,* see p.170).

acorns may not develop into mature fruits

leaves persist far into winter

densely hairy shoots

small teeth at leaf margin point forward

Height 20m (65ft)	Shape Broadly spreading	Leaf persistence Deciduous	Leaf type

| Family FAGACEAE | Species *Quercus variabilis* | Author Blume |

QUERCUS VARIABILIS

Leaves Oblong, to 20cm (8in) long and 5cm (2in) across, pointed at the tip, with numerous parallel veins ending in bristle-tipped teeth, glossy dark green and smooth above, grey and thinly hairy beneath. *Bark* Pale grey-brown, thick and corky, deeply fissured. *Flowers* Males in yellow-green, drooping catkins, females inconspicuous, separately on the same plant in late spring. *Fruit* An acorn, to 2cm (¾in) long, almost enclosed in a cup, the cup covered in long, curly scales.
• NATIVE REGION
China, Japan, Korea.
• HABITAT
Mountain woods.

broad, rounded acorns

hairy, grey leaf under-side

thick bark fissured into deep ridges

many bristle-tipped teeth at leaf margin

| Height 25m (80ft) | Shape Broadly spreading | Leaf persistence Deciduous | Leaf type |

| Family FAGACEAE | Species *Quercus velutina* | Author Lamarck |

BLACK OAK

Leaves Ovate to elliptic, to 25cm (10in) or more long and 15cm (6in) across, with five to seven finely pointed lobes, glossy dark green and smooth above, paler and hairy becoming smooth with tufts of brown hairs in the vein axils beneath. *Bark* Dark brown and ridged. *Flowers* Males in yellow-green, drooping catkins, females inconspicuous, separately on the same plant in late spring. *Fruit* An acorn, to 2.5cm (1in) long, one-half enclosed in a cup.
• NATIVE REGION
E. North America.
• HABITAT Dry woods, sand dunes.

leaf lobes end in long, bristle-like tip

glossy upper leaf surface

deep acorn cup covered in loose scales

| Height 25m (80ft) | Shape Broadly spreading | Leaf persistence Deciduous | Leaf type |

FLACOURTIACEAE

T HIS LARGELY TROPICAL and sub-tropical family occurs in both hemispheres, and contains about 90 genera and 900 species of evergreen and deciduous trees and shrubs. As well as the plants described here, the family includes species of the South-east Asian genus, *Hydnocarpus*. These yield chaulmoogra oil, which is used to treat some types of skin disease.

Family FLACOURTIACEAE	Species *Azara microphylla*	Author J.D. Hooker

AZARA MICROPHYLLA

Leaves Obovate to elliptic, to 2.5cm (1in) long, toothed, glossy dark green above, paler beneath, smooth, with a smaller, leaf-like stipule at the base. *Bark* Grey, with horizontal lenticels, cracking into thin flakes. *Flowers* Small, without petals, but with green sepals and conspicuous yellow stamens, in the leaf axils in late winter or early spring. *Fruit* A small, orange-red berry.
• **NATIVE REGION** Argentina, Chile.
• **HABITAT** Deciduous forests.

smaller stipule at leaf base

leaves edged with few small teeth

tiny, fragrant flowers clustered in leaf axils

Height 10m (33ft)	Shape Narrowly conical	Leaf persistence Evergreen	Leaf type

Family FLACOURTIACEAE	Species *Idesia polycarpa*	Author Maximowicz

IDESIA POLYCARPA

Leaves Broadly heart-shaped, to 20cm (8in) long and nearly the same across, heart-shaped at the base, with a short, tapered tip, toothed, bronze-purple becoming dark green above, blue-white beneath, smooth, on long stalks. *Bark* Grey-white. *Flowers* Small and yellow-green, without petals, in large, drooping panicles at the ends of the shoots, on separate plants in early summer. *Fruit* A small, red berry, borne in hanging clusters.
• **NATIVE REGION** China, Japan.
• **HABITAT** Mountain slopes.
• **REMARK** Favours sunny situations.

red leaf stalks bear conspicuous glands

prominent veins on leaf under-side

Height 15m (50ft)	Shape Broadly spreading	Leaf persistence Deciduous	Leaf type

HAMAMELIDACEAE

A FAMILY OF ABOUT 25 genera and 100 species of deciduous and evergreen trees and shrubs, distributed widely in temperate and subtropical regions, yet unknown in the wild throughout the whole of Europe, most of South America, and Africa. As well as the five species described here, this family contains genera of ornamental shrubs, such as the witch hazels *(Hamamelis)*, which usually flower in winter, *Corylopsis*, and *Fothergilla*.

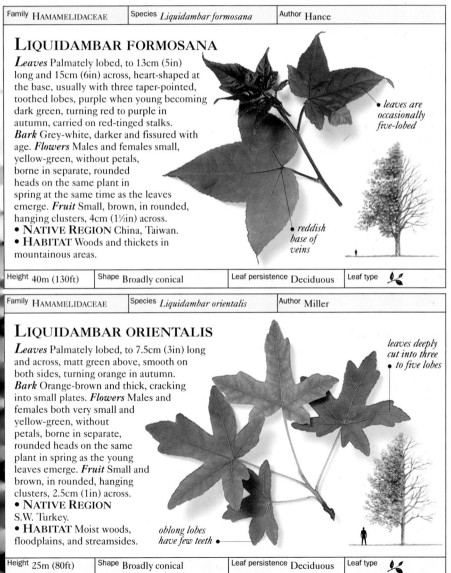

Family HAMAMELIDACEAE	Species *Liquidambar formosana*	Author Hance

LIQUIDAMBAR FORMOSANA

Leaves Palmately lobed, to 13cm (5in) long and 15cm (6in) across, heart-shaped at the base, usually with three taper-pointed, toothed lobes, purple when young becoming dark green, turning red to purple in autumn, carried on red-tinged stalks. **Bark** Grey-white, darker and fissured with age. **Flowers** Males and females small, yellow-green, without petals, borne in separate, rounded heads on the same plant in spring at the same time as the leaves emerge. **Fruit** Small, brown, in rounded, hanging clusters, 4cm (1½in) across.
• NATIVE REGION China, Taiwan.
• HABITAT Woods and thickets in mountainous areas.

• *leaves are occasionally five-lobed*

• *reddish base of veins*

Height 40m (130ft)	Shape Broadly conical	Leaf persistence Deciduous	Leaf type

Family HAMAMELIDACEAE	Species *Liquidambar orientalis*	Author Miller

LIQUIDAMBAR ORIENTALIS

Leaves Palmately lobed, to 7.5cm (3in) long and across, matt green above, smooth on both sides, turning orange in autumn. **Bark** Orange-brown and thick, cracking into small plates. **Flowers** Males and females both very small and yellow-green, without petals, borne in separate, rounded heads on the same plant in spring as the young leaves emerge. **Fruit** Small and brown, in rounded, hanging clusters, 2.5cm (1in) across.
• NATIVE REGION S.W. Turkey.
• HABITAT Moist woods, floodplains, and streamsides.

leaves deeply cut into three • *to five lobes*

oblong lobes have few teeth •

Height 25m (80ft)	Shape Broadly conical	Leaf persistence Deciduous	Leaf type

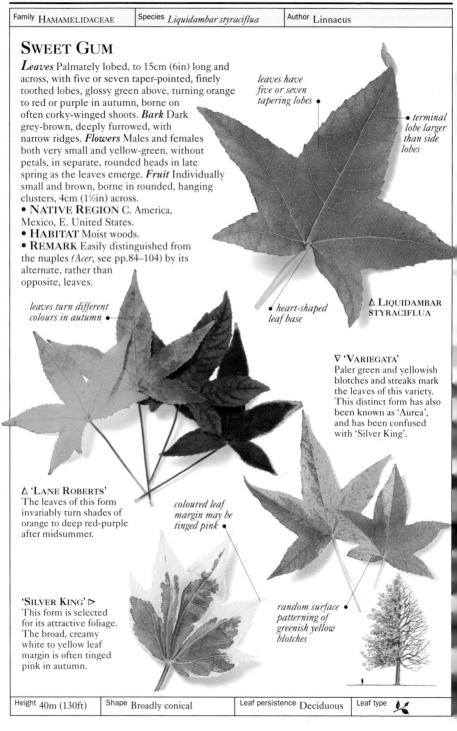

Family HAMAMELIDACEAE	Species *Liquidambar styraciflua*	Author Linnaeus

SWEET GUM

Leaves Palmately lobed, to 15cm (6in) long and across, with five or seven taper-pointed, finely toothed lobes, glossy green above, turning orange to red or purple in autumn, borne on often corky-winged shoots. *Bark* Dark grey-brown, deeply furrowed, with narrow ridges. *Flowers* Males and females both very small and yellow-green, without petals, in separate, rounded heads in late spring as the leaves emerge. *Fruit* Individually small and brown, borne in rounded, hanging clusters, 4cm (1½in) across.
• NATIVE REGION C. America, Mexico, E. United States.
• HABITAT Moist woods.
• REMARK Easily distinguished from the maples *(Acer,* see pp.84–104) by its alternate, rather than opposite, leaves.

leaves have five or seven tapering lobes

terminal lobe larger than side lobes

heart-shaped leaf base

△ LIQUIDAMBAR STYRACIFLUA

leaves turn different colours in autumn

▽ 'VARIEGATA'
Paler green and yellowish blotches and streaks mark the leaves of this variety. This distinct form has also been known as 'Aurea', and has been confused with 'Silver King'.

△ 'LANE ROBERTS'
The leaves of this form invariably turn shades of orange to deep red-purple after midsummer.

coloured leaf margin may be tinged pink

'SILVER KING' ▷
This form is selected for its attractive foliage. The broad, creamy white to yellow leaf margin is often tinged pink in autumn.

random surface patterning of greenish yellow blotches

| Height 40m (130ft) | Shape Broadly conical | Leaf persistence Deciduous | Leaf type |

Family HAMAMELIDACEAE	Species *Parrotia persica*	Author (Candolle) C.A. Meyer

PERSIAN IRONWOOD

Leaves Elliptic to obovate, to 12cm (4¾in) long and 6cm (2½in) across, wavy at the margin, toothed above the middle, bright glossy green and smooth above, thinly hairy beneath. **Bark** Grey-brown, flaking. **Flowers** Small, without petals, but with red anthers, in late winter to early spring. **Fruit** A nut-like, brown capsule, 8mm (⅜in) long.
• **NATIVE REGION** E. Caucasus, N. Iran.
• **HABITAT** Forests.
• **REMARK** Can be either a tree of medium height or a large shrub.

colourful autumn foliage •

• leaves broaden above middle

• rounded teeth edge upper half of leaf

Height 20m (65ft)	Shape Broadly spreading	Leaf persistence Deciduous	Leaf type

Family HAMAMELIDACEAE	Species *Parrotiopsis jacquemontiana*	Author (Decaisne) Rehder

PARROTIOPSIS JACQUEMONTIANA

Leaves Rounded, to 7.5cm (3in) long, toothed, glossy green becoming smooth or nearly so above, hairy beneath, carried on short stalks. **Bark** Grey and smooth. **Flowers** Small and without petals, with numerous stamens, the stamens with yellow anthers, borne in dense clusters, each cluster surrounded by up to six white bracts, the bracts dotted with numerous tiny brown scales beneath, forming a head to 5cm (2in) across, in mid- to late spring. **Fruit** A small, bristly, brown capsule, borne in clusters.
• **NATIVE REGION** W. Himalayas.
• **HABITAT** Forests.
• **REMARK** This shrub-like plant is the only species of *Parrotiopsis*. Flowers usually persist to early or midsummer.

• rounded leaves

toothed leaf • margin

tiny clustered flowers have • yellow anthers

dark scales • on underside of bracts

• white bracts surround each flower

Height 6m (20ft)	Shape Broadly conical	Leaf persistence Deciduous	Leaf type

HIPPOCASTANACEAE

T HIS FAMILY HAS ONLY two genera. Its 15 species of deciduous trees and shrubs are native plants in North America, south-east Europe, and east Asia. They have palmately compound, opposite leaves, and conspicuous, four- or five-petalled flowers, borne in large clusters at the ends of the shoots.

Family HIPPOCASTANACEAE	Species *Aesculus californica*	Author (Spach) Nuttall

CALIFORNIA BUCKEYE

Leaves Palmately compound, with five to seven oblong, toothed leaflets, to 15cm (6in) long, deep blue-green above, grey-green beneath. **Bark** Pale grey, nearly smooth, thinly scaly. **Flowers** White or pale pink, with four petals, in dense, cylindrical, upright panicles to 20cm (8in) long, in summer. **Fruit** Smooth, pear-shaped, to 7cm (2¾in) long, with one glossy brown seed, on a long stalk.
• **NATIVE REGION** USA: California.
• **HABITAT** Dry slopes and canyons in hills.

leaflets have long, tapered • point

flowers borne in very dense • panicles

• long, exserted flower stamens

Height 10m (33ft)	Shape Broadly spreading	Leaf persistence Deciduous	Leaf type

Family HIPPOCASTANACEAE	Species *Aesculus x carnea*	Author Hayne

RED HORSE CHESTNUT

Leaves Palmately compound, with five to seven obovate, sharply toothed, stalkless or short-stalked leaflets, to 25cm (10in) long, dark green, on long stalks. **Bark** Reddish brown. **Flowers** Creamy white blotched yellow becoming pink blotched red, with five petals, in conical, upright, or slightly spreading panicles to 20cm (8in) long, in late spring. **Fruit** Smooth or only slightly spiny, 4cm (1½in) across.
• **NATIVE REGION** Of garden origin.
• **REMARK** A hybrid between common horse chestnut *(Aesculus hippo-castanum, see p.179)* and red buckeye *(Aesculus pavia, see p.181).*

sharply toothed • leaflets

leaflets are often • twisted

AESCULUS x CARNEA

fruits contain • up to three seeds

◁ 'BRIOTII'
Brighter red flowers distinguish this form.

Height 20m (65ft)	Shape Broadly columnar	Leaf persistence Deciduous	Leaf type

Family HIPPOCASTANACEAE	Species *Aesculus flava*	Author Solander

SWEET BUCKEYE

Leaves Palmately compound, with usually five sharply toothed, short-stalked leaflets, to 15cm (6in) long, dark green, turning orange-red in autumn. **Bark** Grey-brown, peeling in large, smooth scales. **Flowers** Yellow, with four petals, in conical, upright panicles to 15cm (6in) long, in late spring to early summer. **Fruit** Smooth, rounded, to 6cm (2½in) across, covered in brown scales, usually with two seeds.
• **NATIVE REGION** E. United States.
• **HABITAT** Moist, rich woods.
• **REMARK** Also known as *Aesculus octandra*, yellow buckeye. The best buckeye for autumn colour.

taper-pointed leaflets

distinctly stalked leaflets

leaves colour early in autumn

flowers have pink blotch

Height 30m (100ft)	Shape Broadly conical	Leaf persistence Deciduous	Leaf type

Family HIPPOCASTANACEAE	Species *Aesculus hippocastanum*	Author Linnaeus

COMMON HORSE CHESTNUT

Leaves Palmately compound, with five to seven obovate, sharply toothed, unstalked leaflets, to 30cm (12in) long, dark green, usually turning yellow in autumn, on long stalks. **Bark** Red-brown or grey, scaly. **Flowers** Creamy yellow blotched yellow becoming white blotched red, with four petals, in large, conical, upright panicles to 30cm (12in) long, in late spring. **Fruit** Rounded, spiny, and green, with up to three glossy brown seeds.
• **NATIVE REGION** Albania, N. Greece.
• **HABITAT** Mountain woods.
• **REMARK** The native region of this species was unknown for many years, because of its introduction to European gardens via cultivation in Turkey.

yellow flower blotch becomes red

large flower panicles borne upright

'BAUMANNII' △
The double flowers of this form set no fruit.

unstalked leaflets

AESCULUS ▷
HIPPOCASTANUM

Height 30m (100ft)	Shape Broadly columnar	Leaf persistence Deciduous	Leaf type

Family HIPPOCASTANACEAE	Species *Aesculus indica*	Author (Cambessèdes) J.D. Hooker

INDIAN HORSE CHESTNUT

Leaves Palmately compound, with usually seven but occasionally five obovate to lanceolate, stalked and finely toothed leaflets, to 25cm (10in) long, bronze when young becoming glossy green above, turning orange or yellow in autumn. **Bark** Grey and smooth. **Flowers** White to pale pink blotched bright yellow, the blotch becoming red, with long, protruding stamens, in conical, upright panicles to 30cm (12in) long, in midsummer. **Fruit** Pear-shaped, scaly, and brown, with up to three seeds, on a stout stalk.
• **NATIVE REGION** N.W. Himalayas.
• **HABITAT** Forests and shady ravines.
• **REMARK** Flowers much later than the common horse chestnut *(Aesculus hippocastanum,* see p.179).

scaly, spineless husk encloses seeds

some leaflets narrow towards tip

some leaflets have broader shape

leaflets edged with fine teeth

small point at leaflet tip

short stalk joins each leaflet to leaf-stalk

yellow blotch turns red as flower ages

Height 30m (100ft)	Shape Broadly columnar	Leaf persistence Deciduous	Leaf type

Family HIPPOCASTANACEAE	Species *Aesculus x neglecta*	Author Lindley

AESCULUS X NEGLECTA

Leaves Palmately compound, with usually five elliptic, taper-pointed, finely toothed, stalked leaflets, to 20cm (8in) long and 9cm (3½in) across, smooth except for hairs on the veins above, thinly hairy beneath. **Bark** Grey-brown, with shallow fissures. **Flowers** 2.5cm (1in) long, whitish, borne in conical, upright panicles in late spring to early summer. **Fruit** Rounded and smooth, about 4cm (1½in) across.
• **NATIVE REGION** S.E. United States.
• **HABITAT** Mainly the coastal plain.
• **REMARK** A hybrid between sweet buckeye *(Aesculus flava*, see p.179) and *Aesculus sylvatica*, most well-known for the cultivar, 'Erythroblastos'.

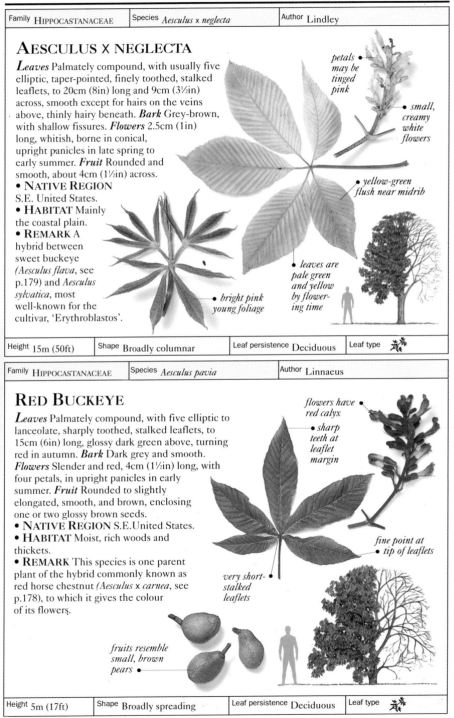

petals may be tinged pink

small, creamy white flowers

yellow-green flush near midrib

leaves are pale green and yellow by flowering time

bright pink young foliage

Height 15m (50ft)	Shape Broadly columnar	Leaf persistence Deciduous	Leaf type

Family HIPPOCASTANACEAE	Species *Aesculus pavia*	Author Linnaeus

RED BUCKEYE

Leaves Palmately compound, with five elliptic to lanceolate, sharply toothed, stalked leaflets, to 15cm (6in) long, glossy dark green above, turning red in autumn. **Bark** Dark grey and smooth. **Flowers** Slender and red, 4cm (1½in) long, with four petals, in upright panicles in early summer. **Fruit** Rounded to slightly elongated, smooth, and brown, enclosing one or two glossy brown seeds.
• **NATIVE REGION** S.E.United States.
• **HABITAT** Moist, rich woods and thickets.
• **REMARK** This species is one parent plant of the hybrid commonly known as red horse chestnut *(Aesculus x carnea*, see p.178), to which it gives the colour of its flowers.

flowers have red calyx

sharp teeth at leaflet margin

fine point at tip of leaflets

very short-stalked leaflets

fruits resemble small, brown pears

Height 5m (17ft)	Shape Broadly spreading	Leaf persistence Deciduous	Leaf type

JUGLANDACEAE

MOST MEMBERS OF this family are deciduous plants. Seven genera with some 60 species grow wild in the Americas, and from south-east Europe to Japan and South-east Asia. The leaves are usually alternate and pinnate. The small flowers lack petals, and are clustered in catkins, males and females on the same plant. The fruit is either a large nut, or small and winged.

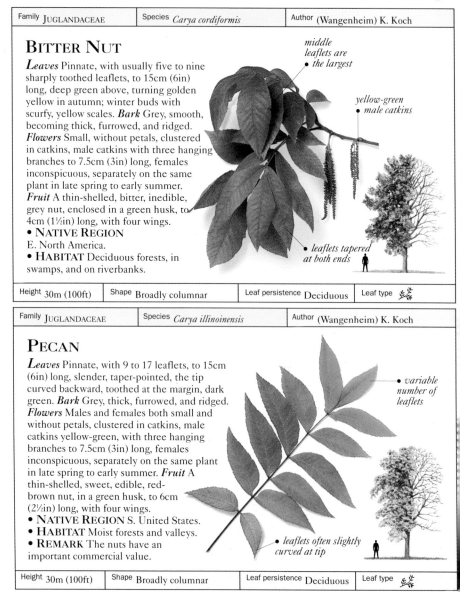

Family JUGLANDACEAE	Species *Carya cordiformis*	Author (Wangenheim) K. Koch

BITTER NUT

Leaves Pinnate, with usually five to nine sharply toothed leaflets, to 15cm (6in) long, deep green above, turning golden yellow in autumn; winter buds with scurfy, yellow scales. **Bark** Grey, smooth, becoming thick, furrowed, and ridged. **Flowers** Small, without petals, clustered in catkins, male catkins with three hanging branches to 7.5cm (3in) long, females inconspicuous, separately on the same plant in late spring to early summer. **Fruit** A thin-shelled, bitter, inedible, grey nut, enclosed in a green husk, to 4cm (1½in) long, with four wings.
- **NATIVE REGION** E. North America.
- **HABITAT** Deciduous forests, in swamps, and on riverbanks.

middle leaflets are the largest

yellow-green male catkins

leaflets tapered at both ends

Height 30m (100ft)	Shape Broadly columnar	Leaf persistence Deciduous	Leaf type

Family JUGLANDACEAE	Species *Carya illinoinensis*	Author (Wangenheim) K. Koch

PECAN

Leaves Pinnate, with 9 to 17 leaflets, to 15cm (6in) long, slender, taper-pointed, the tip curved backward, toothed at the margin, dark green. **Bark** Grey, thick, furrowed, and ridged. **Flowers** Males and females both small and without petals, clustered in catkins, male catkins yellow-green, with three hanging branches to 7.5cm (3in) long, females inconspicuous, separately on the same plant in late spring to early summer. **Fruit** A thin-shelled, sweet, edible, red-brown nut, in a green husk, to 6cm (2½in) long, with four wings.
- **NATIVE REGION** S. United States.
- **HABITAT** Moist forests and valleys.
- **REMARK** The nuts have an important commercial value.

variable number of leaflets

leaflets often slightly curved at tip

Height 30m (100ft)	Shape Broadly columnar	Leaf persistence Deciduous	Leaf type

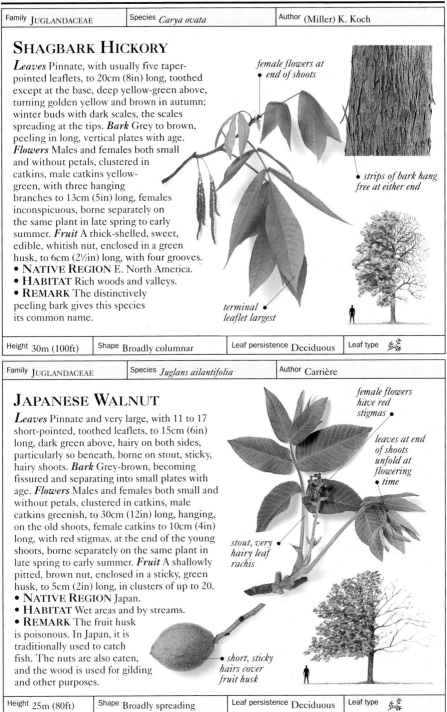

| Family JUGLANDACEAE | Species *Carya ovata* | Author (Miller) K. Koch |

SHAGBARK HICKORY

Leaves Pinnate, with usually five taper-pointed leaflets, to 20cm (8in) long, toothed except at the base, deep yellow-green above, turning golden yellow and brown in autumn; winter buds with dark scales, the scales spreading at the tips. ***Bark*** Grey to brown, peeling in long, vertical plates with age. ***Flowers*** Males and females both small and without petals, clustered in catkins, male catkins yellow-green, with three hanging branches to 13cm (5in) long, females inconspicuous, borne separately on the same plant in late spring to early summer. ***Fruit*** A thick-shelled, sweet, edible, whitish nut, enclosed in a green husk, to 6cm (2½in) long, with four grooves.
• **NATIVE REGION** E. North America.
• **HABITAT** Rich woods and valleys.
• **REMARK** The distinctively peeling bark gives this species its common name.

female flowers at end of shoots

strips of bark hang free at either end

terminal leaflet largest

| Height 30m (100ft) | Shape Broadly columnar | Leaf persistence Deciduous | Leaf type |

| Family JUGLANDACEAE | Species *Juglans ailantifolia* | Author Carrière |

JAPANESE WALNUT

Leaves Pinnate and very large, with 11 to 17 short-pointed, toothed leaflets, to 15cm (6in) long, dark green above, hairy on both sides, particularly so beneath, borne on stout, sticky, hairy shoots. ***Bark*** Grey-brown, becoming fissured and separating into small plates with age. ***Flowers*** Males and females both small and without petals, clustered in catkins, male catkins greenish, to 30cm (12in) long, hanging, on the old shoots, female catkins to 10cm (4in) long, with red stigmas, at the end of the young shoots, borne separately on the same plant in late spring to early summer. ***Fruit*** A shallowly pitted, brown nut, enclosed in a sticky, green husk, to 5cm (2in) long, in clusters of up to 20.
• **NATIVE REGION** Japan.
• **HABITAT** Wet areas and by streams.
• **REMARK** The fruit husk is poisonous. In Japan, it is traditionally used to catch fish. The nuts are also eaten, and the wood is used for gilding and other purposes.

female flowers have red stigmas

leaves at end of shoots unfold at flowering time

stout, very hairy leaf rachis

short, sticky hairs cover fruit husk

| Height 25m (80ft) | Shape Broadly spreading | Leaf persistence Deciduous | Leaf type |

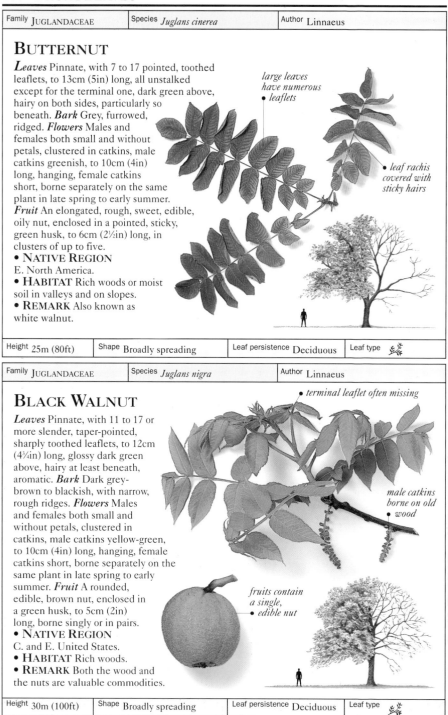

Family JUGLANDACEAE	Species *Juglans cinerea*	Author Linnaeus

BUTTERNUT

Leaves Pinnate, with 7 to 17 pointed, toothed leaflets, to 13cm (5in) long, all unstalked except for the terminal one, dark green above, hairy on both sides, particularly so beneath. **Bark** Grey, furrowed, ridged. **Flowers** Males and females both small and without petals, clustered in catkins, male catkins greenish, to 10cm (4in) long, hanging, female catkins short, borne separately on the same plant in late spring to early summer. **Fruit** An elongated, rough, sweet, edible, oily nut, enclosed in a pointed, sticky, green husk, to 6cm (2½in) long, in clusters of up to five.
• **NATIVE REGION**
E. North America.
• **HABITAT** Rich woods or moist soil in valleys and on slopes.
• **REMARK** Also known as white walnut.

large leaves have numerous leaflets

leaf rachis covered with sticky hairs

Height 25m (80ft)	Shape Broadly spreading	Leaf persistence Deciduous	Leaf type

Family JUGLANDACEAE	Species *Juglans nigra*	Author Linnaeus

BLACK WALNUT

terminal leaflet often missing

Leaves Pinnate, with 11 to 17 or more slender, taper-pointed, sharply toothed leaflets, to 12cm (4¾in) long, glossy dark green above, hairy at least beneath, aromatic. **Bark** Dark grey-brown to blackish, with narrow, rough ridges. **Flowers** Males and females both small and without petals, clustered in catkins, male catkins yellow-green, to 10cm (4in) long, hanging, female catkins short, borne separately on the same plant in late spring to early summer. **Fruit** A rounded, edible, brown nut, enclosed in a green husk, to 5cm (2in) long, borne singly or in pairs.
• **NATIVE REGION**
C. and E. United States.
• **HABITAT** Rich woods.
• **REMARK** Both the wood and the nuts are valuable commodities.

male catkins borne on old wood

fruits contain a single, edible nut

Height 30m (100ft)	Shape Broadly spreading	Leaf persistence Deciduous	Leaf type

Family JUGLANDACEAE	Species *Juglans regia*	Author Linnaeus

WALNUT

Leaves Pinnate, with five to nine short-pointed leaflets, to 15cm (6in) long, the terminal leaflet largest, bronze when young becoming dark green, smooth, aromatic when bruised. **Bark** Pale grey, smooth, fissured on old plants. **Flowers** Males and females both small, without petals, clustered in catkins, male catkins yellow-green, to 10cm (4in) long, hanging, females short, borne separately on the same plant in late spring to early summer. **Fruit** An edible nut, creamy white becoming brown, enclosed in a green husk, to 5cm (2in) long.
• **NATIVE REGION** China to S.E. Europe.
• **HABITAT** Valleys and streambanks.

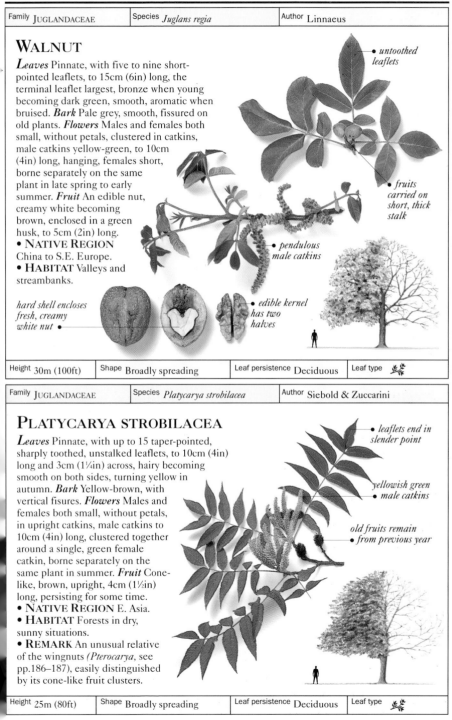

untoothed leaflets

fruits carried on short, thick stalk

pendulous male catkins

hard shell encloses fresh, creamy white nut •

edible kernel has two halves

Height 30m (100ft)	Shape Broadly spreading	Leaf persistence Deciduous	Leaf type

Family JUGLANDACEAE	Species *Platycarya strobilacea*	Author Siebold & Zuccarini

PLATYCARYA STROBILACEA

Leaves Pinnate, with up to 15 taper-pointed, sharply toothed, unstalked leaflets, to 10cm (4in) long and 3cm (1¼in) across, hairy becoming smooth on both sides, turning yellow in autumn. **Bark** Yellow-brown, with vertical fisures. **Flowers** Males and females both small, without petals, in upright catkins, male catkins to 10cm (4in) long, clustered together around a single, green female catkin, borne separately on the same plant in summer. **Fruit** Cone-like, brown, upright, 4cm (1½in) long, persisting for some time.
• **NATIVE REGION** E. Asia.
• **HABITAT** Forests in dry, sunny situations.
• **REMARK** An unusual relative of the wingnuts *(Pterocarya,* see pp.186–187), easily distinguished by its cone-like fruit clusters.

leaflets end in slender point

yellowish green male catkins

old fruits remain from previous year

Height 25m (80ft)	Shape Broadly spreading	Leaf persistence Deciduous	Leaf type

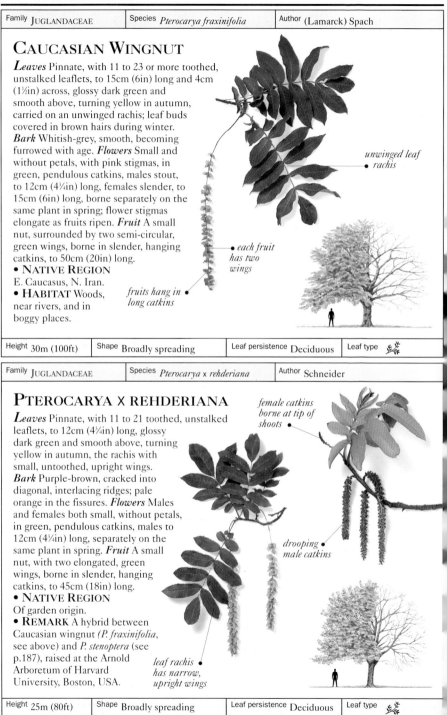

Family JUGLANDACEAE	Species *Pterocarya fraxinifolia*	Author (Lamarck) Spach

CAUCASIAN WINGNUT

Leaves Pinnate, with 11 to 23 or more toothed, unstalked leaflets, to 15cm (6in) long and 4cm (1½in) across, glossy dark green and smooth above, turning yellow in autumn, carried on an unwinged rachis; leaf buds covered in brown hairs during winter. **Bark** Whitish-grey, smooth, becoming furrowed with age. **Flowers** Small and without petals, with pink stigmas, in green, pendulous catkins, males stout, to 12cm (4¾in) long, females slender, to 15cm (6in) long, borne separately on the same plant in spring; flower stigmas elongate as fruits ripen. **Fruit** A small nut, surrounded by two semi-circular, green wings, borne in slender, hanging catkins, to 50cm (20in) long.
• **NATIVE REGION**
E. Caucasus, N. Iran.
• **HABITAT** Woods, near rivers, and in boggy places.

unwinged leaf rachis

each fruit has two wings

fruits hang in long catkins

Height 30m (100ft)	Shape Broadly spreading	Leaf persistence Deciduous	Leaf type

Family JUGLANDACEAE	Species *Pterocarya x rehderiana*	Author Schneider

PTEROCARYA X REHDERIANA

Leaves Pinnate, with 11 to 21 toothed, unstalked leaflets, to 12cm (4¾in) long, glossy dark green and smooth above, turning yellow in autumn, the rachis with small, untoothed, upright wings. **Bark** Purple-brown, cracked into diagonal, interlacing ridges; pale orange in the fissures. **Flowers** Males and females both small, without petals, in green, pendulous catkins, males to 12cm (4¾in) long, separately on the same plant in spring. **Fruit** A small nut, with two elongated, green wings, borne in slender, hanging catkins, to 45cm (18in) long.
• **NATIVE REGION**
Of garden origin.
• **REMARK** A hybrid between Caucasian wingnut *(P. fraxinifolia,* see above) and *P. stenoptera* (see p.187), raised at the Arnold Arboretum of Harvard University, Boston, USA.

female catkins borne at tip of shoots

drooping male catkins

leaf rachis has narrow, upright wings

Height 25m (80ft)	Shape Broadly spreading	Leaf persistence Deciduous	Leaf type

Family JUGLANDACEAE	Species *Pterocarya rhoifolia*	Author Siebold & Zuccarini

JAPANESE WINGNUT

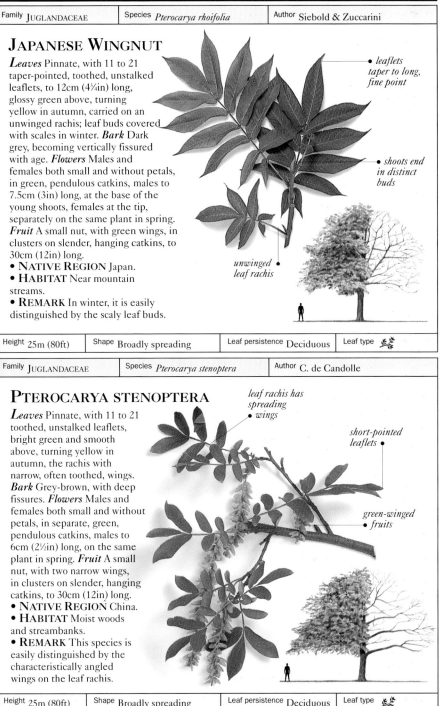

Leaves Pinnate, with 11 to 21 taper-pointed, toothed, unstalked leaflets, to 12cm (4¾in) long, glossy green above, turning yellow in autumn, carried on an unwinged rachis; leaf buds covered with scales in winter. **Bark** Dark grey, becoming vertically fissured with age. **Flowers** Males and females both small and without petals, in green, pendulous catkins, males to 7.5cm (3in) long, at the base of the young shoots, females at the tip, separately on the same plant in spring. **Fruit** A small nut, with green wings, in clusters on slender, hanging catkins, to 30cm (12in) long.
• **NATIVE REGION** Japan.
• **HABITAT** Near mountain streams.
• **REMARK** In winter, it is easily distinguished by the scaly leaf buds.

leaflets taper to long, fine point

shoots end in distinct buds

unwinged leaf rachis

Height 25m (80ft)	Shape Broadly spreading	Leaf persistence Deciduous	Leaf type

Family JUGLANDACEAE	Species *Pterocarya stenoptera*	Author C. de Candolle

PTEROCARYA STENOPTERA

Leaves Pinnate, with 11 to 21 toothed, unstalked leaflets, bright green and smooth above, turning yellow in autumn, the rachis with narrow, often toothed, wings. **Bark** Grey-brown, with deep fissures. **Flowers** Males and females both small and without petals, in separate, green, pendulous catkins, males to 6cm (2½in) long, on the same plant in spring. **Fruit** A small nut, with two narrow wings, in clusters on slender, hanging catkins, to 30cm (12in) long.
• **NATIVE REGION** China.
• **HABITAT** Moist woods and streambanks.
• **REMARK** This species is easily distinguished by the characteristically angled wings on the leaf rachis.

leaf rachis has spreading wings

short-pointed leaflets

green-winged fruits

Height 25m (80ft)	Shape Broadly spreading	Leaf persistence Deciduous	Leaf type

LAURACEAE

S OME 40 GENERA and more than 2,000 species belong to this widespread family; many grow wild in tropical South America and South-east Asia. The deciduous and evergreen, usually aromatic, trees and shrubs have untoothed, either opposite or alternate, leaves. Flower petals and sepals, which resemble each other, are arranged in threes. The fruit is usually fleshy.

Family LAURACEAE	Species *Laurus nobilis*	Author Linnaeus

BAY LAUREL

Leaves Elliptic to ovate, to 10cm (4in) long and 4cm (1½in) across, pointed at the tip, with a wavy margin, glossy dark green above, paler beneath, smooth, leathery, aromatic when crushed.
Bark Dark grey, smooth.
Flowers About 1cm (⅜in) across, yellow-green, males with numerous yellow stamens, in clusters in the leaf axils, on separate plants in spring.
Fruit A rounded berry, about 1cm (⅜in) long, green ripening to black.
• **NATIVE REGION** Mediterranean.
• **HABITAT** Evergreen woods, thickets and rocky places.
• **REMARK** Also known as sweet bay. This species and the related Canary Island laurel *(Laurus azorica)* are the only members of the family native to Europe.

leaves taper gradually towards base

male flowers have many yellow anthers

small female flowers

wavy, untoothed leaf margin

berries ripen from green to black

flower buds form in autumn

Height 15m (50ft)	Shape Broadly conical	Leaf persistence Evergreen	Leaf type

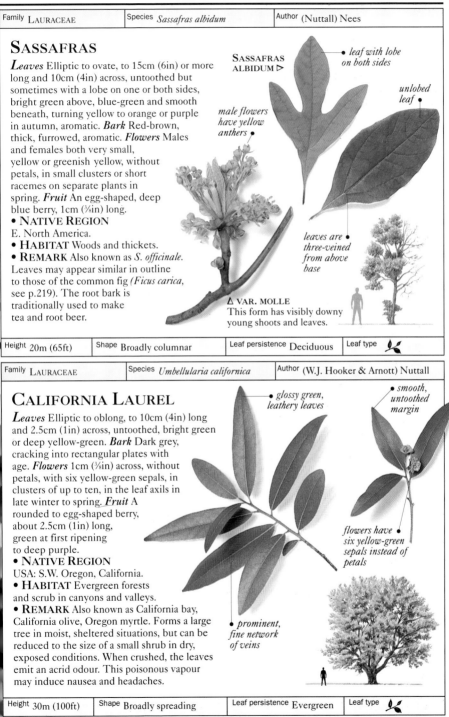

Family LAURACEAE	Species *Sassafras albidum*	Author (Nuttall) Nees

SASSAFRAS

Leaves Elliptic to ovate, to 15cm (6in) or more long and 10cm (4in) across, untoothed but sometimes with a lobe on one or both sides, bright green above, blue-green and smooth beneath, turning yellow to orange or purple in autumn, aromatic. **Bark** Red-brown, thick, furrowed, aromatic. **Flowers** Males and females both very small, yellow or greenish yellow, without petals, in small clusters or short racemes on separate plants in spring. **Fruit** An egg-shaped, deep blue berry, 1cm (⅜in) long.
• **NATIVE REGION** E. North America.
• **HABITAT** Woods and thickets.
• **REMARK** Also known as *S. officinale*. Leaves may appear similar in outline to those of the common fig *(Ficus carica, see p.219)*. The root bark is traditionally used to make tea and root beer.

SASSAFRAS
ALBIDUM ▷

leaf with lobe on both sides

unlobed leaf

male flowers have yellow anthers

leaves are three-veined from above base

△ VAR. MOLLE
This form has visibly downy young shoots and leaves.

Height 20m (65ft)	Shape Broadly columnar	Leaf persistence Deciduous	Leaf type

Family LAURACEAE	Species *Umbellularia californica*	Author (W.J. Hooker & Arnott) Nuttall

CALIFORNIA LAUREL

Leaves Elliptic to oblong, to 10cm (4in) long and 2.5cm (1in) across, untoothed, bright green or deep yellow-green. **Bark** Dark grey, cracking into rectangular plates with age. **Flowers** 1cm (⅜in) across, without petals, with six yellow-green sepals, in clusters of up to ten, in the leaf axils in late winter to spring. **Fruit** A rounded to egg-shaped berry, about 2.5cm (1in) long, green at first ripening to deep purple.
• **NATIVE REGION** USA: S.W. Oregon, California.
• **HABITAT** Evergreen forests and scrub in canyons and valleys.
• **REMARK** Also known as California bay, California olive, Oregon myrtle. Forms a large tree in moist, sheltered situations, but can be reduced to the size of a small shrub in dry, exposed conditions. When crushed, the leaves emit an acrid odour. This poisonous vapour may induce nausea and headaches.

glossy green, leathery leaves

smooth, untoothed margin

flowers have six yellow-green sepals instead of petals

prominent, fine network of veins

Height 30m (100ft)	Shape Broadly spreading	Leaf persistence Evergreen	Leaf type

LEGUMINOSAE

T HE PEA FAMILY contains about 700 genera and over 15,000 species of trees, shrubs, and herbaceous plants, found worldwide. The leaves are often compound, and frequently pinnate or with three leaflets. Species that grow in cool temperate regions have pealike flowers. The fruit, usually a pod, splits open along both sides or breaks into portions to release its seeds.

Family LEGUMINOSAE	Species *Acacia dealbata*	Author Link

SILVER WATTLE

Leaves Bipinnate, to 12cm (4¾in) long, with numerous linear leaflets, to 5mm (³⁄₁₆in) long, the leaflets untoothed, blue-green, and finely hairy. *Bark* Smooth and green or blue-green, becoming nearly black with age. *Flowers* Very small, with bright yellow petals and numerous conspicuous stamens, fragrant, in panicles of small, rounded clusters in late winter to early spring. *Fruit* A flattened pod, to 7.5cm (3in) long, green becoming blue-white ripening to brown.
• **NATIVE REGION**
S.E. Australia, Tasmania.
• **HABITAT** Mainly mountain gullies and streambanks.

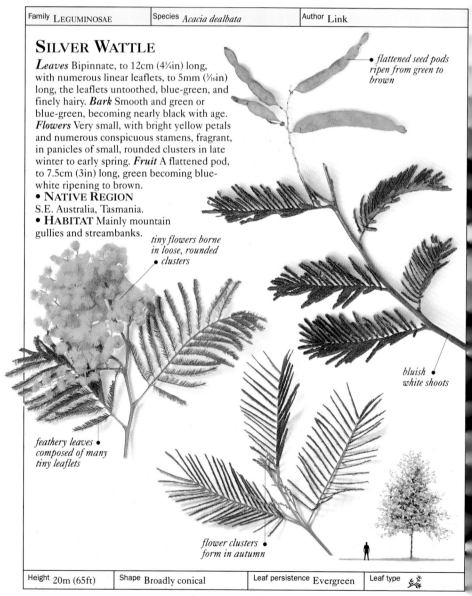

flattened seed pods ripen from green to brown

tiny flowers borne in loose, rounded clusters

bluish white shoots

feathery leaves composed of many tiny leaflets

flower clusters form in autumn

Height 20m (65ft)	Shape Broadly conical	Leaf persistence Evergreen	Leaf type

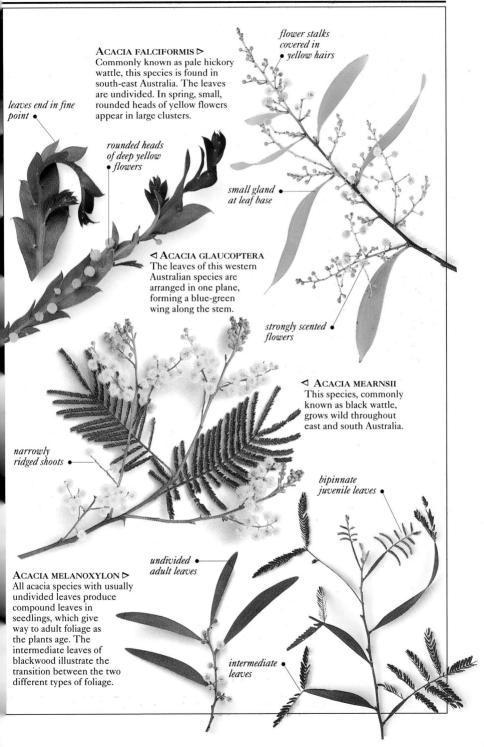

ACACIA FALCIFORMIS ▷
Commonly known as pale hickory
wattle, this species is found in
south-east Australia. The leaves
are undivided. In spring, small,
rounded heads of yellow flowers
appear in large clusters.

*flower stalks
covered in
yellow hairs*

*leaves end in fine
point*

*rounded heads
of deep yellow
flowers*

*small gland
at leaf base*

◁ ACACIA GLAUCOPTERA
The leaves of this western
Australian species are
arranged in one plane,
forming a blue-green
wing along the stem.

*strongly scented
flowers*

◁ ACACIA MEARNSII
This species, commonly
known as black wattle,
grows wild throughout
east and south Australia.

*narrowly
ridged shoots*

*bipinnate
juvenile leaves*

*undivided
adult leaves*

ACACIA MELANOXYLON ▷
All acacia species with usually
undivided leaves produce
compound leaves in
seedlings, which give
way to adult foliage as
the plants age. The
intermediate leaves of
blackwood illustrate the
transition between the two
different types of foliage.

*intermediate
leaves*

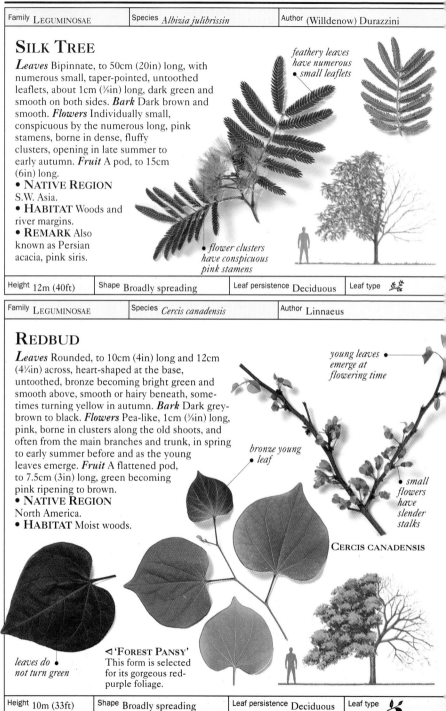

Family LEGUMINOSAE	Species *Albizia julibrissin*	Author (Willdenow) Durazzini

SILK TREE

Leaves Bipinnate, to 50cm (20in) long, with numerous small, taper-pointed, untoothed leaflets, about 1cm (⅜in) long, dark green and smooth on both sides. *Bark* Dark brown and smooth. *Flowers* Individually small, conspicuous by the numerous long, pink stamens, borne in dense, fluffy clusters, opening in late summer to early autumn. *Fruit* A pod, to 15cm (6in) long.
• NATIVE REGION S.W. Asia.
• HABITAT Woods and river margins.
• REMARK Also known as Persian acacia, pink siris.

feathery leaves have numerous small leaflets

• flower clusters have conspicuous pink stamens

Height 12m (40ft)	Shape Broadly spreading	Leaf persistence Deciduous	Leaf type

Family LEGUMINOSAE	Species *Cercis canadensis*	Author Linnaeus

REDBUD

Leaves Rounded, to 10cm (4in) long and 12cm (4¾in) across, heart-shaped at the base, untoothed, bronze becoming bright green and smooth above, smooth or hairy beneath, sometimes turning yellow in autumn. *Bark* Dark grey-brown to black. *Flowers* Pea-like, 1cm (⅜in) long, pink, borne in clusters along the old shoots, and often from the main branches and trunk, in spring to early summer before and as the young leaves emerge. *Fruit* A flattened pod, to 7.5cm (3in) long, green becoming pink ripening to brown.
• NATIVE REGION North America.
• HABITAT Moist woods.

young leaves • emerge at flowering time

bronze young • leaf

• small flowers have slender stalks

CERCIS CANADENSIS

leaves do • not turn green

◁ 'FOREST PANSY'
This form is selected for its gorgeous red-purple foliage.

Height 10m (33ft)	Shape Broadly spreading	Leaf persistence Deciduous	Leaf type

Family LEGUMINOSAE	Species *Cercis racemosa*	Author Oliver

CERCIS RACEMOSA

Leaves Rounded, to 13cm (5in) long and 10cm (4in) across, rounded at the base, dark green above, hairy beneath. *Bark* Pale grey, flaking with age. *Flowers* Pea-like, 1cm (⅜in) long, pale pink, borne in racemes from the old shoots in mid- to late spring or early summer. *Fruit* A flattened pod, to 10cm (4in) long, green becoming pink-tinged ripening to brown.
• **NATIVE REGION** China.
• **HABITAT** Woods and stream-banks in mountains.
• **REMARK** A rarely seen species, distinguished by its flowers borne in racemes.

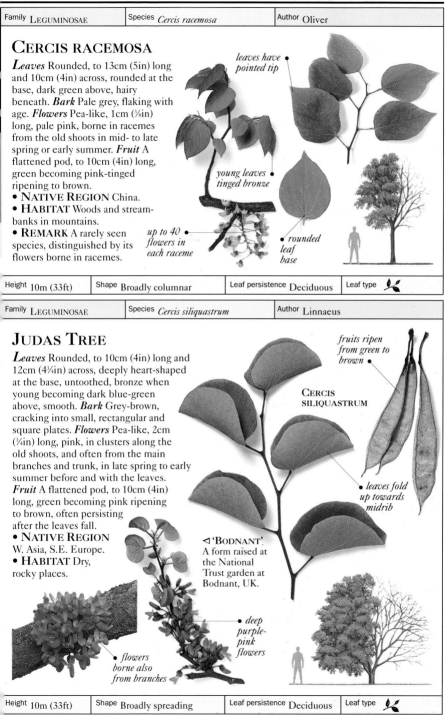

leaves have pointed tip

young leaves tinged bronze

up to 40 flowers in each raceme

rounded leaf base

Height 10m (33ft)	Shape Broadly columnar	Leaf persistence Deciduous	Leaf type

Family LEGUMINOSAE	Species *Cercis siliquastrum*	Author Linnaeus

JUDAS TREE

Leaves Rounded, to 10cm (4in) long and 12cm (4¾in) across, deeply heart-shaped at the base, untoothed, bronze when young becoming dark blue-green above, smooth. *Bark* Grey-brown, cracking into small, rectangular and square plates. *Flowers* Pea-like, 2cm (¾in) long, pink, in clusters along the old shoots, and often from the main branches and trunk, in late spring to early summer before and with the leaves. *Fruit* A flattened pod, to 10cm (4in) long, green becoming pink ripening to brown, often persisting after the leaves fall.
• **NATIVE REGION** W. Asia, S.E. Europe.
• **HABITAT** Dry, rocky places.

fruits ripen from green to brown

CERCIS SILIQUASTRUM

leaves fold up towards midrib

◁ '**BODNANT**'.
A form raised at the National Trust garden at Bodnant, UK.

deep purple-pink flowers

flowers borne also from branches

Height 10m (33ft)	Shape Broadly spreading	Leaf persistence Deciduous	Leaf type

Family LEGUMINOSAE	Species *Cladrastis lutea*	Author K. Koch

YELLOW WOOD

Leaves Pinnate, with 7 to 11 elliptic to ovate, untoothed leaflets, to 10cm (4in) long, the terminal one largest, bright green above and smooth on both sides, turning bright yellow in autumn, the stalk swollen at the base and enclosing the bud. **Bark** Grey and smooth, often horizontally wrinkled. **Flowers** Pea-like, 3cm (1¼in) long, white, slightly fragrant, in large, hanging panicles to 45cm (18in) long, at the ends of the shoots in early summer. **Fruit** A flattened, brown pod, to 10cm (4in) long.
• **NATIVE REGION** S.E. United States.
• **HABITAT** Rich woods and rocky bluffs.
• **REMARK** Also known as virgilia. This species is rare in the wild, with a restricted distribution in only a few States. The wood produces a yellow dye.

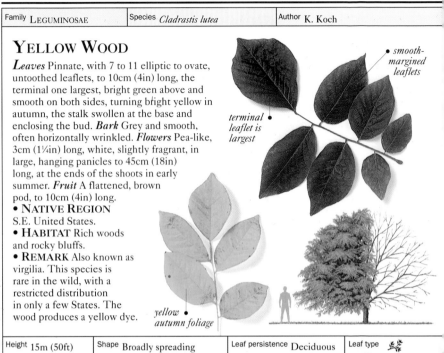

smooth-margined leaflets

terminal leaflet is largest

yellow autumn foliage

Height 15m (50ft)	Shape Broadly spreading	Leaf persistence Deciduous	Leaf type

Family LEGUMINOSAE	Species *Genista aetnensis*	Author (Bivona) Candolle

MOUNT ETNA BROOM

Leaves Linear and small, 1cm (⅜in) long, borne sparsely on slender, bright green shoots; on mature plants usually absent by flowering time. **Bark** Grey-brown, deeply fissured at the base. **Flowers** Pea-like, 1.5cm (⅝in) long, bright golden yellow, fragrant, profuse, singly along the new shoots in mid- to late summer. **Fruit** A small, blackish brown pod, about 1cm (⅜in) long, ending in a short, slender, pointed tip, and containing two or three seeds.
• **NATIVE REGION** Sardinia, Sicily.
• **HABITAT** Rocky slopes.
• **REMARK** This species can be either a large shrub or a small tree. In the wild, it is found particularly on the slopes of Mount Etna, in Sicily, where it grows on old volcanic lava. The rush-like shoots take over the role of photosynthesis from the leaves. They are green even during winter, giving the tree an evergreen appearance.

flowers borne on slender, leafless shoots

fragrant, golden flowers

young plants have few leaves

Height 10m (33ft)	Shape Broadly spreading	Leaf persistence Deciduous	Leaf type

| Family LEGUMINOSAE | Species *Gleditsia triacanthos* | Author Linnaeus |

HONEY LOCUST

GLEDITSIA TRIACANTHOS

Leaves First leaves from spurs on the old wood pinnate, later leaves on new shoots usually bipinnate, with numerous small leaflets, to 4cm (1½in) long, minutely toothed, bright green, turning yellow in autumn; shoots usually spiny. *Bark* Dark grey, scaly, with clusters of branched spines. *Flowers* Males and females both very small and yellow-green, in separate small, cylindrical, mainly upright racemes to 5cm (2in) long, from the old shoots, on the same plant in early summer. *Fruit* A large, often twisted, brown, hanging pod, to 45cm (18in) long.
• **NATIVE REGION** North America.
• **HABITAT** Rich, moist woods.
• **REMARK** The fruits contain a sweet, edible flesh.

'SUNBURST' ▷
The foliage of this form matures from golden yellow to dark green.

some leaves pinnate

some leaves bipinnate

bright young leaves

| Height 30m (100ft) | Shape Broadly spreading | Leaf persistence Deciduous | Leaf type |

| Family LEGUMINOSAE | Species *Gymnocladus dioica* | Author (Linnaeus) K. Koch |

KENTUCKY COFFEE TREE

Leaves Bipinnate and very large, to 1m (39in) long, with numerous ovate leaflets, to 7.5cm (3in) long, untoothed, bronze becoming dark green above, bluish beneath, becoming smooth on both sides, on very stout shoots. *Bark* Dark brown and rough, with scaly ridges. *Flowers* Whitish, fragrant, about 2.5cm (1in) across, in conical panicles, males to 10cm (4in) long, females to 30cm (12in) long, usually on separate plants in late spring to early summer. *Fruit* A large, leathery, red-brown, hanging pod, to 25cm (10in) long, persisting for some time.
• **NATIVE REGION** C. and E. United States.
• **HABITAT** Moist woods.

terminal leaflet often missing

leaflets are alternate or opposite

simple leaflets at leaf base

| Height 25m (80ft) | Shape Broadly columnar | Leaf persistence Deciduous | Leaf type |

Family LEGUMINOSAE	Species + *Laburnocytisus adamii*	Author (Poiteau) Schneider

+ LABURNOCYTISUS ADAMII

Leaves Variable, with three leaflets, resembling one parent or intermediate between both parents. **Bark** Dark grey, smooth, shallowly fissured with age. **Flowers** Pea-like, of three sorts, either yellow laburnum or purple broom, resembling one parent, or between the two, the intermediate flowers pale purple-pink flushed yellow, borne in short, hanging racemes to 15cm (6in) long, in late spring to early summer. **Fruit** A brown pod, to 7.5cm (3in) long, hanging in clusters, with black seeds, produced from the yellow flowers.

• **NATIVE REGION**
Of garden origin.

• **REMARK** A chimera, or graft hybrid, between the common laburnum (*Laburnum anagyroides*, see p.197) and the shrubby purple broom (*Cytisus purpureus*). A graft hybrid is not a true hybrid, because it contains a mixture of the tissues of the two genetically distinct parents. All parts of this tree are poisonous.

intermediate leaves are dark green above, paler beneath •

Δ + LABURNOCYTISUS ADAMII

• intermediate flowers carried on most branches

◁ LABURNUM ANAGYROIDES
Common laburnum (*Laburnum anagyroides*) forms the inner core of the plant.

laburnum leaves are dull grey-green •

• yellow laburnum flowers borne in drooping racemes

dense • clusters of purple broom flowers borne on some branches

purple broom • leaves have tiny leaflets

Δ CYTISUS PURPUREUS
The outer envelope of the tree is formed by purple broom (*Cytisus purpureus*).

Height 6m (20ft)	Shape Broadly spreading	Leaf persistence Deciduous	Leaf type

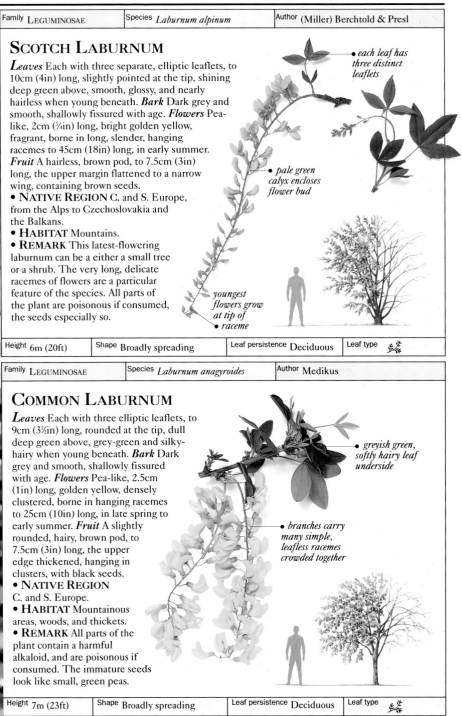

Family LEGUMINOSAE	Species *Laburnum alpinum*	Author (Miller) Berchtold & Presl

SCOTCH LABURNUM

Leaves Each with three separate, elliptic leaflets, to 10cm (4in) long, slightly pointed at the tip, shining deep green above, smooth, glossy, and nearly hairless when young beneath. *Bark* Dark grey and smooth, shallowly fissured with age. *Flowers* Pea-like, 2cm (¾in) long, bright golden yellow, fragrant, borne in long, slender, hanging racemes to 45cm (18in) long, in early summer. *Fruit* A hairless, brown pod, to 7.5cm (3in) long, the upper margin flattened to a narrow wing, containing brown seeds.
• **NATIVE REGION** C. and S. Europe, from the Alps to Czechoslovakia and the Balkans.
• **HABITAT** Mountains.
• **REMARK** This latest-flowering laburnum can be a either a small tree or a shrub. The very long, delicate racemes of flowers are a particular feature of the species. All parts of the plant are poisonous if consumed, the seeds especially so.

each leaf has three distinct leaflets

pale green calyx encloses flower bud

youngest flowers grow at tip of • raceme

Height 6m (20ft)	Shape Broadly spreading	Leaf persistence Deciduous	Leaf type

Family LEGUMINOSAE	Species *Laburnum anagyroides*	Author Medikus

COMMON LABURNUM

Leaves Each with three elliptic leaflets, to 9cm (3½in) long, rounded at the tip, dull deep green above, grey-green and silky-hairy when young beneath. *Bark* Dark grey and smooth, shallowly fissured with age. *Flowers* Pea-like, 2.5cm (1in) long, golden yellow, densely clustered, borne in hanging racemes to 25cm (10in) long, in late spring to early summer. *Fruit* A slightly rounded, hairy, brown pod, to 7.5cm (3in) long, the upper edge thickened, hanging in clusters, with black seeds.
• **NATIVE REGION** C. and S. Europe.
• **HABITAT** Mountainous areas, woods, and thickets.
• **REMARK** All parts of the plant contain a harmful alkaloid, and are poisonous if consumed. The immature seeds look like small, green peas.

greyish green, softly hairy leaf underside

branches carry many simple, leafless racemes crowded together

Height 7m (23ft)	Shape Broadly spreading	Leaf persistence Deciduous	Leaf type

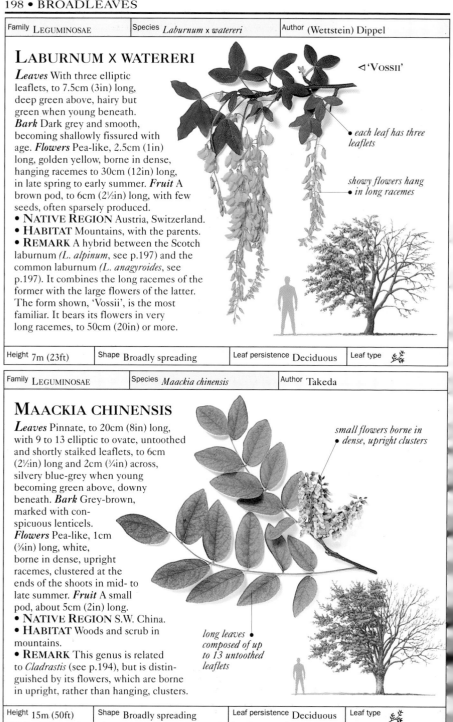

Family LEGUMINOSAE	Species *Laburnum x watereri*	Author (Wettstein) Dippel

LABURNUM X WATERERI

◁ 'VOSSII'

Leaves With three elliptic leaflets, to 7.5cm (3in) long, deep green above, hairy but green when young beneath. **Bark** Dark grey and smooth, becoming shallowly fissured with age. **Flowers** Pea-like, 2.5cm (1in) long, golden yellow, borne in dense, hanging racemes to 30cm (12in) long, in late spring to early summer. **Fruit** A brown pod, to 6cm (2½in) long, with few seeds, often sparsely produced.
- **NATIVE REGION** Austria, Switzerland.
- **HABITAT** Mountains, with the parents.
- **REMARK** A hybrid between the Scotch laburnum *(L. alpinum*, see p.197) and the common laburnum *(L. anagyroides*, see p.197). It combines the long racemes of the former with the large flowers of the latter. The form shown, 'Vossii', is the most familiar. It bears its flowers in very long racemes, to 50cm (20in) or more.

each leaf has three leaflets

showy flowers hang in long racemes

Height 7m (23ft)	Shape Broadly spreading	Leaf persistence Deciduous	Leaf type

Family LEGUMINOSAE	Species *Maackia chinensis*	Author Takeda

MAACKIA CHINENSIS

Leaves Pinnate, to 20cm (8in) long, with 9 to 13 elliptic to ovate, untoothed and shortly stalked leaflets, to 6cm (2½in) long and 2cm (¾in) across, silvery blue-grey when young becoming green above, downy beneath. **Bark** Grey-brown, marked with conspicuous lenticels. **Flowers** Pea-like, 1cm (⅜in) long, white, borne in dense, upright racemes, clustered at the ends of the shoots in mid- to late summer. **Fruit** A small pod, about 5cm (2in) long.
- **NATIVE REGION** S.W. China.
- **HABITAT** Woods and scrub in mountains.
- **REMARK** This genus is related to *Cladrastis* (see p.194), but is distinguished by its flowers, which are borne in upright, rather than hanging, clusters.

small flowers borne in dense, upright clusters

long leaves composed of up to 13 untoothed leaflets

Height 15m (50ft)	Shape Broadly spreading	Leaf persistence Deciduous	Leaf type

Family LEGUMINOSAE	Species *Robinia x holdtii*	Author Beissner

ROBINIA X HOLDTII

Leaves Pinnate, to 45cm (18in) long, with up to 21 oblong leaflets, to 5cm (2in) long and 2.5cm (1in) across, often indented at the tip with a very fine point, deep green above, grey-green beneath, thinly hairy on both sides. **Bark** Grey-brown, deeply furrowed, with scaly ridges. **Flowers** Pea-like, 2cm (¾in) long, white flushed purplish pink, faintly fragrant, borne in hanging clusters over a long period in summer. **Fruit** A slightly sticky, bristly, red pod, about 6cm (2½in) long.
• **NATIVE REGION** Of garden origin.
• **REMARK** This vigorous tree is a hybrid between the pink-flowered, often shrubby, *Robinia luxurians* and the black locust *(Robinia pseudoacacia*, see below). Of the two parent plants, it is most similar in appearance and habit to *R. pseudoacacia*, from which it is distinguished by the colour of its flowers.

very long leaves have leaflets arranged • opposite

• flowers often produced into early autumn

very fine • point at tip of leaflet

Height 20m (65ft)	Shape Broadly columnar	Leaf persistence Deciduous	Leaf type

Family LEGUMINOSAE	Species *Robinia pseudoacacia*	Author Linnaeus

BLACK LOCUST

Leaves Pinnate, to 30cm (12in) long, with 11 to 21 elliptic to ovate, untoothed leaflets, to 5cm (2in) long, often indented and ending in a slender point, blue-green above, grey-green and thinly hairy becoming smooth beneath, the shoot often with two spines at the base of each leaf. **Bark** Grey-brown, deeply furrowed, with scaly ridges. **Flowers** Pea-like, 2cm (¾in) long, white, with a yellow-green blotch, fragrant, in dense, hanging racemes to 20cm (8in) long, in early to midsummer. **Fruit** A smooth, dark brown, hanging pod, to 10cm (4in) long.
• **NATIVE REGION** S.E. United States.
• **HABITAT** Woods and thickets.
• **REMARK** Widely planted and naturalized in North America.

reddish brown calyx has five teeth •

△ ROBINIA PSEUDOACACIA

thin, soft • leaves

△ 'FRISIA'
This smaller form is less vigorous. It has golden yellow foliage from spring to early autumn.

Height 25m (80ft)	Shape Broadly columnar	Leaf persistence Deciduous	Leaf type

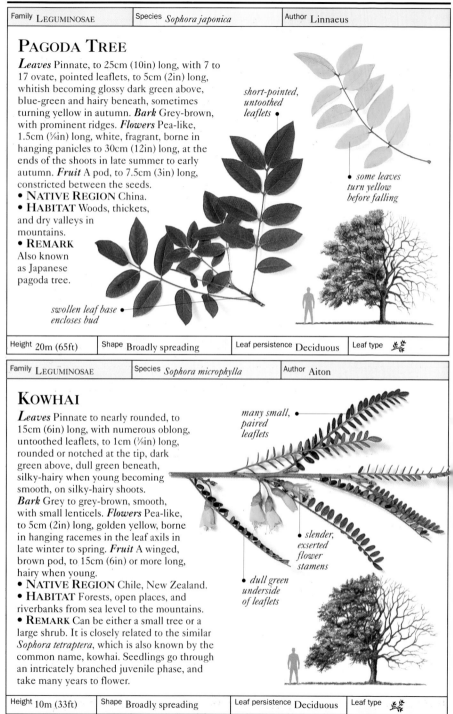

| Family LEGUMINOSAE | Species *Sophora japonica* | Author Linnaeus |

PAGODA TREE

Leaves Pinnate, to 25cm (10in) long, with 7 to 17 ovate, pointed leaflets, to 5cm (2in) long, whitish becoming glossy dark green above, blue-green and hairy beneath, sometimes turning yellow in autumn. **Bark** Grey-brown, with prominent ridges. **Flowers** Pea-like, 1.5cm (⅝in) long, white, fragrant, borne in hanging panicles to 30cm (12in) long, at the ends of the shoots in late summer to early autumn. **Fruit** A pod, to 7.5cm (3in) long, constricted between the seeds.
• **NATIVE REGION** China.
• **HABITAT** Woods, thickets, and dry valleys in mountains.
• **REMARK** Also known as Japanese pagoda tree.

short-pointed, untoothed leaflets •

• some leaves turn yellow before falling

• swollen leaf base encloses bud

| Height 20m (65ft) | Shape Broadly spreading | Leaf persistence Deciduous | Leaf type |

| Family LEGUMINOSAE | Species *Sophora microphylla* | Author Aiton |

KOWHAI

Leaves Pinnate to nearly rounded, to 15cm (6in) long, with numerous oblong, untoothed leaflets, to 1cm (⅜in) long, rounded or notched at the tip, dark green above, dull green beneath, silky-hairy when young becoming smooth, on silky-hairy shoots. **Bark** Grey to grey-brown, smooth, with small lenticels. **Flowers** Pea-like, to 5cm (2in) long, golden yellow, borne in hanging racemes in the leaf axils in late winter to spring. **Fruit** A winged, brown pod, to 15cm (6in) or more long, hairy when young.
• **NATIVE REGION** Chile, New Zealand.
• **HABITAT** Forests, open places, and riverbanks from sea level to the mountains.
• **REMARK** Can be either a small tree or a large shrub. It is closely related to the similar *Sophora tetraptera*, which is also known by the common name, kowhai. Seedlings go through an intricately branched juvenile phase, and take many years to flower.

many small, • paired leaflets

• slender, exserted flower stamens

• dull green underside of leaflets

| Height 10m (33ft) | Shape Broadly spreading | Leaf persistence Deciduous | Leaf type |

MAGNOLIACEAE

T HIS FAMILY of 12 genera and about 200 species is distributed in two main areas. Most species are found in east Asia, from the Himalayas through China to Japan, and in South-east Asia to New Guinea; relatively few occur from the eastern United States through Mexico to tropical South America. The deciduous and evergreen trees and shrubs have alternate, untoothed, and (only occasionally) lobed leaves. The showy flowers are borne singly.

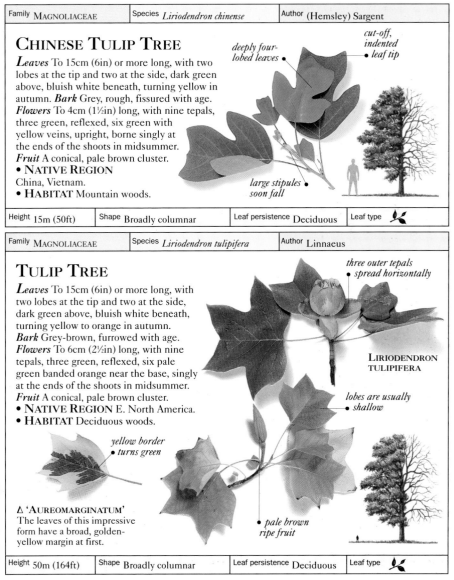

Family MAGNOLIACEAE	Species *Liriodendron chinense*	Author (Hemsley) Sargent

CHINESE TULIP TREE

Leaves To 15cm (6in) or more long, with two lobes at the tip and two at the side, dark green above, bluish white beneath, turning yellow in autumn. **Bark** Grey, rough, fissured with age. **Flowers** To 4cm (1½in) long, with nine tepals, three green, reflexed, six green with yellow veins, upright, borne singly at the ends of the shoots in midsummer. **Fruit** A conical, pale brown cluster.
• **NATIVE REGION** China, Vietnam.
• **HABITAT** Mountain woods.

deeply four-lobed leaves

cut-off, indented leaf tip

large stipules soon fall

Height 15m (50ft)	Shape Broadly columnar	Leaf persistence Deciduous	Leaf type

Family MAGNOLIACEAE	Species *Liriodendron tulipifera*	Author Linnaeus

TULIP TREE

Leaves To 15cm (6in) or more long, with two lobes at the tip and two at the side, dark green above, bluish white beneath, turning yellow to orange in autumn. **Bark** Grey-brown, furrowed with age. **Flowers** To 6cm (2½in) long, with nine tepals, three green, reflexed, six pale green banded orange near the base, singly at the ends of the shoots in midsummer. **Fruit** A conical, pale brown cluster.
• **NATIVE REGION** E. North America.
• **HABITAT** Deciduous woods.

three outer tepals spread horizontally

LIRIODENDRON TULIPIFERA

lobes are usually shallow

yellow border turns green

△ 'AUREOMARGINATUM'
The leaves of this impressive form have a broad, golden-yellow margin at first.

pale brown ripe fruit

Height 50m (164ft)	Shape Broadly columnar	Leaf persistence Deciduous	Leaf type

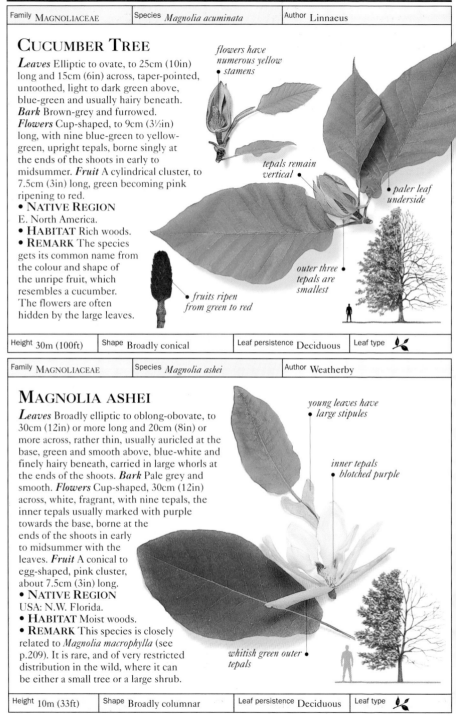

Family MAGNOLIACEAE	Species *Magnolia acuminata*	Author Linnaeus

CUCUMBER TREE

Leaves Elliptic to ovate, to 25cm (10in) long and 15cm (6in) across, taper-pointed, untoothed, light to dark green above, blue-green and usually hairy beneath. **Bark** Brown-grey and furrowed. **Flowers** Cup-shaped, to 9cm (3½in) long, with nine blue-green to yellow-green, upright tepals, borne singly at the ends of the shoots in early to midsummer. **Fruit** A cylindrical cluster, to 7.5cm (3in) long, green becoming pink ripening to red.

• **NATIVE REGION**
E. North America.
• **HABITAT** Rich woods.
• **REMARK** The species gets its common name from the colour and shape of the unripe fruit, which resembles a cucumber. The flowers are often hidden by the large leaves.

flowers have numerous yellow stamens

tepals remain vertical

paler leaf underside

outer three tepals are smallest

fruits ripen from green to red

Height 30m (100ft)	Shape Broadly conical	Leaf persistence Deciduous	Leaf type

Family MAGNOLIACEAE	Species *Magnolia ashei*	Author Weatherby

MAGNOLIA ASHEI

Leaves Broadly elliptic to oblong-obovate, to 30cm (12in) or more long and 20cm (8in) or more across, rather thin, usually auricled at the base, green and smooth above, blue-white and finely hairy beneath, carried in large whorls at the ends of the shoots. **Bark** Pale grey and smooth. **Flowers** Cup-shaped, 30cm (12in) across, white, fragrant, with nine tepals, the inner tepals usually marked with purple towards the base, borne at the ends of the shoots in early to midsummer with the leaves. **Fruit** A conical to egg-shaped, pink cluster, about 7.5cm (3in) long.

• **NATIVE REGION**
USA: N.W. Florida.
• **HABITAT** Moist woods.
• **REMARK** This species is closely related to *Magnolia macrophylla* (see p.209). It is rare, and of very restricted distribution in the wild, where it can be either a small tree or a large shrub.

young leaves have large stipules

inner tepals blotched purple

whitish green outer tepals

Height 10m (33ft)	Shape Broadly columnar	Leaf persistence Deciduous	Leaf type

Family MAGNOLIACEAE	Species *Magnolia campbellii*	Author J.D. Hooker & Thomson

MAGNOLIA CAMPBELLII

Leaves Oblong to ovate or obovate, to 25cm (10in) or more long, usually abruptly pointed, untoothed, bronze when young becoming dark green and smooth above, paler and smooth or hairy beneath. **Bark** Grey and smooth. **Flowers** Very large, 30cm (12in) across, pale to deep pink to purplish pink or white, slightly fragrant, with up to 16 tepals, the outer tepals spreading, the inner tepals upright, giving the flower its characteristic cup-and-saucer shape, carried on smooth stalks, opening in late winter to early spring before the leaves. **Fruit** A cylindrical, cone-like, red cluster, to 15cm (6in) long.
• **NATIVE REGION** S.W. China, Himalayas.
• **HABITAT** Forests in mountainous areas.
• **REMARK** A magnificent, large tree, much sought after in gardens for its huge flowers. On plants raised from seed, flowers are produced only after 20 years.

MAGNOLIA
CAMPBELLII

smooth flower stalks

inner tepals remain upright

large, smooth leaves emerge after flowers

△ MAGNOLIA
CAMPBELLII

△ SUBSP. MOLLICOMATA
The flowers of this subspecies are produced slightly earlier in the year, on younger plants.

outer tepals spread widely

Height 30m (100ft)	Shape Broadly conical	Leaf persistence Deciduous	Leaf type

Family MAGNOLIACEAE	Species *Magnolia dawsoniana*	Author Rehder & Wilson

MAGNOLIA DAWSONIANA

Leaves Elliptic to obovate, to 15cm (6in) long and 7.5cm (3in) across, rounded at the tip, dark green and smooth above, paler and smooth except for hairs along the veins beneath. **Bark** Grey, smooth, with conspicuous raised lenticels, fissured at the base. **Flowers** Held horizontally, to 12cm (4¾in) long, pale pink, slightly fragrant, with 9 to 12 drooping tepals, opening in late winter or early spring before the leaves. **Fruit** A cylindrical, reddish green cluster, to 10cm (4in) long.
• **NATIVE REGION** China.
• **HABITAT**
Mountain woods.
• **REMARK**
One of the earliest-flowering magnolias.

colour becomes paler as flowers age

dark green leaf upperside

paler leaf underside

leaf buds unfold after flowers open

Height 12m (40ft)	Shape Broadly conical	Leaf persistence Deciduous	Leaf type

Family MAGNOLIACEAE	Species *Magnolia delavayi*	Author Franchet

MAGNOLIA DELAVAYI

Leaves Elliptic to oblong, to 30cm (12in) long and 15cm (6in) across, dark green above, downy when young becoming more or less smooth on both sides. **Bark** Dark brown, vertically fissured. **Flowers** Saucer-shaped, to 20cm (8in) across, fragrant, with nine fleshy tepals, the outer three greenish white, reflexed, the inner six creamy white, spreading, opening in late summer. **Fruit** A cylindrical cluster, to 10cm (4in) long, green ripening to pale brown.
• **NATIVE REGION**
S.W. China.
• **HABITAT** Scrubland and open places.

rigid, glossy dark green leaves

creamy white flowers open at night and fade the next day

grey-green, hairy young leaves eventually become smooth on underside

Height 10m (33ft)	Shape Broadly spreading	Leaf persistence Evergreen	Leaf type

Family MAGNOLIACEAE	Species *Magnolia fraseri*	Author Walter

MAGNOLIA FRASERI

Leaves Obovate, to 40cm (16in) long and 20cm (8in) across, auricled at the base, pointed at the tip, bronze when young becoming pale green, smooth on both sides. **Bark** Brown or grey, smooth. **Flowers** Vase-shaped in bud, to 12cm (4¾in) long, opening saucer-shaped, the nine tepals creamy white flushed green on the outer surface, borne singly at the ends of the shoots in late spring to early summer. **Fruit** A cone-like, red cluster, to 10cm (4in) long.
• **NATIVE REGION** S.E. United States.
• **HABITAT** Rich mountain forests.

• *creamy yellowish white flowers open after leaves unfold*

large, thin, soft leaves whorled at shoot end •

Height 14m (46ft)	Shape Broadly spreading	Leaf persistence Deciduous	Leaf type

Family MAGNOLIACEAE	Species *Magnolia grandiflora*	Author Linnaeus

BULL BAY

Leaves Elliptic to ovate or lanceolate, to 25cm (10in) long and 10cm (4in) across, rigid and leathery, glossy dark green and smooth above, paler or covered in rusty hairs beneath. **Bark** Grey, cracking into small plates. **Flowers** Cup-shaped, to 30cm (12in) across, creamy white, very fragrant, with 9 to 12 or more thick tepals, borne singly at the ends of the shoots in early summer. **Fruit** An egg-shaped, red cluster, to 10cm (4in) long.
• **NATIVE REGION** S.E. United States.
• **HABITAT** Riverbanks and moist places on coastal plain.
• **REMARK** Plants cultivated in areas that are cooler than the native region flower in late summer to autumn.

• *very fragrant, large white flowers*

leaf underside often covered in rust-coloured • hairs

• *flowers have 9 to 12 or more tepals*

• *glossy dark green leaf upperside*

Height 25m (80ft)	Shape Broadly conical	Leaf persistence Evergreen	Leaf type

Family MAGNOLIACEAE	Species *Magnolia* 'Heaven Scent'	Author None

MAGNOLIA 'HEAVEN SCENT'

Leaves Broadly elliptic, to 20cm (8in) long, pointed at the tip, glossy green above, paler beneath. *Bark* Grey and smooth. *Flowers* Upright and vase-shaped, 13cm (5in) long, narrow at first later opening more widely, strongly fragrant, the nine tepals pale pink but more deeply shaded towards the base, with a distinct, darker pink band on the back, opening in spring to early summer before and with the leaves. *Fruit* Cone-like, the ripe seeds protruding and hanging for some time.
• **NATIVE REGION** Of garden origin.
• **REMARK** This hybrid between the shrubby *M. liliiflora* 'Nigra' and *M.* x *veitchii* (see p.214) is one of the Gresham Hybrids that resulted from Drury Todd Gresham's programme of hybridization in California in the 1950s. By careful selection of both parents and offspring, he produced small trees that combine attributes of some of the best magnolias. 'Peppermint Stick' and 'Sayonara' belong also to this group.

pointed tepals spread slightly as flower ages

'HEAVEN SCENT'

◁ 'PEPPERMINT STICK'
The buds of this hybrid between *M. liliiflora* and *M.* x *veitchii* are 11cm (4½in) long.

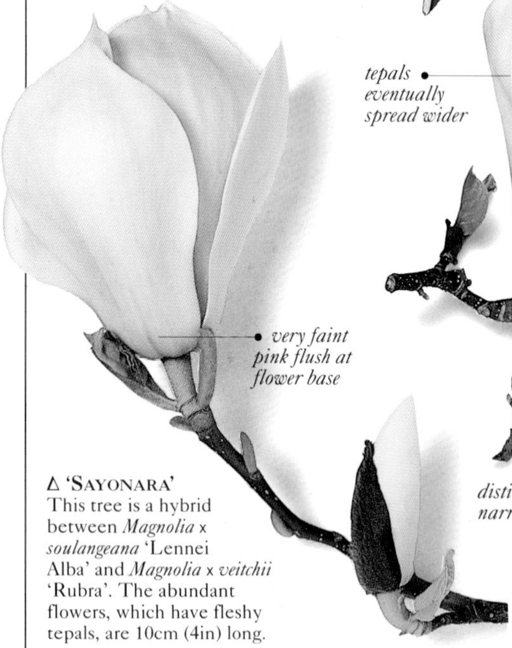

tepals eventually spread wider

very faint pink flush at flower base

△ 'SAYONARA'
This tree is a hybrid between *Magnolia* x *soulangeana* 'Lennei Alba' and *Magnolia* x *veitchii* 'Rubra'. The abundant flowers, which have fleshy tepals, are 10cm (4in) long.

distinctively narrow buds

Height 10m (33ft)	Shape Broadly spreading	Leaf persistence Deciduous	Leaf type

Family MAGNOLIACEAE	Species *Magnolia hypoleuca*	Author Siebold & Zuccarini

MAGNOLIA HYPOLEUCA

Leaves Obovate, to 45cm (18in) long and 20cm (8in) across, short-pointed at the tip, deep green and smooth above, pale blue-green and hairy at least when young beneath, in large whorls at the ends of the shoots. *Bark* Grey and smooth.
Flowers Large, cup-shaped, 20cm (8in) across, very strongly fragrant, with 9 to 12 creamy white tepals, the outer tepals sometimes tinged pink, the filaments and stigmas bright red, opening in summer.
Fruit A cylindrical, large, red cluster, to 20cm (8in) long, from which red seeds hang when ripe.
• **NATIVE REGION** Japan.
• **HABITAT** Woods in mountainous areas.
• **REMARK** Also known as *Magnolia obovata*. The powerful scent of the flowers provides an easy clue to distinguishing this species. In Japan, the large leaves are used to wrap food.

• *large leaves whorled beneath flowers*

• *outer tepals may have pink tinge*

Height 30m (100ft)	Shape Broadly columnar	Leaf persistence Deciduous	Leaf type

Family MAGNOLIACEAE	Species *Magnolia kobus*	Author Candolle

MAGNOLIA KOBUS

Leaves Elliptic to obovate, to 15cm (6in) long and 9cm (3½in) across, tapered at the base, short-pointed at the tip, dark green and smooth above, paler and hairy along the veins beneath. *Bark* Grey and smooth. *Flowers* Usually held horizontally, to 10cm (4in) across, creamy white sometimes flushed pink at the base, slightly fragrant, with six petal-like tepals and three smaller, sepal-like tepals, opening in early spring before the leaves emerge.
Fruit A cylindrical, pink to red cluster, to 10cm (4in) long, from which red seeds hang when ripe.
• **NATIVE REGION** Japan, S. Korea.
• **HABITAT** Mountain forests.

very small outer tepals •

• *smooth leaf buds open after flowers*

• *leaves taper towards base*

Height 20m (65ft)	Shape Broadly conical	Leaf persistence Deciduous	Leaf type

Family MAGNOLIACEAE	Species *Magnolia x loebneri*	Author Kache

MAGNOLIA X LOEBNERI

Leaves Oblanceolate to elliptic, to 15cm (6in) long, glossy dark green to paler green, usually smooth. *Bark* Grey, smooth. *Flowers* Variable, upright to horizontal, to 15cm (6in) across, white to pink, with up to 16 or more tepals and three small, sepal-like tepals, opening in early to mid-spring. *Fruit* A cylindrical, pinkish red cluster, to 10cm (4in) long.
• **NATIVE REGION**
Of garden origin.
• **REMARK** A group of hybrids between *Magnolia kobus* (see p.207) and the usually shrubby *Magnolia stellata*, first raised in Germany, with many selected forms that combine the best qualities of both parents. The starry flowers are inherited from the aptly named *M. stellata*.

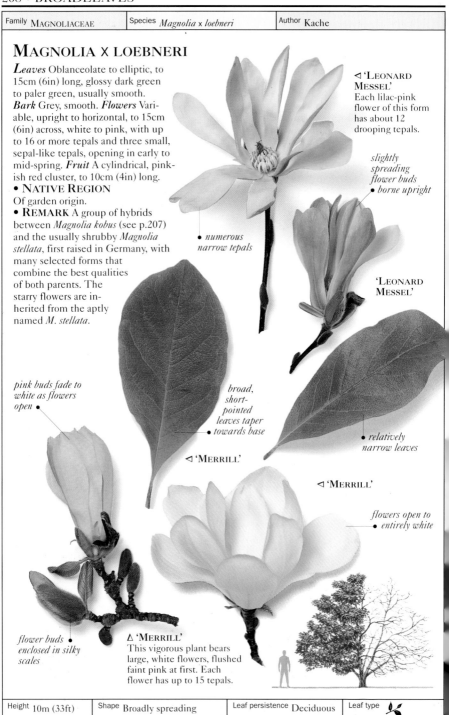

◁ 'LEONARD MESSEL'
Each lilac-pink flower of this form has about 12 drooping tepals.

slightly spreading flower buds
• *borne upright*

• *numerous narrow tepals*

'LEONARD MESSEL'

pink buds fade to white as flowers open •

broad, short-pointed leaves taper
• *towards base*

◁ 'MERRILL'

• *relatively narrow leaves*

◁ 'MERRILL'

flowers open to
• *entirely white*

flower buds •
enclosed in silky scales

△ 'MERRILL'
This vigorous plant bears large, white flowers, flushed faint pink at first. Each flower has up to 15 tepals.

Height 10m (33ft)	Shape Broadly spreading	Leaf persistence Deciduous	Leaf type

Family MAGNOLIACEAE	Species *Magnolia macrophylla*	Author A. Michaux

MAGNOLIA MACROPHYLLA

Leaves Very large and rather thin, broadly elliptic to oblong-ovate, to 60cm (24in) or more long and 30cm (12in) across, usually auricled at the base, green and smooth above, blue-green to blue-white and finely hairy beneath, in large whorls at the ends of stout shoots. *Bark* Pale grey and smooth. *Flowers* Very large and broadly cup-shaped, 30cm (12in) across, creamy white to yellowish, fragrant, with nine tepals, the inner tepals petal-like, usually marked with purple towards the base, the outer tepals sepal-like, held upright, at the ends of the shoots in early to midsummer with the leaves. *Fruit* A rounded, pink cluster, about 7.5cm (3in) long, from which red seeds hang when ripe.
• NATIVE REGION S.E. United States.
• HABITAT Rich, moist woods.
• REMARK The enormous leaves and flowers of this species are among the largest of those of all deciduous trees that are native to temperate regions.

distinctively large leaves

outer tepals streaked green

grey young shoot covered with soft hairs

bluish green leaf underside shows strong midrib

twin auricles at leaf base

Height 15m (50ft)	Shape Broadly columnar	Leaf persistence Deciduous	Leaf type

Family MAGNOLIACEAE	Species *Magnolia officinalis*	Author Rehder & Wilson

MAGNOLIA OFFICINALIS

Leaves Obovate, to 45cm (18in) long and 20cm (8in) across, tapered at the base, rounded to short-pointed at the tip, rather pale green and smooth above, whitish and softly hairy when young beneath, carried in whorls at the ends of the shoots. *Bark* Pale grey and smooth. *Flowers* Cup- to saucer-shaped, 15cm (6in) across, creamy white, fragrant, the stamens with red filaments, at the ends of the shoots in late spring to early summer. *Fruit* An oblong, pinkish red cluster, to 15cm (6in) long, from which bright red seeds emerge and hang.
• **NATIVE REGION** C. China.
• **HABITAT** Now known only in cultivation.
• **REMARK** The form shown here, var. *biloba*, differs only in the large notch at the tip of the leaves. The bark was traditionally used for medicinal purposes. The practice of stripping it from the trees, thus killing them, may be responsible for the probable extinction of the species in the wild.

large fruits develop in autumn

△ VAR. BILOBA

VAR. BILOBA ▷

flowers soon fade and wither

large leaves whorled around flower

wavy leaf margin

Height 20m (65ft)	Shape Broadly columnar	Leaf persistence Deciduous	Leaf type

Family MAGNOLIACEAE	Species *Magnolia x soulangeana*	Author Soulange-Bodin

MAGNOLIA X SOULANGEANA

Leaves Elliptic to obovate, to 20cm (8in) long and 12cm (4¾in) across, tapered at the base, usually rounded at the tip, with a short point, dark green and nearly smooth above, paler and finely hairy beneath. *Bark* Grey and smooth. *Flowers* Variable, from goblet- to cup- or saucer-shaped, to 25cm (10in) across, with usually nine white to pink or deep purple-pink tepals, in spring to early summer from before to after the leaves emerge. *Fruit* A cylindrical cluster, to 10cm (4in) long, green ripening to pink.
• **NATIVE REGION** Of garden origin.
• **REMARK** A hybrid between *Magnolia denudata* and *Magnolia liliiflora*.

leaves end in abruptly short-pointed tip

inner tepals spread more or less widely

leaves taper to narrowed base

three smaller outer tepals

deep pink flush at base of tepals fades to pale streak at tip

shoots marked with pale lenticels

flowers open from cylindrical buds

fruit clusters ripen from green to pink

silky-hairy flower buds

Height 9m (30ft)	Shape Broadly spreading	Leaf persistence Deciduous	Leaf type

Family MAGNOLIACEAE	Species *Magnolia* x *soulangeana*	Author Soulange-Bodin

▽ 'BROZZONII'
This conical tree has large, white flowers, faintly flushed pink at the base. They can reach 25cm (10in) across and are produced continuously over a long period from mid-spring to early summer.

• centre of tepals coloured rich purplish pink

large flowers have six tepals •

• edge of tepals coloured nearly white

narrow • buds later open more widely

merest pink flush at base of tepals •

△ 'PICTURE'
The flowers of this form are strongly marked with purplish pink. The plant tends towards a compact and upright, rather than broadly spreading, habit.

silky bud scales • enclose new leaves

• richly coloured tepals

goblet-shaped • flowers open from broad buds

'RUSTICA RUBRA' ▷
This form bears large, goblet-shaped flowers. The tepals are shaded deep purplish pink on the outer surface, particularly at the base. The colour fades to cream flushed pink at the tip.

• first flowers open before leaves emerge

Height 9m (30ft)	Shape Broadly spreading	Leaf persistence Deciduous	Leaf type

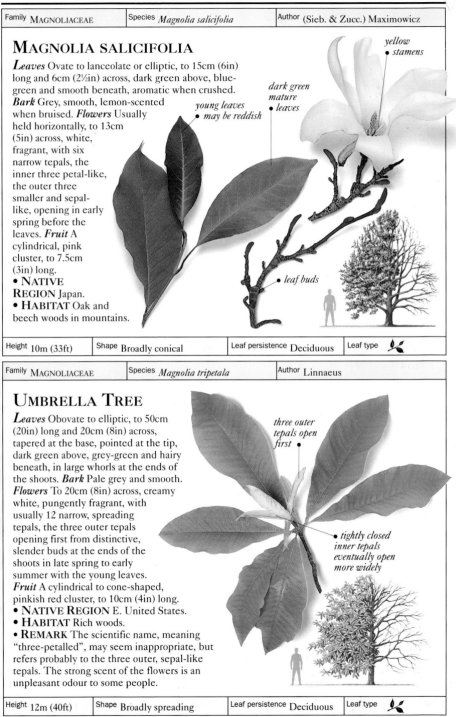

Family MAGNOLIACEAE	Species *Magnolia salicifolia*	Author (Sieb. & Zucc.) Maximowicz

MAGNOLIA SALICIFOLIA

Leaves Ovate to lanceolate or elliptic, to 15cm (6in) long and 6cm (2½in) across, dark green above, blue-green and smooth beneath, aromatic when crushed. *Bark* Grey, smooth, lemon-scented when bruised. *Flowers* Usually held horizontally, to 13cm (5in) across, white, fragrant, with six narrow tepals, the inner three petal-like, the outer three smaller and sepal-like, opening in early spring before the leaves. *Fruit* A cylindrical, pink cluster, to 7.5cm (3in) long.
• **NATIVE REGION** Japan.
• **HABITAT** Oak and beech woods in mountains.

yellow stamens

dark green mature leaves

young leaves may be reddish

leaf buds

Height 10m (33ft)	Shape Broadly conical	Leaf persistence Deciduous	Leaf type

Family MAGNOLIACEAE	Species *Magnolia tripetala*	Author Linnaeus

UMBRELLA TREE

Leaves Obovate to elliptic, to 50cm (20in) long and 20cm (8in) across, tapered at the base, pointed at the tip, dark green above, grey-green and hairy beneath, in large whorls at the ends of the shoots. *Bark* Pale grey and smooth. *Flowers* To 20cm (8in) across, creamy white, pungently fragrant, with usually 12 narrow, spreading tepals, the three outer tepals opening first from distinctive, slender buds at the ends of the shoots in late spring to early summer with the young leaves. *Fruit* A cylindrical to cone-shaped, pinkish red cluster, to 10cm (4in) long.
• **NATIVE REGION** E. United States.
• **HABITAT** Rich woods.
• **REMARK** The scientific name, meaning "three-petalled", may seem inappropriate, but refers probably to the three outer, sepal-like tepals. The strong scent of the flowers is an unpleasant odour to some people.

three outer tepals open first

tightly closed inner tepals eventually open more widely

Height 12m (40ft)	Shape Broadly spreading	Leaf persistence Deciduous	Leaf type

Family MAGNOLIACEAE	Species *Magnolia x veitchii*	Author Bean

MAGNOLIA X VEITCHII

Leaves Obovate to oblong, to 30cm (12in) long and 15cm (6in) across, short-pointed at the tip, bronze-purple at first becoming dark green and smooth above, downy at least on the veins beneath. *Bark* Grey and smooth. *Flowers* Vase-shaped, to 15cm (6in) long, white to pink, fragrant, with usually nine tepals, opening in mid-spring usually before the leaves. *Fruit* A cylindrical cluster, to 10cm (4in) long, pinkish green ripening to purple-brown.

• **NATIVE REGION**
Of garden origin.

• **REMARK** One of a number of hybrids between the often shrubby yulan *(Magnolia denudata)* and *Magnolia campbellii* (see p.203). These vigorous trees owe their large size to the latter parent, which can also reach 30m (100ft) in the wild. They are attractive plants, usually producing abundant flowers and pretty young

• inner and outer tepals are upright

△ 'ISCA'
This cultivar flowers in mid-spring.

lustrous young leaves tinged bronze •

• flowers flushed slightly pink at base

• white flowers flushed deep pink appear pale pink from a distance

△ 'PETER VEITCH'
The goblet-shaped, soft pink blooms of this hardy magnolia appear in mid-spring before the leaves. Flowers are produced even on young plants.

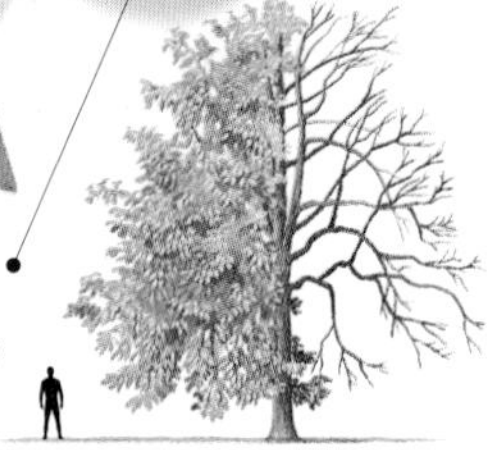

mature leaves • are dark green and smooth on upper surface

Height 30m (100ft)	Shape Broadly columnar	Leaf persistence Deciduous	Leaf type

Family MAGNOLIACEAE	Species *Magnolia* 'Wada's Memory'	Author None

MAGNOLIA 'WADA'S MEMORY'

Leaves Obovate to narrowly ovate, to 17.5cm (7in) long, tapered at the base, abruptly pointed, red-purple when young becoming glossy dark green above, blue-green beneath, smooth on both sides. ***Bark*** Grey, smooth. ***Flowers*** Held horizontally, 15cm (6in) across, creamy white becoming white, fragrant, the tepals soon drooping, opening from felted buds. ***Fruit*** A cylindrical, pink to red cluster, to 10cm (4in) long, not usually produced.
• **NATIVE REGION** Of garden origin.
• **REMARK** Probably a hybrid between *Magnolia kobus* (see p.207) and *Magnolia salicifolia* (see p.213), which originated in Japan. It is named after the Japanese nurseryman, Koichiro Wada.

tepals soon flop as flower buds open

much smaller tepals at base of flower

young leaves coloured reddish purple

silky scales enclose flower bud

young leaves emerge just after first flowers

leaves mature to olive green

Height 9m (30ft)	Shape Broadly conical	Leaf persistence Deciduous	Leaf type

MALVACEAE

W ITH MORE THAN 100 GENERA and 1,500 species, the mallow family is found worldwide, except in the very coldest parts. The plants are deciduous and evergreen trees and shrubs, as well as herbaceous. The alternate leaves are often palmately lobed. Flowers vary from large and showy to very small.

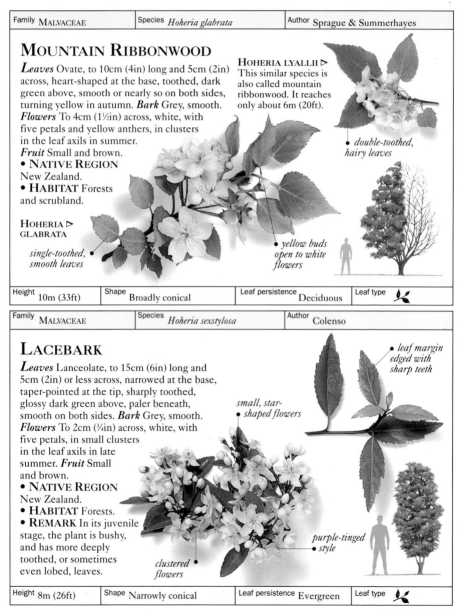

Family MALVACEAE	Species *Hoheria glabrata*	Author Sprague & Summerhayes

MOUNTAIN RIBBONWOOD

Leaves Ovate, to 10cm (4in) long and 5cm (2in) across, heart-shaped at the base, toothed, dark green above, smooth or nearly so on both sides, turning yellow in autumn. **Bark** Grey, smooth. **Flowers** To 4cm (1½in) across, white, with five petals and yellow anthers, in clusters in the leaf axils in summer. **Fruit** Small and brown.
• **NATIVE REGION** New Zealand.
• **HABITAT** Forests and scrubland.

HOHERIA ▷ GLABRATA

single-toothed, smooth leaves

HOHERIA LYALLII ▷ This similar species is also called mountain ribbonwood. It reaches only about 6m (20ft).

double-toothed, hairy leaves

yellow buds open to white flowers

Height 10m (33ft)	Shape Broadly conical	Leaf persistence Deciduous	Leaf type

Family MALVACEAE	Species *Hoheria sexstylosa*	Author Colenso

LACEBARK

Leaves Lanceolate, to 15cm (6in) long and 5cm (2in) or less across, narrowed at the base, taper-pointed at the tip, sharply toothed, glossy dark green above, paler beneath, smooth on both sides. **Bark** Grey, smooth. **Flowers** To 2cm (¾in) across, white, with five petals, in small clusters in the leaf axils in late summer. **Fruit** Small and brown.
• **NATIVE REGION** New Zealand.
• **HABITAT** Forests.
• **REMARK** In its juvenile stage, the plant is bushy, and has more deeply toothed, or sometimes even lobed, leaves.

leaf margin edged with sharp teeth

small, star- shaped flowers

purple-tinged style

clustered flowers

Height 8m (26ft)	Shape Narrowly conical	Leaf persistence Evergreen	Leaf type

MELIACEAE

O CCURRING IN TEMPERATE regions of east Asia, this largely tropical and subtropical family is composed of some 50 genera and nearly 600 species. The plants, which are evergreen and deciduous trees and shrubs, have leaves that are most often pinnate, arranged alternately. The flowers are usually small, frequently borne in large clusters. The fruit is a woody capsule. Many trees that belong to Meliaceae have an important commercial value for their timber: several of the species produce the hardwood, mahogany.

Family MELIACEAE	Species *Toona sinensis*	Author (Jussieu) Roemer

TOONA SINENSIS

Leaves Pinnate, to 60cm (24in) long, with up to 26 oblong-lanceolate, taper-pointed, remotely toothed leaflets, to 15cm (6in) long, the terminal leaflet often missing, bronze to pinkish and downy when young becoming dark green and smooth or nearly so, tinged yellow in autumn, smelling of onions when crushed. *Bark* Brown, peeling in long strips. *Flowers* Small and white, fragrant, in large, drooping panicles 30cm (12in) or more long, from the ends of the shoots in midsummer. *Fruit* A woody, brown capsule, 3cm (1¼in) long.
• **NATIVE REGION** China.
• **HABITAT** Woods.
• **REMARK** Also known as *Cedrela sinensis*.

terminal leaflet is sometimes absent •

leaflets edged with very small teeth •

bark peels in long strips on older plants •

smallest leaflets at leaf base •

Height 20m (65ft)	Shape Broadly columnar	Leaf persistence Deciduous	Leaf type

MORACEAE

THIS LARGE FAMILY includes the figs *(Ficus,* see p.219) and mulberries *(Morus,* see p.220). Its 50 genera and some 1,200 species of deciduous and evergreen trees, shrubs, and climbing and herbaceous plants are distributed worldwide. The leaves are usually alternate and simple, and, occasionally, lobed. Male and female flowers are borne separately, in small clusters.

Family MORACEAE	Species *Broussonetia papyrifera*	Author (Linnaeus) Ventenat

PAPER MULBERRY

Leaves Ovate to broadly ovate, to 20cm (8in) long and 15cm (6in) across, sometimes lobed, coarsely toothed, purplish at first becoming matt dark green, roughly hairy above, softly hairy beneath. *Bark* Grey-brown, shallowly fissured. *Flowers* Males and females both small, males white, in stout, drooping catkins, females green, with slender, purple, protruding stigmas, borne in dense, rounded heads on separate plants in late spring to early summer. *Fruit* Red, protruding from a rounded cluster, 2cm (¾in) across.
• NATIVE REGION China, Japan.
• HABITAT Sunny, fertile situations.
• REMARK In Japan, the bark is traditionally used to make paper.

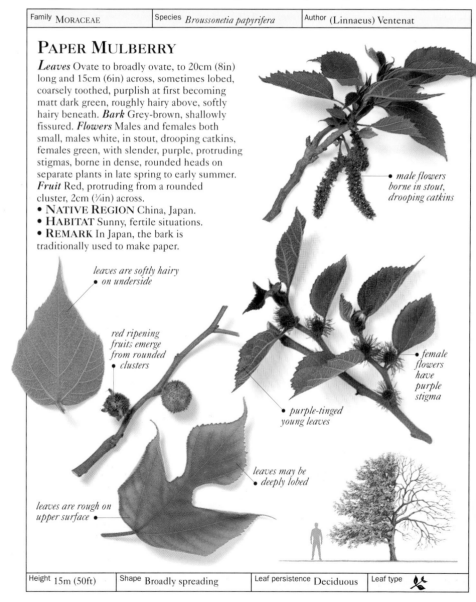

• *male flowers borne in stout, drooping catkins*

leaves are softly hairy on underside •

red ripening fruits emerge from rounded clusters •

• *female flowers have purple stigma*

• *purple-tinged young leaves*

leaves may be deeply lobed •

leaves are rough on upper surface •

Height 15m (50ft)	Shape Broadly spreading	Leaf persistence Deciduous	Leaf type

Family MORACEAE	Species *Ficus carica*	Author Linnaeus

COMMON FIG

Leaves Rounded in outline, to 30cm (12in) long and across, deeply cut into three to five lobes, heart-shaped at the base, toothed, glossy green above, rough with hairs on both sides, turning yellow in autumn. *Bark* Grey and smooth. *Flowers* Males and females both very small, borne inconspicuously inside a fleshy, green receptacle, on separate plants in late spring. *Fruit* Numerous small seeds borne inside a receptacle, the whole green ripening to brown or purple, forming the edible fig.
• **NATIVE REGION** S.W. Asia.
• **HABITAT** Broadleaf forests.
• **REMARK** This species is commonly naturalized in the Mediterranean. It favours rocky places, including old walls. Plants are fertilized by female wasps, which take pollen from the tree in which they hatched to one in which they lay their eggs. Most cultivated plants produce fruit without pollination.

fleshy receptacle contains many • tiny seeds

fruits of some forms ripen to purple

green unripe • fruit

long • leaf stalk

leathery leaves have • visible ribs and network of veins

Height 10m (33ft)	Shape Broadly spreading	Leaf persistence Deciduous	Leaf type

| Family MORACEAE | Species *Maclura pomifera* | Author (Rafinesque) Schneider |

OSAGE ORANGE

Leaves Ovate, to 10cm (4in) long and 5cm (2in) across, untoothed, glossy bright green above, smooth, turning yellow in autumn. *Bark* Orange-brown, fissured. *Flowers* Males and females small, yellow-green, in clusters 1cm (⅜in) long, on separate plants in early summer. *Fruit* A wrinkled, yellow-green cluster, to 10cm (4in) across.
• **NATIVE REGION**
C. and S. United States.
• **HABITAT** Rich, moist soil.

small fruits fuse to form heavy fruit mass

leaves taper to long, slender point

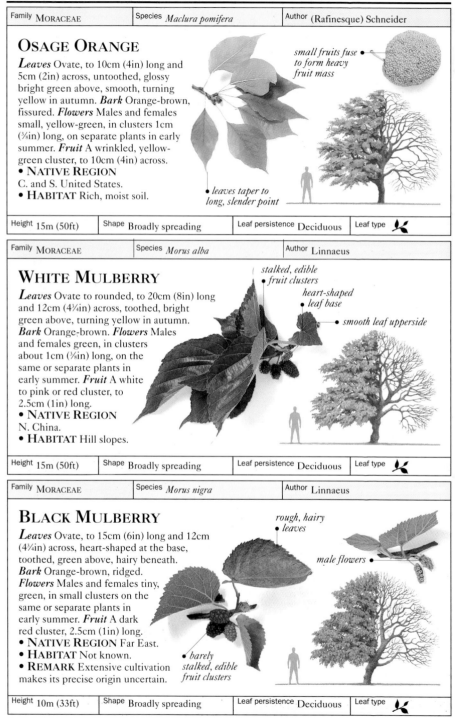

| Height 15m (50ft) | Shape Broadly spreading | Leaf persistence Deciduous | Leaf type |

| Family MORACEAE | Species *Morus alba* | Author Linnaeus |

WHITE MULBERRY

Leaves Ovate to rounded, to 20cm (8in) long and 12cm (4¾in) across, toothed, bright green above, turning yellow in autumn. *Bark* Orange-brown. *Flowers* Males and females green, in clusters about 1cm (⅜in) long, on the same or separate plants in early summer. *Fruit* A white to pink or red cluster, to 2.5cm (1in) long.
• **NATIVE REGION**
N. China.
• **HABITAT** Hill slopes.

stalked, edible fruit clusters

heart-shaped leaf base

smooth leaf upperside

| Height 15m (50ft) | Shape Broadly spreading | Leaf persistence Deciduous | Leaf type |

| Family MORACEAE | Species *Morus nigra* | Author Linnaeus |

BLACK MULBERRY

Leaves Ovate, to 15cm (6in) long and 12cm (4¾in) across, heart-shaped at the base, toothed, green above, hairy beneath. *Bark* Orange-brown, ridged. *Flowers* Males and females tiny, green, in small clusters on the same or separate plants in early summer. *Fruit* A dark red cluster, 2.5cm (1in) long.
• **NATIVE REGION** Far East.
• **HABITAT** Not known.
• **REMARK** Extensive cultivation makes its precise origin uncertain.

rough, hairy leaves

male flowers

barely stalked, edible fruit clusters

| Height 10m (33ft) | Shape Broadly spreading | Leaf persistence Deciduous | Leaf type |

MYRTACEAE

T HIS LARGE FAMILY is distributed most widely in the southern hemisphere. Despite the fact that it extends to temperate regions of the northern hemisphere, it does not grow wild in North America, and is represented in Europe only by the myrtle *(Myrtus communis)*. It contains nearly 4,000 species of usually evergreen, frequently aromatic, trees and shrubs, in over 100 genera. The leaves are often opposite. The flowers have usually four or five petals and numerous stamens. In eucalyptus species, the petals form a cap over the flower, which falls as the flower opens.

Family MYRTACEAE	Species *Callistemon* species	Author None

CALLISTEMONS

The callistemons, or bottlebrushes, are all native to Australia, and can be found growing usually in moist habitats. Some make small trees, reaching about 10m (33ft), for example *C. salignus* and *C. viminalis*, although most are shrubby. These evergreen plants have usually narrow, pointed leaves, often coloured bronze or red when young. The flowers have very small petals, but their numerous long stamens, which range in colour from creamy white or yellow to red, pink, or purplish, radiate around the stem, forming dense spikes, and giving the flower clusters their characteristic appearance.

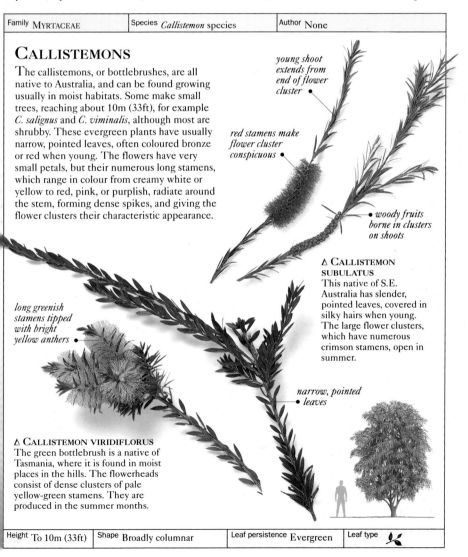

young shoot extends from end of flower cluster •

red stamens make flower cluster conspicuous •

• woody fruits borne in clusters on shoots

△ CALLISTEMON SUBULATUS
This native of S.E. Australia has slender, pointed leaves, covered in silky hairs when young. The large flower clusters, which have numerous crimson stamens, open in summer.

long greenish stamens tipped with bright yellow anthers •

narrow, pointed • leaves

△ CALLISTEMON VIRIDIFLORUS
The green bottlebrush is a native of Tasmania, where it is found in moist places in the hills. The flowerheads consist of dense clusters of pale yellow-green stamens. They are produced in the summer months.

Height To 10m (33ft)	Shape Broadly columnar	Leaf persistence Evergreen	Leaf type

Family MYRTACEAE	Species *Eucalyptus coccifera*	Author J.D. Hooker

MOUNT WELLINGTON PEPPERMINT

Leaves Juvenile leaves rounded, usually glaucous, unstalked, adult leaves lanceolate, to 5cm (2in) long and 2cm (¾in) across, with a hooked tip, green to blue-green, smooth on both sides, aromatic, carried on often bloomy shoots. **Bark** Grey and white, smooth, peeling in long strips; creamy white when freshly exposed. **Flowers** White, with numerous stamens, borne in clusters of three to seven in the leaf axils in early summer. **Fruit** Resembling an inverted cone, small and woody, 1cm (⅜in) long.
• **NATIVE REGION** Tasmania.
• **HABITAT** Mountains.
• **REMARK** Also known as Tasmanian snow gum. Juvenile leaves are opposite, adult leaves alternate: plants often bear both stages together. On mature plants, juvenile foliage is produced on shoots from the base of the trunk.

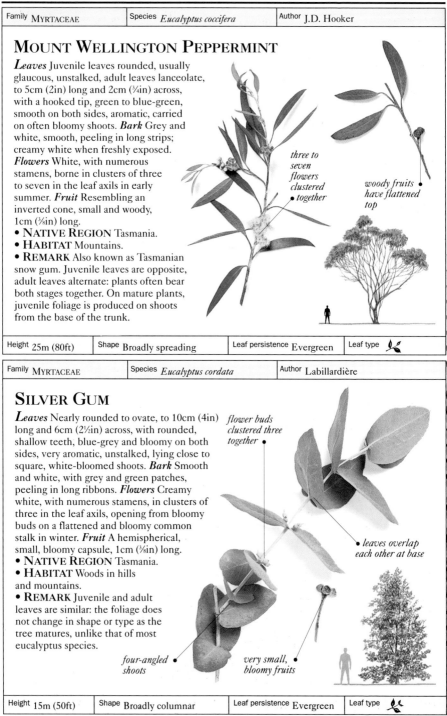

three to seven flowers clustered together

woody fruits have flattened top

Height 25m (80ft)	Shape Broadly spreading	Leaf persistence Evergreen	Leaf type

Family MYRTACEAE	Species *Eucalyptus cordata*	Author Labillardière

SILVER GUM

Leaves Nearly rounded to ovate, to 10cm (4in) long and 6cm (2½in) across, with rounded, shallow teeth, blue-grey and bloomy on both sides, very aromatic, unstalked, lying close to square, white-bloomed shoots. **Bark** Smooth and white, with grey and green patches, peeling in long ribbons. **Flowers** Creamy white, with numerous stamens, in clusters of three in the leaf axils, opening from bloomy buds on a flattened and bloomy common stalk in winter. **Fruit** A hemispherical, small, bloomy capsule, 1cm (⅜in) long.
• **NATIVE REGION** Tasmania.
• **HABITAT** Woods in hills and mountains.
• **REMARK** Juvenile and adult leaves are similar: the foliage does not change in shape or type as the tree matures, unlike that of most eucalyptus species.

flower buds clustered three together

leaves overlap each other at base

four-angled shoots

very small, bloomy fruits

Height 15m (50ft)	Shape Broadly columnar	Leaf persistence Evergreen	Leaf type

Family MYRTACEAE	Species *Eucalyptus dalrympleana*	Author Maiden

MOUNTAIN GUM

Leaves Juvenile leaves rounded, unstalked, adult leaves lanceolate, to 17.5cm (7in) long and 3cm (1¼in) across, tapered to a fine point, bronze when young becoming blue-green and smooth on both sides. **Bark** Grey-brown and smooth, peeling in large flakes; creamy white when freshly exposed. **Flowers** White, with numerous stamens, in clusters of three in the leaf axils in late summer. **Fruit** Hemispherical, small, woody, 1cm (⅜in) long.
• **NATIVE REGION** S.E. Australia, Tasmania.
• **HABITAT** Mountain slopes.
• **REMARK** Juvenile leaves are opposite, adult leaves alternate: plants often bear both stages together.

juvenile leaves

leaf shape changes as plant matures

peeling bark exposes creamy layer beneath

slender, curved adult leaves

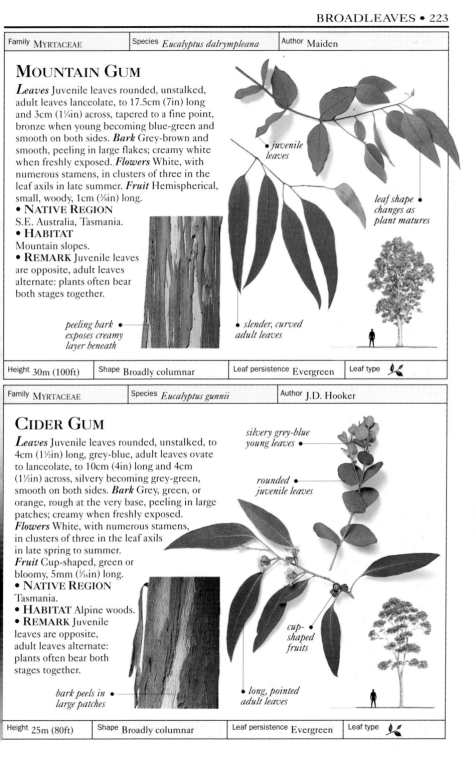

Height 30m (100ft)	Shape Broadly columnar	Leaf persistence Evergreen	Leaf type

Family MYRTACEAE	Species *Eucalyptus gunnii*	Author J.D. Hooker

CIDER GUM

Leaves Juvenile leaves rounded, unstalked, to 4cm (1½in) long, grey-blue, adult leaves ovate to lanceolate, to 10cm (4in) long and 4cm (1½in) across, silvery becoming grey-green, smooth on both sides. **Bark** Grey, green, or orange, rough at the very base, peeling in large patches; creamy when freshly exposed. **Flowers** White, with numerous stamens, in clusters of three in the leaf axils in late spring to summer. **Fruit** Cup-shaped, green or bloomy, 5mm (³⁄₁₆in) long.
• **NATIVE REGION** Tasmania.
• **HABITAT** Alpine woods.
• **REMARK** Juvenile leaves are opposite, adult leaves alternate: plants often bear both stages together.

silvery grey-blue young leaves

rounded juvenile leaves

cup-shaped fruits

bark peels in large patches

long, pointed adult leaves

Height 25m (80ft)	Shape Broadly columnar	Leaf persistence Evergreen	Leaf type

Family MYRTACEAE	Species *Eucalyptus pauciflora*	Author Siebold ex Sprengel

SNOW GUM

Leaves Juvenile leaves ovate to rounded, to 6cm (2½in) long, leathery, grey, adult leaves lanceolate, to 15cm (6in) long and 4cm (1½in) across, often curved, glossy green and smooth. ***Bark*** Grey and white, peeling in large flakes. ***Flowers*** White, with numerous stamens, in clusters in the leaf axils in summer. ***Fruit*** Rounded, woody, 6mm (¼in) long.
• **NATIVE REGION** S.E. Australia, Tasmania.
• **HABITAT** From sea level to the tree line.

flowers borne in clusters of up to 12

◁ **EUCALYPTUS PAUCIFLORA**

adult leaves carried on red shoots

◁ SUBSP. NIPHOPHILA

◁ SUBSP. NIPHOPHILA
This high mountain form is often shrubby.

Height 15m (50ft)	Shape Broadly spreading	Leaf persistence Evergreen	Leaf type

Family MYRTACEAE	Species *Eucalyptus perriniana*	Author Mueller ex Rodway

SPINNING GUM

Leaves Juvenile leaves blue-grey, joined at the base forming a circular disk around the shoot, adult leaves lanceolate, to 12cm (4¾in) long and 2.5cm (1in) across, often purple when young becoming deep blue-green and smooth on both sides, pendulous. ***Bark*** Grey and brown, peeling. ***Flowers*** White, with numerous stamens, in clusters in the leaf axils in late summer. ***Fruit*** Small, woody, 5mm (³⁄₁₆in) long.
• **NATIVE REGION** S.E. Australia, Tasmania.
• **HABITAT** Mountains, on moist soil.

adult leaves taper to fine point at end

very small, cup-shaped, woody fruits

juvenile leaves joined at base

withered juvenile leaves form spinning disk

tiny flowers borne in threes

Height 7m (23ft)	Shape Broadly spreading	Leaf persistence Evergreen	Leaf type

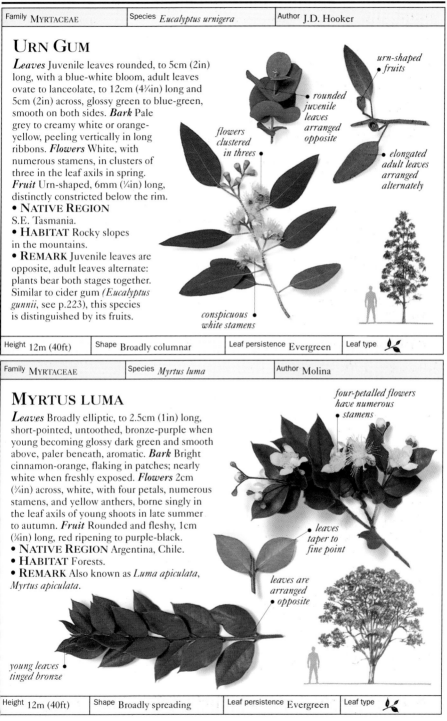

Family MYRTACEAE	Species *Eucalyptus urnigera*	Author J.D. Hooker

URN GUM

Leaves Juvenile leaves rounded, to 5cm (2in) long, with a blue-white bloom, adult leaves ovate to lanceolate, to 12cm (4¾in) long and 5cm (2in) across, glossy green to blue-green, smooth on both sides. **Bark** Pale grey to creamy white or orange-yellow, peeling vertically in long ribbons. **Flowers** White, with numerous stamens, in clusters of three in the leaf axils in spring. **Fruit** Urn-shaped, 6mm (¼in) long, distinctly constricted below the rim.
• **NATIVE REGION** S.E. Tasmania.
• **HABITAT** Rocky slopes in the mountains.
• **REMARK** Juvenile leaves are opposite, adult leaves alternate: plants bear both stages together. Similar to cider gum *(Eucalyptus gunnii*, see p.223), this species is distinguished by its fruits.

urn-shaped fruits

rounded juvenile leaves arranged opposite

flowers clustered in threes

elongated adult leaves arranged alternately

conspicuous white stamens

Height 12m (40ft)	Shape Broadly columnar	Leaf persistence Evergreen	Leaf type

Family MYRTACEAE	Species *Myrtus luma*	Author Molina

MYRTUS LUMA

Leaves Broadly elliptic, to 2.5cm (1in) long, short-pointed, untoothed, bronze-purple when young becoming glossy dark green and smooth above, paler beneath, aromatic. **Bark** Bright cinnamon-orange, flaking in patches; nearly white when freshly exposed. **Flowers** 2cm (¾in) across, white, with four petals, numerous stamens, and yellow anthers, borne singly in the leaf axils of young shoots in late summer to autumn. **Fruit** Rounded and fleshy, 1cm (⅜in) long, red ripening to purple-black.
• **NATIVE REGION** Argentina, Chile.
• **HABITAT** Forests.
• **REMARK** Also known as *Luma apiculata*, *Myrtus apiculata*.

four-petalled flowers have numerous stamens

leaves taper to fine point

leaves are arranged opposite

young leaves tinged bronze

Height 12m (40ft)	Shape Broadly spreading	Leaf persistence Evergreen	Leaf type

NYSSACEAE

T HE THREE GENERA and seven species of the tupelo family are native to North America and east Asia. The best-known genus is *Nyssa*, whose species display brilliant autumn colour. The leaves are alternate, and the small flowers petalless, but those of *Davidia involucrata* have conspicuous bracts.

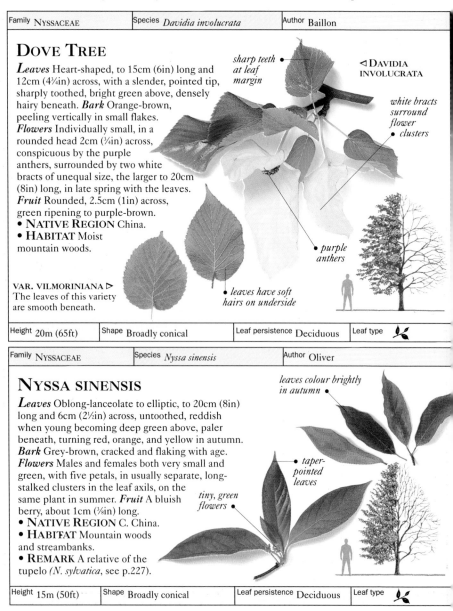

Family NYSSACEAE	Species *Davidia involucrata*	Author Baillon

DOVE TREE

Leaves Heart-shaped, to 15cm (6in) long and 12cm (4¾in) across, with a slender, pointed tip, sharply toothed, bright green above, densely hairy beneath. **Bark** Orange-brown, peeling vertically in small flakes. **Flowers** Individually small, in a rounded head 2cm (¾in) across, conspicuous by the purple anthers, surrounded by two white bracts of unequal size, the larger to 20cm (8in) long, in late spring with the leaves. **Fruit** Rounded, 2.5cm (1in) across, green ripening to purple-brown.
• **NATIVE REGION** China.
• **HABITAT** Moist mountain woods.

VAR. VILMORINIANA ▷
The leaves of this variety are smooth beneath.

sharp teeth at leaf margin

◁ **DAVIDIA INVOLUCRATA**

white bracts surround flower clusters

purple anthers

leaves have soft hairs on underside

Height 20m (65ft)	Shape Broadly conical	Leaf persistence Deciduous	Leaf type

Family NYSSACEAE	Species *Nyssa sinensis*	Author Oliver

NYSSA SINENSIS

Leaves Oblong-lanceolate to elliptic, to 20cm (8in) long and 6cm (2½in) across, untoothed, reddish when young becoming deep green above, paler beneath, turning red, orange, and yellow in autumn. **Bark** Grey-brown, cracked and flaking with age. **Flowers** Males and females both very small and green, with five petals, in usually separate, long-stalked clusters in the leaf axils, on the same plant in summer. **Fruit** A bluish berry, about 1cm (⅜in) long.
• **NATIVE REGION** C. China.
• **HABITAT** Mountain woods and streambanks.
• **REMARK** A relative of the tupelo (*N. sylvatica*, see p.227).

leaves colour brightly in autumn

taper-pointed leaves

tiny, green flowers

Height 15m (50ft)	Shape Broadly conical	Leaf persistence Deciduous	Leaf type

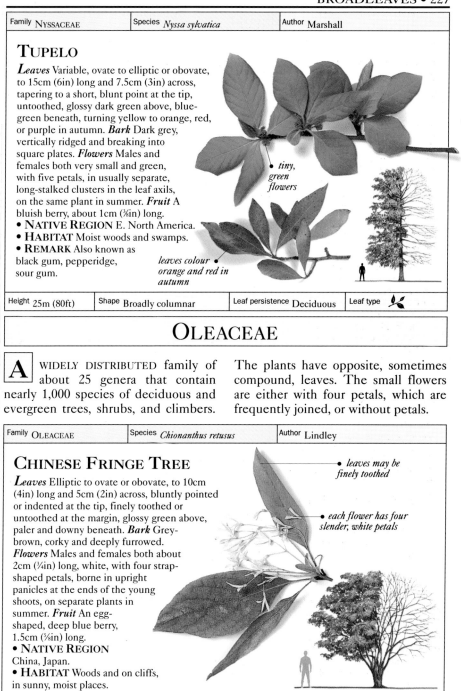

| Family NYSSACEAE | Species *Nyssa sylvatica* | Author Marshall |

TUPELO

Leaves Variable, ovate to elliptic or obovate, to 15cm (6in) long and 7.5cm (3in) across, tapering to a short, blunt point at the tip, untoothed, glossy dark green above, blue-green beneath, turning yellow to orange, red, or purple in autumn. **Bark** Dark grey, vertically ridged and breaking into square plates. **Flowers** Males and females both very small and green, with five petals, in usually separate, long-stalked clusters in the leaf axils, on the same plant in summer. **Fruit** A bluish berry, about 1cm (⅜in) long.
• **NATIVE REGION** E. North America.
• **HABITAT** Moist woods and swamps.
• **REMARK** Also known as black gum, pepperidge, sour gum.

tiny, green flowers

leaves colour orange and red in autumn

| Height 25m (80ft) | Shape Broadly columnar | Leaf persistence Deciduous | Leaf type |

OLEACEAE

A WIDELY DISTRIBUTED family of about 25 genera that contain nearly 1,000 species of deciduous and evergreen trees, shrubs, and climbers. The plants have opposite, sometimes compound, leaves. The small flowers are either with four petals, which are frequently joined, or without petals.

| Family OLEACEAE | Species *Chionanthus retusus* | Author Lindley |

CHINESE FRINGE TREE

Leaves Elliptic to ovate or obovate, to 10cm (4in) long and 5cm (2in) across, bluntly pointed or indented at the tip, finely toothed or untoothed at the margin, glossy green above, paler and downy beneath. **Bark** Grey-brown, corky and deeply furrowed. **Flowers** Males and females both about 2cm (¾in) long, white, with four strap-shaped petals, borne in upright panicles at the ends of the young shoots, on separate plants in summer. **Fruit** An egg-shaped, deep blue berry, 1.5cm (⅝in) long.
• **NATIVE REGION** China, Japan.
• **HABITAT** Woods and on cliffs, in sunny, moist places.

leaves may be finely toothed

each flower has four slender, white petals

| Height 10m (33ft) | Shape Broadly spreading | Leaf persistence Deciduous | Leaf type |

Family OLEACEAE	Species *Chionanthus virginicus*	Author Linnaeus

FRINGE TREE

Leaves Elliptic, to 20cm (8in) long and 10cm (4in) across, tapered to a short point at the tip, untoothed, glossy green above, turning yellow in autumn. **Bark** Grey and smooth, becoming furrowed with age. **Flowers** Males and females both to 3cm (1¼in) long, white, slightly fragrant, with four to six slender, strap-shaped petals, on slender, drooping stalks, borne in conical, upright panicles, male panicles to 20cm (8in) long, females somewhat shorter, usually on separate plants in summer. **Fruit** An egg-shaped, bloomy, deep blue berry, 2cm (¾in) long.
• **NATIVE REGION** E. United States.
• **HABITAT** Moist woods and riverbanks.
• **REMARK** Also known as old man's beard. This species can be either a shrub or a small tree.

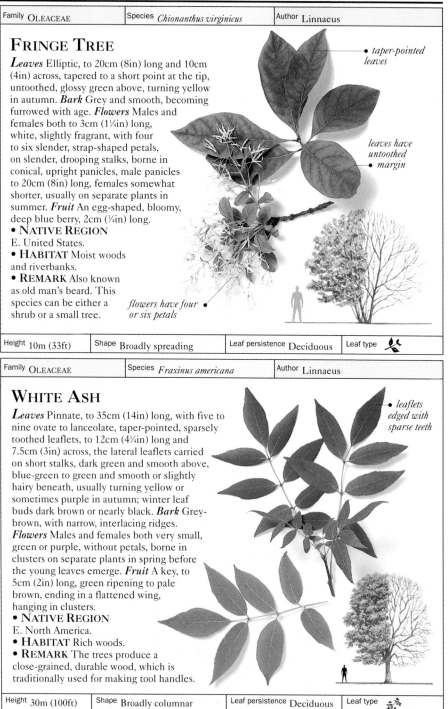

taper-pointed leaves

leaves have untoothed margin

flowers have four or six petals

Height 10m (33ft)	Shape Broadly spreading	Leaf persistence Deciduous	Leaf type

Family OLEACEAE	Species *Fraxinus americana*	Author Linnaeus

WHITE ASH

Leaves Pinnate, to 35cm (14in) long, with five to nine ovate to lanceolate, taper-pointed, sparsely toothed leaflets, to 12cm (4¾in) long and 7.5cm (3in) across, the lateral leaflets carried on short stalks, dark green and smooth above, blue-green to green and smooth or slightly hairy beneath, usually turning yellow or sometimes purple in autumn; winter leaf buds dark brown or nearly black. **Bark** Grey-brown, with narrow, interlacing ridges. **Flowers** Males and females both very small, green or purple, without petals, borne in clusters on separate plants in spring before the young leaves emerge. **Fruit** A key, to 5cm (2in) long, green ripening to pale brown, ending in a flattened wing, hanging in clusters.
• **NATIVE REGION** E. North America.
• **HABITAT** Rich woods.
• **REMARK** The trees produce a close-grained, durable wood, which is traditionally used for making tool handles.

leaflets edged with sparse teeth

Height 30m (100ft)	Shape Broadly columnar	Leaf persistence Deciduous	Leaf type

Family OLEACEAE	Species *Fraxinus angustifolia*	Author Vahl

NARROW-LEAVED ASH

Leaves Pinnate, to 25cm (10in) long, with 7 to 13 lanceolate leaflets, to 7.5cm (3in) long and 2cm (¾in) across, with a slender, tapered point at the tip, sharply toothed, glossy bright green and smooth above, the lateral leaflets unstalked; winter buds dark brown. **Bark** Grey-brown, with prominent ridges. **Flowers** Very small, green or purple, without petals, borne in clusters in spring before the leaves. **Fruit** With a flattened wing at the end, to 4cm (1½in) long, green ripening to pale brown, in hanging clusters.
• **NATIVE REGION** N. Africa, S.W. Europe.
• **HABITAT** Woods and riversides.

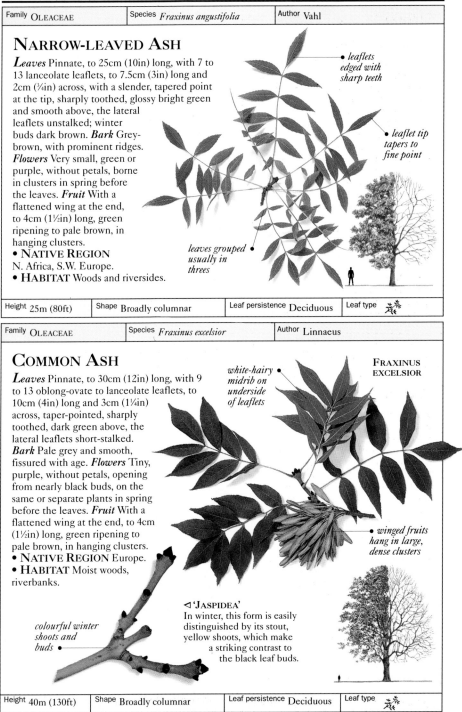

• *leaflets edged with sharp teeth*

• *leaflet tip tapers to fine point*

leaves grouped usually in threes

Height 25m (80ft)	Shape Broadly columnar	Leaf persistence Deciduous	Leaf type

Family OLEACEAE	Species *Fraxinus excelsior*	Author Linnaeus

COMMON ASH

Leaves Pinnate, to 30cm (12in) long, with 9 to 13 oblong-ovate to lanceolate leaflets, to 10cm (4in) long and 3cm (1¼in) across, taper-pointed, sharply toothed, dark green above, the lateral leaflets short-stalked. **Bark** Pale grey and smooth, fissured with age. **Flowers** Tiny, purple, without petals, opening from nearly black buds, on the same or separate plants in spring before the leaves. **Fruit** With a flattened wing at the end, to 4cm (1½in) long, green ripening to pale brown, in hanging clusters.
• **NATIVE REGION** Europe.
• **HABITAT** Moist woods, riverbanks.

FRAXINUS EXCELSIOR

white-hairy midrib on underside of leaflets •

• *winged fruits hang in large, dense clusters*

◁ 'JASPIDEA'
In winter, this form is easily distinguished by its stout, yellow shoots, which make a striking contrast to the black leaf buds.

colourful winter shoots and buds •

Height 40m (130ft)	Shape Broadly columnar	Leaf persistence Deciduous	Leaf type

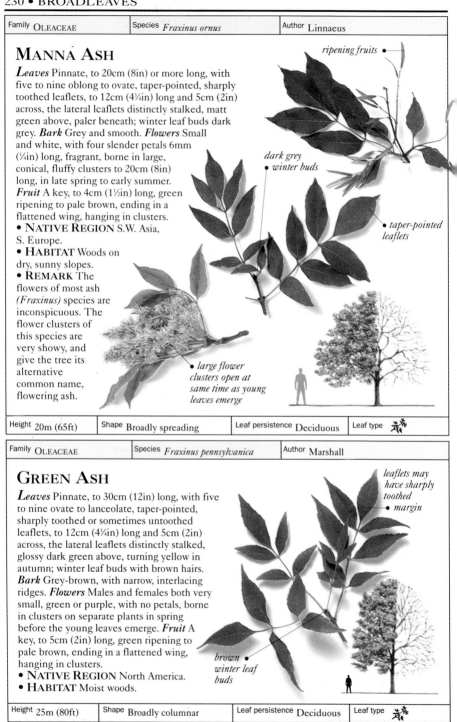

| Family OLEACEAE | Species *Fraxinus ornus* | Author Linnaeus |

MANNA ASH

Leaves Pinnate, to 20cm (8in) or more long, with five to nine oblong to ovate, taper-pointed, sharply toothed leaflets, to 12cm (4¾in) long and 5cm (2in) across, the lateral leaflets distinctly stalked, matt green above, paler beneath; winter leaf buds dark grey. *Bark* Grey and smooth. *Flowers* Small and white, with four slender petals 6mm (¼in) long, fragrant, borne in large, conical, fluffy clusters to 20cm (8in) long, in late spring to early summer. *Fruit* A key, to 4cm (1½in) long, green ripening to pale brown, ending in a flattened wing, hanging in clusters.
• **NATIVE REGION** S.W. Asia, S. Europe.
• **HABITAT** Woods on dry, sunny slopes.
• **REMARK** The flowers of most ash *(Fraxinus)* species are inconspicuous. The flower clusters of this species are very showy, and give the tree its alternative common name, flowering ash.

ripening fruits •

dark grey • winter buds

• taper-pointed leaflets

• large flower clusters open at same time as young leaves emerge

| Height 20m (65ft) | Shape Broadly spreading | Leaf persistence Deciduous | Leaf type |

| Family OLEACEAE | Species *Fraxinus pennsylvanica* | Author Marshall |

GREEN ASH

Leaves Pinnate, to 30cm (12in) long, with five to nine ovate to lanceolate, taper-pointed, sharply toothed or sometimes untoothed leaflets, to 12cm (4¾in) long and 5cm (2in) across, the lateral leaflets distinctly stalked, glossy dark green above, turning yellow in autumn; winter leaf buds with brown hairs. *Bark* Grey-brown, with narrow, interlacing ridges. *Flowers* Males and females both very small, green or purple, with no petals, borne in clusters on separate plants in spring before the young leaves emerge. *Fruit* A key, to 5cm (2in) long, green ripening to pale brown, ending in a flattened wing, hanging in clusters.
• **NATIVE REGION** North America.
• **HABITAT** Moist woods.

leaflets may have sharply toothed • margin

brown • winter leaf buds

| Height 25m (80ft) | Shape Broadly columnar | Leaf persistence Deciduous | Leaf type |

Family OLEACEAE	Species *Ligustrum lucidum*	Author Aiton f.

LIGUSTRUM LUCIDUM

Leaves Ovate, to 10cm (4in) long and 5cm (2in) across, tapering to a fine point at the tip, untoothed, bronze when young becoming glossy dark green above, paler and dull beneath, smooth on both sides. **Bark** Grey and smooth.
Flowers Small and white, fragrant, with four joined petals, profusely borne in large, conical, upright panicles to 20cm (8in) long, over a long period in late summer and autumn. **Fruit** A blue-black berry, 1cm (⅜in) long.
• **NATIVE REGION** China.
• **HABITAT** Hillside woods and river valleys in mountains.
• **REMARK** This species, which can be either a large shrub or a small to medium-sized tree, is one of the evergreen privets. Its flowering season is unusually long.

'EXCELSUM SUPERBUM' ▷
The leaves of this form are tinged bronze when young. They mature to bright green with a yellow margin, which becomes creamy white.

• *small, clustered flowers*

pale leaf under-side •

• *glossy green mature leaves*

LIGUSTRUM LUCIDUM

▽ **'TRICOLOR'**
The young foliage of this form is flushed pink.

Height 12m (40ft)	Shape Broadly conical	Leaf persistence Evergreen	Leaf type

Family OLEACEAE	Species *Phillyrea latifolia*	Author Linnaeus

PHILLYREA LATIFOLIA

Leaves Ovate to lanceolate, to 5cm (2in) long and 4cm (1½in) across, toothed, glossy very dark green above, paler beneath, smooth on both sides; on juvenile plants, variable in shape and size. **Bark** Pale grey and smooth, becoming dark grey and cracking into small, square plates with age.
Flowers Very small and greenish white, the exserted stamens with yellow anthers, borne in clusters in the leaf axils in late spring to early summer. **Fruit** A small, rounded, blue-black berry, about 1cm (⅜in) across.
• **NATIVE REGION** S. Europe.
• **HABITAT** Evergreen woods.

yellow anthers make tiny flowers • *conspicuous*

• *dark green, leathery leaves*

Height 10m (33ft)	Shape Broadly spreading	Leaf persistence Evergreen	Leaf type

PALMAE

THE PALMS FORM A distinct group of more than 200 genera, with over 2,500 species of mainly tropical distribution. In North America they are native to the southern States alone; Europe has two native species, in the western Mediterranean and in Crete.

Palms are trees or shrubs, sometimes climbing, that differ from other trees in several ways. With few exceptions, they have a single, unbranched stem which, once formed, does not increase in girth. The often very large leaves are mainly one of two types, either palmately divided, as in the fan palms (eg *Trachycarpus*), or pinnately divided, as in the feather palms (eg *Phoenix*). The small flowers have three sepals and three petals, and are often carried in very large, heavy clusters, males and females sometimes on separate plants.

Family PALMAE	Species *Trachycarpus fortunei*	Author (W.J. Hooker) Wendland

CHUSAN PALM

Leaves Fan-shaped, to 120cm (4ft) across, segmented, dark green above, blue-green beneath. *Bark* Densely covered with brown, fibrous remnants of old leaves. *Flowers* Very small and yellow, fragrant, in large, drooping panicles on separate plants in early summer. *Fruit* A rounded to kidney-shaped, three-lobed, blue-black berry, 1.2cm (½in) across.
• NATIVE REGION C. and S. China.
• HABITAT Mountain slopes.

V-shaped leaf tip soon withers

long, stout leaf stalk edged with sharp teeth

yellow anthers indicate male flowers

large bracts enclose flower cluster before opening

stout flower stalks emerge from among leaves

sides of narrow leaf segments fold up towards each other

Height 10m (33ft)	Shape Unique	Leaf persistence Evergreen	Leaf type

PITTOSPORACEAE

T HE NINE GENERA and more than 200 species in this family of evergreen trees, shrubs, and climbing plants are native to tropical regions, particularly Australasia. The leaves are alternate, most often untoothed. Small, usually tubular, five-lobed flowers develop into a dry or fleshy fruit.

Family PITTOSPORACEAE	Species *Pittosporum tenuifolium*	Author Gaertner

PITTOSPORUM TENUIFOLIUM

Leaves Oblong to elliptic, to 6cm (2½in) long and 2cm (¾in) across, with a wavy margin, glossy rather light green, smooth, on deep purple-black shoots. *Bark* Dark grey, smooth. *Flowers* Small and tubular, about 1cm (⅜in) long, whitish, with five reflexed, deep red-purple lobes and yellow anthers, strongly fragrant, borne singly or in clusters in the leaf axils in late spring. *Fruit* A rounded capsule, about 1.2cm (½in) across, green ripening to nearly black.
• **NATIVE REGION** New Zealand.
• **HABITAT** Forests from coastline to mountain level.

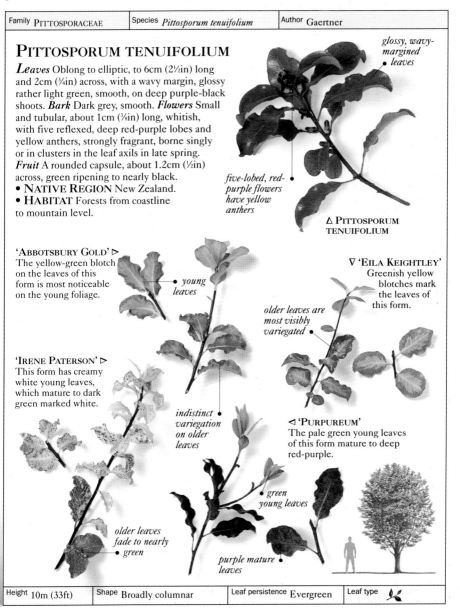

glossy, wavy-margined leaves

five-lobed, red-purple flowers have yellow anthers

△ PITTOSPORUM TENUIFOLIUM

'ABBOTSBURY GOLD' ▷
The yellow-green blotch on the leaves of this form is most noticeable on the young foliage.

young leaves

▽ **'EILA KEIGHTLEY'**
Greenish yellow blotches mark the leaves of this form.

older leaves are most visibly variegated

'IRENE PATERSON' ▷
This form has creamy white young leaves, which mature to dark green marked white.

indistinct variegation on older leaves

◁ **'PURPUREUM'**
The pale green young leaves of this form mature to deep red-purple.

green young leaves

older leaves fade to nearly green

purple mature leaves

Height 10m (33ft)	Shape Broadly columnar	Leaf persistence Evergreen	Leaf type

PLATANACEAE

T HE PLANE FAMILY CONSISTS of only one genus, *Platanus*, and seven species. The large, deciduous trees grow wild mainly in the United States and Mexico. The leaves are alternate and palmately lobed, except for those of the South-east Asian *Platanus kerrii*, which are unlobed. The dense clusters of tiny flowers hang on slender stalks, either singly or in groups.

Family PLATANACEAE	Species *Platanus x hispanica*	Author Miller ex Münchhausen

LONDON PLANE

Leaves Palmately lobed, to 20cm (8in) long and 25cm (10in) across, with three to five large, toothed lobes, glossy bright green above, paler beneath, covered in scurfy brown hairs when young.
Bark Brown, grey, and cream, flaking in patches. **Flowers** Males and females both very small, males yellow, females reddish, borne in separate, small, rounded clusters on the same plant in late spring.
Fruit A rounded, dense cluster, 2.5cm (1in) across, green ripening to brown, covered in spiky, brown bristles, hanging two to four together, persisting over winter.
• **NATIVE REGION**
Of garden origin.
• **REMARK** Also known as *Platanus x acerifolia*. This species is probably a hybrid between the American sycamore (*Platanus occidentalis*, see p.235) and the oriental plane (*Platanus orientalis*, see p.235).

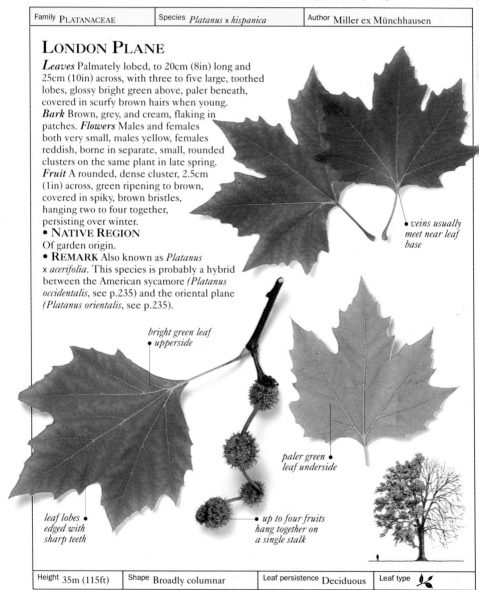

veins usually meet near leaf base

bright green leaf upperside

paler green leaf underside

leaf lobes edged with sharp teeth

up to four fruits hang together on a single stalk

Height 35m (115ft)	Shape Broadly columnar	Leaf persistence Deciduous	Leaf type

Family PLATANACEAE	Species *Platanus occidentalis*	Author Linnaeus

AMERICAN SYCAMORE

Leaves Palmately lobed, to 20cm (8in) long and across, with three lobes, glossy green above, paler beneath. **Bark** Grey, brown, cream, flaking. **Flowers** Very small, males yellow, females reddish, in separate, rounded clusters on the same plant in late spring. **Fruit** A rounded, dense, brown cluster, 2.5cm (1in) across.
• **NATIVE REGION**
E. North America.
• **HABITAT** Rich, moist soil.

shallow lobes usually edged with sharp teeth

leaf base may be heart-shaped

Height 35m (115ft)	Shape Broadly columnar	Leaf persistence Deciduous	Leaf type

Family PLATANACEAE	Species *Platanus orientalis*	Author Linnaeus

ORIENTAL PLANE

Leaves Palmately lobed, to 20cm (8in) long and 25cm (10in) across, cut to below the middle into usually five toothed lobes, glossy green above, paler beneath, with scurfy brown hairs when young. **Bark** Grey, pinkish brown, and cream, flaking in patches. **Flowers** Males and females both very small, males yellow, females reddish, borne in separate, small, rounded clusters on the same plant in late spring. **Fruit** A rounded, dense, brown cluster, 2.5cm (1in) across, hanging up to six on each stalk, persisting on the plant over winter.
• **NATIVE REGION** S.E. Europe.
• **HABITAT** Mountain woods, riversides, and moist places.

deeply cut, slender leaf lobes

leaves become smooth on underside

bristly fruits break up before falling

up to six fruit clusters hang on a single stalk

Height 30m (100ft)	Shape Broadly columnar	Leaf persistence Deciduous	Leaf type

PROTEACEAE

S OME 75 GENERA and over 1,000 species of evergreen trees and shrubs are included in this family. Native to the southern hemisphere, they grow wild throughout this part of the world; some species extend also to warm regions of the northern hemisphere. The leaves are alternate, simple to pinnate; the flowers have a petal-like calyx divided into four lobes, although the petals themselves are very small and inconspicuous.

—— ✍ ——

Proteaceae is best known for its ornamental plants (eg species of *Grevillea*, *Banksia*, *Protea*, and *Telopea*), and for *Macadamia* species, cultivated in Australia and Hawaii for their edible nuts.

Family PROTEACEAE	Species *Embothrium coccineum*	Author J.R. & J.G. Forster

CHILEAN FIRE BUSH

Leaves Elliptic to oblong, variable, to 15cm (6in) long and 3cm (1¼in) across, untoothed, dark green to blue-green above, paler beneath, leathery, smooth on both sides. **Bark** Purple-brown, smooth, flaking with age. **Flowers** Tubular at first, to 5cm (2in) long, splitting into four lobes, the lobes curling backward leaving the style protruding, bright orange-red, borne in clusters in late spring to early summer. **Fruit** A woody capsule, to 3cm (1¼in) long, with a long beak.
• **NATIVE REGION** Argentina, Chile.
• **HABITAT** Open places, at all altitudes from the coast to the mountains.
• **REMARK** This species is one of the most striking representatives of its family.

open flowers have curled lobes

flower lobes closed over long style

leaves are evergreen only in mild climates

flowers borne in axillary racemes

young shoot in leaf axil

Height 9m (30ft)	Shape Broadly columnar	Leaf persistence Evergreen	Leaf type

RHAMNACEAE

T HE 60 GENERA AND around 900 species of deciduous and evergreen trees, shrubs, and climbing plants belonging to this family grow wild in all parts of the world. They are sometimes spiny, bearing alternate or opposite leaves, and small male and female flowers, found sometimes on separate plants. Several species of buckthorn *(Rhamnus)* yield dyes.

Family RHAMNACEAE	Species *Rhamnus cathartica*	Author Linnaeus

COMMON BUCKTHORN

Leaves Broadly ovate to nearly rounded, to 6cm (2½in) long and 4cm (1½in) across, with a short point at the tip, finely toothed, glossy green above, paler beneath, turning yellow in autumn, borne on sparsely spiny shoots. **Bark** Dark orange-brown and scaly. **Flowers** Small, with tiny petals and a green, four-lobed calyx, fragrant, in clusters in early to midsummer. **Fruit** Rounded, fleshy, berry-like, to 1cm (⅜in) across, green ripening to black.
• **NATIVE REGION** Asia, Europe.
• **HABITAT** Woods, thickets, and hedgerows, on chalky soil.

dense clusters of ripe fruits

rounded teeth at leaf margin

tiny, green flowers

Height 10m (33ft)	Shape Broadly spreading	Leaf persistence Deciduous	Leaf type

Family RHAMNACEAE	Species *Rhamnus frangula*	Author Linnaeus

ALDER BUCKTHORN

Leaves Obovate, to 7cm (2¾in) long and 4cm (1½in) across, with a short, blunt point, untoothed, glossy dark green above, paler beneath, turning red in autumn. **Bark** Grey, smooth, with vertical, shallow, pale cracks. **Flowers** Very small, with tiny petals and a green, five-lobed calyx, in clusters in early to late summer. **Fruit** Rounded, fleshy, and berry-like, to 1cm (⅜in) across, green becoming red ripening to black.
• **NATIVE REGION** N. Africa, W. Asia, Europe.
• **HABITAT** Woods and scrub, usually on wet soil.
• **REMARK** Also known as *Frangula alnus.*

glossy dark leaf surface

fruits ripen from red to black

untoothed leaves

tiny, pink-tinged flowers

Height 5m (17ft)	Shape Broadly spreading	Leaf persistence Deciduous	Leaf type

ROSACEAE

THIS FAMILY is a widely distributed and very important collection of deciduous and evergreen trees, shrubs, and herbaceous plants, containing over 100 genera and 3,000 species.

The leaves are usually alternate, and vary from simple and untoothed to pinnate. The flowers are usually five-petalled. Several different types of fruit are produced, and the family is divided into groups on the basis of their structure. The trees in this book fall into two of these groups. Both have fleshy, often edible, fruits, but whereas those of *Prunus* species contain only a single seed, those of *Amelanchier*, *Cotoneaster*, *Crataegus*, *Malus*, *Mespilus*, *Photinia*, *Pyrus*, and *Sorbus* contain two or more seeds.

Family ROSACEAE	Species *Amelanchier arborea*	Author (A. Michaux) Fernald

AMELANCHIER ARBOREA

Leaves Ovate to obovate, to 7.5cm (3in) long and 4cm (1½in) across, rounded to heart-shaped at the base, usually short-pointed at the tip, finely toothed, becoming deep green above, folded and white with hairs when young becoming smooth beneath, turning orange to red in autumn. *Bark* Grey and smooth when young, becoming ridged and scaly with age. *Flowers* White, with five narrow petals, borne in upright racemes to 5cm (2in) long, in spring before the leaves are fully open. *Fruit* A rounded, dry or juicy, sweet, edible, reddish purple berry, to 8mm (5/16 in) across, ripening in summer.
• **NATIVE REGION** C. and E. United States.
• **HABITAT** Woods and thickets, on moist soil.

slender leaf stalks

leaf margin edged with small teeth

mature leaves are smooth on both sides

white flowers borne in dense clusters

hairy young leaves unfold at flowering time

Height 12m (40ft)	Shape Broadly spreading	Leaf persistence Deciduous	Leaf type

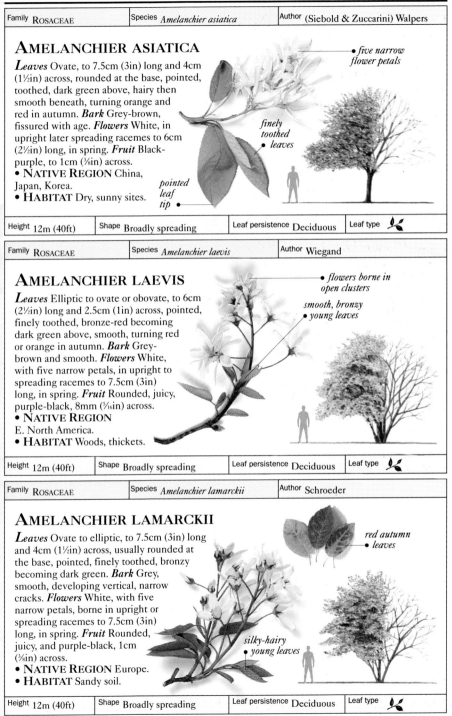

Family ROSACEAE	Species *Amelanchier asiatica*	Author (Siebold & Zuccarini) Walpers

AMELANCHIER ASIATICA

Leaves Ovate, to 7.5cm (3in) long and 4cm (1½in) across, rounded at the base, pointed, toothed, dark green above, hairy then smooth beneath, turning orange and red in autumn. *Bark* Grey-brown, fissured with age. *Flowers* White, in upright later spreading racemes to 6cm (2½in) long, in spring. *Fruit* Black-purple, to 1cm (⅜in) across.
• NATIVE REGION China, Japan, Korea.
• HABITAT Dry, sunny sites.

five narrow flower petals

finely toothed leaves

pointed leaf tip

Height 12m (40ft)	Shape Broadly spreading	Leaf persistence Deciduous	Leaf type

Family ROSACEAE	Species *Amelanchier laevis*	Author Wiegand

AMELANCHIER LAEVIS

Leaves Elliptic to ovate or obovate, to 6cm (2½in) long and 2.5cm (1in) across, pointed, finely toothed, bronze-red becoming dark green above, smooth, turning red or orange in autumn. *Bark* Grey-brown and smooth. *Flowers* White, with five narrow petals, in upright to spreading racemes to 7.5cm (3in) long, in spring. *Fruit* Rounded, juicy, purple-black, 8mm (⅜in) across.
• NATIVE REGION E. North America.
• HABITAT Woods, thickets.

flowers borne in open clusters

smooth, bronzy young leaves

Height 12m (40ft)	Shape Broadly spreading	Leaf persistence Deciduous	Leaf type

Family ROSACEAE	Species *Amelanchier lamarckii*	Author Schroeder

AMELANCHIER LAMARCKII

Leaves Ovate to elliptic, to 7.5cm (3in) long and 4cm (1½in) across, usually rounded at the base, pointed, finely toothed, bronzy becoming dark green. *Bark* Grey, smooth, developing vertical, narrow cracks. *Flowers* White, with five narrow petals, borne in upright or spreading racemes to 7.5cm (3in) long, in spring. *Fruit* Rounded, juicy, and purple-black, 1cm (⅜in) across.
• NATIVE REGION Europe.
• HABITAT Sandy soil.

red autumn leaves

silky-hairy young leaves

Height 12m (40ft)	Shape Broadly spreading	Leaf persistence Deciduous	Leaf type

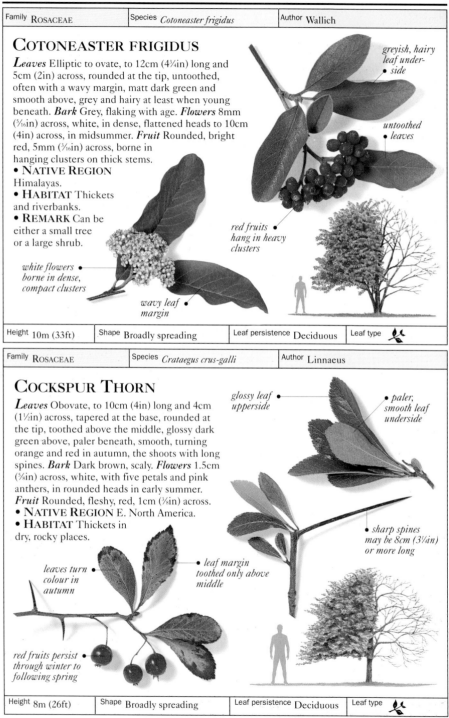

Family ROSACEAE	Species *Cotoneaster frigidus*	Author Wallich

COTONEASTER FRIGIDUS

Leaves Elliptic to ovate, to 12cm (4¾in) long and 5cm (2in) across, rounded at the tip, untoothed, often with a wavy margin, matt dark green and smooth above, grey and hairy at least when young beneath. **Bark** Grey, flaking with age. **Flowers** 8mm (⁵⁄₁₆in) across, white, in dense, flattened heads to 10cm (4in) across, in midsummer. **Fruit** Rounded, bright red, 5mm (³⁄₁₆in) across, borne in hanging clusters on thick stems.
• **NATIVE REGION** Himalayas.
• **HABITAT** Thickets and riverbanks.
• **REMARK** Can be either a small tree or a large shrub.

greyish, hairy leaf underside

untoothed leaves

red fruits hang in heavy clusters

white flowers borne in dense, compact clusters

wavy leaf margin

Height 10m (33ft)	Shape Broadly spreading	Leaf persistence Deciduous	Leaf type

Family ROSACEAE	Species *Crataegus crus-galli*	Author Linnaeus

COCKSPUR THORN

Leaves Obovate, to 10cm (4in) long and 4cm (1½in) across, tapered at the base, rounded at the tip, toothed above the middle, glossy dark green above, paler beneath, smooth, turning orange and red in autumn, the shoots with long spines. **Bark** Dark brown, scaly. **Flowers** 1.5cm (⅝in) across, white, with five petals and pink anthers, in rounded heads in early summer. **Fruit** Rounded, fleshy, red, 1cm (⅜in) across.
• **NATIVE REGION** E. North America.
• **HABITAT** Thickets in dry, rocky places.

glossy leaf upperside

paler, smooth leaf underside

sharp spines may be 8cm (3¼in) or more long

leaves turn colour in autumn

leaf margin toothed only above middle

red fruits persist through winter to following spring

Height 8m (26ft)	Shape Broadly spreading	Leaf persistence Deciduous	Leaf type

Family ROSACEAE	Species *Crataegus laciniata*	Author Ucria

CRATAEGUS LACINIATA

Leaves Diamond-shaped, to 5cm (2in) long and across, deeply lobed, the lobes often toothed at the tip, glossy dark green above, grey and hairy beneath. **Bark** Grey, flaking in thin plates. **Flowers** 2cm (¾in) across, white, with five petals and pink anthers, in dense clusters in early summer. **Fruit** Rounded or slightly oblong, red or red flushed yellow, 2cm (¾in) long, with a flattened top.
• **NATIVE REGION** S.W. Asia, S.E. Europe.
• **HABITAT** Wood margins and thickets.

sharply toothed stipules

three or four lobes each side of leaf

ornamental fruits

Height 6m (20ft)	Shape Broadly spreading	Leaf persistence Deciduous	Leaf type

Family ROSACEAE	Species *Crataegus laevigata*	Author (Poiret) Candolle

MIDLAND HAWTHORN

Leaves Ovate to obovate, to 5cm (2in) long and across, shallowly lobed, toothed, glossy dark green above, paler beneath, becoming smooth. **Bark** Grey, smooth, cracking with age. **Flowers** 2cm (¾in) across, usually white, with five petals, borne in small clusters in late spring. **Fruit** Rounded to oval, red, to 2cm (¾in) long.
• **NATIVE REGION** Europe.
• **HABITAT** Woods and hedgerows.

▽ 'GIREOUDII'
The green young leaves of this form are later followed by variegated foliage.

each fruit has two stones

vibrantly deep pink double flowers

◁ 'PAUL'S SCARLET'
This lovely cultivar is selected for its flowers, borne through late spring and early summer.

creamy-mottled leaves

Height 10m (33ft)	Shape Broadly spreading	Leaf persistence Deciduous	Leaf type

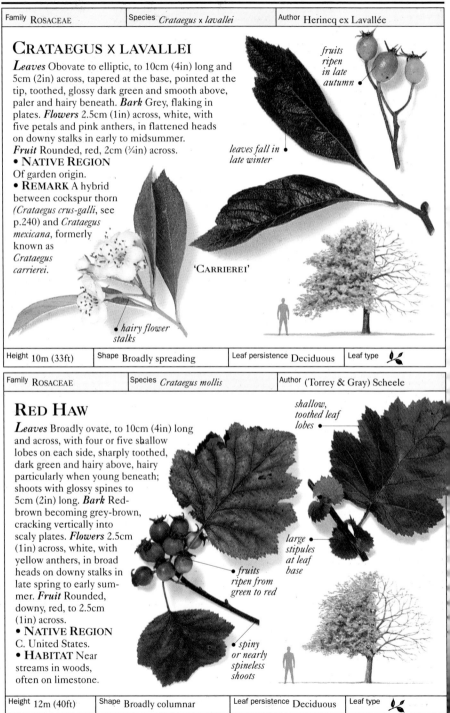

Family ROSACEAE	Species *Crataegus x lavallei*	Author Herincq ex Lavallée

CRATAEGUS X LAVALLEI

Leaves Obovate to elliptic, to 10cm (4in) long and 5cm (2in) across, tapered at the base, pointed at the tip, toothed, glossy dark green and smooth above, paler and hairy beneath. **Bark** Grey, flaking in plates. **Flowers** 2.5cm (1in) across, white, with five petals and pink anthers, in flattened heads on downy stalks in early to midsummer. **Fruit** Rounded, red, 2cm (¾in) across.
• NATIVE REGION Of garden origin.
• REMARK A hybrid between cockspur thorn (*Crataegus crus-galli*, see p.240) and *Crataegus mexicana*, formerly known as *Crataegus carrierei*.

fruits ripen in late autumn

leaves fall in late winter

'CARRIEREI'

hairy flower stalks

Height 10m (33ft)	Shape Broadly spreading	Leaf persistence Deciduous	Leaf type

Family ROSACEAE	Species *Crataegus mollis*	Author (Torrey & Gray) Scheele

RED HAW

Leaves Broadly ovate, to 10cm (4in) long and across, with four or five shallow lobes on each side, sharply toothed, dark green and hairy above, hairy particularly when young beneath; shoots with glossy spines to 5cm (2in) long. **Bark** Red-brown becoming grey-brown, cracking vertically into scaly plates. **Flowers** 2.5cm (1in) across, white, with yellow anthers, in broad heads on downy stalks in late spring to early summer. **Fruit** Rounded, downy, red, to 2.5cm (1in) across.
• NATIVE REGION C. United States.
• HABITAT Near streams in woods, often on limestone.

shallow, toothed leaf lobes

large stipules at leaf base

fruits ripen from green to red

spiny or nearly spineless shoots

Height 12m (40ft)	Shape Broadly columnar	Leaf persistence Deciduous	Leaf type

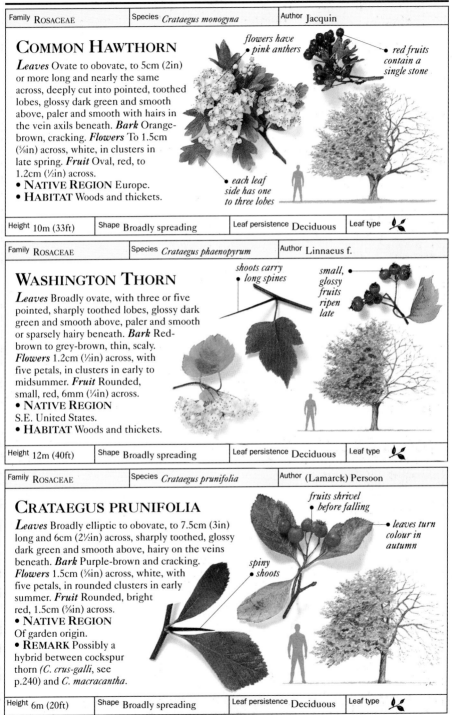

Family ROSACEAE	Species *Crataegus monogyna*	Author Jacquin

COMMON HAWTHORN

Leaves Ovate to obovate, to 5cm (2in) or more long and nearly the same across, deeply cut into pointed, toothed lobes, glossy dark green and smooth above, paler and smooth with hairs in the vein axils beneath. **Bark** Orange-brown, cracking. **Flowers** To 1.5cm (⅝in) across, white, in clusters in late spring. **Fruit** Oval, red, to 1.2cm (½in) across.
• **NATIVE REGION** Europe.
• **HABITAT** Woods and thickets.

flowers have pink anthers

red fruits contain a single stone

each leaf side has one to three lobes

Height 10m (33ft)	Shape Broadly spreading	Leaf persistence Deciduous	Leaf type

Family ROSACEAE	Species *Crataegus phaenopyrum*	Author Linnaeus f.

WASHINGTON THORN

Leaves Broadly ovate, with three or five pointed, sharply toothed lobes, glossy dark green and smooth above, paler and smooth or sparsely hairy beneath. **Bark** Red-brown to grey-brown, thin, scaly. **Flowers** 1.2cm (½in) across, with five petals, in clusters in early to midsummer. **Fruit** Rounded, small, red, 6mm (¼in) across.
• **NATIVE REGION** S.E. United States.
• **HABITAT** Woods and thickets.

shoots carry long spines

small, glossy fruits ripen late

Height 12m (40ft)	Shape Broadly spreading	Leaf persistence Deciduous	Leaf type

Family ROSACEAE	Species *Crataegus prunifolia*	Author (Lamarck) Persoon

CRATAEGUS PRUNIFOLIA

Leaves Broadly elliptic to obovate, to 7.5cm (3in) long and 6cm (2½in) across, sharply toothed, glossy dark green and smooth above, hairy on the veins beneath. **Bark** Purple-brown and cracking. **Flowers** 1.5cm (⅝in) across, with five petals, in rounded clusters in early summer. **Fruit** Rounded, bright red, 1.5cm (⅝in) across.
• **NATIVE REGION** Of garden origin.
• **REMARK** Possibly a hybrid between cockspur thorn *(C. crus-galli*, see p.240) and *C. macracantha*.

fruits shrivel before falling

leaves turn colour in autumn

spiny shoots

Height 6m (20ft)	Shape Broadly spreading	Leaf persistence Deciduous	Leaf type

Family ROSACEAE	Species x *Crataemespilus grandiflora*	Author (W.W. Smith) E.G. Camus

x CRATAEMESPILUS GRANDIFLORA

Leaves Elliptic to obovate, to 7.5cm (3in) long
and 5cm (2in) across, glossy green above,
turning bright orange in autumn; on vigorous
shoots deeply lobed. **Bark** Pale orange-brown,
flaking in thin plates. **Flowers** 2.5cm (1in)
across, white, with five petals, borne in
clusters of up to three in late spring.
Fruit Rounded, slightly hairy, glossy
orange-brown, 2cm (¾in) across.
• **NATIVE REGION** Of garden origin.
• **REMARK** Thought to be a hybrid
between the Midland hawthorn
(Crataegus laevigata, see p.241)
and the medlar *(Mespilus
germanica,* see p.255).

+ **CRATAEGOMESPILUS** ▽
**DARDARII 'JULES
D'ASNIÈRES'**
This graft hybrid
has rounded leaf
lobes, smaller flowers,
and small, brown fruits.

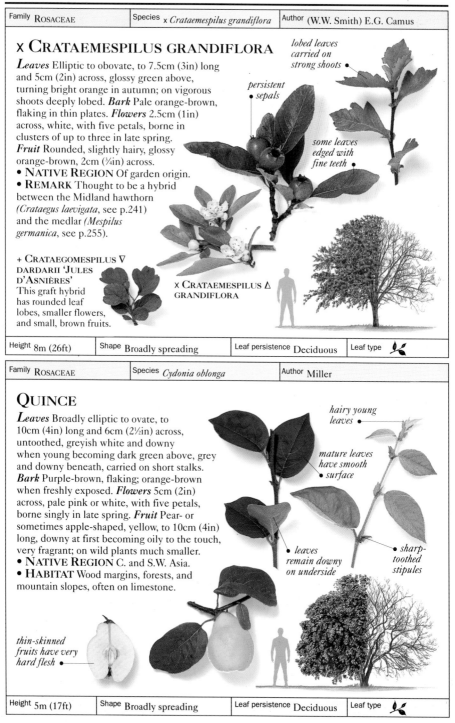

*lobed leaves
carried on
strong shoots* •

*persistent
• sepals*

*some leaves
edged with
fine teeth* •

x **CRATAEMESPILUS** △
GRANDIFLORA

Height 8m (26ft)	Shape Broadly spreading	Leaf persistence Deciduous	Leaf type

Family ROSACEAE	Species *Cydonia oblonga*	Author Miller

QUINCE

Leaves Broadly elliptic to ovate, to
10cm (4in) long and 6cm (2½in) across,
untoothed, greyish white and downy
when young becoming dark green above, grey
and downy beneath, carried on short stalks.
Bark Purple-brown, flaking; orange-brown
when freshly exposed. **Flowers** 5cm (2in)
across, pale pink or white, with five petals,
borne singly in late spring. **Fruit** Pear- or
sometimes apple-shaped, yellow, to 10cm (4in)
long, downy at first becoming oily to the touch,
very fragrant; on wild plants much smaller.
• **NATIVE REGION** C. and S.W. Asia.
• **HABITAT** Wood margins, forests, and
mountain slopes, often on limestone.

*hairy young
leaves* •

*mature leaves
have smooth
• surface*

*• leaves
remain downy
on underside*

*• sharp-
toothed
stipules*

*thin-skinned
fruits have very
hard flesh* •

Height 5m (17ft)	Shape Broadly spreading	Leaf persistence Deciduous	Leaf type

| Family ROSACEAE | Species *Malus baccata* | Author (Linnaeus) Borkhausen |

SIBERIAN CRAB APPLE

Leaves Elliptic to ovate, to 7.5cm (3in) long and 4cm (1½in) across, tapered to a pointed tip, finely toothed, dark green above, paler beneath, smooth on both sides. *Bark* Grey-brown, flaking in square plates; red-brown when freshly exposed. *Flowers* Individually to 4cm (1½in) across, white tinged pink opening white, with five petals and yellow anthers, fragrant, borne in clusters in mid-spring at the same time as the young leaves emerge. *Fruit* Rounded, small, red or yellow, 1cm (⅜in) across.
• **NATIVE REGION** E. Asia.
• **HABITAT** Woods and scrub.

pale green young leaves unfold as flowers open

small fruits carried on slender stalks

leaf margin edged with fine teeth

| Height 15m (50ft) | Shape Broadly spreading | Leaf persistence Deciduous | Leaf type |

| Family ROSACEAE | Species *Malus coronaria* | Author (Linnaeus) Miller |

WILD SWEET CRAB APPLE

fragrant flowers

Leaves Ovate, to 10cm (4in) long and 6cm (2½in) across, sharply often double-toothed, reddish and downy becoming deep green above, smooth; on vigorous shoots lobed towards the base. *Bark* Red-brown and scaly, with vertical fissures. *Flowers* 5cm (2in) across, pink, in clusters in late spring. *Fruit* Rounded, green, 4cm (1½in) across, slightly broader than long.
• **NATIVE REGION** E. North America.
• **HABITAT** Woods and thickets.

leaves often colour in autumn

MALUS CORONARIA

hairy under-side of young leaf

hard fruits remain green

◁ 'CHARLOTTAE'
This form has double, violet-scented flowers.

| Height 9m (30ft) | Shape Broadly spreading | Leaf persistence Deciduous | Leaf type |

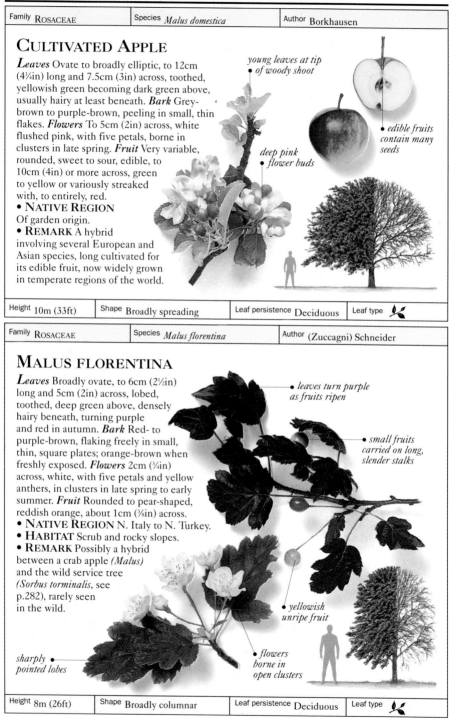

Family ROSACEAE	Species *Malus domestica*	Author Borkhausen

CULTIVATED APPLE

Leaves Ovate to broadly elliptic, to 12cm (4¼in) long and 7.5cm (3in) across, toothed, yellowish green becoming dark green above, usually hairy at least beneath. **Bark** Grey-brown to purple-brown, peeling in small, thin flakes. **Flowers** To 5cm (2in) across, white flushed pink, with five petals, borne in clusters in late spring. **Fruit** Very variable, rounded, sweet to sour, edible, to 10cm (4in) or more across, green to yellow or variously streaked with, to entirely, red.
• **NATIVE REGION** Of garden origin.
• **REMARK** A hybrid involving several European and Asian species, long cultivated for its edible fruit, now widely grown in temperate regions of the world.

young leaves at tip • of woody shoot

deep pink • flower buds

• edible fruits contain many seeds

Height 10m (33ft)	Shape Broadly spreading	Leaf persistence Deciduous	Leaf type

Family ROSACEAE	Species *Malus florentina*	Author (Zuccagni) Schneider

MALUS FLORENTINA

Leaves Broadly ovate, to 6cm (2½in) long and 5cm (2in) across, lobed, toothed, deep green above, densely hairy beneath, turning purple and red in autumn. **Bark** Red- to purple-brown, flaking freely in small, thin, square plates; orange-brown when freshly exposed. **Flowers** 2cm (¾in) across, white, with five petals and yellow anthers, in clusters in late spring to early summer. **Fruit** Rounded to pear-shaped, reddish orange, about 1cm (⅜in) across.
• **NATIVE REGION** N. Italy to N. Turkey.
• **HABITAT** Scrub and rocky slopes.
• **REMARK** Possibly a hybrid between a crab apple *(Malus)* and the wild service tree *(Sorbus torminalis*, see p.282), rarely seen in the wild.

• leaves turn purple as fruits ripen

• small fruits carried on long, slender stalks

• yellowish unripe fruit

sharply • pointed lobes

• flowers borne in open clusters

Height 8m (26ft)	Shape Broadly columnar	Leaf persistence Deciduous	Leaf type

| Family ROSACEAE | Species *Malus floribunda* | Author Siebold ex van Houtte |

JAPANESE CRAB APPLE

Leaves Elliptic, to 10cm (4in) long and 5cm
(2in) across, taper-pointed, sharply toothed,
dark green and smooth above, hairy when
young beneath; on vigorous shoots sometimes
lobed. *Bark* Purple-brown, flaking in thin
plates with age. *Flowers* 2.5cm (1in) across,
deep red in bud opening pale pink becoming
white, with five petals, very profuse, in clusters
in mid-spring. *Fruit* Rounded and yellow, 2cm
(¾in) across.
• NATIVE REGION Of garden origin.
• REMARK A hybrid of
unknown origin,
introduced to
the West from
Japan.

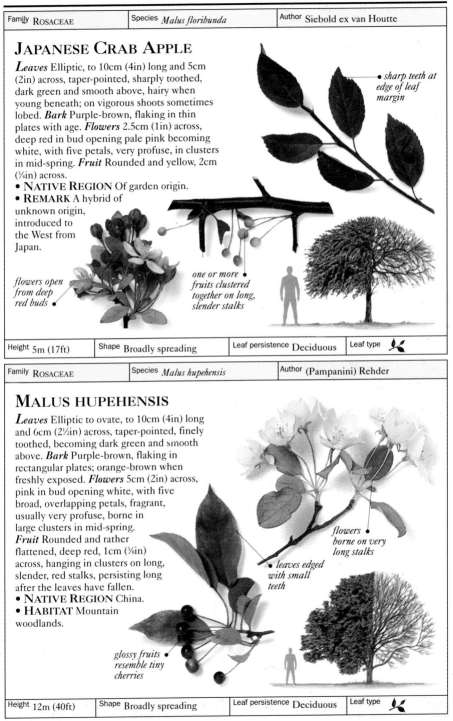

*sharp teeth at
edge of leaf
margin*

*flowers open
from deep
red buds*

*one or more
fruits clustered
together on long,
slender stalks*

| Height 5m (17ft) | Shape Broadly spreading | Leaf persistence Deciduous | Leaf type |

| Family ROSACEAE | Species *Malus hupehensis* | Author (Pampanini) Rehder |

MALUS HUPEHENSIS

Leaves Elliptic to ovate, to 10cm (4in) long
and 6cm (2½in) across, taper-pointed, finely
toothed, becoming dark green and smooth
above. *Bark* Purple-brown, flaking in
rectangular plates; orange-brown when
freshly exposed. *Flowers* 5cm (2in) across,
pink in bud opening white, with five
broad, overlapping petals, fragrant,
usually very profuse, borne in
large clusters in mid-spring.
Fruit Rounded and rather
flattened, deep red, 1cm (⅜in)
across, hanging in clusters on long,
slender, red stalks, persisting long
after the leaves have fallen.
• NATIVE REGION China.
• HABITAT Mountain
woodlands.

*flowers
borne on very
long stalks*

*leaves edged
with small
teeth*

*glossy fruits
resemble tiny
cherries*

| Height 12m (40ft) | Shape Broadly spreading | Leaf persistence Deciduous | Leaf type |

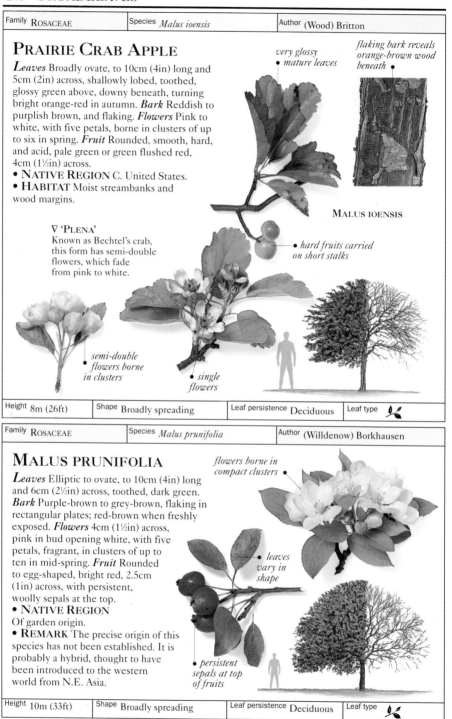

Family ROSACEAE	Species *Malus ioensis*	Author (Wood) Britton

PRAIRIE CRAB APPLE

Leaves Broadly ovate, to 10cm (4in) long and 5cm (2in) across, shallowly lobed, toothed, glossy green above, downy beneath, turning bright orange-red in autumn. **Bark** Reddish to purplish brown, and flaking. **Flowers** Pink to white, with five petals, borne in clusters of up to six in spring. **Fruit** Rounded, smooth, hard, and acid, pale green or green flushed red, 4cm (1½in) across.
• **NATIVE REGION** C. United States.
• **HABITAT** Moist streambanks and wood margins.

very glossy • mature leaves

flaking bark reveals orange-brown wood beneath •

MALUS IOENSIS

▽ '**PLENA**'
Known as Bechtel's crab, this form has semi-double flowers, which fade from pink to white.

• hard fruits carried on short stalks

semi-double • flowers borne in clusters

• single flowers

Height 8m (26ft)	Shape Broadly spreading	Leaf persistence Deciduous	Leaf type

Family ROSACEAE	Species *Malus prunifolia*	Author (Willdenow) Borkhausen

MALUS PRUNIFOLIA

Leaves Elliptic to ovate, to 10cm (4in) long and 6cm (2½in) across, toothed, dark green. **Bark** Purple-brown to grey-brown, flaking in rectangular plates; red-brown when freshly exposed. **Flowers** 4cm (1½in) across, pink in bud opening white, with five petals, fragrant, in clusters of up to ten in mid-spring. **Fruit** Rounded to egg-shaped, bright red, 2.5cm (1in) across, with persistent, woolly sepals at the top.
• **NATIVE REGION** Of garden origin.
• **REMARK** The precise origin of this species has not been established. It is probably a hybrid, thought to have been introduced to the western world from N.E. Asia.

flowers borne in compact clusters •

• leaves vary in shape

• persistent sepals at top of fruits

Height 10m (33ft)	Shape Broadly spreading	Leaf persistence Deciduous	Leaf type

Family ROSACEAE	Species *Malus* x *purpurea*	Author (Barbier) Rehder

MALUS X PURPUREA

Leaves Elliptic to narrowly ovate, to 7.5cm (3in) long, pointed, toothed, purplish green. *Bark* Purple-brown, cracked, flaking. *Flowers* 4cm (1½in) across, opening deep purple-pink, borne in clusters in spring. *Fruit* Rounded, deep reddish purple, 2.5cm (1in) across.
• **NATIVE REGION** Of garden origin.
• **REMARK** A hybrid between *M.* x *atrosanguinea* and *M. niedzwetzkyana*.

flowers have • five petals

Height 8m (26ft)	Shape Broadly spreading	Leaf persistence Deciduous	Leaf type

Family ROSACEAE	Species *Malus sieboldii*	Author (Regel) Rehder

MALUS SIEBOLDII

Leaves Elliptic to ovate, to 6cm (2½in) long and 3cm (1¼in) across, taper-pointed, toothed, matt deep green above, paler beneath, downy on both sides when young becoming nearly smooth; on vigorous shoots with three to five lobes. *Bark* Dark grey, cracking into small plates. *Flowers* 2cm (¾in) across, pink in bud opening white, with five petals, fragrant, in small clusters in mid-spring. *Fruit* Rounded, red or yellow, 1cm (⅜in) across, with no sepals when ripe, on slender stalks, persisting for some time.
• **NATIVE REGION** Japan.
• **HABITAT** Moist, sunny situations.

• strong shoots have deeply lobed leaves

small flowers carried • on slender stalks

coarsely • toothed lobes

green stalks become • red as fruits ripen

Height 10m (33ft)	Shape Broadly weeping	Leaf persistence Deciduous	Leaf type

Family ROSACEAE	Species *Malus transitoria*	Author (Batalin) Schneider

MALUS TRANSITORIA

Leaves Variable, small and oblong, to 2.5cm (1in) long on short shoots, larger, to 7.5cm (3in) long and 6cm (2½in) across on vigorous shoots, deeply cut into three lobes, the central lobe with a lobe on each side, sharply toothed, bright green above, paler beneath, thinly hairy. *Bark* Purple-brown, cracking into smooth, vertical, rectangular plates. *Flowers* 2cm (¾in) across, white, with five petals, in small clusters in late spring. *Fruit* Small, yellow, 8mm (⁵⁄₁₆in) across, slightly flattened, carried on slender, red stalks.
• NATIVE REGION N.W. China.
• HABITAT Woods and thickets.

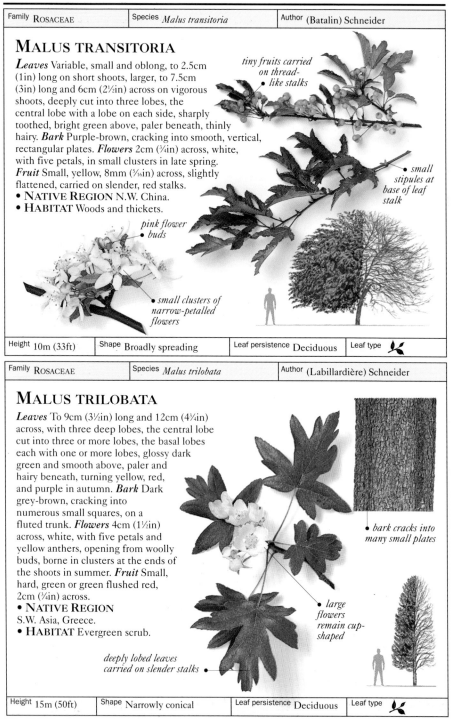

tiny fruits carried on thread-like stalks

small stipules at base of leaf stalk

pink flower buds

small clusters of narrow-petalled flowers

Height 10m (33ft)	Shape Broadly spreading	Leaf persistence Deciduous	Leaf type

Family ROSACEAE	Species *Malus trilobata*	Author (Labillardière) Schneider

MALUS TRILOBATA

Leaves To 9cm (3½in) long and 12cm (4¾in) across, with three deep lobes, the central lobe cut into three or more lobes, the basal lobes each with one or more lobes, glossy dark green and smooth above, paler and hairy beneath, turning yellow, red, and purple in autumn. *Bark* Dark grey-brown, cracking into numerous small squares, on a fluted trunk. *Flowers* 4cm (1½in) across, white, with five petals and yellow anthers, opening from woolly buds, borne in clusters at the ends of the shoots in summer. *Fruit* Small, hard, green or green flushed red, 2cm (¾in) across.
• NATIVE REGION S.W. Asia, Greece.
• HABITAT Evergreen scrub.

bark cracks into many small plates

large flowers remain cup-shaped

deeply lobed leaves carried on slender stalks

Height 15m (50ft)	Shape Narrowly conical	Leaf persistence Deciduous	Leaf type

Family ROSACEAE	Species *Malus tschonoskii*	Author (Maximowicz) Schneider

MALUS TSCHONOSKII

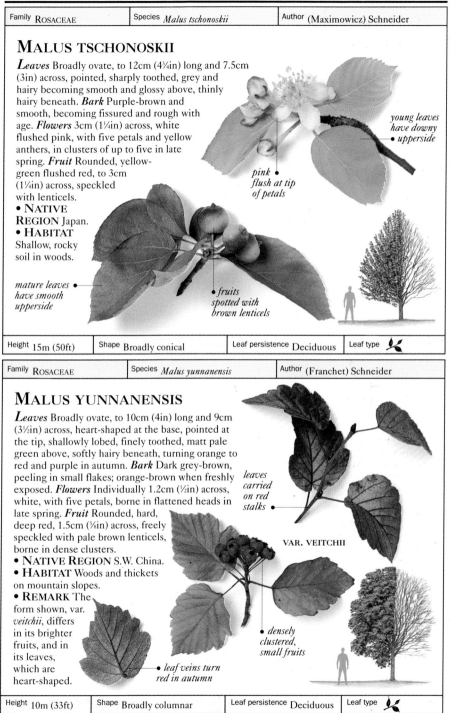

Leaves Broadly ovate, to 12cm (4¾in) long and 7.5cm (3in) across, pointed, sharply toothed, grey and hairy becoming smooth and glossy above, thinly hairy beneath. **Bark** Purple-brown and smooth, becoming fissured and rough with age. **Flowers** 3cm (1¼in) across, white flushed pink, with five petals and yellow anthers, in clusters of up to five in late spring. **Fruit** Rounded, yellow-green flushed red, to 3cm (1¼in) across, speckled with lenticels.
• **NATIVE REGION** Japan.
• **HABITAT** Shallow, rocky soil in woods.

young leaves have downy • upperside

pink • flush at tip of petals

mature leaves • have smooth upperside

• fruits spotted with brown lenticels

Height 15m (50ft)	Shape Broadly conical	Leaf persistence Deciduous	Leaf type

Family ROSACEAE	Species *Malus yunnanensis*	Author (Franchet) Schneider

MALUS YUNNANENSIS

Leaves Broadly ovate, to 10cm (4in) long and 9cm (3½in) across, heart-shaped at the base, pointed at the tip, shallowly lobed, finely toothed, matt pale green above, softly hairy beneath, turning orange to red and purple in autumn. **Bark** Dark grey-brown, peeling in small flakes; orange-brown when freshly exposed. **Flowers** Individually 1.2cm (½in) across, white, with five petals, borne in flattened heads in late spring. **Fruit** Rounded, hard, deep red, 1.5cm (⅝in) across, freely speckled with pale brown lenticels, borne in dense clusters.
• **NATIVE REGION** S.W. China.
• **HABITAT** Woods and thickets on mountain slopes.
• **REMARK** The form shown, var. *veitchii*, differs in its brighter fruits, and in its leaves, which are heart-shaped.

leaves carried on red stalks •

VAR. VEITCHII

• densely clustered, small fruits

• leaf veins turn red in autumn

Height 10m (33ft)	Shape Broadly columnar	Leaf persistence Deciduous	Leaf type

Family ROSACEAE	Species *Malus* hybrids	Author None

CRAB APPLE HYBRIDS

Many of the garden crab apples are hybrids between various species, raised in cultivation and grown for the beauty of their flowers or fruits; the attraction of some of these trees lies in both flowers and the fruits that follow in autumn. The plants usually make small, spreading trees, reaching about 6–8m (20–26ft) in height, and flowering in late spring and early summer. Several species have purplish leaves and flowers. This coloration arises as a result of hybridization with *Malus niedzwetzkyana*, a species found originally in the central Asian region of Turkestan.

pinkish flower buds

◁ **'BUTTERBALL'**
This hybrid was raised in North America. Rounded, yellowish fruits succeed the pink-flushed, white flowers.

▽ **'BUTTERBALL'**

fruits persist through autumn and winter

fruits mature to orange-yellow

▽ **'DARTMOUTH'**
The small, white flowers of this form open from buds tinged faintly pink. The large fruits are 5cm (2in) across, red-purple and bloomy.

white flowers borne profusely

◁ **'CRITTENDEN'**
This plant bears white flowers flushed slightly pink. They are followed by a profusion of bright scarlet fruits.

▽ **'CRITTENDEN'**

clustered flowers open after leaves unfold

• *fruits ripen from yellow to shades of purple and deep red*

◁ **'ELEYI'**
The fruits of this ornamental form are small, conical, and coloured purple.

bronze-purple young leaves •

• *reddish purple flower petals narrow to white base*

Height To 8m (26ft)	Shape Broadly spreading	Leaf persistence Deciduous	Leaf type

white flowers open from deep pink buds

∇ 'JOHN DOWNIE'
The soft pink buds of this form open into small, white flowers with yellow anthers. The egg-shaped fruits are 3cm (1¼in) long and orange-yellow flushed red.

fruits ripen from green to yellow

pale pink buds open to white flowers

△ 'GOLDEN HORNET'
The flowers of this form are 4cm (1½in) across, pink in bud opening white flushed pink. The rounded, deep yellow fruits measure 2.5cm (1in) across.

'GOLDEN HORNET' ▷

purplish-red flowers have broad petals

leaves can be unevenly lobed

distinctive, egg-shaped fruits

fruits carried on short stalks

△ 'JOHN DOWNIE'

◁ 'LEMOINEI'
This colourful hybrid has deep bronze-purple young leaves, which mature to purplish green. The purplish red flowers are 4cm (1½in) across, and the deep purple fruits 1.5cm (⅝in) long.

flowers open as leaves mature

cherry-like fruits

∇ 'LISET'
The bronze-purple young leaves of this form become dark green, contrasting with the deep purple-pink flowers.

very dark red flower buds

shiny shoots speckled with lenticels

△ 'LISET'

Family ROSACEAE	Species *Malus* hybrids	Author None

small fruits carried on slender stalks

◁ 'PROFUSION'
The purplish red flowers of this plant are 4cm (1½in) across, borne profusely in large clusters. The dark green, red-veined leaves are bronze-purple when young. Deep reddish purple, rounded fruits, 1.2cm (½in) across, are produced in autumn.

leaves are often lobed on strong shoots

fruits are red when ripe

'RED SENTINEL' ▷
The pink buds of this hybrid open into white flowers 3cm (1¼in) across, which set rounded, long-persistent, glossy deep red fruits, 2.5cm (1in) across.

petals flushed pink at base

△ 'RED JADE'
This mushroom-shaped tree bears clusters of pink buds, which open to white flowers. The bright red fruits are carried on the branches into late autumn.

△ 'RED JADE'

▽ 'ROYALTY'
The glossy red-purple leaves of this compact tree turn red in late autumn. Deep red flower buds open deep red-purple.

'ROYALTY' ▷

double flowers have 15 petals each

'VAN ESELTINE' ▷
This form is distinguished by its upright habit, double flowers, and the small, yellow or yellow flushed red fruits that follow in autumn.

leaves still reddish as fruits ripen

Height To 8m (26ft)	Shape Variable	Leaf persistence Deciduous	Leaf type

Family ROSACEAE	Species *Mespilus germanica*	Author Linnaeus

MEDLAR

Leaves Elliptic to oblong, to 15cm (6in) long and 5cm (2in) across, untoothed or finely toothed, dark green above, usually hairy on both sides, turning yellow and brown in autumn, on very short stalks; shoots often thorny. *Bark* Grey-brown and smooth at first, cracking into thin plates with age; orange-brown when freshly exposed. *Flowers* To 5cm (2in) across, white, with five petals, borne singly on short stalks in late spring to early summer; vigorous plants often flower again in late summer. *Fruit* Rounded, flat-topped to pear-shaped, fleshy, brown, to 3cm (1¼in) across, with persistent sepals at the top.

• **NATIVE REGION**
S.W. Asia, S.E. Europe.
• **HABITAT** Forests, wood margins, and mountain thickets.
• **REMARK** Wild plants tend to be more shrubby than cultivated forms. The fruit becomes edible only after exposure to frost.

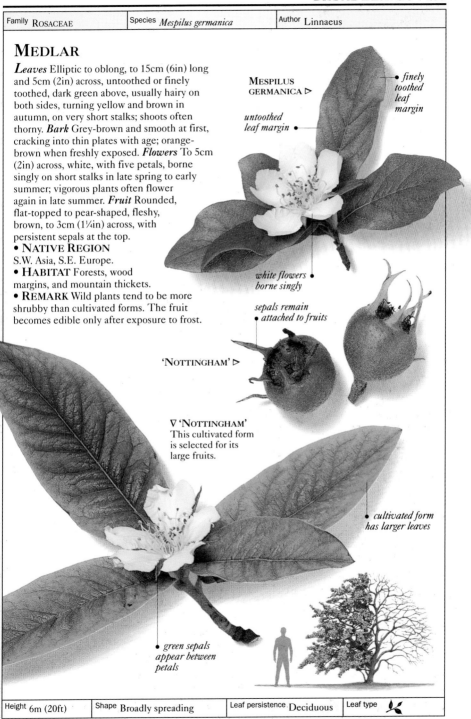

MESPILUS GERMANICA ▷

• *finely toothed leaf margin*

untoothed leaf margin •

white flowers borne singly •

sepals remain • attached to fruits

'NOTTINGHAM' ▷

▽ 'NOTTINGHAM'
This cultivated form is selected for its large fruits.

• *cultivated form has larger leaves*

• *green sepals appear between petals*

Height 6m (20ft)	Shape Broadly spreading	Leaf persistence Deciduous	Leaf type

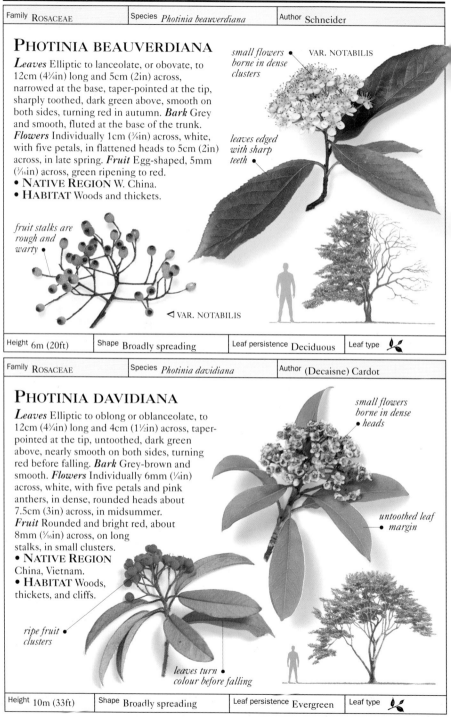

| Family ROSACEAE | Species *Photinia beauverdiana* | Author Schneider |

PHOTINIA BEAUVERDIANA

Leaves Elliptic to lanceolate, or obovate, to 12cm (4¾in) long and 5cm (2in) across, narrowed at the base, taper-pointed at the tip, sharply toothed, dark green above, smooth on both sides, turning red in autumn. **Bark** Grey and smooth, fluted at the base of the trunk. **Flowers** Individually 1cm (⅜in) across, white, with five petals, in flattened heads to 5cm (2in) across, in late spring. **Fruit** Egg-shaped, 5mm (³⁄₁₆in) across, green ripening to red.
• **NATIVE REGION** W. China.
• **HABITAT** Woods and thickets.

small flowers borne in dense clusters

VAR. NOTABILIS

leaves edged with sharp teeth

fruit stalks are rough and warty

◁ VAR. NOTABILIS

| Height 6m (20ft) | Shape Broadly spreading | Leaf persistence Deciduous | Leaf type |

| Family ROSACEAE | Species *Photinia davidiana* | Author (Decaisne) Cardot |

PHOTINIA DAVIDIANA

Leaves Elliptic to oblong or oblanceolate, to 12cm (4¾in) long and 4cm (1½in) across, taper-pointed at the tip, untoothed, dark green above, nearly smooth on both sides, turning red before falling. **Bark** Grey-brown and smooth. **Flowers** Individually 6mm (¼in) across, white, with five petals and pink anthers, in dense, rounded heads about 7.5cm (3in) across, in midsummer. **Fruit** Rounded and bright red, about 8mm (⁵⁄₁₆in) across, on long stalks, in small clusters.
• **NATIVE REGION** China, Vietnam.
• **HABITAT** Woods, thickets, and cliffs.

small flowers borne in dense • heads

untoothed leaf • margin

ripe fruit • clusters

leaves turn • colour before falling

| Height 10m (33ft) | Shape Broadly spreading | Leaf persistence Evergreen | Leaf type |

Family ROSACEAE	Species *Photinia x fraseri*	Author Dress

PHOTINIA X FRASERI

Leaves Oblong to obovate, to 15cm (6in) long and 6cm (2½in) across, toothed, glossy dark green above, smooth. **Bark** Grey-brown and smooth, peeling on large trunks. **Flowers** White, in flattened heads 12cm (4¾in) across, from late spring to summer. **Fruit** Rounded, red, 5mm (³⁄₁₆in) across.
• **NATIVE REGION** Of garden origin.
• **REMARK** A hybrid between *Photinia glabra* and *P. serratifolia* (see below).

mature leaf

flowers have five petals and pink anthers

bronzy young foliage

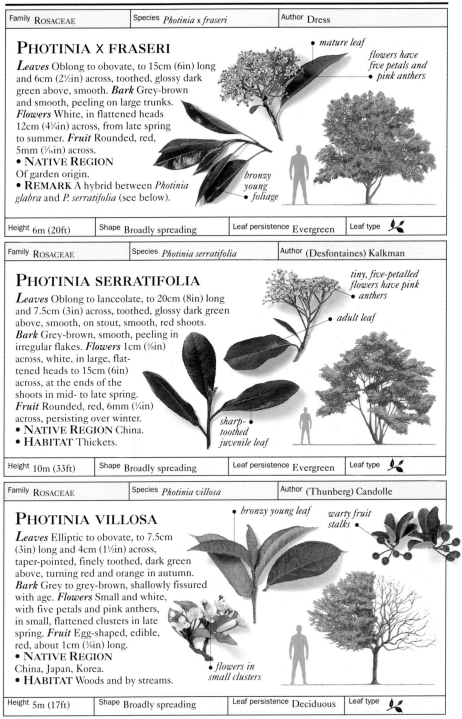

Height 6m (20ft)	Shape Broadly spreading	Leaf persistence Evergreen	Leaf type

Family ROSACEAE	Species *Photinia serratifolia*	Author (Desfontaines) Kalkman

PHOTINIA SERRATIFOLIA

Leaves Oblong to lanceolate, to 20cm (8in) long and 7.5cm (3in) across, toothed, glossy dark green above, smooth, on stout, smooth, red shoots. **Bark** Grey-brown, smooth, peeling in irregular flakes. **Flowers** 1cm (⅜in) across, white, in large, flattened heads to 15cm (6in) across, at the ends of the shoots in mid- to late spring. **Fruit** Rounded, red, 6mm (¼in) across, persisting over winter.
• **NATIVE REGION** China.
• **HABITAT** Thickets.

tiny, five-petalled flowers have pink anthers

adult leaf

sharp-toothed juvenile leaf

Height 10m (33ft)	Shape Broadly spreading	Leaf persistence Evergreen	Leaf type

Family ROSACEAE	Species *Photinia villosa*	Author (Thunberg) Candolle

PHOTINIA VILLOSA

Leaves Elliptic to obovate, to 7.5cm (3in) long and 4cm (1½in) across, taper-pointed, finely toothed, dark green above, turning red and orange in autumn. **Bark** Grey to grey-brown, shallowly fissured with age. **Flowers** Small and white, with five petals and pink anthers, in small, flattened clusters in late spring. **Fruit** Egg-shaped, edible, red, about 1cm (⅜in) long.
• **NATIVE REGION** China, Japan, Korea.
• **HABITAT** Woods and by streams.

bronzy young leaf

warty fruit stalks

flowers in small clusters

Height 5m (17ft)	Shape Broadly spreading	Leaf persistence Deciduous	Leaf type

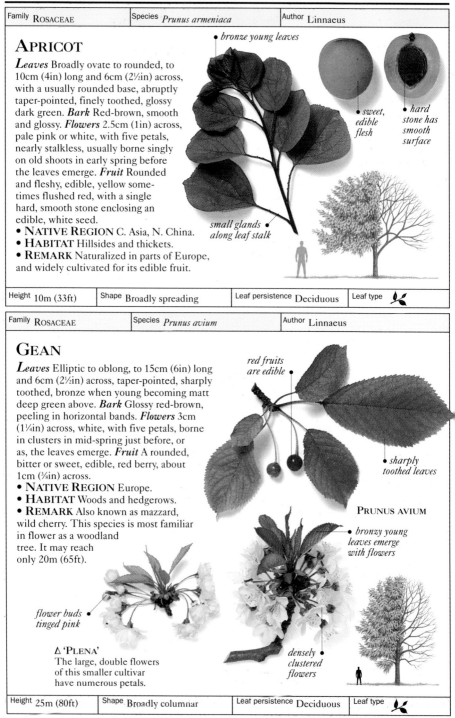

| Family | ROSACEAE | Species | *Prunus armeniaca* | Author | Linnaeus |

APRICOT

bronze young leaves

Leaves Broadly ovate to rounded, to 10cm (4in) long and 6cm (2½in) across, with a usually rounded base, abruptly taper-pointed, finely toothed, glossy dark green. **Bark** Red-brown, smooth and glossy. **Flowers** 2.5cm (1in) across, pale pink or white, with five petals, nearly stalkless, usually borne singly on old shoots in early spring before the leaves emerge. **Fruit** Rounded and fleshy, edible, yellow sometimes flushed red, with a single hard, smooth stone enclosing an edible, white seed.

sweet, edible flesh

hard stone has smooth surface

- **NATIVE REGION** C. Asia, N. China.
- **HABITAT** Hillsides and thickets.
- **REMARK** Naturalized in parts of Europe, and widely cultivated for its edible fruit.

small glands along leaf stalk

| Height 10m (33ft) | Shape Broadly spreading | Leaf persistence Deciduous | Leaf type |

| Family | ROSACEAE | Species | *Prunus avium* | Author | Linnaeus |

GEAN

red fruits are edible

Leaves Elliptic to oblong, to 15cm (6in) long and 6cm (2½in) across, taper-pointed, sharply toothed, bronze when young becoming matt deep green above. **Bark** Glossy red-brown, peeling in horizontal bands. **Flowers** 3cm (1¼in) across, white, with five petals, borne in clusters in mid-spring just before, or as, the leaves emerge. **Fruit** A rounded, bitter or sweet, edible, red berry, about 1cm (⅜in) across.

sharply toothed leaves

- **NATIVE REGION** Europe.
- **HABITAT** Woods and hedgerows.
- **REMARK** Also known as mazzard, wild cherry. This species is most familiar in flower as a woodland tree. It may reach only 20m (65ft).

PRUNUS AVIUM

bronzy young leaves emerge with flowers

flower buds tinged pink

△ 'PLENA'
The large, double flowers of this smaller cultivar have numerous petals.

densely clustered flowers

| Height 25m (80ft) | Shape Broadly columnar | Leaf persistence Deciduous | Leaf type |

Family ROSACEAE	Species *Prunus cerasifera*	Author Ehrhart

CHERRY PLUM

Leaves Ovate to obovate, to 6cm (2½in) long and 3cm (1¼in) across, toothed at the margin, glossy dark green and smooth above, downy on the veins beneath. **Bark** Purple-brown, thinly scaly, with horizontal, orange lenticels, fissured with age. **Flowers** 2.5cm (1in) across, white, with five petals and reflexed sepals, borne singly or in small clusters in early spring before the leaves emerge. **Fruit** Rounded, plum-like, edible, and red, 3cm (1¼in) across.
• **NATIVE REGION** Of garden origin.
• **REMARK** Also known as myrobalan. A similar species is the yellow-fruiting *Prunus divaricata*, which is native to S.E. Europe, and C. and S.W. Asia.

white flowers open before leaves •

PRUNUS CERASIFERA

very dark green shoots and leaves •

◁ **'NIGRA'**
Deep red-purple leaves and pink flowers distinguish this form.

pink flowers have dark • centre

• stamens have pink anthers

△ **'PISSARDII'**
This form has pink flower buds, opening to white, and purple leaves.

△ **'ROSEA'**
This hybrid has red-purple foliage and small, pink flowers.

Height 8m (26ft)	Shape Broadly spreading	Leaf persistence Deciduous	Leaf type

Family ROSACEAE	Species *Prunus cerasus*	Author Linnaeus

SOUR CHERRY

Leaves Elliptic to ovate, to 7.5cm (3in) long and 5cm (2in) across, taper-pointed, sharply toothed, dark green above, smooth on both sides. **Bark** Purple-brown, with horizontal, orange-brown lenticels, peeling horizontally. **Flowers** 2cm (¾in) across, white, with five petals, in small clusters in mid-spring. **Fruit** An edible, red to black cherry, 2cm (¾in) across.
• **NATIVE REGION** Of garden origin.
• **REMARK** The species is related to the gean *(Prunus avium, see p.258)*.

leaves emerge • after flowers open

• ripe fruits remain sour

PRUNUS CERASUS

• green sepals

△ **'RHEXII'**
This form has large, rosette-like flowers.

Height 8m (26ft)	Shape Broadly spreading	Leaf persistence Deciduous	Leaf type

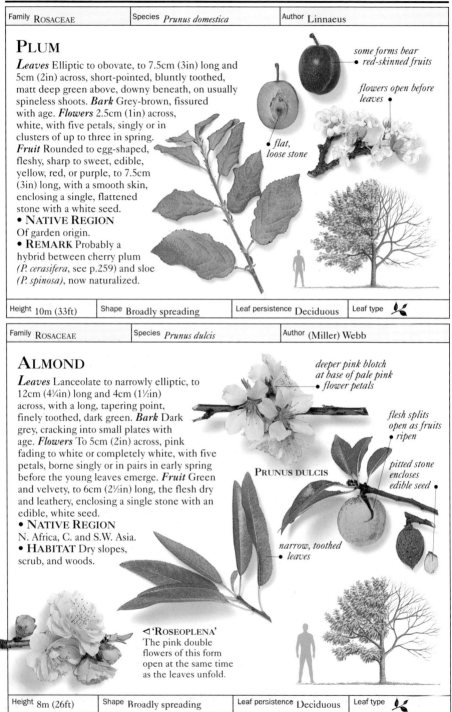

Family ROSACEAE	Species *Prunus domestica*	Author Linnaeus

PLUM

Leaves Elliptic to obovate, to 7.5cm (3in) long and 5cm (2in) across, short-pointed, bluntly toothed, matt deep green above, downy beneath, on usually spineless shoots. **Bark** Grey-brown, fissured with age. **Flowers** 2.5cm (1in) across, white, with five petals, singly or in clusters of up to three in spring. **Fruit** Rounded to egg-shaped, fleshy, sharp to sweet, edible, yellow, red, or purple, to 7.5cm (3in) long, with a smooth skin, enclosing a single, flattened stone with a white seed.
• **NATIVE REGION** Of garden origin.
• **REMARK** Probably a hybrid between cherry plum (*P. cerasifera*, see p.259) and sloe (*P. spinosa*), now naturalized.

some forms bear red-skinned fruits

flowers open before leaves

flat, loose stone

Height 10m (33ft)	Shape Broadly spreading	Leaf persistence Deciduous	Leaf type

Family ROSACEAE	Species *Prunus dulcis*	Author (Miller) Webb

ALMOND

Leaves Lanceolate to narrowly elliptic, to 12cm (4¾in) long and 4cm (1½in) across, with a long, tapering point, finely toothed, dark green. **Bark** Dark grey, cracking into small plates with age. **Flowers** To 5cm (2in) across, pink fading to white or completely white, with five petals, borne singly or in pairs in early spring before the young leaves emerge. **Fruit** Green and velvety, to 6cm (2½in) long, the flesh dry and leathery, enclosing a single stone with an edible, white seed.
• **NATIVE REGION** N. Africa, C. and S.W. Asia.
• **HABITAT** Dry slopes, scrub, and woods.

deeper pink blotch at base of pale pink flower petals

flesh splits open as fruits ripen

PRUNUS DULCIS

pitted stone encloses edible seed

narrow, toothed leaves

◁ 'ROSEOPLENA'
The pink double flowers of this form open at the same time as the leaves unfold.

Height 8m (26ft)	Shape Broadly spreading	Leaf persistence Deciduous	Leaf type

Family ROSACEAE	Species *Prunus incisa*	Author Thunberg

FUJI CHERRY

Leaves Ovate to obovate, to 6cm (2½in) long and 3cm (1¼in) across, taper-pointed at the tip, very sharply toothed at the margin, bronze-red when young becoming dark green, hairy on both sides. *Bark* Dark grey and vertically fissured. *Flowers* 2cm (¾in) across, white or very pale pink, with five notched petals, in small clusters of two or three in mid-spring before the leaves emerge. *Fruit* An egg-shaped, purple-black cherry, to 8mm (⁵⁄₁₆in) long.
• **NATIVE REGION** S.W. Japan.
• **HABITAT** Mountain woods.

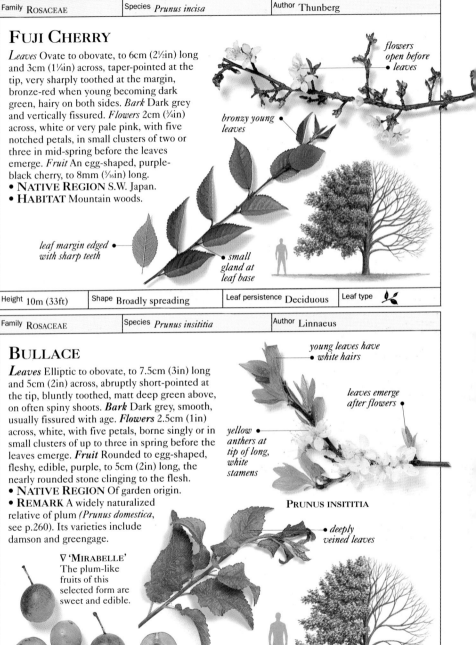

flowers open before • leaves

bronzy young leaves

leaf margin edged • with sharp teeth

• small gland at leaf base

Height 10m (33ft)	Shape Broadly spreading	Leaf persistence Deciduous	Leaf type

Family ROSACEAE	Species *Prunus insititia*	Author Linnaeus

BULLACE

Leaves Elliptic to obovate, to 7.5cm (3in) long and 5cm (2in) across, abruptly short-pointed at the tip, bluntly toothed, matt deep green above, on often spiny shoots. *Bark* Dark grey, smooth, usually fissured with age. *Flowers* 2.5cm (1in) across, white, with five petals, borne singly or in small clusters of up to three in spring before the leaves emerge. *Fruit* Rounded to egg-shaped, fleshy, edible, purple, to 5cm (2in) long, the nearly rounded stone clinging to the flesh.
• **NATIVE REGION** Of garden origin.
• **REMARK** A widely naturalized relative of plum *(Prunus domestica, see p.260).* Its varieties include damson and greengage.

∇ '**MIRABELLE**'
The plum-like fruits of this selected form are sweet and edible.

young leaves have • white hairs

leaves emerge after flowers •

yellow • anthers at tip of long, white stamens

PRUNUS INSITITIA

• deeply veined leaves

Height 7m (23ft)	Shape Broadly spreading	Leaf persistence Deciduous	Leaf type

Family ROSACEAE	Species *Prunus* forms or hybrids	Author None

JAPANESE CHERRIES

The Japanese cherries, or *Sato-zakura*, are ornamental, flowering garden trees raised or selected in Japan. They are thought to be forms or hybrids of two native Japanese species, the hill cherry *(Prunus jamasakura,* see p.265) and the Oshima cherry *(Prunus speciosa)*: trees similar to some of them grow wild in the hills and mountains of Japan. They have been cultivated in Japanese gardens for more than 1,500 years, yet are of relatively recent introduction to the West. Most have a spreading habit, but some are weeping or narrowly upright. The showy flowers are single to semi-double or fully double, and range from white to deep pink.

▽ 'AMANOGAWA'
A distinct tree of narrow, upright habit, to about 8m (26ft) tall. The pale pink double flowers are 4cm (1½in) across, and open in mid-spring before or with the bronze-tinged young leaves.

pale pink flowers have yellow anthers

deep bronze young leaves

double flowers borne in dense clusters

sharply toothed leaves

double flowers have numerous petals

bronze-green young leaves

'KANZAN' △
By far the most popular and commonly planted Japanese cherry, this tree is vase-shaped at first, the branches eventually spreading and arching, to 10m (33ft) or more tall.

teeth at leaf margin end in long, slender point

△ 'KANZAN'

△ 'CHEAL'S WEEPING'
This form usually reaches about 2.5m (8ft). Its long branches arch to the ground, giving the tree a mushroom shape.

Height To 10m (33ft)	Shape Variable		Leaf persistence Deciduous	Leaf type

⊲ 'SHIROFUGEN'
One of the most beautiful of Japanese cherries, this spreading tree grows to 10m (33ft) tall. The double flowers are pink in bud, and open white in late spring. They turn again to pink before they fall.

flowers fade to white after opening •

flowers hang in clusters beneath • shoots

sharply toothed • petals

young leaves mature to dark green •

large, white flowers have pink stamens •

△ 'SHOGETSU'
The large, white double flowers of this spreading tree open from pink-tinged buds in late spring, and form drooping clusters among the pale green young leaves.

'TAI HAKU' ⊳
The great white cherry was found in an English garden and re-introduced to Japan, where at one time it had been thought lost to cultivation. Its single flowers are the largest of those of any flowering cherry. They open in mid-spring among bronzy leaves.

petals tinged green •

• leaves edged with fine-pointed teeth

△ 'UKON'
The distinctive double flowers of this form are pale yellow-green flushed at first with pink. They open in mid-spring with the bronze-tinged young leaves.

Family ROSACEAE	Species *Prunus* hybrids	Author None

PRUNUS HYBRIDS

Apart from the Japanese cherries, there are in
gardens many other hybrids between various
species, either intentionally or accidentally
raised and grown for their ornamental
flowers and foliage. Their parentage
involves several different species and
hybrids, including *P. sargentii* (see p.268)
and *P.* x *subhirtella* (see pp.270–271), and
so these trees are more diverse than
the Japanese cherries. They can be
upright or spreading, usually reach
no more than 10m (33ft), and are
always deciduous; some produce
good autumn colour. The flowers
are single to semi-double or fully
double, usually opening in early
to late spring.

*double flowers
have yellow
anthers*

*sharp-
pointed,
toothed leaves*

△ 'ACCOLADE'
This small tree is thought
to be a hybrid between
Prunus sargentii (see
p.268) and *Prunus* x
subhirtella (see p.270).

*small glands at
base of leaf*

*pink buds fade to
nearly white on
opening*

△ 'PANDORA'
This tree has pale pink
single flowers, each with
five petals. They open in
early spring before the
leaves emerge.

*single-
flower petals
have notch
at tip*

*leaves end
in short point*

*leaf margin edged
with coarse teeth*

△ 'SPIRE'
The matt dark green foliage
of this form turns orange and
red in autumn.

Height To 10m (33ft)	Shape Variable	Leaf persistence Deciduous	Leaf type

Family ROSACEAE	Species *Prunus jamasakura*	Author Siebold ex Koidzumi

HILL CHERRY

Leaves Oblong to obovate, to 12cm (4¾in) long and 5cm (2in) across, abruptly taper-pointed at the tip, sharply toothed, bronze or red becoming deep green above, blue-green beneath, smooth on both sides, turning yellow to red in autumn. **Bark** Purple-brown, with horizontal lenticels. **Flowers** 3cm (1¼in) across, pale pink to nearly white, with five petals notched at the tip, opening in small clusters in mid-spring as the young leaves emerge. **Fruit** A fleshy, deep purple-black berry, 2.5cm (1in) long.
• **NATIVE REGION** China, Japan, Korea.
• **HABITAT** Woods in hills and low mountains.
• **REMARK** Also known as *Prunus serrulata* var. *spontanea*.

notch at tip of petal

sharply toothed leaf margin

folded, soft young leaves

coloured autumn leaves carried on red stalks

Height 20m (65ft)	Shape Broadly spreading	Leaf persistence Deciduous	Leaf type

Family ROSACEAE	Species *Prunus laurocerasus*	Author Linnaeus

CHERRY LAUREL

Leaves Elliptic to oblong or obovate, to 20cm (8in) long and 6cm (2½in) across, abruptly short-pointed, usually shallowly toothed at least above the middle, glossy yellowish to very dark green above, pale green beneath, smooth, on short, stout stalks. **Bark** Grey-brown and smooth. **Flowers** 8mm (⁵⁄₁₆in) across, white, with five petals, fragrant, borne in upright racemes to 12cm (4¾in) long, in the leaf axils in mid-spring, sometimes flowering again in autumn. **Fruit** A rounded berry, 1.2cm (½in) across, green becoming red ripening to black.
• **NATIVE REGION** S.W. Asia, E. Europe.
• **HABITAT** Thickets in forests.

yellowish leaf stalks

fruits ripen from green through red to black

long flower clusters emerge from leaf axils

Height 10m (33ft)	Shape Broadly spreading	Leaf persistence Evergreen	Leaf type

Family ROSACEAE	Species *Prunus lusitanica*	Author Linnaeus

PORTUGAL LAUREL

Leaves Ovate to elliptic, to 12cm (4¾in) long and 5cm (2in) across, taper-pointed at the tip, toothed, glossy dark green above, smooth on both sides, on slender, red stalks. **Bark** Dark grey-brown and smooth. **Flowers** Individually 1cm (⅜in) across, white, with five petals, fragrant, numerous, borne in spreading racemes to 25cm (10in) long, in midsummer. **Fruit** Egg-shaped, 1.2cm (½in) long, green becoming red ripening to black.
• **NATIVE REGION** S.W. France, Portugal, Spain.
• **HABITAT** Mountain woods.

SUBSP. AZORICA ▷
This form is native to the North Atlantic islands, the Azores. Its flowers are borne in shorter racemes.

flowers borne in long, slender racemes

PRUNUS LUSITANICA

broader leaves

fewer flowers in upright racemes

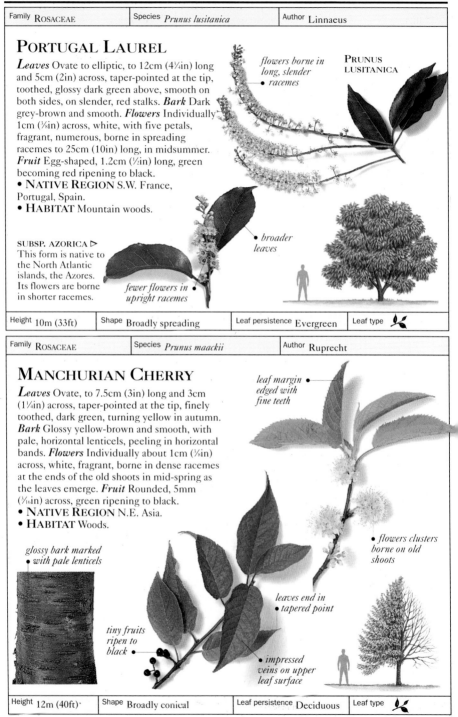

Height 10m (33ft)	Shape Broadly spreading	Leaf persistence Evergreen	Leaf type

Family ROSACEAE	Species *Prunus maackii*	Author Ruprecht

MANCHURIAN CHERRY

Leaves Ovate, to 7.5cm (3in) long and 3cm (1¼in) across, taper-pointed at the tip, finely toothed, dark green, turning yellow in autumn. **Bark** Glossy yellow-brown and smooth, with pale, horizontal lenticels, peeling in horizontal bands. **Flowers** Individually about 1cm (⅜in) across, white, fragrant, borne in dense racemes at the ends of the old shoots in mid-spring as the leaves emerge. **Fruit** Rounded, 5mm (³⁄₁₆in) across, green ripening to black.
• **NATIVE REGION** N.E. Asia.
• **HABITAT** Woods.

leaf margin edged with fine teeth

glossy bark marked with pale lenticels

flowers clusters borne on old shoots

leaves end in tapered point

tiny fruits ripen to black

impressed veins on upper leaf surface

Height 12m (40ft)	Shape Broadly conical	Leaf persistence Deciduous	Leaf type

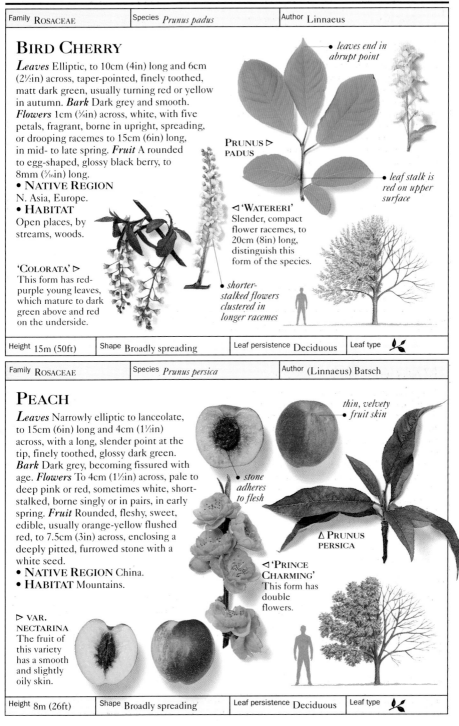

Family ROSACEAE	Species *Prunus padus*	Author Linnaeus

BIRD CHERRY

Leaves Elliptic, to 10cm (4in) long and 6cm (2½in) across, taper-pointed, finely toothed, matt dark green, usually turning red or yellow in autumn. ***Bark*** Dark grey and smooth. ***Flowers*** 1cm (⅜in) across, white, with five petals, fragrant, borne in upright, spreading, or drooping racemes to 15cm (6in) long, in mid- to late spring. ***Fruit*** A rounded to egg-shaped, glossy black berry, to 8mm (5⁄16in) long.

• **NATIVE REGION** N. Asia, Europe.

• **HABITAT** Open places, by streams, woods.

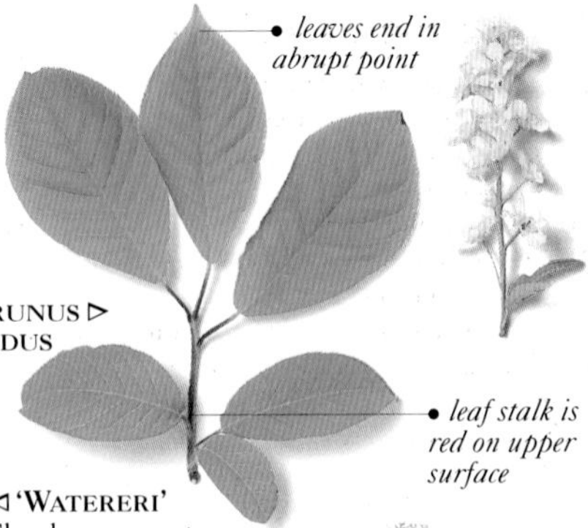
leaves end in abrupt point
leaf stalk is red on upper surface

PRUNUS ▷ PADUS

shorter-stalked flowers clustered in longer racemes

◁ 'WATERERI' Slender, compact flower racemes, to 20cm (8in) long, distinguish this form of the species.

'COLORATA' ▷ This form has red-purple young leaves, which mature to dark green above and red on the underside.

Height 15m (50ft)	Shape Broadly spreading	Leaf persistence Deciduous	Leaf type

Family ROSACEAE	Species *Prunus persica*	Author (Linnaeus) Batsch

PEACH

Leaves Narrowly elliptic to lanceolate, to 15cm (6in) long and 4cm (1½in) across, with a long, slender point at the tip, finely toothed, glossy dark green. ***Bark*** Dark grey, becoming fissured with age. ***Flowers*** To 4cm (1½in) across, pale to deep pink or red, sometimes white, short-stalked, borne singly or in pairs, in early spring. ***Fruit*** Rounded, fleshy, sweet, edible, usually orange-yellow flushed red, to 7.5cm (3in) across, enclosing a deeply pitted, furrowed stone with a white seed.

• **NATIVE REGION** China.

• **HABITAT** Mountains.

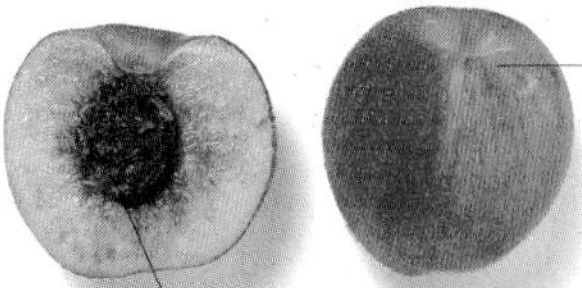
thin, velvety fruit skin
stone adheres to flesh

△ PRUNUS PERSICA

◁ 'PRINCE CHARMING' This form has double flowers.

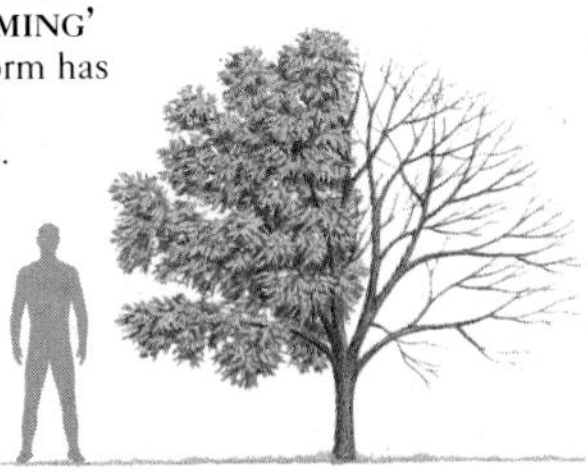

▷ VAR. NECTARINA The fruit of this variety has a smooth and slightly oily skin.

Height 8m (26ft)	Shape Broadly spreading	Leaf persistence Deciduous	Leaf type

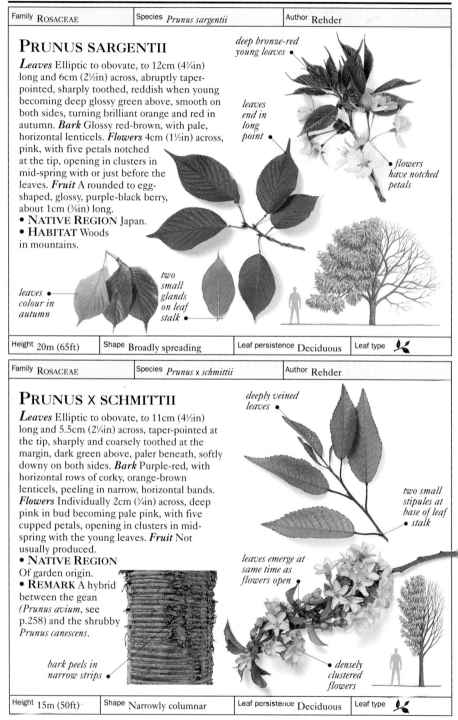

Family ROSACEAE	Species *Prunus sargentii*	Author Rehder

PRUNUS SARGENTII

Leaves Elliptic to obovate, to 12cm (4¾in) long and 6cm (2½in) across, abruptly taper-pointed, sharply toothed, reddish when young becoming deep glossy green above, smooth on both sides, turning brilliant orange and red in autumn. **Bark** Glossy red-brown, with pale, horizontal lenticels. **Flowers** 4cm (1½in) across, pink, with five petals notched at the tip, opening in clusters in mid-spring with or just before the leaves. **Fruit** A rounded to egg-shaped, glossy, purple-black berry, about 1cm (⅜in) long.
• **NATIVE REGION** Japan.
• **HABITAT** Woods in mountains.

deep bronze-red young leaves

leaves end in long point

flowers have notched petals

leaves colour in autumn

two small glands on leaf stalk

Height 20m (65ft)	Shape Broadly spreading	Leaf persistence Deciduous	Leaf type

Family ROSACEAE	Species *Prunus x schmittii*	Author Rehder

PRUNUS X SCHMITTII

Leaves Elliptic to obovate, to 11cm (4½in) long and 5.5cm (2¼in) across, taper-pointed at the tip, sharply and coarsely toothed at the margin, dark green above, paler beneath, softly downy on both sides. **Bark** Purple-red, with horizontal rows of corky, orange-brown lenticels, peeling in narrow, horizontal bands. **Flowers** Individually 2cm (¾in) across, deep pink in bud becoming pale pink, with five cupped petals, opening in clusters in mid-spring with the young leaves. **Fruit** Not usually produced.
• **NATIVE REGION** Of garden origin.
• **REMARK** A hybrid between the gean *(Prunus avium*, see p.258) and the shrubby *Prunus canescens.*

deeply veined leaves

two small stipules at base of leaf stalk

leaves emerge at same time as flowers open

bark peels in narrow strips

densely clustered flowers

Height 15m (50ft)	Shape Narrowly columnar	Leaf persistence Deciduous	Leaf type

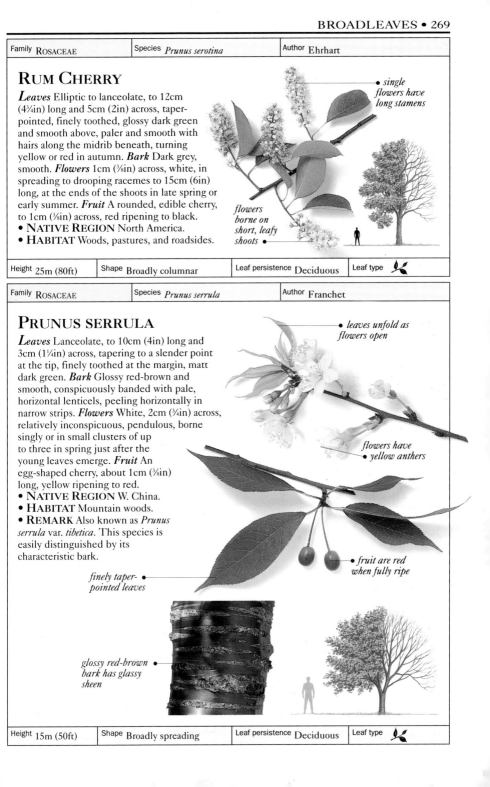

Family	ROSACEAE	Species	*Prunus serotina*	Author	Ehrhart

RUM CHERRY

Leaves Elliptic to lanceolate, to 12cm (4¾in) long and 5cm (2in) across, taper-pointed, finely toothed, glossy dark green and smooth above, paler and smooth with hairs along the midrib beneath, turning yellow or red in autumn. **Bark** Dark grey, smooth. **Flowers** 1cm (⅜in) across, white, in spreading to drooping racemes to 15cm (6in) long, at the ends of the shoots in late spring or early summer. **Fruit** A rounded, edible cherry, to 1cm (⅜in) across, red ripening to black.
• **NATIVE REGION** North America.
• **HABITAT** Woods, pastures, and roadsides.

single flowers have long stamens

flowers borne on short, leafy shoots

Height	25m (80ft)	Shape	Broadly columnar	Leaf persistence	Deciduous	Leaf type	

Family	ROSACEAE	Species	*Prunus serrula*	Author	Franchet

PRUNUS SERRULA

Leaves Lanceolate, to 10cm (4in) long and 3cm (1¼in) across, tapering to a slender point at the tip, finely toothed at the margin, matt dark green. **Bark** Glossy red-brown and smooth, conspicuously banded with pale, horizontal lenticels, peeling horizontally in narrow strips. **Flowers** White, 2cm (¾in) across, relatively inconspicuous, pendulous, borne singly or in small clusters of up to three in spring just after the young leaves emerge. **Fruit** An egg-shaped cherry, about 1cm (⅜in) long, yellow ripening to red.
• **NATIVE REGION** W. China.
• **HABITAT** Mountain woods.
• **REMARK** Also known as *Prunus serrula* var. *tibetica*. This species is easily distinguished by its characteristic bark.

leaves unfold as flowers open

flowers have yellow anthers

finely taper-pointed leaves

fruit are red when fully ripe

glossy red-brown bark has glassy sheen

Height	15m (50ft)	Shape	Broadly spreading	Leaf persistence	Deciduous	Leaf type	

Family ROSACEAE	Species *Prunus* x *subhirtella*	Author Miquel

SPRING CHERRY

Leaves Elliptic to ovate, to 7.5cm (3in) long and 5cm (2in) across, taper-pointed, sharply toothed, pale bronze when young becoming deep green above, paler beneath, turning yellow in autumn. **Bark** Grey-brown and smooth, banded with horizontal lenticels. **Flowers** Individually 2cm (¾in) across, pale pink or white, with five petals notched at the tip, opening from pink buds, in small clusters in early spring either before or as the young leaves emerge. **Fruit** A nearly black cherry, 8mm (⁵⁄₁₆in) across, sparsely borne.

- **NATIVE REGION** Japan.
- **HABITAT** In woods with the parents.
- **REMARK** A naturally occurring hybrid between Fuji cherry *(Prunus incisa*, see p.261) and *Prunus pendula*. It is seen only rarely in the wild, but has many garden forms. 'Autumnalis' is one of the most commonly cultivated varieties.

flowers open from pink buds

'AUTUMNALIS'

semi-double white flowers may open during winter

'AUTUMNALIS' ▷
The semi-double flowers of this form are white, tinged with pale pink. They open in autumn, during mild periods in winter, and in spring.

stipules at leaf base

bronze-green young leaves

sharply toothed leaf margin

leaves mature to dark green

△ **'AUTUMNALIS ROSEA'**
The semi-double flowers of this cultivar are very similar to those of 'Autumnalis', but are deeper pink both in bud and when open. Like 'Autumnalis', it flowers during mild weather in winter, and in spring.

spring flowers open as young leaves emerge

Height 6m (20ft)	Shape Broadly spreading	Leaf persistence Deciduous	Leaf type

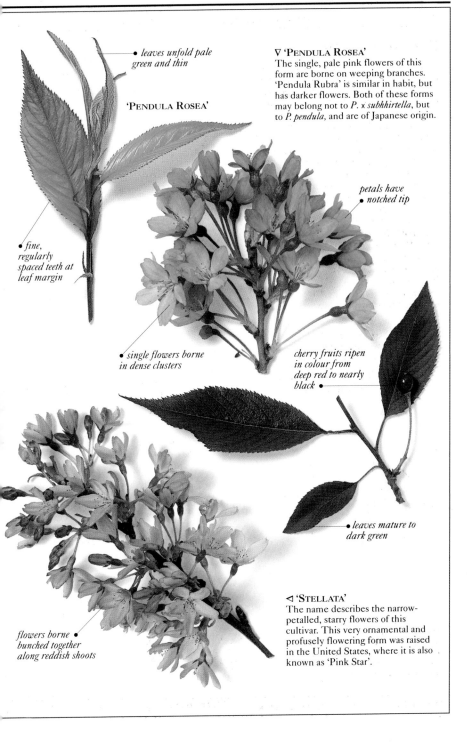

leaves unfold pale green and thin

'PENDULA ROSEA'

▽ 'PENDULA ROSEA'
The single, pale pink flowers of this form are borne on weeping branches. 'Pendula Rubra' is similar in habit, but has darker flowers. Both of these forms may belong not to *P.* x *subhirtella*, but to *P. pendula*, and are of Japanese origin.

petals have notched tip

• fine, regularly spaced teeth at leaf margin

• single flowers borne in dense clusters

cherry fruits ripen in colour from deep red to nearly black •

leaves mature to dark green

flowers borne bunched together along reddish shoots

◁ 'STELLATA'
The name describes the narrow-petalled, starry flowers of this cultivar. This very ornamental and profusely flowering form was raised in the United States, where it is also known as 'Pink Star'.

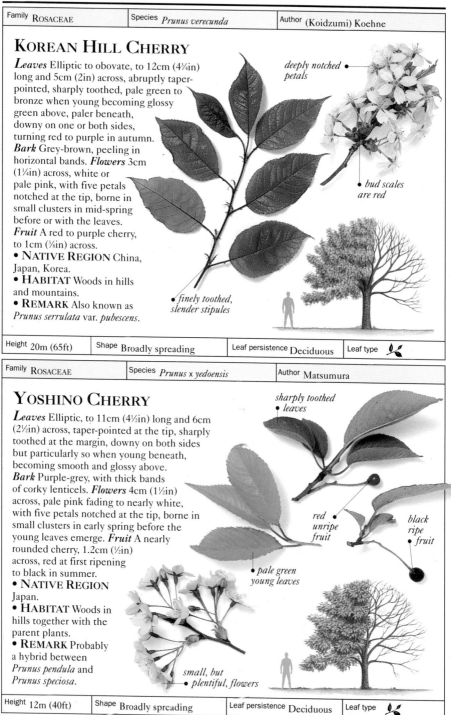

Family ROSACEAE	Species *Prunus verecunda*	Author (Koidzumi) Koehne

KOREAN HILL CHERRY

Leaves Elliptic to obovate, to 12cm (4¾in) long and 5cm (2in) across, abruptly taper-pointed, sharply toothed, pale green to bronze when young becoming glossy green above, paler beneath, downy on one or both sides, turning red to purple in autumn. **Bark** Grey-brown, peeling in horizontal bands. **Flowers** 3cm (1¼in) across, white or pale pink, with five petals notched at the tip, borne in small clusters in mid-spring before or with the leaves. **Fruit** A red to purple cherry, to 1cm (⅜in) across.
• **NATIVE REGION** China, Japan, Korea.
• **HABITAT** Woods in hills and mountains.
• **REMARK** Also known as *Prunus serrulata* var. *pubescens*.

deeply notched petals

bud scales are red

finely toothed, slender stipules

Height 20m (65ft)	Shape Broadly spreading	Leaf persistence Deciduous	Leaf type

Family ROSACEAE	Species *Prunus x yedoensis*	Author Matsumura

YOSHINO CHERRY

Leaves Elliptic, to 11cm (4½in) long and 6cm (2½in) across, taper-pointed at the tip, sharply toothed at the margin, downy on both sides but particularly so when young beneath, becoming smooth and glossy above. **Bark** Purple-grey, with thick bands of corky lenticels. **Flowers** 4cm (1½in) across, pale pink fading to nearly white, with five petals notched at the tip, borne in small clusters in early spring before the young leaves emerge. **Fruit** A nearly rounded cherry, 1.2cm (½in) across, red at first ripening to black in summer.
• **NATIVE REGION** Japan.
• **HABITAT** Woods in hills together with the parent plants.
• **REMARK** Probably a hybrid between *Prunus pendula* and *Prunus speciosa*.

sharply toothed leaves

red unripe fruit

black ripe fruit

pale green young leaves

small, but plentiful, flowers

Height 12m (40ft)	Shape Broadly spreading	Leaf persistence Deciduous	Leaf type

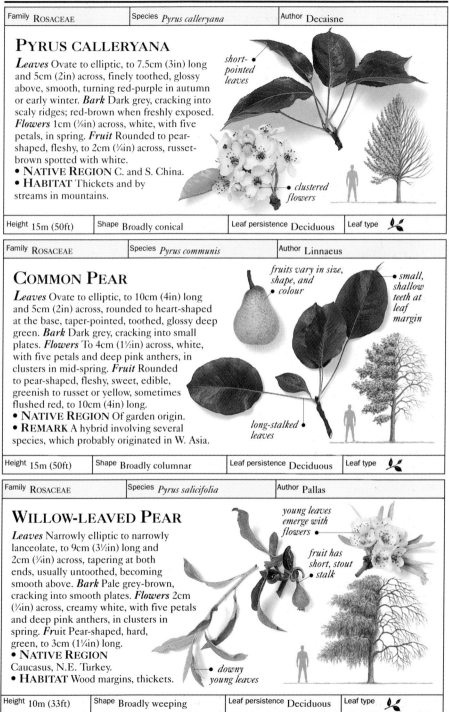

| Family ROSACEAE | Species *Pyrus calleryana* | Author Decaisne |

PYRUS CALLERYANA

Leaves Ovate to elliptic, to 7.5cm (3in) long and 5cm (2in) across, finely toothed, glossy above, smooth, turning red-purple in autumn or early winter. **Bark** Dark grey, cracking into scaly ridges; red-brown when freshly exposed. **Flowers** 1cm (⅜in) across, white, with five petals, in spring. **Fruit** Rounded to pear-shaped, fleshy, to 2cm (¾in) across, russet-brown spotted with white.
• **NATIVE REGION** C. and S. China.
• **HABITAT** Thickets and by streams in mountains.

short-pointed leaves

clustered flowers

| Height 15m (50ft) | Shape Broadly conical | Leaf persistence Deciduous | Leaf type |

| Family ROSACEAE | Species *Pyrus communis* | Author Linnaeus |

COMMON PEAR

Leaves Ovate to elliptic, to 10cm (4in) long and 5cm (2in) across, rounded to heart-shaped at the base, taper-pointed, toothed, glossy deep green. **Bark** Dark grey, cracking into small plates. **Flowers** To 4cm (1½in) across, white, with five petals and deep pink anthers, in clusters in mid-spring. **Fruit** Rounded to pear-shaped, fleshy, sweet, edible, greenish to russet or yellow, sometimes flushed red, to 10cm (4in) long.
• **NATIVE REGION** Of garden origin.
• **REMARK** A hybrid involving several species, which probably originated in W. Asia.

fruits vary in size, shape, and colour

small, shallow teeth at leaf margin

long-stalked leaves

| Height 15m (50ft) | Shape Broadly columnar | Leaf persistence Deciduous | Leaf type |

| Family ROSACEAE | Species *Pyrus salicifolia* | Author Pallas |

WILLOW-LEAVED PEAR

Leaves Narrowly elliptic to narrowly lanceolate, to 9cm (3½in) long and 2cm (¾in) across, tapering at both ends, usually untoothed, becoming smooth above. **Bark** Pale grey-brown, cracking into smooth plates. **Flowers** 2cm (¾in) across, creamy white, with five petals and deep pink anthers, in clusters in spring. **Fruit** Pear-shaped, hard, green, to 3cm (1¼in) long.
• **NATIVE REGION** Caucasus, N.E. Turkey.
• **HABITAT** Wood margins, thickets.

young leaves emerge with flowers

fruit has short, stout stalk

downy young leaves

| Height 10m (33ft) | Shape Broadly weeping | Leaf persistence Deciduous | Leaf type |

Family	ROSACEAE	Species	*Sorbus alnifolia*	Author	(Siebold & Zuccarini) K. Koch

SORBUS ALNIFOLIA

Leaves Ovate to elliptic, to 10cm (4in) long and 4cm (1½in) across, pointed, toothed, dark green above, downy becoming smooth beneath, turning yellow, orange, or red in autumn. *Bark* Dark brown, smooth, with shallow fissures. *Flowers* 1cm (⅜in) across, white, in clusters in mid-spring. *Fruit* A rounded, reddish berry, about 1cm (⅜in) across.
• NATIVE REGION China, Japan, Korea, Taiwan.
• HABITAT Woods.

fruits marked with lenticels

five-petalled flowers

Height	20m (65ft)	Shape	Broadly conical	Leaf persistence	Deciduous	Leaf type

Family	ROSACEAE	Species	*Sorbus americana*	Author	Marshall

AMERICAN MOUNTAIN ASH

Leaves Pinnate, to 25cm (10in) long, with about 15 oblong to lanceolate, pointed, toothed leaflets, to 10cm (4in) long and 2.5cm (1in) across, turning yellow or red in late autumn. *Bark* Grey and smooth. *Flowers* 5mm (³⁄₁₆in) across, white, in dense heads to 20cm (8in) across, in late spring to early summer. *Fruit* An orange-red berry, about 5mm (³⁄₁₆in) across.
• NATIVE REGION E. North America.
• HABITAT Woods.

fruit clusters hang down

pale green leaflets

Height	8m (26ft)	Shape	Broadly spreading	Leaf persistence	Deciduous	Leaf type

Family	ROSACEAE	Species	*Sorbus aria*	Author	(Linnaeus) Crantz

WHITEBEAM

Leaves Elliptic to ovate, to 12cm (4¾in) long and 6cm (2½in) across, sharply toothed, pale green with hairs when young becoming glossy dark green above, white with hairs beneath. *Bark* Grey and smooth, developing rugged cracks with age. *Flowers* About 1cm (⅜in) across, white, with five petals, borne in flattened clusters in late spring. *Fruit* A rounded, bright red berry, about 1.2cm (½in) across, speckled with pale lenticels.
• NATIVE REGION Europe.
• HABITAT From lowland to mountains, on chalk and limestone.

clustered ripe fruits

mature leaves are glossy dark olive green

Height	15m (50ft)	Shape	Broadly columnar	Leaf persistence	Deciduous	Leaf type

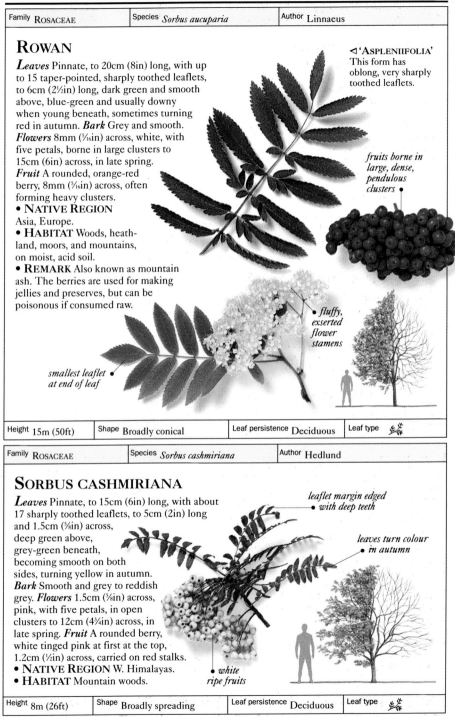

| Family ROSACEAE | Species *Sorbus aucuparia* | Author Linnaeus |

ROWAN

Leaves Pinnate, to 20cm (8in) long, with up to 15 taper-pointed, sharply toothed leaflets, to 6cm (2½in) long, dark green and smooth above, blue-green and usually downy when young beneath, sometimes turning red in autumn. **Bark** Grey and smooth. **Flowers** 8mm (⁵⁄₁₆in) across, white, with five petals, borne in large clusters to 15cm (6in) across, in late spring. **Fruit** A rounded, orange-red berry, 8mm (⁵⁄₁₆in) across, often forming heavy clusters.
• **NATIVE REGION** Asia, Europe.
• **HABITAT** Woods, heathland, moors, and mountains, on moist, acid soil.
• **REMARK** Also known as mountain ash. The berries are used for making jellies and preserves, but can be poisonous if consumed raw.

◁ '**ASPLENIIFOLIA**' This form has oblong, very sharply toothed leaflets.

fruits borne in large, dense, pendulous clusters •

fluffy, exserted flower stamens

smallest leaflet at end of leaf •

| Height 15m (50ft) | Shape Broadly conical | Leaf persistence Deciduous | Leaf type |

| Family ROSACEAE | Species *Sorbus cashmiriana* | Author Hedlund |

SORBUS CASHMIRIANA

Leaves Pinnate, to 15cm (6in) long, with about 17 sharply toothed leaflets, to 5cm (2in) long and 1.5cm (⅝in) across, deep green above, grey-green beneath, becoming smooth on both sides, turning yellow in autumn. **Bark** Smooth and grey to reddish grey. **Flowers** 1.5cm (⅝in) across, pink, with five petals, in open clusters to 12cm (4¾in) across, in late spring. **Fruit** A rounded berry, white tinged pink at first at the top, 1.2cm (½in) across, carried on red stalks.
• **NATIVE REGION** W. Himalayas.
• **HABITAT** Mountain woods.

leaflet margin edged • *with deep teeth*

leaves turn colour • *in autumn*

white ripe fruits

| Height 8m (26ft) | Shape Broadly spreading | Leaf persistence Deciduous | Leaf type |

Family ROSACEAE	Species *Sorbus commixta*	Author Hedlund

SORBUS COMMIXTA

Leaves Pinnate, to 20cm (8in) long, with up to 15 taper-pointed leaflets, to 7.5cm (3in) long and 2.5cm (1in) across, glossy above, blue-green beneath, turning yellow to reddish purple in autumn. **Bark** Grey and smooth. **Flowers** 8mm (⁵⁄₁₆in) across, white, with five petals, in clusters to 15cm (6in) across, in late spring. **Fruit** Rounded, orange-red, 8mm (⁵⁄₁₆in) across.
• **NATIVE REGION** Japan, Korea.
• **HABITAT** Mountain forests.

flowers borne in large clusters •

• leaflets edged with fine, sharp teeth

Height 10m (33ft)	Shape Broadly conical	Leaf persistence Deciduous	Leaf type

Family ROSACEAE	Species *Sorbus domestica*	Author Linnaeus

SERVICE TREE

Leaves Pinnate, to 22cm (8¼in) long, with up to 21 oblong, toothed leaflets, to 6cm (2½in) long and about 1cm (⅜in) across, yellow-green and smooth above, downy when young beneath, turning yellow or red in autumn. **Bark** Dark brown, scaly, cracking into plates. **Flowers** To 1.5cm (⅝in) across, white, with five petals, in rounded clusters about 10cm (4in) across, in late spring. **Fruit** Rounded or pear-shaped, yellow-green flushed red, to 3cm (1¼in) long.
• **NATIVE REGION** S.W. Asia, E. and S. Europe.
• **HABITAT** Mountain slopes, deciduous forests.

flowers borne in rounded • heads

◁ **SORBUS DOMESTICA**

• parallel-sided leaflets

fruits may be • rounded or pear-shaped

VAR. PYRIFERA ▷
This form has bright red fruits shaped like miniature pears.

VAR. POMIFERA ▷
The fruits of this form resemble tiny apples.

fruits broaden • above centre

teeth at top half of leaflet margin • point forward

Height 20m (65ft)	Shape Broadly columnar	Leaf persistence Deciduous	Leaf type

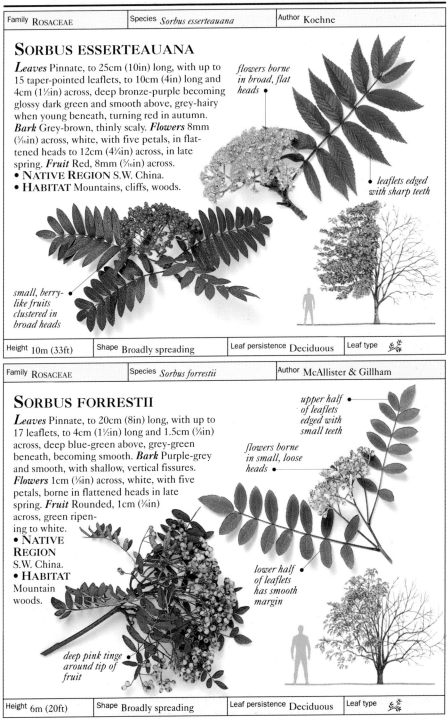

Family ROSACEAE	Species *Sorbus esserteauana*	Author Koehne

SORBUS ESSERTEAUANA

Leaves Pinnate, to 25cm (10in) long, with up to 15 taper-pointed leaflets, to 10cm (4in) long and 4cm (1½in) across, deep bronze-purple becoming glossy dark green and smooth above, grey-hairy when young beneath, turning red in autumn. **Bark** Grey-brown, thinly scaly. **Flowers** 8mm (⁵⁄₁₆in) across, white, with five petals, in flattened heads to 12cm (4¾in) across, in late spring. **Fruit** Red, 8mm (⁵⁄₁₆in) across.
• **NATIVE REGION** S.W. China.
• **HABITAT** Mountains, cliffs, woods.

flowers borne in broad, flat heads

leaflets edged with sharp teeth

small, berry-like fruits clustered in broad heads

Height 10m (33ft)	Shape Broadly spreading	Leaf persistence Deciduous	Leaf type

Family ROSACEAE	Species *Sorbus forrestii*	Author McAllister & Gillham

SORBUS FORRESTII

Leaves Pinnate, to 20cm (8in) long, with up to 17 leaflets, to 4cm (1½in) long and 1.5cm (⅝in) across, deep blue-green above, grey-green beneath, becoming smooth. **Bark** Purple-grey and smooth, with shallow, vertical fissures. **Flowers** 1cm (⅜in) across, white, with five petals, borne in flattened heads in late spring. **Fruit** Rounded, 1cm (⅜in) across, green ripening to white.
• **NATIVE REGION** S.W. China.
• **HABITAT** Mountain woods.

upper half of leaflets edged with small teeth

flowers borne in small, loose heads

lower half of leaflets has smooth margin

deep pink tinge around tip of fruit

Height 6m (20ft)	Shape Broadly spreading	Leaf persistence Deciduous	Leaf type

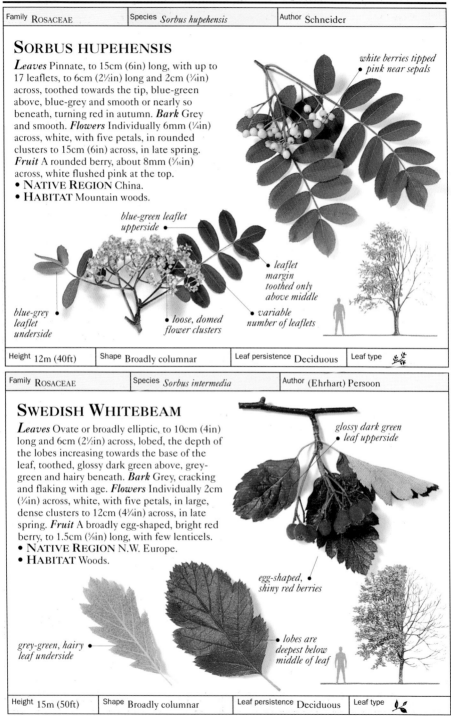

| Family ROSACEAE | | Species *Sorbus hupehensis* | | Author Schneider |

SORBUS HUPEHENSIS

Leaves Pinnate, to 15cm (6in) long, with up to 17 leaflets, to 6cm (2½in) long and 2cm (¾in) across, toothed towards the tip, blue-green above, blue-grey and smooth or nearly so beneath, turning red in autumn. **Bark** Grey and smooth. **Flowers** Individually 6mm (¼in) across, white, with five petals, in rounded clusters to 15cm (6in) across, in late spring. **Fruit** A rounded berry, about 8mm (⁵⁄₁₆in) across, white flushed pink at the top.
• **NATIVE REGION** China.
• **HABITAT** Mountain woods.

white berries tipped pink near sepals

blue-green leaflet upperside

leaflet margin toothed only above middle

blue-grey leaflet underside

loose, domed flower clusters

variable number of leaflets

| Height 12m (40ft) | Shape Broadly columnar | Leaf persistence Deciduous | Leaf type |

| Family ROSACEAE | | Species *Sorbus intermedia* | | Author (Ehrhart) Persoon |

SWEDISH WHITEBEAM

Leaves Ovate or broadly elliptic, to 10cm (4in) long and 6cm (2½in) across, lobed, the depth of the lobes increasing towards the base of the leaf, toothed, glossy dark green above, grey-green and hairy beneath. **Bark** Grey, cracking and flaking with age. **Flowers** Individually 2cm (¾in) across, white, with five petals, in large, dense clusters to 12cm (4¾in) across, in late spring. **Fruit** A broadly egg-shaped, bright red berry, to 1.5cm (⅝in) long, with few lenticels.
• **NATIVE REGION** N.W. Europe.
• **HABITAT** Woods.

glossy dark green leaf upperside

egg-shaped, shiny red berries

grey-green, hairy leaf underside

lobes are deepest below middle of leaf

| Height 15m (50ft) | Shape Broadly columnar | Leaf persistence Deciduous | Leaf type |

Family ROSACEAE	Species *Sorbus* 'Joseph Rock'	Author None

SORBUS 'JOSEPH ROCK'

Leaves Pinnate, to 15cm (6in) long, with up to 17 sharply toothed leaflets, to 4cm (1½in) long and 1.2cm (½in) across, bright green above, grey-green beneath, becoming nearly smooth, turning orange, red, and purple in autumn. *Bark* Grey, nearly smooth, with small, orange lenticels. *Flowers* 1cm (⅜in) across, white, with five petals, borne in flattened heads 10cm (4in) across, in late spring to early summer. *Fruit* Rounded, 1cm (⅜in) across, green then yellow-white ripening to orange-yellow.
• **NATIVE REGION** Probably China.
• **HABITAT** Not known. This species may not occur in the wild.

fruits borne on red stalks

leaflets edged with small teeth

leaves turn colour in autumn

Height 10m (33ft)	Shape Broadly columnar	Leaf persistence Deciduous	Leaf type

Family ROSACEAE	Species *Sorbus latifolia*	Author (Lamarck) Persoon

SERVICE TREE OF FONTAINEBLEAU

smooth leaf upperside

Leaves Broadly ovate, to 10cm (4in) long and the same across, with shallow, pointed lobes towards the base, sharply toothed, glossy dark green above, grey and downy beneath. *Bark* Dark grey, cracked, flaking. *Flowers* Individually 1.5cm (⅝in) across, white, with five petals, borne in flattened heads in late spring. *Fruit* Rounded, yellow-brown, 1.2cm (½in) across, with conspicuous lenticels.
• **NATIVE REGION** C. and W. Europe.
• **HABITAT** Woods.
• **REMARK** The species probably originated as a hybrid between the whitebeam *(Sorbus aria,* see p.274) and the wild service tree *(Sorbus torminalis,* see p.282).

leaves turn yellow in autumn

leaf underside felted with grey hairs

shallow leaf lobes edged with sharp teeth

Height 12m (40ft)	Shape Broadly columnar	Leaf persistence Deciduous	Leaf type

Family ROSACEAE	Species *Sorbus sargentiana*	Author Koehne

SORBUS SARGENTIANA

Leaves Pinnate, to 35cm (14in) long, with about 11 oblong, taper-pointed, toothed leaflets, to 12cm (4¾in) long and 5cm (2in) across, matt deep green above, grey-green and hairy beneath, turning orange and red in autumn. *Bark* Purple-brown, cracked and flaking with age. *Flowers* 6mm (¼in) across, white, in rounded heads to 20cm (8in) across, in early summer. *Fruit* Rounded, bright red, 6mm (¼in) across, borne in large clusters.
• **NATIVE REGION** S.W. China.
• **HABITAT** Mountain woods.

terminal pair of leaflets points forward

small fruits borne in broad heads

Height 10m (33ft)	Shape Broadly columnar	Leaf persistence Deciduous	Leaf type

Family ROSACEAE	Species *Sorbus scalaris*	Author Koehne

SORBUS SCALARIS

Leaves Pinnate, to 20cm (8in) long, with numerous narrowly oblong leaflets, to 4cm (1½in) long and 1cm (⅜in) across, toothed towards the tip, glossy deep green above, grey and hairy beneath, turning red and purple in late autumn. *Bark* Smooth and grey, with shallow fissures. *Flowers* 6mm (¼in) across, white, with five petals, in broad, flattened heads to 15cm (6in) across, in late spring or early summer. *Fruit* Rounded, bright red, 6mm (¼in) across, in large clusters.
• **NATIVE REGION** S.W. China.
• **HABITAT** Mountain woods.

sparse, shallow teeth only at tip of leaflets

small flowers borne in dense clusters

small, deep red fruits

Height 10m (33ft)	Shape Broadly spreading	Leaf persistence Deciduous	Leaf type

Family ROSACEAE	Species *Sorbus thibetica*	Author (Cardot) Handel-Mazzetti

SORBUS THIBETICA

Leaves Elliptic to obovate or nearly rounded, to 15cm (6in) long and 10cm (4in) across, tapered at the base, pointed at the tip, sharply toothed, hairy at first becoming smooth or only thinly hairy and dark green above, densely covered in white hairs beneath, with up to 14 pairs of veins. **Bark** Grey-brown, thinly scaly, cracked, flaking at the base. **Flowers** White, with five petals, in clusters to 6cm (2½in) across, in late spring to early summer. **Fruit** A rounded berry, 1.5cm (⅝in) across, green ripening to orange or yellow.
• **NATIVE REGION** S.W. China, Himalayas.
• **HABITAT** Evergreen and deciduous mountain forests.
• **REMARK** 'John Mitchell', shown here, is the form seen most commonly.

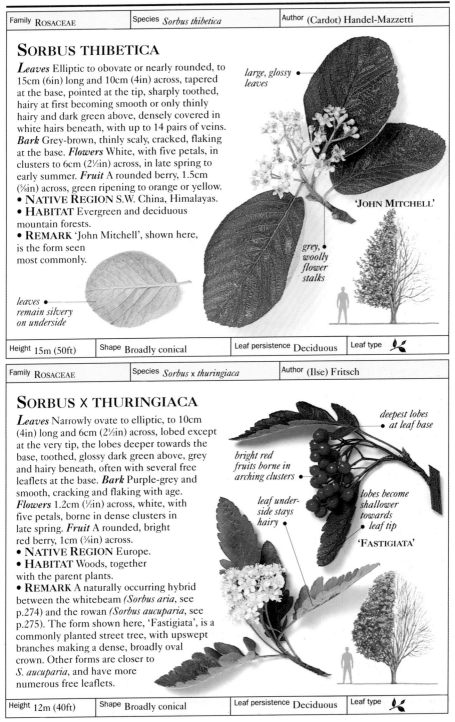

large, glossy leaves

'JOHN MITCHELL'

grey, woolly flower stalks

leaves remain silvery on underside

Height 15m (50ft)	Shape Broadly conical	Leaf persistence Deciduous	Leaf type

Family ROSACEAE	Species *Sorbus x thuringiaca*	Author (Ilse) Fritsch

SORBUS X THURINGIACA

Leaves Narrowly ovate to elliptic, to 10cm (4in) long and 6cm (2½in) across, lobed except at the very tip, the lobes deeper towards the base, toothed, glossy dark green above, grey and hairy beneath, often with several free leaflets at the base. **Bark** Purple-grey and smooth, cracking and flaking with age. **Flowers** 1.2cm (½in) across, white, with five petals, borne in dense clusters in late spring. **Fruit** A rounded, bright red berry, 1cm (⅜in) across.
• **NATIVE REGION** Europe.
• **HABITAT** Woods, together with the parent plants.
• **REMARK** A naturally occurring hybrid between the whitebeam *(Sorbus aria*, see p.274) and the rowan *(Sorbus aucuparia*, see p.275). The form shown here, 'Fastigiata', is a commonly planted street tree, with upswept branches making a dense, broadly oval crown. Other forms are closer to *S. aucuparia*, and have more numerous free leaflets.

deepest lobes at leaf base

bright red fruits borne in arching clusters

leaf under-side stays hairy

lobes become shallower towards leaf tip

'FASTIGIATA'

Height 12m (40ft)	Shape Broadly conical	Leaf persistence Deciduous	Leaf type

Family ROSACEAE	Species *Sorbus torminalis*	Author (Linnaeus) Crantz

WILD SERVICE TREE

Leaves Broadly ovate, to 10cm (4in) long and nearly the same across, deeply cut into sharply toothed lobes, glossy dark green above, paler beneath, downy when young, turning yellow, red, or purple in autumn. **Bark** Dark brown, cracking into scaly plates. **Flowers** 1.2cm (½in) across, white, in flattened clusters in late spring to early summer. **Fruit** A rounded, russet-brown berry, 1.2cm (½in) long.
• **NATIVE REGION** N. Africa, S.W. Asia, Europe.
• **HABITAT** Woods.

ripe fruits speckled with lenticels

maple-like leaves

open flower clusters

Height 15m (50ft)	Shape Broadly columnar	Leaf persistence Deciduous	Leaf type

Family ROSACEAE	Species *Sorbus vestita*	Author (G. Don) Loddiges

SORBUS VESTITA

Leaves Elliptic, to 20cm (8in) or more long and 15cm (6in) across, sometimes with small lobes, sharply toothed, white-hairy when young becoming glossy dark green above, densely covered with white hairs beneath, with up to 11 pairs of veins. **Bark** Pale grey, peeling in thick flakes. **Flowers** 2cm (¾in) across, white, with five petals, in flattened clusters to 10cm (4in) across, in late spring to early summer. **Fruit** A rounded to pear-shaped berry, 2cm (¾in) across, green speckled with brown.
• **NATIVE REGION** Himalayas.
• **HABITAT** Mountain forests.

fruits dotted with brown lenticels

fruits borne on stout stalks

Height 15m (50ft)	Shape Broadly conical	Leaf persistence Deciduous	Leaf type

Family ROSACEAE	Species *Sorbus vilmorinii*	Author Schneider

SORBUS VILMORINII

Leaves Pinnate, to 15cm (6in) long, with up to about 25 oblong leaflets, to 2cm (¾in) long, toothed towards the tip, glossy dark green above, grey-green beneath. **Bark** Smooth, dark grey. **Flowers** 6mm (¼in) across, white, with five petals, in clusters to 10cm (4in) across, in late spring to early summer. **Fruit** A roundish berry, 1cm (⅜in) long, deep red at first ripening to white.
• **NATIVE REGION** S.W. China.
• **HABITAT** Mountain woods.

crimson young fruits

fruits ripen through many shades of pink

Height 8m (26ft)	Shape Broadly spreading	Leaf persistence Deciduous	Leaf type

RUTACEAE

T HE 1,500 SPECIES OF TREES, shrubs, and climbing plants belonging to this family are contained in over 150 genera. They are found worldwide, but particularly in tropical and warm temperate regions. The leaves are usually alternate and often compound, and release an aromatic vapour when crushed. Flowers are green to white or yellow, with usually four or five petals.

Family RUTACEAE	Species *Phellodendron amurense*	Author Ruprecht

AMUR CORK TREE

Leaves Pinnate, to 35cm (14in) long, with up to 13 ovate to lanceolate, taper-pointed, untoothed or minutely toothed leaflets, to 10cm (4in) long and 5cm (2in) across, glossy deep green and smooth above, blue-green with hairs at the base of the midrib beneath, turning yellow in autumn. *Bark* Grey-brown, thick, corky, with prominent ridges. *Flowers* Males and females both small and greenish, males with yellow, protruding anthers, borne in conical clusters about 7.5cm (3in) long, on separate plants in mid-summer. *Fruit* Rounded, 1cm (⅜in) across, green ripening to black.
• **NATIVE REGION** N.E. Asia.
• **HABITAT** Moist places near streams in mountains.

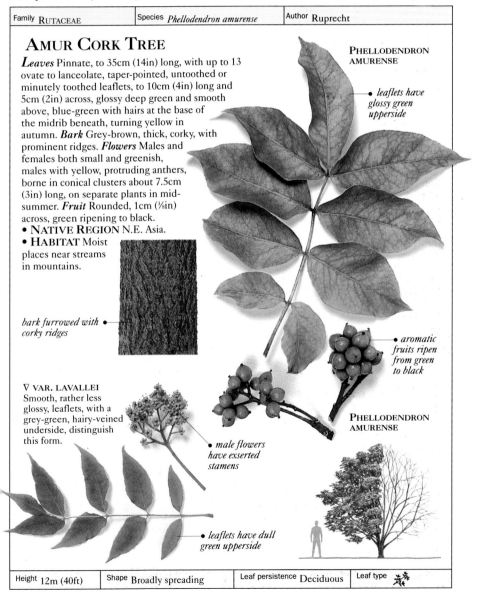

PHELLODENDRON
AMURENSE

• *leaflets have glossy green upperside*

bark furrowed with corky ridges

• *aromatic fruits ripen from green to black*

∇ **VAR. LAVALLEI**
Smooth, rather less glossy, leaflets, with a grey-green, hairy-veined underside, distinguish this form.

• *male flowers have exserted stamens*

PHELLODENDRON
AMURENSE

• *leaflets have dull green upperside*

Height 12m (40ft)	Shape Broadly spreading	Leaf persistence Deciduous	Leaf type

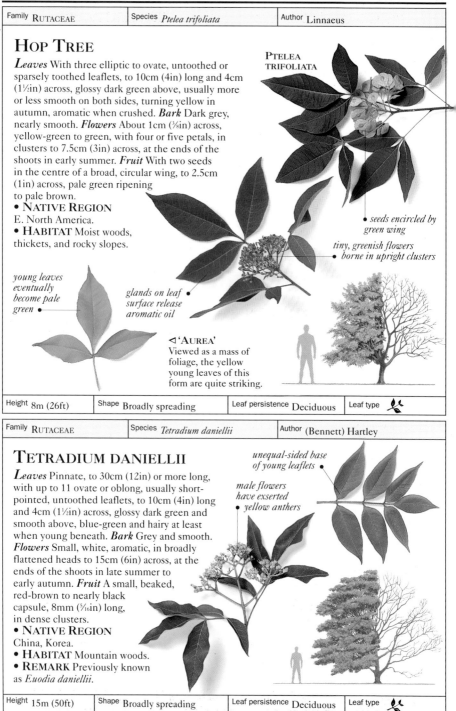

Family RUTACEAE	Species *Ptelea trifoliata*	Author Linnaeus

HOP TREE

PTELEA TRIFOLIATA

Leaves With three elliptic to ovate, untoothed or sparsely toothed leaflets, to 10cm (4in) long and 4cm (1½in) across, glossy dark green above, usually more or less smooth on both sides, turning yellow in autumn, aromatic when crushed. *Bark* Dark grey, nearly smooth. *Flowers* About 1cm (⅜in) across, yellow-green to green, with four or five petals, in clusters to 7.5cm (3in) across, at the ends of the shoots in early summer. *Fruit* With two seeds in the centre of a broad, circular wing, to 2.5cm (1in) across, pale green ripening to pale brown.
• **NATIVE REGION** E. North America.
• **HABITAT** Moist woods, thickets, and rocky slopes.

• *seeds encircled by green wing*

tiny, greenish flowers borne in upright clusters

young leaves eventually become pale green •

glands on leaf surface release aromatic oil •

◁ **'AUREA'** Viewed as a mass of foliage, the yellow young leaves of this form are quite striking.

Height 8m (26ft)	Shape Broadly spreading	Leaf persistence Deciduous	Leaf type

Family RUTACEAE	Species *Tetradium daniellii*	Author (Bennett) Hartley

TETRADIUM DANIELLII

unequal-sided base of young leaflets •

Leaves Pinnate, to 30cm (12in) or more long, with up to 11 ovate or oblong, usually short-pointed, untoothed leaflets, to 10cm (4in) long and 4cm (1½in) across, glossy dark green and smooth above, blue-green and hairy at least when young beneath. *Bark* Grey and smooth. *Flowers* Small, white, aromatic, in broadly flattened heads to 15cm (6in) across, at the ends of the shoots in late summer to early autumn. *Fruit* A small, beaked, red-brown to nearly black capsule, 8mm (⁵⁄₁₆in) long, in dense clusters.
• **NATIVE REGION** China, Korea.
• **HABITAT** Mountain woods.
• **REMARK** Previously known as *Euodia daniellii*.

male flowers have exserted • *yellow anthers*

Height 15m (50ft)	Shape Broadly spreading	Leaf persistence Deciduous	Leaf type

Family RUTACEAE	Species *Zanthoxylum ailanthoides*	Author Siebold & Zuccarini

ZANTHOXYLUM AILANTHOIDES

Leaves Pinnate, 30cm (12in) or more long, with up to 15 pairs of oblong, pointed leaflets, to 15cm (6in) long and 5cm (2in) across, light green above, blue-green beneath. **Bark** Grey and green, striped, with spiny protuberances. **Flowers** Males and females yellow-green, in broad heads at the ends of the shoots, on separate plants in late summer. **Fruit** Small, green, with black seeds.
• **NATIVE REGION**
E. Asia.
• **HABITAT** Woods.

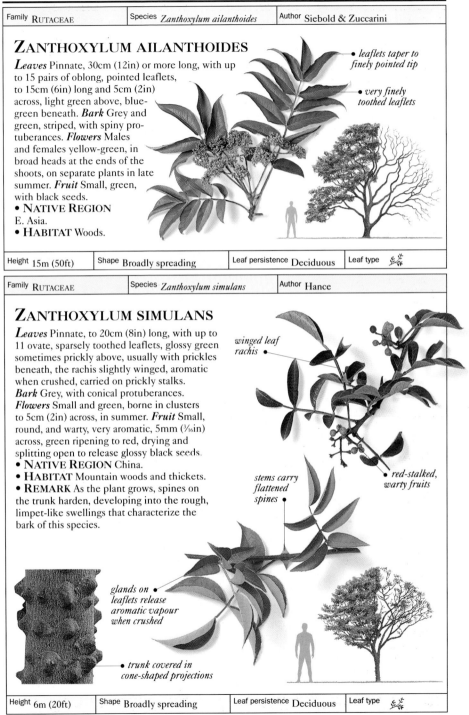

leaflets taper to finely pointed tip

very finely toothed leaflets

Height 15m (50ft)	Shape Broadly spreading	Leaf persistence Deciduous	Leaf type

Family RUTACEAE	Species *Zanthoxylum simulans*	Author Hance

ZANTHOXYLUM SIMULANS

Leaves Pinnate, to 20cm (8in) long, with up to 11 ovate, sparsely toothed leaflets, glossy green sometimes prickly above, usually with prickles beneath, the rachis slightly winged, aromatic when crushed, carried on prickly stalks. **Bark** Grey, with conical protuberances. **Flowers** Small and green, borne in clusters to 5cm (2in) across, in summer. **Fruit** Small, round, and warty, very aromatic, 5mm (³⁄₁₆in) across, green ripening to red, drying and splitting open to release glossy black seeds.
• **NATIVE REGION** China.
• **HABITAT** Mountain woods and thickets.
• **REMARK** As the plant grows, spines on the trunk harden, developing into the rough, limpet-like swellings that characterize the bark of this species.

winged leaf rachis

stems carry flattened spines

red-stalked, warty fruits

glands on leaflets release aromatic vapour when crushed

trunk covered in cone-shaped projections

Height 6m (20ft)	Shape Broadly spreading	Leaf persistence Deciduous	Leaf type

SALICACEAE

T HE TWO GENERA and about 350 species of trees and shrubs in this family occur throughout the world, except in Australasia, most commonly in northern temperate regions. Leaves are alternate or, occasionally, opposite. The tiny, petalless flowers are borne in catkins, males and females nearly always on separate plants. The fruit is a capsule, containing small seeds.

Family SALICACEAE	Species *Populus alba*	Author Linnaeus

WHITE POPLAR

Leaves Variable, on vigorous shoots maple-like, with three to five lobes, to 10cm (4in) long and 7.5cm (3in) across, on short shoots shallow-ly lobed to wavy-edged, both types white with hairs when young becoming smooth and dark green above, densely covered in white hairs beneath. *Bark* Grey, fissured, dark at the base. *Flowers* In drooping catkins, males to 7.5cm (3in) long, grey with red anthers, females to 5cm (2in) long, green, on separate plants in early spring before the young leaves. *Fruit* Small, green capsules, borne in catkins to 10cm (4in) long, opening to release tiny seeds held in white, cotton wool-like hairs.
• **NATIVE REGION** N. Africa, C. and W. Asia, Europe.
• **HABITAT** Woods, in moist and dry places.
• **REMARK** Also known as abele.

white, hairy
• *young leaves*

• *mature leaves have smooth upper surface*

• *strong shoots carry maple-like leaves*

less vigorous •
shoots have
shallowly lobed
leaves

• *dense, white hairs cover underside of leaves*

Height 30m (100ft)	Shape Broadly columnar	Leaf persistence Deciduous	Leaf type

Family SALICACEAE	Species *Populus balsamifera*	Author Linnaeus

BALSAM POPLAR

Leaves Ovate, to 12cm (4¾in) long and 10cm (4in) across, taper-pointed, finely toothed, glossy green above, whitish and net-veined beneath, smooth on both sides, balsam-scented when young. **Bark** Grey, ridged. **Flowers** In catkins, males to 5cm (2in) long, females to 7.5cm (3in) long, green, on separate plants in early spring. **Fruit** Small green capsules, in catkins to 30cm (12in) long.
• **NATIVE REGION** North America.
• **HABITAT** Moist woods.

leaves end in long, slender point

fine network of veins on under-side of leaves

Height 30m (100ft)	Shape Broadly columnar	Leaf persistence Deciduous	Leaf type

Family SALICACEAE	Species *Populus x canadensis*	Author Moench

POPULUS X CANADENSIS

Leaves Broadly triangular, to 10cm (4in) long and across, with a short point at the tip, finely toothed, glossy green above. **Bark** Pale grey, with deep, vertical fissures. **Flowers** In catkins, males to 10cm (4in) long, females green, on separate plants in early spring before the leaves. **Fruit** Small green capsules, opening to release tiny seeds held in fluffy, white hairs.
• **NATIVE REGION** Of garden origin.
• **REMARK** This group of hybrids between the North American species, cotton-wood *(Populus deltoides)*, and the black poplar *(Populus nigra, see p.289)*, has many forms, including some of the most commonly grown poplars.

'MARILANDICA' ▷ Deep furrows give the bark of this form a craggy appearance.

irregularly ridged, pale grey bark

leaves are edged with larger teeth towards • base

◁ **'ROBUSTA'** The bronze-red young leaves of this male form emerge in mid-spring, and mature by late summer to glossy deep green.

strikingly bright young leaves

vertically ridged bark •

△ **'SEROTINA AUREA'** This male form, which has bright yellow summer foliage, comes into leaf in late spring.

Height 30m (100ft)	Shape Broadly columnar	Leaf persistence Deciduous	Leaf type

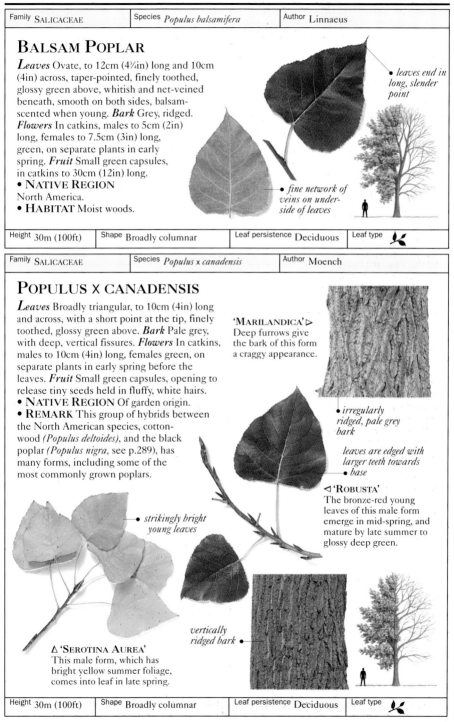

Family SALICACEAE	Species *Populus x candicans*	Author Aiton

BALM OF GILEAD

Leaves Broadly ovate, to 15cm (6in) long and 10cm (4in) across, usually heart-shaped at the base, taper-pointed, toothed, dark green above, whitish and net-veined beneath, slightly downy on both sides. *Bark* Grey and smooth, becoming ridged with age. *Flowers* Females only, green, in drooping catkins in early spring. *Fruit* Small, green capsules, borne in catkins to 15cm (6in) long, opening to release tiny seeds held in white, cotton wool-like hairs.
• **NATIVE REGION**
Of garden origin.
• **REMARK** Also known as Ontario poplar. This species is thought to be a hybrid of the balsam poplar *(Populus balsamifera*, see p.287), naturalized from gardens on riverbanks in E. North America. 'Aurora', a common form, has leaves blotched white, cream, and pink.

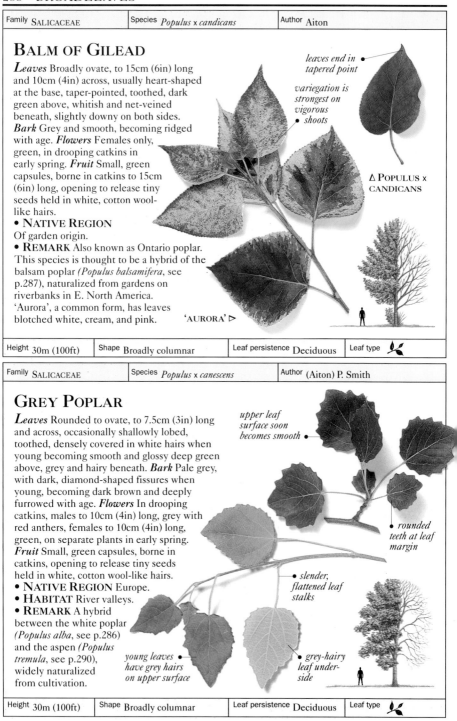

leaves end in tapered point

variegation is strongest on vigorous shoots

△ POPULUS x CANDICANS

'AURORA' ▷

Height 30m (100ft)	Shape Broadly columnar	Leaf persistence Deciduous	Leaf type

Family SALICACEAE	Species *Populus x canescens*	Author (Aiton) P. Smith

GREY POPLAR

Leaves Rounded to ovate, to 7.5cm (3in) long and across, occasionally shallowly lobed, toothed, densely covered in white hairs when young becoming smooth and glossy deep green above, grey and hairy beneath. *Bark* Pale grey, with dark, diamond-shaped fissures when young, becoming dark brown and deeply furrowed with age. *Flowers* In drooping catkins, males to 10cm (4in) long, grey with red anthers, females to 10cm (4in) long, green, on separate plants in early spring. *Fruit* Small, green capsules, borne in catkins, opening to release tiny seeds held in white, cotton wool-like hairs.
• **NATIVE REGION** Europe.
• **HABITAT** River valleys.
• **REMARK** A hybrid between the white poplar *(Populus alba*, see p.286) and the aspen *(Populus tremula*, see p.290), widely naturalized from cultivation.

upper leaf surface soon becomes smooth

rounded teeth at leaf margin

slender, flattened leaf stalks

young leaves have grey hairs on upper surface

grey-hairy leaf underside

Height 30m (100ft)	Shape Broadly columnar	Leaf persistence Deciduous	Leaf type

Family SALICACEAE	Species *Populus lasiocarpa*	Author Oliver

POPULUS LASIOCARPA

Leaves Broadly ovate and large, to 30cm (12in) long and 20cm (8in) across, deeply heart-shaped at the base, edged with small, rounded teeth at the margin, downy on both sides when young becoming deep green and smooth above, with red veins and stalk, carried on very stout shoots. **Bark** Grey-brown and vertically fissured. **Flowers** Males and females both yellow-green, males with red anthers, borne in stout, drooping catkins to 10cm (4in) long, sometimes on the same spike, usually on separate plants in mid-spring. **Fruit** Small, green capsules, borne in catkins, opening to release tiny seeds held in white, cotton wool-like hairs.
• **NATIVE REGION** C. China.
• **HABITAT** Moist woods in mountains.
• **REMARK** The very large, long-stalked leaves easily distinguish this species from others of its genus.

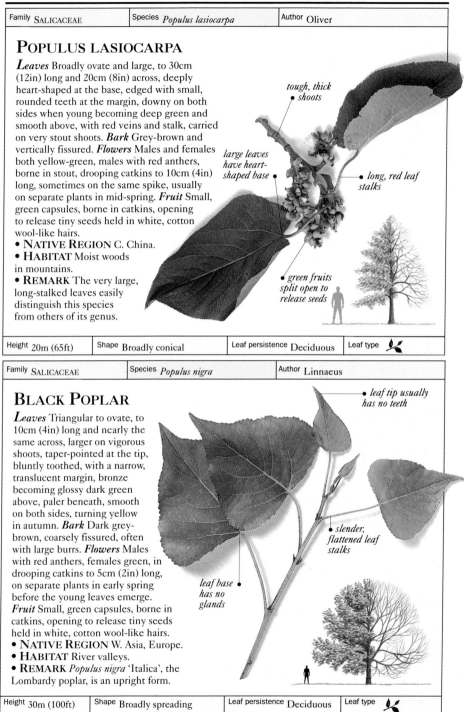

tough, thick shoots

large leaves have heart-shaped base

long, red leaf stalks

green fruits split open to release seeds

Height 20m (65ft)	Shape Broadly conical	Leaf persistence Deciduous	Leaf type

Family SALICACEAE	Species *Populus nigra*	Author Linnaeus

BLACK POPLAR

Leaves Triangular to ovate, to 10cm (4in) long and nearly the same across, larger on vigorous shoots, taper-pointed at the tip, bluntly toothed, with a narrow, translucent margin, bronze becoming glossy dark green above, paler beneath, smooth on both sides, turning yellow in autumn. **Bark** Dark grey-brown, coarsely fissured, often with large burrs. **Flowers** Males with red anthers, females green, in drooping catkins to 5cm (2in) long, on separate plants in early spring before the young leaves emerge. **Fruit** Small, green capsules, borne in catkins, opening to release tiny seeds held in white, cotton wool-like hairs.
• **NATIVE REGION** W. Asia, Europe.
• **HABITAT** River valleys.
• **REMARK** *Populus nigra* 'Italica', the Lombardy poplar, is an upright form.

leaf tip usually has no teeth

slender, flattened leaf stalks

leaf base has no glands

Height 30m (100ft)	Shape Broadly spreading	Leaf persistence Deciduous	Leaf type

Family SALICACEAE	Species *Populus szechuanica*	Author Schneider

POPULUS SZECHUANICA

VAR. THIBETICA ▷

Leaves Ovate, to 30cm (12in) long and 20cm (8in) or more across on vigorous shoots, usually much smaller on short shoots, rounded to heart-shaped at the base, tapered at the tip, blunt-toothed, reddish to bronzy when young becoming dark green above, paler beneath, smooth on both sides. **Bark** Pinkish grey, cracking into large, smooth flakes with age. **Flowers** Small and without petals, males with deep red anthers, females green, borne in drooping catkins on separate plants in mid-spring before the young leaves emerge. **Fruit** Small, green capsules, in catkins to 16cm (6¼in) long, opening to release tiny seeds held in white, cotton wool-like hairs.
• **NATIVE REGION** W. China.
• **HABITAT** Moist mountain woods.
• **REMARK** The leaves of the form shown here, var. *thibetica*, are slightly hairy on the underside.

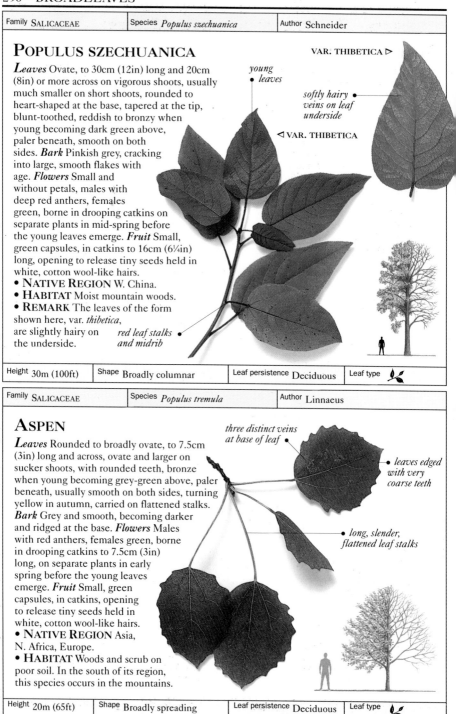

young leaves

softly hairy veins on leaf underside

◁ **VAR. THIBETICA**

red leaf stalks and midrib

Height 30m (100ft)	Shape Broadly columnar	Leaf persistence Deciduous	Leaf type

Family SALICACEAE	Species *Populus tremula*	Author Linnaeus

ASPEN

Leaves Rounded to broadly ovate, to 7.5cm (3in) long and across, ovate and larger on sucker shoots, with rounded teeth, bronze when young becoming grey-green above, paler beneath, usually smooth on both sides, turning yellow in autumn, carried on flattened stalks. **Bark** Grey and smooth, becoming darker and ridged at the base. **Flowers** Males with red anthers, females green, borne in drooping catkins to 7.5cm (3in) long, on separate plants in early spring before the young leaves emerge. **Fruit** Small, green capsules, in catkins, opening to release tiny seeds held in white, cotton wool-like hairs.
• **NATIVE REGION** Asia, N. Africa, Europe.
• **HABITAT** Woods and scrub on poor soil. In the south of its region, this species occurs in the mountains.

three distinct veins at base of leaf

leaves edged with very coarse teeth

long, slender, flattened leaf stalks

Height 20m (65ft)	Shape Broadly spreading	Leaf persistence Deciduous	Leaf type

| Family SALICACEAE | Species *Salix alba* | Author Linnaeus |

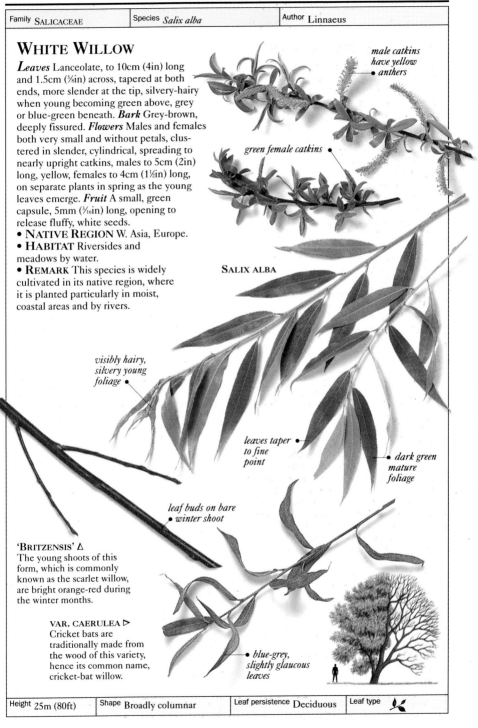

WHITE WILLOW

Leaves Lanceolate, to 10cm (4in) long and 1.5cm (⅝in) across, tapered at both ends, more slender at the tip, silvery-hairy when young becoming green above, grey or blue-green beneath. **Bark** Grey-brown, deeply fissured. **Flowers** Males and females both very small and without petals, clustered in slender, cylindrical, spreading to nearly upright catkins, males to 5cm (2in) long, yellow, females to 4cm (1½in) long, on separate plants in spring as the young leaves emerge. **Fruit** A small, green capsule, 5mm (³⁄₁₆in) long, opening to release fluffy, white seeds.
• **NATIVE REGION** W. Asia, Europe.
• **HABITAT** Riversides and meadows by water.
• **REMARK** This species is widely cultivated in its native region, where it is planted particularly in moist, coastal areas and by rivers.

male catkins have yellow anthers

green female catkins

SALIX ALBA

visibly hairy, silvery young foliage

leaves taper to fine point

dark green mature foliage

leaf buds on bare winter shoot

'BRITZENSIS' △
The young shoots of this form, which is commonly known as the scarlet willow, are bright orange-red during the winter months.

VAR. CAERULEA ▷
Cricket bats are traditionally made from the wood of this variety, hence its common name, cricket-bat willow.

blue-grey, slightly glaucous leaves

| Height 25m (80ft) | Shape Broadly columnar | Leaf persistence Deciduous | Leaf type |

Family SALICACEAE	Species *Salix babylonica*	Author Linnaeus

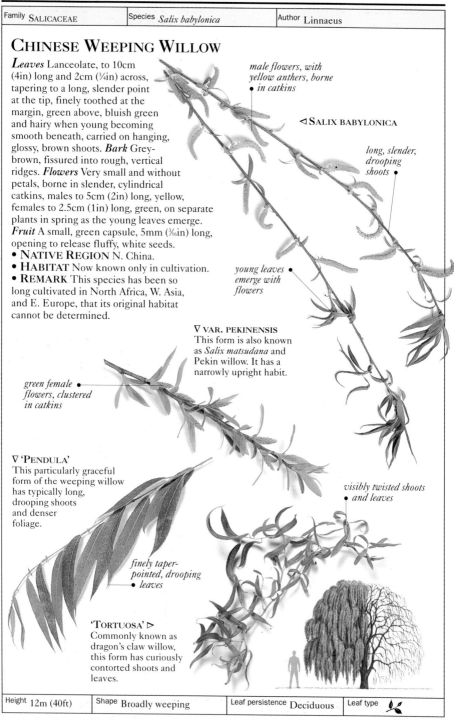

CHINESE WEEPING WILLOW

Leaves Lanceolate, to 10cm (4in) long and 2cm (¾in) across, tapering to a long, slender point at the tip, finely toothed at the margin, green above, bluish green and hairy when young becoming smooth beneath, carried on hanging, glossy, brown shoots. **Bark** Grey-brown, fissured into rough, vertical ridges. **Flowers** Very small and without petals, borne in slender, cylindrical catkins, males to 5cm (2in) long, yellow, females to 2.5cm (1in) long, green, on separate plants in spring as the young leaves emerge. **Fruit** A small, green capsule, 5mm (³⁄₁₆in) long, opening to release fluffy, white seeds.
• **NATIVE REGION** N. China.
• **HABITAT** Now known only in cultivation.
• **REMARK** This species has been so long cultivated in North Africa, W. Asia, and E. Europe, that its original habitat cannot be determined.

male flowers, with yellow anthers, borne in catkins

◁ **SALIX BABYLONICA**

long, slender, drooping shoots

young leaves emerge with flowers

▽ **VAR. PEKINENSIS**
This form is also known as *Salix matsudana* and Pekin willow. It has a narrowly upright habit.

green female flowers, clustered in catkins

▽ **'PENDULA'**
This particularly graceful form of the weeping willow has typically long, drooping shoots and denser foliage.

visibly twisted shoots and leaves

finely taper-pointed, drooping leaves

'TORTUOSA' ▷
Commonly known as dragon's claw willow, this form has curiously contorted shoots and leaves.

Height 12m (40ft)	Shape Broadly weeping	Leaf persistence Deciduous	Leaf type

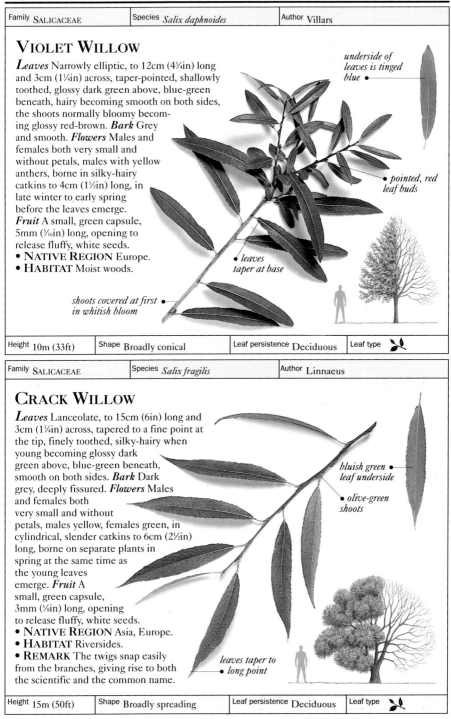

| Family SALICACEAE | Species *Salix daphnoides* | Author Villars |

VIOLET WILLOW

Leaves Narrowly elliptic, to 12cm (4¾in) long and 3cm (1¼in) across, taper-pointed, shallowly toothed, glossy dark green above, blue-green beneath, hairy becoming smooth on both sides, the shoots normally bloomy becoming glossy red-brown. **Bark** Grey and smooth. **Flowers** Males and females both very small and without petals, males with yellow anthers, borne in silky-hairy catkins to 4cm (1½in) long, in late winter to early spring before the leaves emerge. **Fruit** A small, green capsule, 5mm (³⁄₁₆in) long, opening to release fluffy, white seeds.
• **NATIVE REGION** Europe.
• **HABITAT** Moist woods.

underside of leaves is tinged blue

pointed, red leaf buds

leaves taper at base

shoots covered at first in whitish bloom

| Height 10m (33ft) | Shape Broadly conical | Leaf persistence Deciduous | Leaf type |

| Family SALICACEAE | Species *Salix fragilis* | Author Linnaeus |

CRACK WILLOW

Leaves Lanceolate, to 15cm (6in) long and 3cm (1¼in) across, tapered to a fine point at the tip, finely toothed, silky-hairy when young becoming glossy dark green above, blue-green beneath, smooth on both sides. **Bark** Dark grey, deeply fissured. **Flowers** Males and females both very small and without petals, males yellow, females green, in cylindrical, slender catkins to 6cm (2½in) long, borne on separate plants in spring at the same time as the young leaves emerge. **Fruit** A small, green capsule, 3mm (⅛in) long, opening to release fluffy, white seeds.
• **NATIVE REGION** Asia, Europe.
• **HABITAT** Riversides.
• **REMARK** The twigs snap easily from the branches, giving rise to both the scientific and the common name.

bluish green leaf underside

olive-green shoots

leaves taper to long point

| Height 15m (50ft) | Shape Broadly spreading | Leaf persistence Deciduous | Leaf type |

Family SALICACEAE	Species *Salix pentandra*	Author Linnaeus

BAY WILLOW

Leaves Elliptic to narrowly ovate, to 12cm (4¾in) long and 5cm (2in) across, tapering to a short point, finely toothed, glossy very dark green above, paler beneath, smooth on both sides, slightly aromatic. **Bark** Grey-brown, with shallow fissures. **Flowers** Males and females both very small and without petals, males bright yellow, females green, in cylindrical catkins to 5cm (2in) long, on separate plants in early summer after the young leaves emerge. **Fruit** A small, green capsule, 6mm (¼in) long, opening to release fluffy, white seeds.
• **NATIVE REGION** Asia, Europe.
• **HABITAT** Riverbanks and meadows.

dull leaf underside

slender female catkins

glossy upper leaf surface

male catkins have broad base

catkins borne at end of leafy shoots

Height 15m (50ft)	Shape Broadly spreading	Leaf persistence Deciduous	Leaf type

Family SALICACEAE	Species *Salix x sepulcralis*	Author Simonkai

SALIX X SEPULCRALIS

'CHRYSOCOMA'

Leaves Narrowly lanceolate, to 12cm (4¾in) long and 2cm (¾in) across, taper-pointed, finely toothed, thinly hairy when young becoming bright green above, blue-green beneath, smooth, on slender, hanging, yellowish shoots. **Bark** Pale grey-brown, with shallow fissures. **Flowers** Small and without petals, in catkins to 7.5cm (3in) long, often on the same spike, in spring. **Fruit** A small, green capsule, 3mm (⅛in) long, opening to release fluffy, white seeds.
• **NATIVE REGION** Of garden origin.
• **REMARK** A hybrid between white willow *(Salix alba, see p.291)* and Chinese weeping willow *(Salix babylonica, see p.292).* Of its many different forms, 'Chrysocoma' – the familiar weeping willow shown here – is the most well known.

long, fine point at tip of slender leaves

upright, curved catkins

blue-green leaf underside

Height 20m (65ft)	Shape Broadly weeping	Leaf persistence Deciduous	Leaf type

SAPINDACEAE

W IDELY DISTRIBUTED MAINLY in tropical and subtropical regions, this family has 1,500 or so species of deciduous trees, shrubs, and climbers, collected in about 150 genera. The leaves are alternate, simple, pinnate, bipinnate, or with three leaflets. The small male or female flowers have usually five petals. The fruit is dry and winged, a capsule, nut, or berry.

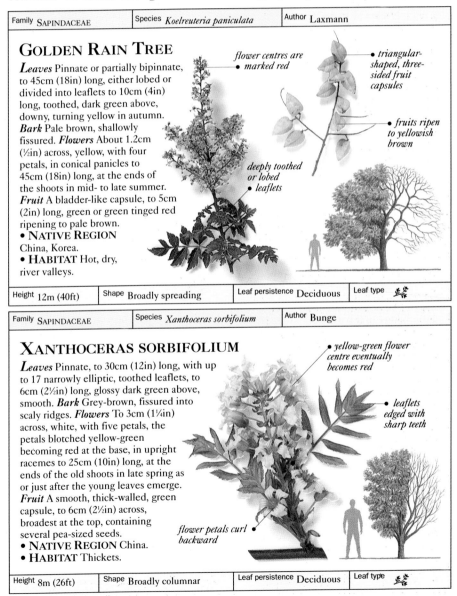

Family SAPINDACEAE	Species *Koelreuteria paniculata*	Author Laxmann

GOLDEN RAIN TREE

Leaves Pinnate or partially bipinnate, to 45cm (18in) long, either lobed or divided into leaflets to 10cm (4in) long, toothed, dark green above, downy, turning yellow in autumn. **Bark** Pale brown, shallowly fissured. **Flowers** About 1.2cm (½in) across, yellow, with four petals, in conical panicles to 45cm (18in) long, at the ends of the shoots in mid- to late summer. **Fruit** A bladder-like capsule, to 5cm (2in) long, green or green tinged red ripening to pale brown.
• **NATIVE REGION** China, Korea.
• **HABITAT** Hot, dry, river valleys.

flower centres are marked red

triangular-shaped, three-sided fruit capsules

fruits ripen to yellowish brown

deeply toothed or lobed leaflets

Height 12m (40ft)	Shape Broadly spreading	Leaf persistence Deciduous	Leaf type

Family SAPINDACEAE	Species *Xanthoceras sorbifolium*	Author Bunge

XANTHOCERAS SORBIFOLIUM

Leaves Pinnate, to 30cm (12in) long, with up to 17 narrowly elliptic, toothed leaflets, to 6cm (2½in) long, glossy dark green above, smooth. **Bark** Grey-brown, fissured into scaly ridges. **Flowers** To 3cm (1¼in) across, white, with five petals, the petals blotched yellow-green becoming red at the base, in upright racemes to 25cm (10in) long, at the ends of the old shoots in late spring as or just after the young leaves emerge. **Fruit** A smooth, thick-walled, green capsule, to 6cm (2½in) across, broadest at the top, containing several pea-sized seeds.
• **NATIVE REGION** China.
• **HABITAT** Thickets.

yellow-green flower centre eventually becomes red

leaflets edged with sharp teeth

flower petals curl backward

Height 8m (26ft)	Shape Broadly columnar	Leaf persistence Deciduous	Leaf type

SCROPHULARIACEAE

T HIS LARGE FAMILY has about 4,500 species and 220 genera of woody and herbaceous plants, found world-wide. The alternate or opposite leaves can be simple or lobed. The flowers have usually a five-lobed, two-lipped corolla. The fruit is a capsule. The trees are all in the genus *Paulownia*.

Family SCROPHULARIACEAE	Species *Paulownia tomentosa*	Author (Thunberg) Steudel

PAULOWNIA TOMENTOSA

Leaves Ovate, to 30cm (12in) long and 25cm (10in) across, heart-shaped at the base, taper-pointed, sometimes lobed, dark green and hairy above, hairy beneath. *Bark* Grey, smooth. *Flowers* To 5cm (2in) long, pale purple marked deeper purple and yellow inside, in upright panicles to 40cm (16in) long, in spring. *Fruit* A pale brown, woody capsule, to 5cm (2in) long.
• **NATIVE REGION** China.
• **HABITAT** Mountains.

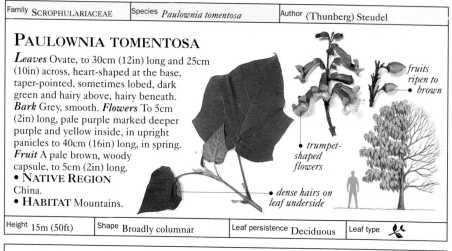

fruits ripen to brown

• *trumpet-shaped flowers*

• *dense hairs on leaf underside*

Height 15m (50ft)	Shape Broadly columnar	Leaf persistence Deciduous	Leaf type

SIMAROUBACEAE

T HIS FAMILY OF SOME 20 genera and 150 species of trees and shrubs occurs in both tropical and subtropical regions, and temperate regions of Asia. The alternate leaves are often pinnate. The small flowers have five petals; females develop into the fruit, which is dry and winged or a capsule.

Family SIMAROUBACEAE	Species *Ailanthus altissima*	Author (Miller) Swingle

TREE OF HEAVEN

Leaves Pinnate, to 60cm (24in) long, with 15 or more pairs of leaflets, to 12cm (4¾in) long and 5cm (2in) across, glossy. *Bark* Grey-brown, with pale streaks. *Flowers* Males and females greenish yellow, with five or six petals, in large panicles at the ends of the shoots, usually on separate plants in mid- to late summer. *Fruit* Winged, to 4cm (1½in) long.
• **NATIVE REGION** China.
• **HABITAT** Mountain woods.

notch near base of leaflets

• *leaflets end in tapered point*

• *winged fruits ripen from green to red-brown*

Height 20m (65ft)	Shape Broadly columnar	Leaf persistence Deciduous	Leaf type

STYRACACEAE

THERE ARE ABOUT 12 GENERA and 150 species of deciduous trees and shrubs in this family, found in east Asia, from the southern United States to central and South America, and with a single species in the Mediterranean. Leaves are alternate and simple. The flower corolla is tubular at the base, and is divided into five to seven lobes. The fruit is usually a capsule.

Family STYRACACEAE	Species *Halesia carolina*	Author Linnaeus

SNOWDROP TREE

Leaves Ovate-oblong, to 20cm (8in) long and 10cm (4in) across, taper-pointed at the tip, finely toothed, bright green above, paler beneath, thinly hairy on both sides, turning yellow in autumn. *Bark* Pale brown, with scaly, interlacing ridges. *Flowers* White or white flushed pink, drooping, the bell-shaped corolla 2cm (¾in) long, with four shallow lobes, in small clusters in mid- to late spring as the young leaves emerge. *Fruit* Pear-shaped, to 5cm (2in) long, with four wings, green at first ripening to pale brown.
• **NATIVE REGION** S.E. United States.
• **HABITAT** Rich, moist woods and by streams.
• **REMARK** In unfavourable conditions, this species reaches only about 10m (33ft).

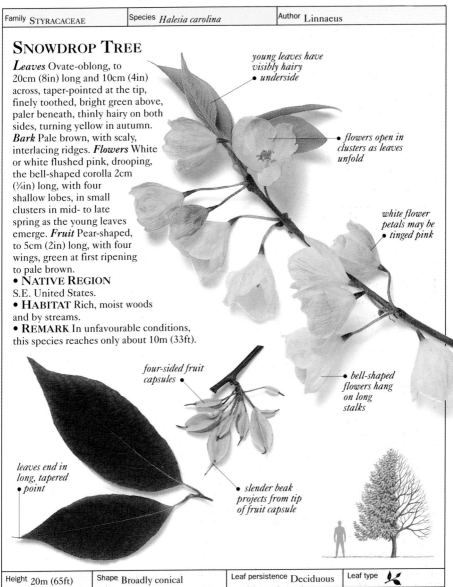

young leaves have visibly hairy underside

flowers open in clusters as leaves unfold

white flower petals may be tinged pink

four-sided fruit capsules

bell-shaped flowers hang on long stalks

leaves end in long, tapered point

slender beak projects from tip of fruit capsule

Height 20m (65ft)	Shape Broadly conical	Leaf persistence Deciduous	Leaf type

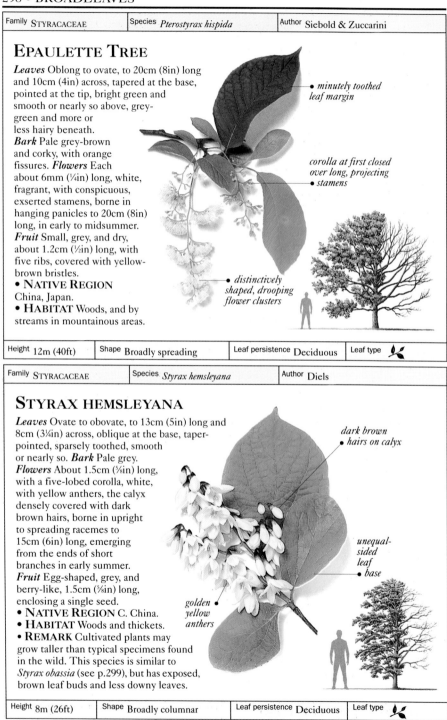

Family STYRACACEAE	Species *Pterostyrax hispida*	Author Siebold & Zuccarini

EPAULETTE TREE

Leaves Oblong to ovate, to 20cm (8in) long and 10cm (4in) across, tapered at the base, pointed at the tip, bright green and smooth or nearly so above, grey-green and more or less hairy beneath.
Bark Pale grey-brown and corky, with orange fissures. **Flowers** Each about 6mm (¼in) long, white, fragrant, with conspicuous, exserted stamens, borne in hanging panicles to 20cm (8in) long, in early to midsummer.
Fruit Small, grey, and dry, about 1.2cm (½in) long, with five ribs, covered with yellow-brown bristles.
• **NATIVE REGION** China, Japan.
• **HABITAT** Woods, and by streams in mountainous areas.

minutely toothed leaf margin

corolla at first closed over long, projecting stamens

distinctively shaped, drooping flower clusters

Height 12m (40ft)	Shape Broadly spreading	Leaf persistence Deciduous	Leaf type

Family STYRACACEAE	Species *Styrax hemsleyana*	Author Diels

STYRAX HEMSLEYANA

Leaves Ovate to obovate, to 13cm (5in) long and 8cm (3¼in) across, oblique at the base, taper-pointed, sparsely toothed, smooth or nearly so. **Bark** Pale grey.
Flowers About 1.5cm (⅝in) long, with a five-lobed corolla, white, with yellow anthers, the calyx densely covered with dark brown hairs, borne in upright to spreading racemes to 15cm (6in) long, emerging from the ends of short branches in early summer.
Fruit Egg-shaped, grey, and berry-like, 1.5cm (⅝in) long, enclosing a single seed.
• **NATIVE REGION** C. China.
• **HABITAT** Woods and thickets.
• **REMARK** Cultivated plants may grow taller than typical specimens found in the wild. This species is similar to *Styrax obassia* (see p.299), but has exposed, brown leaf buds and less downy leaves.

dark brown hairs on calyx

unequal-sided leaf base

golden yellow anthers

Height 8m (26ft)	Shape Broadly columnar	Leaf persistence Deciduous	Leaf type

| Family STYRACACEAE | Species *Styrax japonica* | Author Siebold & Zuccarini |

JAPANESE SNOWBELL

Leaves Elliptic to ovate, to 10cm (4in) long and 5cm (2in) across, narrowed at the base, abruptly taper-pointed at the tip, with a finely or sparsely toothed margin, rich glossy green above, turning yellow or red in autumn. *Bark* Dark grey-brown and smooth, developing orange-brown fissures with age. *Flowers* Individually about 1.5cm (⅝in) long, with a five-lobed corolla, white or pink-tinged, with yellow anthers, slightly fragrant, on slender stalks, in short racemes or hanging singly beneath the branches in early to midsummer. *Fruit* Rounded to egg-shaped, grey, and berry-like, to 1.5cm (⅝in) long, with a single seed.
• **NATIVE REGION** China, Japan, Korea.
• **HABITAT** Sunny places, usually on wet ground.
• **REMARK** This species makes a beautiful, elegant small tree or large shrub.

glossy green leaves have duller underside

bell-like flowers hang beneath branches

| Height 10m (33ft) | Shape Broadly spreading | Leaf persistence Deciduous | Leaf type |

| Family STYRACACEAE | Species *Styrax obassia* | Author Siebold & Zuccarini |

STYRAX OBASSIA

dense hairs cover underside of leaves

Leaves Variable, elliptic to rounded, to 20cm (8in) long and nearly the same across, dark green and smooth above, blue-grey and densely hairy beneath, turning yellow in autumn. *Bark* Grey-brown and smooth, becoming vertically fissured with age. *Flowers* Individually about 2.5cm (1in) long, with a five-lobed corolla, white, with yellow anthers, fragrant, borne in horizontally spreading racemes to 15cm (6in) long, in early to midsummer. *Fruit* Egg-shaped, grey, and berry-like, about 2cm (¾in) long, with a single seed.
• **NATIVE REGION** N. China, Japan, Korea.
• **HABITAT** Moist woods.
• **REMARK** The flower racemes are often almost hidden by the large, broad leaves.

largest leaves are carried at shoot end

loose racemes hang beneath leaves

| Height 12m (40ft) | Shape Broadly columnar | Leaf persistence Deciduous | Leaf type |

THEACEAE

THE TEA FAMILY has 30 genera and over 600 species of deciduous trees and shrubs. They grow mainly in tropical regions, in particular Asia and the Americas, but also in temperate areas of east Asia and the south-east United States. Leaves are simple and usually alternate. Flowers are typically large and showy, with five petals. The fruit is most often a capsule.

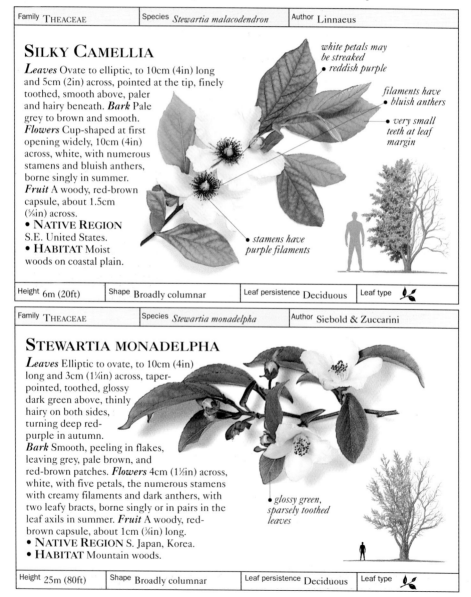

Family THEACEAE	Species *Stewartia malacodendron*	Author Linnaeus

SILKY CAMELLIA

Leaves Ovate to elliptic, to 10cm (4in) long and 5cm (2in) across, pointed at the tip, finely toothed, smooth above, paler and hairy beneath. **Bark** Pale grey to brown and smooth. **Flowers** Cup-shaped at first opening widely, 10cm (4in) across, white, with numerous stamens and bluish anthers, borne singly in summer. **Fruit** A woody, red-brown capsule, about 1.5cm (⅝in) across.
• **NATIVE REGION** S.E. United States.
• **HABITAT** Moist woods on coastal plain.

white petals may be streaked reddish purple

filaments have bluish anthers

very small teeth at leaf margin

stamens have purple filaments

Height 6m (20ft)	Shape Broadly columnar	Leaf persistence Deciduous	Leaf type

Family THEACEAE	Species *Stewartia monadelpha*	Author Siebold & Zuccarini

STEWARTIA MONADELPHA

Leaves Elliptic to ovate, to 10cm (4in) long and 3cm (1¼in) across, taper-pointed, toothed, glossy dark green above, thinly hairy on both sides, turning deep red-purple in autumn. **Bark** Smooth, peeling in flakes, leaving grey, pale brown, and red-brown patches. **Flowers** 4cm (1½in) across, white, with five petals, the numerous stamens with creamy filaments and dark anthers, with two leafy bracts, borne singly or in pairs in the leaf axils in summer. **Fruit** A woody, red-brown capsule, about 1cm (⅜in) long.
• **NATIVE REGION** S. Japan, Korea.
• **HABITAT** Mountain woods.

glossy green, sparsely toothed leaves

Height 25m (80ft)	Shape Broadly columnar	Leaf persistence Deciduous	Leaf type

Family THEACEAE	Species *Stewartia pseudocamellia*	Author Maximowicz

STEWARTIA PSEUDOCAMELLIA

Leaves Broadly ovate to elliptic, to 10cm (4in) long and 6cm (2½in) across, tapered to a short point, finely toothed, dark green and smooth above, smooth or hairy beneath, turning yellow to orange or red in autumn. **Bark** Red-brown, peeling in thin, irregular plates, leaving grey and pink patches. **Flowers** 6cm (2½in) across, white, with five petals, the numerous stamens with yellow filaments and darker anthers, with two leafy bracts outside the sepals, borne singly or in pairs in the leaf axils in summer. **Fruit** A woody, red-brown capsule, about 2cm (¾in) long.

- **NATIVE REGION** Japan.
- **HABITAT** Mountain woods.
- **REMARK** As in other species of *Stewartia*, the five flower petals are joined together at the base and the flowers fall intact.

flaking bark • creates pinkish grey patchwork effect

frilly-petalled flowers •

• finely toothed leaf margin

flowers have bright yellow filaments •

▽ STEWARTIA PSEUDOCAMELLIA

△ VAR. KOREANA
The flowers of this native south Korean variety open more widely than those of the typical form. Its slightly larger leaves colour just as well in autumn, however.

• paler leaf underside may be smooth or hairy

flower petals covered in • silky hairs before opening

dark green leaf • upperside

Height 20m (65ft)	Shape Broadly columnar	Leaf persistence Deciduous	Leaf type

TILIACEAE

T HE LIMES, or lindens, of the genus *Tilia* are well-loved members of this family, which includes more than 700 species of trees, shrubs, and herbaceous plants, in some 50 genera. Most are confined to the tropics, but the limes occur in temperate regions of the northern hemisphere. The leaves are alternate and sometimes lobed, frequently with starry hairs. The often fragrant flowers are small, with usually five petals and sepals, and numerous stamens. The fruit is variable, and may be woody, a dry capsule or a berry.

Family TILIACEAE	Species *Tilia americana*	Author Linnaeus

AMERICAN LIME

Leaves Broadly ovate to nearly rounded, to 20cm (8in) long and 15cm (6in) across, abruptly tapered to a fine point at the tip, with coarse, pointed teeth, matt deep green above, paler and rather glossy beneath, becoming smooth on both sides except for tufts of brown hairs in the vein axils beneath. **Bark** Brown to grey, cracked into long, scaly ridges. **Flowers** 1.5cm (⅝in) across, pale yellow, with five petals, fragrant, in pendulous clusters of up to ten, each cluster with an oblong bract to 10cm (4in) long, in midsummer. **Fruit** Rounded, woody, pale grey-green, about 1cm (⅜in) across.
• **NATIVE REGION** E. North America.
• **HABITAT** Moist woods.
• **REMARK** Also known as basswood.

nearly smooth leaf underside

tufts of brown hairs in vein axils

up to ten fragrant flowers in each cluster

flower cluster stalk joined to pale green bract

abruptly short-pointed leaf tip

leaf margin edged with coarse, pointed teeth

Height 25m (80ft)	Shape Broadly columnar	Leaf persistence Deciduous	Leaf type

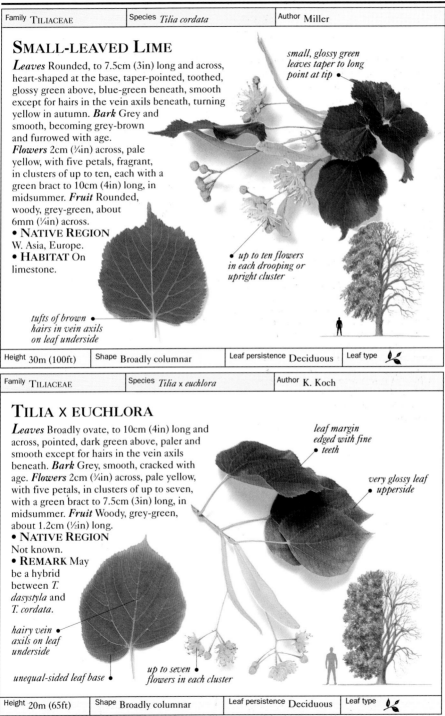

Family TILIACEAE	Species *Tilia cordata*	Author Miller

SMALL-LEAVED LIME

Leaves Rounded, to 7.5cm (3in) long and across, heart-shaped at the base, taper-pointed, toothed, glossy green above, blue-green beneath, smooth except for hairs in the vein axils beneath, turning yellow in autumn. **Bark** Grey and smooth, becoming grey-brown and furrowed with age. **Flowers** 2cm (¾in) across, pale yellow, with five petals, fragrant, in clusters of up to ten, each with a green bract to 10cm (4in) long, in midsummer. **Fruit** Rounded, woody, grey-green, about 6mm (¼in) across.
• **NATIVE REGION** W. Asia, Europe.
• **HABITAT** On limestone.

small, glossy green leaves taper to long point at tip •

• up to ten flowers in each drooping or upright cluster

tufts of brown • hairs in vein axils on leaf underside

Height 30m (100ft)	Shape Broadly columnar	Leaf persistence Deciduous	Leaf type

Family TILIACEAE	Species *Tilia x euchlora*	Author K. Koch

TILIA X EUCHLORA

Leaves Broadly ovate, to 10cm (4in) long and across, pointed, dark green above, paler and smooth except for hairs in the vein axils beneath. **Bark** Grey, smooth, cracked with age. **Flowers** 2cm (¾in) across, pale yellow, with five petals, in clusters of up to seven, with a green bract to 7.5cm (3in) long, in midsummer. **Fruit** Woody, grey-green, about 1.2cm (½in) long.
• **NATIVE REGION** Not known.
• **REMARK** May be a hybrid between *T. dasystyla* and *T. cordata*.

leaf margin edged with fine • teeth

very glossy leaf • upperside

hairy vein axils on leaf underside

unequal-sided leaf base •

up to seven • flowers in each cluster

Height 20m (65ft)	Shape Broadly columnar	Leaf persistence Deciduous	Leaf type

Family TILIACEAE	Species *Tilia x europaea*	Author Linnaeus

COMMON LIME

▽ TILIA × EUROPAEA

tufts of hairs in vein axils on leaf underside

Leaves Broadly ovate to rounded, to 10cm (4in) long and across, heart-shaped at the base, abruptly short-pointed at the tip, coarsely toothed, dark green above, paler beneath, smooth except for tufts of hairs in the vein axils beneath. *Bark* Grey-brown, with shallow fissures. *Flowers* Small, 2cm (¾in) across, pale yellow, fragrant, with five petals, in clusters of up to ten, each cluster with a pale green bract to 10cm (4in) long, in midsummer. *Fruit* Egg-shaped, woody, grey-green, about 1.2cm (½in) long.
• **NATIVE REGION** Europe.
• **HABITAT** With the parents.
• **REMARK** Also known as *Tilia x vulgaris*. A hybrid between small-leaved lime (*Tilia cordata*, see p.303) and broad-leaved lime (*Tilia platyphyllos*, see p.305).

each flower cluster has pale green bract

◁ 'WRATISLAVIENSIS'
The glowing, bright yellow young foliage of this form eventually matures to green.

Height 40m (130ft)	Shape Broadly columnar	Leaf persistence Deciduous	Leaf type

Family TILIACEAE	Species *Tilia mongolica*	Author Maximowicz

MONGOLIAN LIME

lobed leaves edged with sharp teeth

Leaves Broadly ovate, to 7.5cm (3in) long and across, with three to five lobes, taper-pointed at the tip, sharply toothed, reddish when young becoming glossy dark green above, blue-green beneath, smooth on both sides except for tufts of hairs in the vein axils beneath, turning yellow in autumn, carried on red stalks. *Bark* Grey and smooth. *Flowers* Small, 2cm (¾in) across, pale yellow, fragrant, with five petals, borne in drooping clusters of up to 20, each cluster with a narrow, pale green bract to 10cm (4in) long, in midsummer. *Fruit* Rounded, woody, grey-green, about 1.2cm (½in) long.
• **NATIVE REGION** N.E. Asia.
• **HABITAT** Mountain slopes.
• **REMARK** This species is easily identified in season by its distinctively lobed, sharply toothed leaves.

upper leaf surface matures to dark green

tiny tufts of hairs in vein axils

Height 15m (50ft)	Shape Broadly spreading	Leaf persistence Deciduous	Leaf type

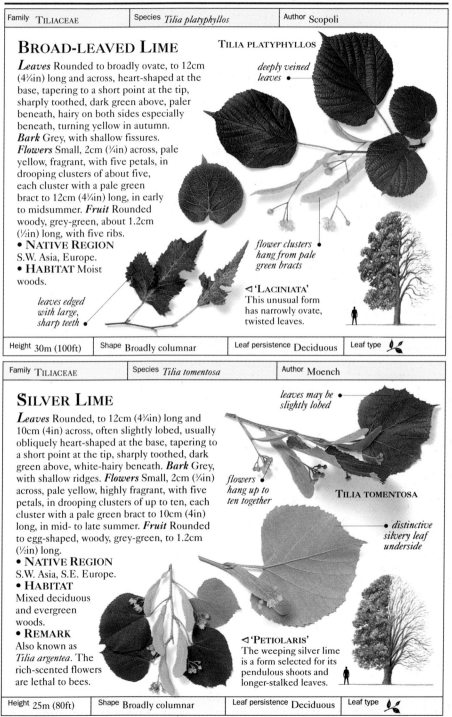

| Family | TILIACEAE | Species | *Tilia platyphyllos* | Author | Scopoli |

BROAD-LEAVED LIME

TILIA PLATYPHYLLOS

Leaves Rounded to broadly ovate, to 12cm (4¾in) long and across, heart-shaped at the base, tapering to a short point at the tip, sharply toothed, dark green above, paler beneath, hairy on both sides especially beneath, turning yellow in autumn. *Bark* Grey, with shallow fissures. *Flowers* Small, 2cm (¾in) across, pale yellow, fragrant, with five petals, in drooping clusters of about five, each cluster with a pale green bract to 12cm (4¾in) long, in early to midsummer. *Fruit* Rounded woody, grey-green, about 1.2cm (½in) long, with five ribs.
• NATIVE REGION S.W. Asia, Europe.
• HABITAT Moist woods.

deeply veined leaves

flower clusters hang from pale green bracts

◁ 'LACINIATA' This unusual form has narrowly ovate, twisted leaves.

leaves edged with large, sharp teeth

| Height | 30m (100ft) | Shape | Broadly columnar | Leaf persistence | Deciduous | Leaf type |

| Family | TILIACEAE | Species | *Tilia tomentosa* | Author | Moench |

SILVER LIME

leaves may be slightly lobed

Leaves Rounded, to 12cm (4¾in) long and 10cm (4in) across, often slightly lobed, usually obliquely heart-shaped at the base, tapering to a short point at the tip, sharply toothed, dark green above, white-hairy beneath. *Bark* Grey, with shallow ridges. *Flowers* Small, 2cm (¾in) across, pale yellow, highly fragrant, with five petals, in drooping clusters of up to ten, each cluster with a pale green bract to 10cm (4in) long, in mid- to late summer. *Fruit* Rounded to egg-shaped, woody, grey-green, to 1.2cm (½in) long.
• NATIVE REGION S.W. Asia, S.E. Europe.
• HABITAT Mixed deciduous and evergreen woods.
• REMARK Also known as *Tilia argentea*. The rich-scented flowers are lethal to bees.

flowers hang up to ten together

TILIA TOMENTOSA

distinctive silvery leaf underside

◁ 'PETIOLARIS' The weeping silver lime is a form selected for its pendulous shoots and longer-stalked leaves.

| Height | 25m (80ft) | Shape | Broadly columnar | Leaf persistence | Deciduous | Leaf type |

TROCHODENDRACEAE

A SINGLE GENUS WITH ONE species, described below, belongs to this family. Its affinities are uncertain, although is generally agreed to be relatively primitive among flowering plants. It is usually thought to be most closely related to either *Cercidiphyllum* (see p.133) or *Drimys* (see p.310).

Family TROCHODENDRACEAE	Species *Trochodendron aralioides*	Author Siebold & Zuccarini

TROCHODENDRON ARALIOIDES

Leaves Narrowly elliptic, to 12cm (4¾in) long and 4cm (1½in) across, toothed except towards the base, dark green above, paler beneath. **Bark** Grey to dark brown, with conspicuous lenticels. **Flowers** 2cm (¾in) across, bright green, without petals, the stamens radiating from a green disk, in racemes to 12cm (4¾in) long, at the ends of the shoots in late spring and early summer. **Fruit** A hemispherical cluster, green ripening to brown, with persistent stigmas.
• **NATIVE REGION** Japan, Korea, Taiwan.
• **HABITAT** Mountain woods.

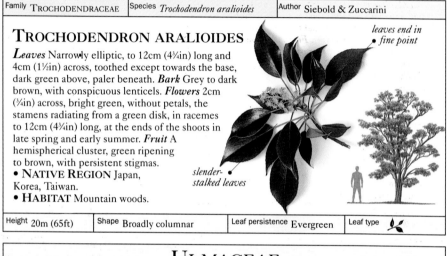

leaves end in fine point

slender-stalked leaves

Height 20m (65ft)	Shape Broadly columnar	Leaf persistence Evergreen	Leaf type

ULMACEAE

T HE ELM FAMILY contains about 15 genera and 150 species of evergreen and deciduous trees and shrubs, growing wild in tropical and northern temperate regions. Leaves are usually alternate. The small flowers have no petals. The fruit may be winged and dry, fleshy with a single seed, or a nut.

Family ULMACEAE	Species *Celtis australis*	Author Linnaeus

SOUTHERN NETTLE TREE

Leaves Lanceolate to ovate, to 15cm (6in) long and 5cm (2in) across, slender-pointed at the tip, light to dark green and roughly hairy above, grey-green and softly hairy beneath. **Bark** Pale grey, smooth. **Flowers** Males and females both small and green, without petals, either singly or in small clusters in the leaf axils, separately on the same plant in spring. **Fruit** Rounded, berry-like, about 1cm (⅜in) across, nearly black when ripe.
• **NATIVE REGION** S.W. Asia, S. Europe.
• **HABITAT** Warm, dry, rocky slopes.

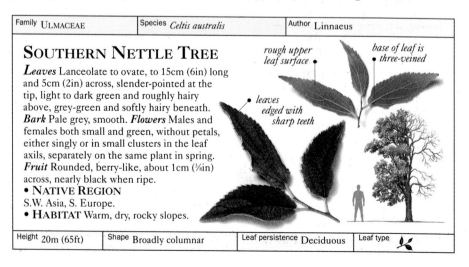

rough upper leaf surface

base of leaf is three-veined

leaves edged with sharp teeth

Height 20m (65ft)	Shape Broadly columnar	Leaf persistence Deciduous	Leaf type

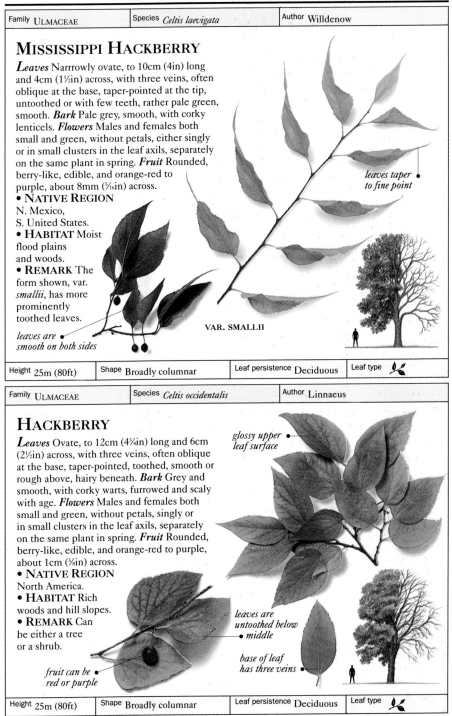

| Family ULMACEAE | Species *Celtis laevigata* | Author Willdenow |

MISSISSIPPI HACKBERRY

Leaves Narrrowly ovate, to 10cm (4in) long and 4cm (1½in) across, with three veins, often oblique at the base, taper-pointed at the tip, untoothed or with few teeth, rather pale green, smooth. *Bark* Pale grey, smooth, with corky lenticels. *Flowers* Males and females both small and green, without petals, either singly or in small clusters in the leaf axils, separately on the same plant in spring. *Fruit* Rounded, berry-like, edible, and orange-red to purple, about 8mm (5⁄16in) across.
• **NATIVE REGION**
N. Mexico,
S. United States.
• **HABITAT** Moist
flood plains
and woods.
• **REMARK** The
form shown, var.
smallii, has more
prominently
toothed leaves.

leaves taper to fine point

leaves are smooth on both sides

VAR. SMALLII

| Height 25m (80ft) | Shape Broadly columnar | Leaf persistence Deciduous | Leaf type |

| Family ULMACEAE | Species *Celtis occidentalis* | Author Linnaeus |

HACKBERRY

Leaves Ovate, to 12cm (4¾in) long and 6cm (2½in) across, with three veins, often oblique at the base, taper-pointed, toothed, smooth or rough above, hairy beneath. *Bark* Grey and smooth, with corky warts, furrowed and scaly with age. *Flowers* Males and females both small and green, without petals, singly or in small clusters in the leaf axils, separately on the same plant in spring. *Fruit* Rounded, berry-like, edible, and orange-red to purple, about 1cm (3⁄8in) across.
• **NATIVE REGION**
North America.
• **HABITAT** Rich
woods and hill slopes.
• **REMARK** Can
be either a tree
or a shrub.

glossy upper leaf surface

leaves are untoothed below middle

base of leaf has three veins

fruit can be red or purple

| Height 25m (80ft) | Shape Broadly columnar | Leaf persistence Deciduous | Leaf type |

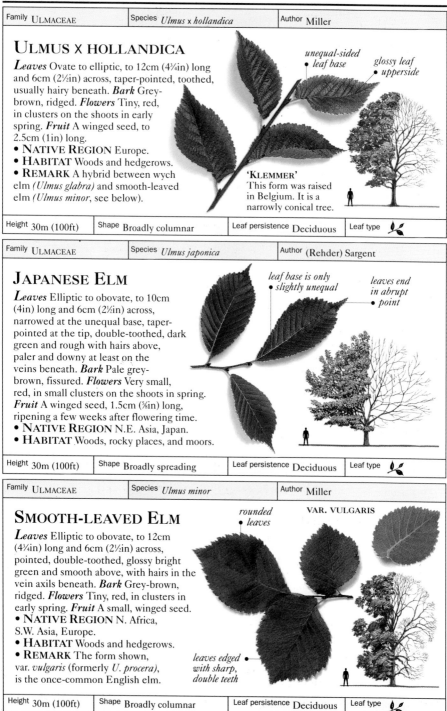

Family ULMACEAE	Species *Ulmus* x *hollandica*	Author Miller

ULMUS X HOLLANDICA

Leaves Ovate to elliptic, to 12cm (4¾in) long and 6cm (2½in) across, taper-pointed, toothed, usually hairy beneath. **Bark** Grey-brown, ridged. **Flowers** Tiny, red, in clusters on the shoots in early spring. **Fruit** A winged seed, to 2.5cm (1in) long.
• **NATIVE REGION** Europe.
• **HABITAT** Woods and hedgerows.
• **REMARK** A hybrid between wych elm *(Ulmus glabra)* and smooth-leaved elm *(Ulmus minor,* see below).

unequal-sided • leaf base

glossy leaf • upperside

'KLEMMER'
This form was raised in Belgium. It is a narrowly conical tree.

Height 30m (100ft)	Shape Broadly columnar	Leaf persistence Deciduous	Leaf type

Family ULMACEAE	Species *Ulmus japonica*	Author (Rehder) Sargent

JAPANESE ELM

Leaves Elliptic to obovate, to 10cm (4in) long and 6cm (2½in) across, narrowed at the unequal base, taper-pointed at the tip, double-toothed, dark green and rough with hairs above, paler and downy at least on the veins beneath. **Bark** Pale grey-brown, fissured. **Flowers** Very small, red, in small clusters on the shoots in spring. **Fruit** A winged seed, 1.5cm (⅝in) long, ripening a few weeks after flowering time.
• **NATIVE REGION** N.E. Asia, Japan.
• **HABITAT** Woods, rocky places, and moors.

leaf base is only • slightly unequal

leaves end in abrupt • point

Height 30m (100ft)	Shape Broadly spreading	Leaf persistence Deciduous	Leaf type

Family ULMACEAE	Species *Ulmus minor*	Author Miller

SMOOTH-LEAVED ELM

Leaves Elliptic to obovate, to 12cm (4¾in) long and 6cm (2½in) across, pointed, double-toothed, glossy bright green and smooth above, with hairs in the vein axils beneath. **Bark** Grey-brown, ridged. **Flowers** Tiny, red, in clusters in early spring. **Fruit** A small, winged seed.
• **NATIVE REGION** N. Africa, S.W. Asia, Europe.
• **HABITAT** Woods and hedgerows.
• **REMARK** The form shown, var. *vulgaris* (formerly *U. procera*), is the once-common English elm.

rounded • leaves

VAR. VULGARIS

leaves edged • with sharp, double teeth

Height 30m (100ft)	Shape Broadly columnar	Leaf persistence Deciduous	Leaf type

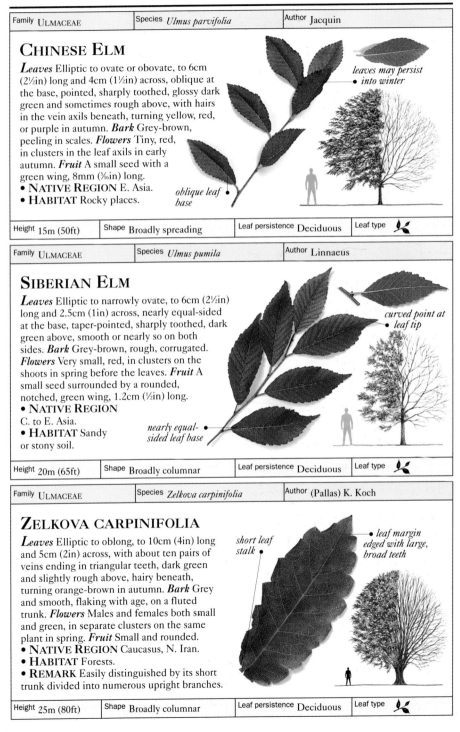

Family ULMACEAE	Species *Ulmus parvifolia*	Author Jacquin

CHINESE ELM

Leaves Elliptic to ovate or obovate, to 6cm (2½in) long and 4cm (1½in) across, oblique at the base, pointed, sharply toothed, glossy dark green and sometimes rough above, with hairs in the vein axils beneath, turning yellow, red, or purple in autumn. **Bark** Grey-brown, peeling in scales. **Flowers** Tiny, red, in clusters in the leaf axils in early autumn. **Fruit** A small seed with a green wing, 8mm (⅜in) long.
- **NATIVE REGION** E. Asia.
- **HABITAT** Rocky places.

leaves may persist into winter

oblique leaf base

Height 15m (50ft)	Shape Broadly spreading	Leaf persistence Deciduous	Leaf type

Family ULMACEAE	Species *Ulmus pumila*	Author Linnaeus

SIBERIAN ELM

Leaves Elliptic to narrowly ovate, to 6cm (2½in) long and 2.5cm (1in) across, nearly equal-sided at the base, taper-pointed, sharply toothed, dark green above, smooth or nearly so on both sides. **Bark** Grey-brown, rough, corrugated. **Flowers** Very small, red, in clusters on the shoots in spring before the leaves. **Fruit** A small seed surrounded by a rounded, notched, green wing, 1.2cm (½in) long.
- **NATIVE REGION** C. to E. Asia.
- **HABITAT** Sandy or stony soil.

curved point at leaf tip

nearly equal-sided leaf base

Height 20m (65ft)	Shape Broadly columnar	Leaf persistence Deciduous	Leaf type

Family ULMACEAE	Species *Zelkova carpinifolia*	Author (Pallas) K. Koch

ZELKOVA CARPINIFOLIA

Leaves Elliptic to oblong, to 10cm (4in) long and 5cm (2in) across, with about ten pairs of veins ending in triangular teeth, dark green and slightly rough above, hairy beneath, turning orange-brown in autumn. **Bark** Grey and smooth, flaking with age, on a fluted trunk. **Flowers** Males and females both small and green, in separate clusters on the same plant in spring. **Fruit** Small and rounded.
- **NATIVE REGION** Caucasus, N. Iran.
- **HABITAT** Forests.
- **REMARK** Easily distinguished by its short trunk divided into numerous upright branches.

short leaf stalk

leaf margin edged with large, broad teeth

Height 25m (80ft)	Shape Broadly columnar	Leaf persistence Deciduous	Leaf type

Family ULMACEAE	Species *Zelkova serrata*	Author (Thunberg) Makino

KEAKI

Leaves Ovate to oblong-ovate, to 12cm (4¾in) long and 5cm (2in) across, rounded at the base, taper-pointed, sharply toothed, the teeth ending in a short point, dark green and slightly rough above, paler and nearly smooth beneath, turning yellow, orange, or red in autumn. **Bark** Pale grey and smooth, flaking with age. **Flowers** Males and females both small and green, on the young shoots on the same plant in spring. **Fruit** Small and rounded.
• **NATIVE REGION** China, Japan, Korea.
• **HABITAT** Moist soil near streams.

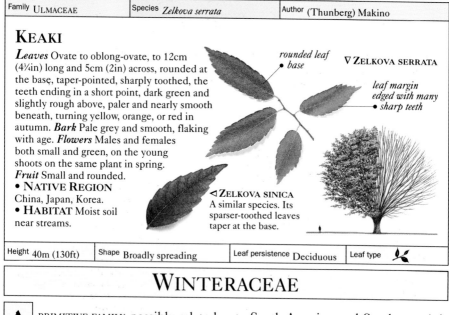

rounded leaf • base

▽ ZELKOVA SERRATA

leaf margin edged with many • sharp teeth

◁ ZELKOVA SINICA
A similar species. Its sparser-toothed leaves taper at the base.

Height 40m (130ft)	Shape Broadly spreading	Leaf persistence Deciduous	Leaf type

WINTERACEAE

A PRIMITIVE FAMILY, possibly related to the magnolias *(Magnolia,* see pp.202–215). About five genera and 60 species of evergreen trees and shrubs occur in Madagascar, and from Mexico to South America, and South-east Asia to Australia and New Zealand. Plants have alternately arranged, untoothed leaves, five- or more petalled flowers, and small, berry-like, clustered fruits.

Family WINTERACEAE	Species *Drimys winteri*	Author J. R. & J. G. Forster

WINTER'S BARK

Leaves Oblong to elliptic, to 20cm (8in) long and 6cm (2½in) across, untoothed, glossy dark green above, bluish green to bluish white beneath, leathery, aromatic when crushed. **Bark** Grey-brown and smooth, very aromatic. **Flowers** 4cm (1½in) across, white, fragrant, with numerous slender petals, borne in large clusters in spring to early summer. **Fruit** A small berry, green ripening to purple-black, in clusters at the end of long stalks.
• **NATIVE REGION** Mexico, South America.
• **HABITAT** Mountains.
• **REMARK** Named after Captain William Winter, who sailed with Sir Francis Drake in the sixteenth century. He used the bark (a source of vitamin C) to treat scurvy, a disease caused by a deficiency of the same vitamin.

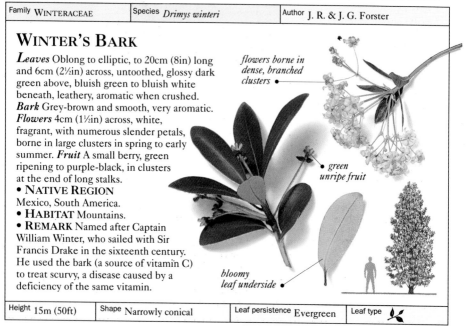

flowers borne in dense, branched clusters •

• green unripe fruit

bloomy leaf underside •

Height 15m (50ft)	Shape Narrowly conical	Leaf persistence Evergreen	Leaf type

GLOSSARY

Technical terms have been kept to a minimum, but a limited use of them is unavoidable in a book of this kind. Words in **bold** in the definitions are explained elsewhere in the glossary.

You may find it useful also to look at Hybrid Plants (p.8), A Family Tree (p.9), What is a Tree? (pp.12–13), The Parts of a Tree (pp.14–15), and Conifer or Broadleaf? (pp.16–17).

- **ANTHER**
Part of a **stamen** that releases **pollen**.
- **ARIL**
Fleshy seed coat.
- **AURICLE**
Small, ear-like **lobe**.
- **BIPINNATE**
Pinnate, with the divisions themselves pinnate.
- **BLOOMY**
Covered with a waxy or powdery, blue-white deposit.
- **BRACT**
Leaf-like structure below a flower or flower cluster.
- **CALYX**
Small part of a flower outside the petals, composed of **sepals**.
- **CAPSULE**
Dry fruit that splits open to release its seeds.
- **CATKIN**
Usually pendulous cluster of **bracts** and tiny flowers, most often of one sex.
- **COMPOUND LEAF**
One that is composed of two or more separate **leaflets**.
- **COROLLA**
Often showy and coloured part of a flower, composed of petals.
- **DECIDUOUS**
Without leaves for part of each year.
- **ENTIRE**
Without teeth or **lobes**.
- **EVERGREEN**
Retaining leaves for more than one year.
- **EXSERTED**
Conspicuously protruding.
- **FILAMENT**
Stalk of an **anther**.

- **GLAUCOUS**
Bluish white.
- **HARDY**
Able to withstand winter temperatures.
- **HERBACEOUS PLANT**
Non-woody plant that dies at the end of the growing season or overwinters by means of underground structures.
- **LEAFLET**
Single division of a **compound leaf**.
- **LEAF AXIL**
Angle formed between a leaf and its stem.
- **LENTICEL**
Usually corky area on a trunk that lets air through the bark.
- **LOBE**
Rounded segment or part.
- **MONOTYPIC**
Of a family: containing a single genus that contains only one species; of a genus: containing a single species.
- **NATIVE**
Growing naturally wild in a specific area.
- **NATURALIZED**
Introduced by man and growing as if naturally wild in a specific area.
- **OVARY**
Organ of a flower's female part that, in fruit, contains the seeds.
- **PALMATE**
Divided into **leaflets** or **lobes** in the manner of a hand.
- **PANICLE**
Raceme in which the branches are themselves branched.
- **PEA-LIKE**
Of a flower: similar in structure to that of a leguminous plant.

- **PERSISTENT**
Remaining attached.
- **PINNATE**
Compound leaf, with **leaflets** arranged on opposite sides of a common stalk.
- **POLLEN**
Spores released from the **anthers**, containing the male reproductive element.
- **RACEME**
Stalked flowers borne singly along a central axis.
- **RACHIS**
Stalk of a **pinnate** leaf on which the **leaflets** are borne.
- **SEPAL**
Individual part of the **calyx**.
- **SIMPLE LEAF**
One that is not divided into **leaflets**.
- **SINUS**
Gap between two **lobes**.
- **SPIKE**
Raceme bearing unstalked flowers.
- **STAMEN**
Anther, usually on a **filament**. A variable number composes the male part of a flower.
- **STIGMA**
Organ of a flower's female part, borne at the tip of the **style**, on which the **pollen** is deposited.
- **STIPULE**
Small, leaf-like structure, most often paired, borne where the leaf stalk joins the stem.
- **STYLE**
Organ of a flower's female part that bears the **stigma**.
- **TEPAL**
Petal or **sepal**, where there is no distinct difference between the two.

INDEX OF PLANTS

ACKNOWLEDGMENTS

THE AUTHOR AND PUBLISHER are greatly indebted to a number of institutions and people, without whom this book could not have been produced. The following supplied and/or collected plant material for photography: Barry Phillips (Curator), Bill George (Head Gardener), and all the staff of the Sir Harold Hillier Gardens and Arboretum, Ampfield, Hampshire; Robert Eburn, P.H.B. Gardner, Bernard and Letty Perrott, and Mrs Eve Taylor; Kate Haywood of The Royal Horticultural Society's Garden Wisley, Woking, Surrey; Hillier Nurseries (Winchester) Limited; Richard Johnston, Mount Annan section of the Royal Botanic Gardens, Sydney, Australia; Longstock Park Gardens; Mike Maunder and Melanie Thomas of the Royal Botanic Gardens, Kew, Surrey; Colin Morgan of the Forestry Commission Research Division, Bedgebury National Pinetum, Cranbrook, Kent; Andrew Pinder (Arboricultural Officer), London Borough of Richmond upon Thames; John White and Margaret Ruskin of the Forestry Commission, Westonbirt Arboretum, Tetbury, Gloucestershire.

The following helped to compile reference material for the illustrators: S. Andrews, T. Kirkham, and Mike Maunder of the Royal Botanic Gardens, Kew, Surrey; the Arnold Arboretum of Harvard University, Jamaica Plain, Massachusetts, USA; Kathie Atkinson; S. Clark and S. Knees of the Royal Botanic Garden Edinburgh, Lothian, Scotland; D. Cooney of the Waite Arboretum, University of Adelaide, S. Australia; B. Davis; Dr T.R. Dudley (Lead Scientist and Research Botanist) of the U.S. National Arboretum, Washington, D.C., USA; M. Flannagan of the Royal Botanic Gardens, Wakehurst Place, Ardingly, West Sussex; the Forestry Commission, Forest Research Station, Alice Holt Lodge, Farnham, Surrey; Anne James of the Parks Department, Dublin County Council, Irish Republic; Roy Lancaster; Scott Leathart; Alan Mitchell; K. Olver; The Royal Horticultural Society's Garden Wisley, Woking, Surrey; V. Schilling of the Tree Register of the British Isles (TROBI), Westmeston, West Sussex; T. Walker of the University of Oxford Botanic Gardens, Oxfordshire; John White and Margaret Ruskin of the Forestry Commission, Westonbirt Arboretum, Tetbury, Gloucestershire; P. Yeo of the University of Cambridge Botanic Garden, Cambridgeshire; Dennis Woodland.

The author would like to express his thanks to: the tremendous team at Dorling Kindersley, especially Vicki James, Gillian Roberts, and Mustafa Sami, for their diligence and commitment to the project; Matthew Ward, for his excellent photography; Roy Lancaster, for reading and commenting on the text; his wife Sue, and daughters Rachel and Ruth, for their support and encouragement.

We acknowledge the invaluable contributions of Mustafa Sami, who shepherded the illustrators with patient good humour, Spencer Holbrook, who gave him vital administrative support, and Donna Rispoli, who researched the references for the illustrators. Special thanks to Mel and Marianne, Witt and Kaye, whose generosity enabled the editor to take a holiday. Thanks also to Michael Allaby, for compiling the index and suggesting words for the glossary; Mike Darton, for reading page proofs, and for commenting on the glossary and introduction; Virginia Fitzgerald, for administrative help with the illustrators' reference material; Angeles Gavira and Ian Hambleton, for cataloguing all the transparencies; Steve Tilling, for commenting on the identification key; Helen Townsend, for caretaking the project while the editor was on holiday; Alastair Wardle, for his computer expertise.

Photographs by Matthew Ward, except: A–Z Botanical Collection 6, 8 *(top)*; Kathie Atkinson 190 *(right & below)*, 191; Bruce Coleman Ltd/Patrick Clement 167 *(Quercus petraea* acorns); Dorling Kindersley/ Peter Chadwick 12 (trunk), 15 (cone section, seed pods), 246 *(top left)*; Harry Smith Photographic Collection/ Polunin Collection 159 *(Quercus canariensis* acorns), 169 *(Quercus pubescens* acorns). **Tree illustrations** by Laura Andrew 200, 201; Marion Appleton 132–143; David Ashby 118–125; Bob Bampton 258–273, 286–297; Anne Child 126, 127, 178–181; Tim Hayward 114–117, 128–131, 144, 145, 154–157, 202–211, 222–237, 274–283, 308–310; Janos Marffy 9, 17, 192–195; David More 158–173, 244–252; Sue Oldfield 12–13, 36–83, 108–113, 188, 189, 196–199, 213–215, 298, 299; Liz Pepperell 182–187, 190, 238–243; Michelle Ross 34, 35, 84–107, 146–152, 300–307; Gill Tomblin 174–177; Barbara Walker 216–221, 255–257, 284, 285. **Leaf type illustrations** by Paul Bailey. **Endpaper illustrations** by Caroline Church.